Huerfano

To Michael + Jane —
Peace + Love (right?)
Roberta Price

Roberta Price

Huerfano

a memoir *of* life *in the* counterculture

UNIVERSITY OF MASSACHUSETTS PRESS   *Amherst & Boston*

Printed in the United States of America
LC 2004018194
ISBN 1-55849-469-3
Set in Mrs. Eaves and Pablo types by
Graphic Composition, Inc.
Printed and bound by Thomson-Shore, Inc.

Library of Congress Cataloging-in-Publication Data
Price, Roberta.
Huerfano : a memoir of life in the counterculture /
Roberta Price.
p. cm.
ISBN 1-55849-469-3 (Cloth : alk. paper)
1. Price, Roberta.
2. Hippies—Colorado—Huerfano County—Biography.
3. Counterculture—Colorado—Huerfano County—
    Biography.
4. Libre (Commune : Colo.) I. Title.
HQ799.72.C6A3 2004
       306 '.1—dc22
              2004018194
British Library Cataloguing in Publication data are
    available.

Contents

Huerfano

Prologue

Last night I had a dream about a dream. It was 1974, the Thanksgiving feast at the Red Rockers, a time when the hippie population of the Huerfano Valley had swelled from the first six at Libre in 1968 to more than three hundred of us. We were at Libre, the Red Rockers, the Triple A, the Ortiviz Farm, Archuletaville. We were in the tiny towns of Gardner, Redwing, Malachite, and Farisita. We were by the butte in the valley's center, up the canyons, on the high mountain meadows and ridges on both sides—in adobes, geodesic domes, log cabins, and shacks studded all over the Huerfano.

The weather was cold and gray, threatening snow, and that year even the Red Rockers' sixty-foot dome couldn't accommodate the circle we traditionally made before Thanksgiving dinner. I don't know who got the idea first, or whether we all just saw that we had to go outdoors to get in a circle. By the time I was headed out of the dome, others were yelling, "Everybody outside!" We poured out without our coats, some stumbling, stoned or drunk already, dressed in our holiday best (fringes and silks and velvets and satin cowboy shirts and hand-sewn leathers), forming a circle in the Red Rock Canyon meadow down from the dome.

Looking down the slot of the canyon, you could see only one or two of the mountains in the Sangre de Cristo Range, but since David and I had been living high up on the ridge at Libre for four years, it was easy to envision the rest of the mountains marching across the curved horizon. Even though our view was cut off by canyon walls, the outline of those mountains on the rim of the world was etched in our heads by then. Behind us was the huge white geodesic dome, dwarfed by the deep red cliffs of the canyon behind it. The generators were still running, and a Taj Mahal record was playing inside. There we were, the wind hitting us and swirling our hair and scarves, our shawls and skirts and fringes, whipping our bell-bottoms against the bones of our legs, and we held hands and looked at one another and grinned.

In the dream, people moved more gracefully and soundlessly than they did when it actually happened, but I still heard the wind blowing down the canyon behind us from the top of Greenhorn and the laughter in the circle that was so fragile, so vivid and tattered in that geography. In the dream I saw how young we all looked, though I didn't notice at the time. David must have been on one side of me. I don't remember who was on the other. We'd split some windowpane LSD with Henry when we got to the Red Rocks, one dose three ways. Or maybe it was one of the thousands of tiny orange tabs in the two-quart canning jar that Owsley, the greatest pure acid chemist of them all, had sent Libre as a commune-warming gift in 1968, but I'm pretty sure they were all gone by then. It hadn't come on yet, but my mouth was dry, my palms sweaty, my heart beating harder, and I was either anticipating or just beginning to feel those electric, surging, sensual waves that flow up your spine, sprouting into chemically induced blossoms of enlightenment.

My Pentax Spotmatic hung from my neck. My arms were crossed over its straps on my chest, and all of our arms crossed our chests as we held hands round the circle. I mostly remember and therefore dreamed about the people on the other side of the circle: Winnie and Mary Red Rocker. Trixie. Lars and Linda. Bella, who had her blouse on (which was remarkable, because she always took it off at parties). Steve, in his handmade deerskin pants and shirt with the deep leather-laced V neck, showing the distinct cleft of his smooth chest muscles. Some are dead now, and some were gone by then, but last night they were back in that circle.

Nobody, not even Peter or Dean, tried to make a speech. We kept smiling and laughing at each other, although our teeth were starting to chatter. Someone, maybe Peter, yelled, "Thank you!" Then more of us shouted, "Thank you!" into the wind, and we dropped hands and ran toward one another, boots crunching in the old snow, the circle collapsing inward, my camera knocking against my chest as I ran. At the center, as close together as we could get, we hugged and laughed and cried all at the same time.

In the dream there were none of the difficulties between David and me that day. I felt the same vague disconnection I'd felt back then as I hugged some of the people who grabbed me, and I was surprised that I didn't know the names of some I embraced. My camera hurt my chest when I pressed against someone too hard. I never took a picture. It was impossible to capture. Part of me was too involved to take pictures, while part of me was too detached, or already too stoned. Then all of us turned, streaming back to the dome and the plank-and-sawhorse serving tables. The tables were laden with elk roasts and wild turkeys poached from the national forest, our gardens' last sweet winter squashes, all sorts of grains and vegetables, and homemade bread and rolls. The smart ones headed for the dessert table first, to get the white sugar and chocolate desserts. They disappeared quickly, leaving only healthy desserts (pies with organic, tooth-breaking, totally whole wheat crusts and natural fruit fillings), so much better for you, but never sweet enough.

When I woke up today, I lay in the sunlight thinking about my dream and the Pilgrims' first Thanksgiving. At our Thanksgiving we were thankful, though not very puritanical, and the only Indians there were one-legged John Pedro and his scrawny son, and maybe one or two other Oklahoma members of the Native American Church. I thought about Sal Paradise and Dean Moriarty driving south from Denver in *On the Road,* and the familial bond of their manic journey. Our roads had ended in the Huerfano, the Orphan Valley, and Kerouac was our John the Baptist, although I doubt he'd have envisioned us trying to take root in the arid, rocky meadows of the mountains he'd driven past en route to Mexico a generation before. I thought about Dylan, resting on the all-night train going west, dreaming about himself and the first few friends he had, who never thought that their road would shatter and split, whose chances were really a million to one.

Then—at first I didn't know why—I thought of Virginia Woolf, *The Waves.* The chapter about an afternoon after World War I, when the children in her family, who were orphaned as young adults, meet at Hampton Court. Virginia sees that each of them is a petal of one flower. The implosion across the Atlantic and deep into our continent more than half a century later outside the Red Rocker dome was something like that, though the scruffy meadow in southern Colorado was less genteel than the manicured gardens of Hampton Court, and our realization was on a sloppy, stoned, jumbo American scale. It's one of the moments I think of when people ask what it was like to be there, what we were doing there, but it's one I've never told them about.

Last night I had a dream of a memory, or maybe it was a memory of a dream. Or a dream about a dream, nearly over even then. The actual moment and last night's glimpse of it were brief, but I've shared that flawed and fleeting vision with the children of the Huerfano ever since, and it makes a difference.

1 : Shop Around

David and I are leaving graduate school at Buffalo for good and moving to a hippie commune in southeastern Colorado. We're twenty-four, and we've come of age in the third quarter of the twentieth century, when many of us have the opportunity to make passionate choices. We haven't told our graduate school friends about our decision straight out, although we've told them about discovering Libre last summer, when we were traveling around Colorado and New Mexico on a SUNY Buffalo faculty fund grant to study the communes that were sprouting up in the Southwest. Libre, which means "free" in Spanish, is in the Huerfano Valley in southern Colorado. The Huerfano—the Orphan Valley. The valley and the Huerfano River running through it share the name of the lone butte that stands east of the valley, looking eastward into the Great Plains.

When we got back to Buffalo, we showed our slides of Libre and Drop City and New Buffalo. The brilliant colors of the Southwest bloomed on the walls of our apartment and classrooms during the long, dark Buffalo winter. We showed pictures of the Huerfano, a relatively narrow valley with sides that slope up like the sides of a teacup, rimmed by mountain ranges. We showed pictures of contemporaries making adobe bricks, irrigating corn, playing guitars, laughing into the camera. We told everyone how in the West you could stand on a mountain and see forever. When we returned to Libre last winter, on another grant to study communes, we felt certain we'd go back there permanently, but we weren't sure when.

On the way back to Buffalo from Libre this winter, we detoured to the Grand Canyon on a late January weekday afternoon. The light was wintry but bright, and there were no other tourists on the south rim. Shoulder to shoulder we looked down through a space that is time to the glinting line of the Colorado River.

"Across the Great Divide," David said.

"So, do you think we'll actually move to Libre?" I asked, looking *down* at a hawk, swooping across the canyon below us.

"I guess so. It's our only real option, don't you think?" David said.

"Yes," I agreed. "It's where I want to wake up every morning. It's where I can be the way I want to be." Against the canyon's grandeur, these words felt like a betrothal to me.

Back in Buffalo, we try to keep our options open, and we don't talk about our future to others much. Some graduate school friends are going to Vancouver Island this summer to start a commune. They sense our paths are forking, but no one's asked us point blank what we're going to do next year, and we haven't told them our plans are definite now. The mountain range that dances across the horizon at sunset in the Huerfano burns in our memory. The people building their houses at Libre can teach us a lot. They have their flaws, like everyone else, but they also have the courage to be the vanguard. They've grown to match their landscape. They are mountain men and women, artists, and free. We want to be like them. Frankly, we don't think our lovable, inexperienced, goofy, intellectual friends in Buffalo will last long in the Canadian woods.

Tonight many of these friends are sprawled in the living room of our second-floor apartment. It's surprisingly warm, and the doors are open onto the balcony overlooking Arlington Park. The elms haven't leafed out yet; in fact, most of them are dying from Dutch elm disease, but their large, graceful skeletons are silhouetted in the streetlights. Rick's gotten some MDA from the army. Actually, Rick got it from someone who got it from someone who supposedly got it from the army—naturally, Rick keeps his sources secret. He says the army developed MDA to dose hostile populations, to make them more docile and manageable. He's taken some before and says it's great. *The Band* is playing on my KLH, and we're all smiling at one another, nodding to "Across the Great Divide": "*Across the Great Divide, / Just grab your hat and take that ride, / Get yourself a bride, / And bring your children down to the riverside . . .*"

Kevin lights a pipe of hash, sucks on it rapidly to get it started, and hands it to David. Kevin's in graduate English with me, but he's a little older. He was a monk for a while, but he's switched his sacraments. His pale blond hair is perfectly trimmed, chin length, and naturally wavy, sort of like a forties starlet's hairdo. His beard and mustache are trimmed neatly too, and his large blue eyes seem even larger through thick, rimless glasses. Do monks still shave their heads? I can't see Kevin without his hair.

Friends gather at our house—it's spacious, with hardwood floors, working fireplaces, and balconies on the park. Kevin, who lives in the apartment downstairs, says this was the actress Katharine Cornell's childhood home, now split up into apartments any graduate student would die for. Friends also gather here because David and I are one of the few long-term couples in the group. We're Peter and Wendy, and this is our gang. Because we haven't told them yet that we're not going to Canada, this evening's bittersweet. David's and my eyes meet occasionally as they chatter, and I just can't believe it—we're going to join Libre and build a home nine thousand two hundred feet up Greenhorn Mountain and live there differently and forever. We'll be psychic pioneers.

On paper, we don't seem prepared for this choice, no more ready to make the change than our friends heading for Vancouver. I graduated from Vassar in 1968, and this is my second year of a teaching fellowship in the English Ph.D. program at SUNY Buffalo, where I came to be with David. He graduated from Yale in 1968, too, and his Yale professor asked him to come with him to help start the new American Studies program up here. This job has the invaluable perk of a graduate school deferment from the draft and Vietnam, at least for a while.

The fact is, neither David nor I have ever built a bookcase before, or anything else for that matter. I suppose David took shop in high school, but I've never seen him with a tool in his hand in the six years I've known him. We've lived the life of the mind in suburbs and cities all our lives. This lack of practical skills doesn't stop us from wanting to head for Libre to build a house by hand, without electricity, on a frequently impassable road halfway up a mountain. We're young and strong, and we can do anything.

At Buffalo I'm studying Blake and teaching journal writing to most of the freshman football team. English is required freshman year, and journal writing is the athletes' course of choice. I'm slim and small and have long, straight blond hair. My students are big and built; each one's neck looks bigger than my waist. I urge them to talk about their feelings while we read Anaïs Nin, who, even in her delusions of grandeur, may not have expected an audience of eighteen-year-old football players from places like North Tonawanda, New York. I try to discuss Vietnam with them in class—many students have brothers or friends there—but they look down at their desks and don't want to talk about it, maybe because they think I'm crazy or stupid or worse. I don't have David's charisma or his leadership abilities. But I'm their teacher, and they flirt with me, awkwardly and politely, humoring me as best they can, confessing more and more in their journal notebooks as the semester progresses. Meanwhile, their uncles and fathers sit in bars along Delaware Avenue with other steelworkers and pray that some hippie will be stupid enough to come in and ask for directions or a beer.

David's across the living room, messing with his guitar and amplifier. He's tall, dark, muscular, and lean. He has high cheekbones, pale skin, wild dark eyes, and black hair and mustache. One grandfather was a North Carolina Cherokee. David is handsome, and his eyes burn. He looks like a cross between Omar Sharif and Henry Fonda with a soupçon of Tonto thrown in. He has the look that visionaries, poets, and some outlaws have—one eye's focused a little further into the future than the other. This may be why he pays a little less attention to the present than I do. In the new American Studies program at Buffalo last year, he taught a class called "The Outsider." This year it's titled "FREAK." On his reading list is Hunter Thompson's *Hell's Angels,* Kerouac's *On the Road,* Tom Wolfe's *Electric Kool-Aid Acid Test,* Ginsberg's *Howl, The Stranger* and all the rest of Kafka, Ralph Ellison's *Invisible Man.* His course is so popular that, even though it's full, many unenrolled students drop in to participate. The large attendance is due to the exciting revolutionary thoughts and insights expressed there, but also because lots of students smoke joints together throughout the class.

This winter, even David's class was canceled when SUNY Buffalo was shut down because of student revolt. The campus ROTC building was burned down one night, and its records were destroyed. Unemployed steelworkers drove through the campus shooting at longhaired hippie-looking students. It was a cloudy, grim winter. While we were away in Colorado, our two cats, Yin and Yang, died from some no doubt environmentally caused disease. JB, a close friend, checked into a mental hospital and detox program last month, not long after he'd organized the clandestine midnight brigade who drove around Buffalo stenciling WAR under STOP on all the stop signs. We didn't see the sun once in

January. Gary Snyder—the Japhy Ryder of Kerouac's *Dharma Bums*—visited, and one long, dark winter night we had a party and danced so exuberantly that the hardwood floor of our apartment shook. Kevin lives downstairs, so no one complained. Snyder knew of Libre and the Huerfano because his friend Nanao, a Japanese poet, was visiting there. We showed Snyder my pictures of Libre and New Buffalo and Morning Star Commune, and he asked, "Why don't you go there?" We couldn't answer. Baba Ram Dass, aka Richard Alpert, Mr. LSD, came through Buffalo, too, dressed in white robes now, drug free and high from two years in India with his guru. We told him about Libre, and he said, "Follow your heart!" It's silly, but when he said that, it felt so simple, so profound.

Beyond the local indications of doom is the tragic, revolting big picture. Che, Malcolm X, Martin, and Bobby are dead. In February, the Weathermen blew up a Bank of America out West. In March, three Weathermen blew themselves up in the East, making a bomb with some sticks of dynamite and an alarm clock in a Greenwich Village brownstone that one of Edith Wharton's eligible bachelors might have lived in late in the previous century. The three were about our age. Nixon expanded the Vietnam War into Cambodia, and last fall at a demonstration at the Pentagon we were teargassed. We were in the front, and one soldier must not have liked the way David looked at him. Or maybe it was the large black and white silk pirate flag I'd made for David to carry. When the order came to gas the crowd, the soldier aimed a canister at David's head, and it knocked him down. The neighboring strangers didn't panic and trample over him. Instead, they helped David's brother Doug and me pick David up. Gasping and choking on gas, we held him up and helped him run. He didn't drop the flag. It's on our apartment wall, by the poster for Cream at Fillmore East.

Bob the Rake, who's sharing a large maroon Naugahyde chair with me, passes a pipe. I take a light puff and smile at him. He's broken five women's hearts in the past three months—and those are only the ones I've heard about. He's got dark brown bedroom eyes, thick eyelashes, wavy brown hair. He's not killingly handsome, a bit stocky even, but he's got a way with the women, and a libido turbocharged by a Catholic boys' school education. The stereo's off, and David's tuning up his electric guitar. Buddy, back from Chicago, where he's been clerking for William Kunstler on the trial of the Chicago Seven, is picking languidly on a bass. Suddenly, I'm overwhelmed with love for everyone in the room. Even Bob the Rake seems harmless and endearing. Joanne, hopelessly in love with Bob, gets up, flicks a cigarette over the balcony, and closes the balcony doors, either because it's getting cold, because she's worried about the electric guitars and the neighbors, or because Bob is driving her crazy.

I stare down at the frayed oriental rug my parents gave me to bring up here. It wasn't new when I crawled on it as a baby. My parents are angry that David and I are living together in sin. It's my mother who's most angry, but my father's going along with her. I've visited over the last two years, but they don't allow David in the house and refuse to speak his name. Maybe it's the MDA that makes me feel a surge of love for them, too, along with love for all the people in the room, and the conviction swells up in me that *it will all work out,* though I'm not sure of the details. If I were a hostile native, I'd drop my Molotov cocktail now.

David plays Leadbelly's "Bourgeois Blues," then a Woody Guthrie tune, "Deportee," then Jerry Lee Lewis's "Great Balls of fire." His soft tenor voice is clear and slightly southern, no matter what he sings. I've heard him practice these songs late into the night. Now he starts "Shop Around," the old Smokey Robinson favorite which he's been playing a lot lately. Everyone's swaying, and Buddy's picking up the bass line surprisingly well. The lights are low, the large candles dripping and flickering.

When I became of age, my mama called me to her side,
She said, "Son, you're growing up now,
Pretty soon you'll take a bride,". . .

David doesn't try to sound like Smokey Robinson. His version is true to who he is, and slightly Appalachian. I feel lucky to be with a person who's so intelligent, such a creative thinker, so handsome and hip. I also feel Bob's hand on my back under my Mexican blouse, and I jump a little, wondering when he put it there, but then he's just been stroking my lower back softly, and it feels good. Not sexual, just good. I smile at David across the room. He looks at me briefly, then looks down at his fingers on the frets.

"This feels so good. You've always been so cool and distant! You're such a weird mix of reserve and passion, I've always wanted to do this," Bob whispers as David plays a bridge between verses, and Clint gives a Texas good ol' boy hoot of approval. Candlelight glints on the thick lenses of Clint's wire-rimmed glasses, and the wire arms disappear into his large, muttonchop sideburns. I should say to Bob that I'm so cool and distant because I'm in love with David and committed to him. Also, I'm friends with Joanne, who has loved Bob forever, and *unlike some people,* I believe in being faithful. But I'm feeling too good to be snide, and David looks up from his guitar meaningfully with his dark, indigenous eyes. I smile back, pretty sure neither he nor anyone else has noticed Bob's arm halfway up my back. Joanne would notice if it weren't so dark.

David sings the chorus in a high falsetto.

"Try to get yourself a bargain son,
Don't be sold on the very first one
Pretty girls come a dime a dozen,
Try to find one who's gonna give you good lovin'. . . ."

He sings and plays with more feeling and flourish than ever. Bob runs his fingers over my back lightly, and I sway a little, to avoid his fingers getting more intimate, and because the music sounds so good I can't sit still. Then David strums his guitar loudly and pauses. Everyone stops swaying and looks up. Clint spills his beer.

"Roberta Price"—David strums dramatically—"Will you marry me?" Bob's hand freezes. Clint's mopping up beer with his sweater and grinning. Everyone's smiling at me, and I smile across the room at David. My face flushes with embarrassment and MDA. I want to get married, but it occurs to me (inappropriately, it seems) that he must be very confident of the answer to ask me in a crowd. Why shouldn't he be confident? I think irritably. But, almost as soon as I think that, I wonder if he's asked me like this because it would really be very hard for me to say no in this situation. Why am I having such foolish thoughts? It must be the wine, the hash, or the MDA. I've been sure that I wanted to marry David all the time he's hesitated and said marriage is too conventional. Have I been so sure because he's been so doubtful?

Everybody's staring. It's been forever since the last guitar chord reverberated in the dark, sweet, smoky air of the apartment. I'm looking at David, and then I remember Bob's hand on my back and wonder if anybody's noticed. Bob's lowered his hand a little and has stopped running his fingers over my skin, so at least my goose bumps are deflating. I look down, blush more, and then I say, "YES!" Clint hoots again, and lurches away to the kitchen in his worn cowboy boots for something to clean up the beer, and Bob puts the arm that was under my blouse around me.

> *"Pretty girls come a dime a dozen,*
> *Try to find one who's gonna give you good lovin',*
> *Before you take a girl and say I do now,*
> *Make sure she's in love with you now,"*
> *My momma told me, "You betta shop around."*

David sings on. Bob looks sideways at me, thick, dark eyelashes at half-mast. He smiles and whispers, "April Fool!"

I get up and cross the room to David, threading through our friends on the floor. I really don't think Bob was kidding.

2 : May Day

Five weeks later, on the way to tell New Haven friends about our wedding, we loop south to White Plains to tell my parents. I call from a gas station on the Merritt Parkway, and Mom sounds a little surprised, but she doesn't say David can't come to the house. Maybe she senses we've got news. We drive up the hill in our 1947 Chrysler Windsor coupe that we bought in Barstow, California, last July, after our Corvair camper died a miserable death in the desert outside Needles. When we found the Chrysler in the first used car lot coming into Barstow, we opened the glove box and found the owner's manual, just slightly worn. It said that the color was Desert Beige, and the cloth pattern on the inside door panels, only a bit torn, was Windsor Plaid. We decided to buy it before we opened the hood to look at the engine, but it all worked out. We've crossed the country three times in it, and it still runs like a top.

"Hey, Berta, David, come on in," Dad says. Glancing past us to the parked Chrysler, he asks, "That old car still running okay? David, last time Berta was here, I told her that her uncle Carl had a Chrysler like that, a black sedan, though. Lately, though, it's only Cadillacs for Carl. He won two, each one in a different lottery, five years apart, remember, Berta? Carl's luck! I've never won any lotteries. . . . Well, here you are! Come on out to the porch," he says cordially. "We just got back from shopping, and we're about to have a drink."

It's fine at first, just a little tense. My mother's acting like Queen Elizabeth, although Queen Elizabeth never unpacks her groceries. Mom's making the best of the situation, being just a bit cold and formal. She finishes putting the food away while the rest of us move through the kitchen onto the side porch looking out at the birches. May's a lot warmer down here than it is in Buffalo, and the large porch windows are open. Dad's got the screens on already.

"Want a beer, David?" asks my dad genially.

"Why, sure." David smiles. He's clean shaven, except for a dark mustache, his black hair pulled back into a ponytail at the base of his neck, so that when you look at him from the front, you notice that his sideburns are a little long, but you don't see the ponytail tucked into the collar of his pin-striped shirt.

The rhododendrons are beginning to bloom near the house, and, despite the tension in the air, I'm happy to be with my parents and the man I love in my childhood home. I look around reflexively for my dog, who died when I was in college. My dad hands David a Heineken and a tall glass, and David sits on a high stool, carefully pouring the beer so it has just the right amount of foam. In the kitchen my dad mixes his martini and then the scotch and water that he pours for Mom every night. She holds her cocktail napkin and her glass in her lap on the Danish modern love seat that replaced the rattan couch we used to sit on while we watched *Walt Disney Presents* every Sunday night. I'm drinking tonic water and lime—what I used to have as a child the summers I traveled with my parents through Europe. Dad's a retired Mobil Oil executive who went all over the world, working in international marketing. Even as I got older, I'd watch Mobil's Flying Red Horse take off in TV ads and think of my father swooping down gracefully over the continents. His quiet, self-effacing manner made him popular with the Europeans, South Americans, Africans, and Caribbeans. He wasn't the Ugly American. Mom's a housewife and a member of the League of Women Voters. They're Rockefeller Republicans.

My mother gets up again to bring us some potato chips and clam dip. I'm nervous, and there are some gaps in the conversation, so I flick on the TV. Walter Cronkite announces that President Nixon invited Peter Brennan, head of the construction workers' union in New York City, to a reception at the White House. There's Brennan giving Nixon an honorary hard hat, and Nixon pinning an American flag on Brennan's lapel.

"Hmphh." My mother says, standing in the doorway from the kitchen. She knows she shouldn't voice her approval of Nixon taking a stand, but she can't control herself.

"I can't believe this!" I blurt out. "That fucker!" This kind of language sets my mother off like a rocket, but I'm out of control. Three days ago, when four Kent State students were shot dead by young National Guardsmen firing at antiwar demonstrators, Nixon had no sympathy for the families of dead or wounded students. His words burn in my memory like battery acid: the deaths should remind us that "when dissent turns to violence, it invites tragedy."

In contrast, in New York City, Mayor Lindsay lowered the flag over City Hall to half-mast to pay tribute to the Kent State dead. Then over a thousand hard hat construction workers, some veterans and all supporters of the war, invaded City Hall and demanded the flag go up again. They beat students rallying at City Hall with clubs and fists, while the New York cops turned their backs. I saw a clip of a construction worker beating a longhaired student over the head with a "Hippies Get Out of America!" sign. Brennan was the union leader of these thugs, and now, if they were Russian, he and Nixon would be kissing on TV.

"Roberta!" my mother exclaims angrily, standing in the doorway, clutching the aluminum chip and dip plate shaped like a huge tropical leaf. "Is that how they talk at Vassar?"

I ignore the question and ask, "What's a little profanity when kids like us are being killed for demonstrating? That's what happens in Hungary, Russia, Czechoslovakia, or China! We're supposed to be free here! Tricky Dick condones mob violence to stop antiwar demonstrations! *That's* profane!" Out of the corner of my eye I see David looking down, and the hand not holding his beer grips his knee tightly as he sits on the stool.

"Those who live by the sword die by the sword," says my dad regretfully.

"What sword?" David asks bitterly. "Of the thirteen students shot at Kent State, eleven were hit in the side or the back, running away, not advancing or threatening the Guards, as was claimed. The four killed weren't even protesters—one girl shot dead was just walking to class!"

"It's unfortunate," my dad says, "it really is, but if you put yourself in the wrong place at the wrong time, you can get hurt." Dad doesn't like to argue. He gets up and reaches around me to turn off the TV.

"Mom and Dad." My voice is shaking, and I'd be crying if I weren't in such a rage. "Can't you see those dead kids are no different from David and me? Do you really, truly think we should be killed for standing up for what we believe in?" They don't seem to remember about the tear gas canister hitting David's head at the Pentagon, knocking him over, but I do.

"Some of those kids are troublemakers and bums!" my mother says, never afraid to escalate. Those are the words Nixon and Agnew used to describe the Kent State students. Looking at David, she adds, "Others are just plain foolish!" I open my mouth but can't think of what to say.

"It's no use, Roberta," David says steadily. "If they aren't convinced by My Lai and everything else on TV about Vietnam, they're not going to get what happened at Kent State."

"Look, Berta, it's horrible what happened to those kids," my father offers, touching my shoulder softly.

"What about those young National Guardsmen who were frightened out of their wits?" my mother persists. She'd use an olive branch to swat somebody she disagreed with.

"What about all those young men dying in Vietnam? For what?" David asks quietly and bitterly. When he leaves graduate school for Colorado, he'll lose his draft deferment.

"Look, why don't we just sit down and talk about something else," my father says gently, almost pleading, trying to smile, touching my mom's arm lightly now.

"There's nothing else to talk about," David says firmly, standing up and staring down at my father. "Come on, Roberta, let's go. We've got to get up to New Haven."

I don't want to go. I want to grab my mother by the shoulders and shake her. I want to put my arms around my father's neck and cry. They've always been loving and kind, and they're angry and hurt now, so they can't see what's right or wrong. We stand on the porch with nothing to say. But they're also hateful and scornful of my brothers and sisters in this struggle. I'm not thinking very clearly. David's put his beer glass and the empty bottle firmly on the kitchen counter. He turns to me.

"Are you coming?" he asks. Then, more gently and sadly, "Nothing more to say right now." Is he implying maybe later there will be?

Staying here without him isn't a possibility, and nothing will stop him from leaving now. I kiss my mother good-bye. She's as angry and as ready to cry as I am. I hug my dad and kiss him quickly on the cheek, smelling his bay rum, and follow David past the potato chips and dip my mother put on the kitchen counter so she could have both arms free to argue. If she were my age, she might deploy her anger on the barricades. We pass through the house I've lived in since I was born. My parents follow slowly behind us in a silent procession. David and I go out the front door and down the walk to the Chrysler and get in. My parents are framed in the doorway. I wave to them as we drive off, and they wave slowly back.

"We didn't even tell them we were getting married," I say to David, tears dimming my vision.

"We couldn't tell them now," says David. He's not sad—he's angry, like he was when he'd been up all night after Kent State and picked up a desk chair and smashed it through a wall like a cowboy in a western. He yelled that he couldn't wait for my father's generation to die, and I didn't know what to say, crying as I cleaned up the pieces of chair and plaster.

Through my tears now I see the big birches by our house in the side mirror. David's angry and troubled about what's going on in the country every day, and that spills over into his own life. He can't argue with his own father—he's half orphaned, so to speak. In March of his senior year at Yale, his father crashed in a snowstorm in West Virginia as he landed a private jet. David and his father hadn't been speaking much for months before that. His father was an ace pilot in World War II, and his and David's Vietnam face-off was even more extreme than in my family. They both had passionate convictions about America, and they were too much alike. They both showed their Native American heritage by not totally buying into the American self-satisfaction of the fifties and early sixties. They both began as Jeffersonian Democrats, but David's father went into the air force and World War II instead of college, while the years at Yale changed David's views. He watched the Vietnam War rage on TV, and he and his friends stayed up late with the chaplain, William Sloane Coffin, talking about whether to burn their draft cards. David's father once said he wasn't happy unless he was over 10,000 feet, while David doesn't seem happy until his mind is eight miles high, as the Byrds' song goes.

At first David's mother was too subdued and gracious and is now too grief stricken to argue. The summer after his father died, she sent David all the love letters his father had written her during the war. David wouldn't read them, but I looked at a few when he wasn't around. His father wrote one from the Pacific before a mission he couldn't talk about—wrote that he didn't know much, but he knew what he was doing was right, and that he loved her, and all that was as certain as the stars he flew under night after night, and if he made it out of this war, they would be together forever. His love for his country and his love for his fiancée were simple, straightforward, cut from the same cloth. Can David, so full of anger at his country and hate for those running it, love me as fully and simply? Can I reciprocate the way his mother did?

"I guess you're right, there's no way we could tell them about getting married after all that," I say, wiping the tears off my cheek.

"No way," says David. He's right, we can't compromise. We turn north at the Old Post Road and head for New Haven. This isn't how I thought things would work out, but nothing's what I expected, and David's my fiancé, my co-pilot, my partner, my inspiration, my hope.

3 : The Wedding Gang

On the morning of our wedding day, as David and I drive up the dirt road above Zoar Valley, Hugh stands waiting for us by the side of the road. David pulls up and leans out the window of the Chrysler, which is washed and polished, its buoyant postwar lines matching our spirits. Hugh smiles and says, "Nice car to drive, after a war!" quoting Dylan's "Talkin' World War III Blues." The DJ on the radio said it's Dylan's birthday this weekend, and this seems significant.

Hugh snuck back from Canada for our wedding, which means a lot to us. Hugh is so true—his boyish, handsome face is pleasingly symmetrical, except for one blue eye and one hazel eye, which look deep into yours, and the difference in their color disconcerts you. The last time I saw him was on film, larger than life, walking across the screen in Haskell Wexler's *Medium Cool,* outside the 1968 Democratic Convention in Chicago. He walked through the mayhem of cops, screams, and smoke carrying a large American flag over his shoulder, like a Revolutionary War soldier, looking steadily into the camera. He burned his draft card with other Yale students in a bonfire on the quad two years ago. David stood by angrily and watched, but didn't burn his.

Hugh and another Yale friend, Ben, slept in our eighteen-foot tipi last night, after they'd helped David, David's brother Doug, and a few other friends pitch the tipi by the river. They placed it by a slip of sandy dirt near a turn in the river which winds through exquisite limestone cliffs and soft eastern forest thirty miles south of Buffalo, a Hudson River school painting come to life. It's a remnant of what our country looked like to the first European settlers. Looking at Zoar Valley's cliffs, you

understand what Nick Carraway said at the end of *Gatsby*: how those settlers "must have held their breath in the presence of the new continent." We'll spend our wedding night here, but the next valley we pitch
our tipi in will be the Huerfano—we'll live in it while we build our
house.

Hugh leans on the car and says quietly, "There's a motorcycle gang
down in the gorge. The Blades. A gang member drowned upriver a few
days ago, and they're looking for his body." It's ironic that Hugh met
the Blades first, because he had a Harley-Davidson at Yale. When David
got the call two years ago that his father had died in a plane crash, Hugh
took David out for a long ride on the Harley on a cold, snowy March day
before I got there from Poughkeepsie. David could hold onto Hugh
that way, crying into the wind. Hugh's looking calm about the bikers,
but he's not getting married, and I'm not so mellow. At the Rolling
Stones Altamont concert last December, the Hell's Angels "body-
guards" stabbed and killed a fan rushing the stage. None of the Angels
looked like Marlon Brando in *The Wild One*.

"Oh," David says, as if Hugh's just said he spotted a flock of Canada
geese. Maybe David's still feeling the Vietnamese opium he and Hugh
ate two days ago. They took it to reconnoiter Zoar Valley, to pick the
spot with the right vibes for the wedding. On the way home, David
leaned out of the Chrysler and puked. Some puke hit the windshield of
the car Hugh was in, but Hugh didn't blink, he just switched on the
windshield wipers.

I'm too uptight. Everything's fine. David's fine, and he looks at
Hugh and me, and we seem to agree silently—*this is our day, we can all live together harmoniously, the bikers aren't a problem*. Still, I'm having trouble swallowing. I start to unload the car, lifting out the two organically raised
geese I stuffed with wild rice and dried fruit and roasted yesterday while
the guys pitched the tipi. Then we take out some cases of May wine, our
wedding clothes, and the dense loaves of *Tassajara Cookbook* bread I baked.

It's better that our families aren't coming to the wedding. I can't
imagine my parents and David's widowed mother coping with our
friends, much less the Blades. The last time we saw my parents was when
we had the Kent State blowup. My mother thinks draft card burners are
sleazy cowards. Hugh's the bravest, most moral person I know. My parents are essentially good, but they're misguided, bourgeois, hypocriti-
cal. We've orphaned ourselves even before we get to the Huerfano. Our

parents' angry disapproval won't fit at our wedding, and the wedding tent can't spread over all of us.

"We're just going to get married quietly with a few friends," I told my mother when I phoned.

"Oh, I see," she said. Our wedding was starting to look like a mini-Woodstock, with over a hundred people, many of whom we barely knew. I'd hoped a little white lie would make it easier for me to tell her, and easier for her to take, but I was wrong.

When I put down the phone, David took my hand and said, "If we're going to get married, we should do it our own way, a revolutionary way."

Our friends are our family now. David's brother Doug is here—real family, of course, but he's younger, just in high school, and there's no question that he's with us. It's bittersweet how old friends have converged from all over, and this is the last time we'll be with them or our Buffalo friends before we go west. Dr. Frank's come from medical school in Chicago, and Harton's back from Vietnam. Ben's come from New Haven and Hugh from Canada. Mark came in last night from Pennsylvania. He's a cub reporter on one of the smaller papers owned by his family. Pam, my childhood friend, married earlier this year in a civil ceremony with no family present either, came with her husband, Don, in a new VW bus. Some Vassar friends drove up from New York. And Henry, who dropped out of Harvard, then the navy, is back from Hawaii via Berkeley, waiting for a draft board hearing in Boston. It's a gathering of our tribe.

Dr. Frank and Doug appear out of the trees, and they and Hugh help us carry the provisions down the trail. Below, the tipi looms ghostlike through the birches. Lots of people are here already, and lots more cars drive up the road, and we hear people laughing and coming down the path behind us. People stand around under the trees. *The Band* plays on our trusty downstairs neighbor Kevin's portable tape deck. The sky's a little hazy, as if it might rain.

"Someone's brought a large batch of THC iced tea in some Igloo jugs, so watch it," Dr. Frank warns, as he sets a glistening goose on a makeshift plank table. He already sounds like a professional. People arrive in a steady stream, carrying platters of food, bottles of wine, guitars, drums, and flowers. Some of David's students show up, and there are others who look only vaguely familiar. David and Doug pour glasses of May wine, and Kevin helps. Two cameras hang from Kevin's neck—he's our official wedding photographer. Everyone's dressed in bright colors, leathers, and fringes, Nehru shirts and Ukrainian blouses, Middle Eastern and African caftans. The sun breaks out and shimmers on the river briefly. Bob the Rake is standing with Joanne, and a student he was with one night last week is across the clearing, trying to catch his glance. Bob's looking down at his feet a lot, as if he dropped something. Weddings must make him nervous.

A couple walks up from downriver. He's short, a little porky, and dressed in dirty leathers. He has red hair, a beard that creeps way up his cheeks over bad skin, small mud-colored eyes, and a black braided-leather headband. The back of his T-shirt says, "If You can Read this, the Bitch fell off!" He doesn't look as scary as the Hell's Angels at Altamont. She's chunky and taller, with dyed black stringy hair, pale white skin, jeans tight as sausage casings, and a leather biker jacket. Gobs of mascara and purple eyeshadow surround her small eyes and make her look like a raccoon in a school play. Her low-cut polyester shirt is too small, and she has big silver earrings and nails painted bruise purple. R. Crumb would love her.

"Hi! Welcome," says David, offering his hand. David assigned Hunter Thompson's *Hell's Angels* for his course and loved the book. I never actually read it.

The biker looks down at David's hand and mumbles, "Hey. I'm Fuzzbo, and this is Marge. We're lookin' for Cheyenne . . . he's a Blade, and he bought it in the river last week. We gotta find him. I promised his old lady we'd find him, so we can, like, bury him, and give him a good send-off." He looks us up and down. "You the ones getting married?"

"Yes," says David, looking Fuzzbo in the eye and handing him a joint. "I'm really sorry about Cheyenne, man. It's horrible . . . Come and join us if you need a break."

Fuzzbo takes a puff and doesn't give the joint back to David. "Maybe we will," he says, looking around at the cases of May wine and the glistening roast geese. "Let us know if you see anything, okay, man? Come on, Marge, let's go."

Everyone should be welcome at our wedding, but I secretly hope Marge and Fuzzbo won't come back. Will a biker corpse float up on shore while we're getting married? That's another reason it's good my mother's not here. Most of our friends have tramped down the trail now, carrying salad, bread, cakes, wine, and fruit, and we hug and laugh. The weather's holding, although it's cloudier, and then I forget about Cheyenne. Jack's singing, "If you're travelin' in the north country fair . . . ," and sounds just like Bob Dylan. He knows all Dylan's songs, every reported detail of Dylan's life, and dresses like Dylan. He even met him once.

"You know, you don't have to smoke much hash to look at these cliffs and hear dinosaurs eating ferns," smiles Dr. Frank, passing David a pipe.

"Yep," says David, sucking on the pipe. David's boss, Larry Chisolm, the head of the American Studies department at Buffalo, walks up. He's an anthropologist, and was David's professor of American Studies at Yale, and is the only middle-aged person here. He's dressed in L. L. Bean and looks relaxed, not seeming to notice the nearly nude girls dancing to Cream or the hash pipe David passes back to Frank. Chisolm probably schmoozed with the headhunters in New Guinea, so this scene is not a big deal. He gives me a white box with a big white satin ribbon on it. David and he shake hands. Chisolm smiles at me.

"Congratulations!" he says in his wry way, holding my hand with both hands. The white gift box with the big satin ribbon looks out of place in the woods, and I don't know where to put it.

After he moves into the crowd, I take a toke from Frank's pipe. These are our friends come to celebrate our marriage, the end of one chapter, the beginning of another. We're acting on the possibilities we've all talked about late at night for years. About living passionately, honestly, fully, openly, truly, creatively. With no pettiness or hypocrisy. Everyone hesitates, but it's really so easy to take the first step. We've seen the Huerfano, and it changes people. We're bound for glory, willing to make mistakes, on our way.

David grabs my hand and we go inside the tipi to change. I put on a nude bodysuit and a turn-of-the-century, intricately embroidered white lawn slip dress that I found in a junk-antique shop in Buffalo. Maybe someone wore it under some more layers at Edith Wharton croquet parties. The fabric is thin, almost transparent, with white embroidered flowers trailing everywhere, and the dress is high necked with puffy sleeves. David puts on a white fitted shirt with a deep V neck and dark blue velvet bell-bottoms. He wears the beads he bought at a reservation store near Cherokee, North Carolina, after his father's funeral.

"It's all right, it's all right, it's awlll right, it's aaaahhhllll right, IT'S ALL RIGHT, IT'S AWLLL RIGHT . . ." someone chants loudly and desperately outside. I lift the door flap and see Tommy the Dwarf yelling, crouched in the dirt. Hugh's beside him, one hand on his

Wedding tipi, 1970. Photo by Dr. Frank.

shoulder. Hugh whispers that Tommy drank the THC tea not knowing what was in it, and Tommy says he freaks out on THC. This doesn't make sense, since THC's what's in marijuana, and he smoked marijuana like a chimney in David's classes. Tommy, dressed in what looks like a jester's shirt and a leather vest, hugs his knees, rocking back and forth, still shouting, "It's all right!" over and over. He's clean shaven, with a pageboy haircut, which makes his large head look larger. His face is red.

I duck back in the tipi. The diffused, creamy yellow light inside is beautiful. I'm a little worried about the weather, and Tommy, and I try not to think about the bikers. Some clouds are building up, but I don't think it'll rain before the ceremony. At the Altamont concert scenes in the Maysles brothers' documentary, the crowd swelled against the stage, and, for a few seconds in the center of a frame, there was the distinct stabbing motion of one of the Hell's Angels' arms. Nothing bad will happen to Tommy. Dr. Frank said the THC tea is weak and diluted.

David buttons the cuffs of his shirt and the tiny buttons down the back of my dress. The air inside the tipi is warm, almost stuffy, and smells of new canvas. The sound of the crowd outside, even Tommy's frantic yelling, is muffled, and I'm moving in a trance. I pull some of my hair back from around my face and stick a barrette in it, leaving the rest loose down my back, and put on a baby's breath tiara and garland a friend wove. Suddenly David sticks his head out the tipi door and shouts at the top of his lungs—"*ALL RIGHT!*" and Tommy stops. People listen to David. Then, hand in hand, we stoop down to get out the small, circular tipi door and walk barefoot to the river's edge, where the smooth dirt is almost beachlike.

"Everyone get in a circle in astrological order!" Jeff Davis shouts, and the crowd stumbles into a wavy amoeba shape.

"Where are the Pisces?" Tommy cries like a lost child.

Since I'm an Aries and David's a Libra, we're opposite each other in the circle. Jeff steps into the center. He's a Universal Life Church minister and looks like his namesake, Jefferson Davis. Anyone can become a minister in the Universal Life Church by sending ten dollars to its Berkeley headquarters. You get a license back in the mail, and you can perform weddings, but it's not enough to get you a 1-0 exemption for conscientious objectors. Jeff's lanky and elegant, with wavy auburn hair and a goatee. He's in the American Studies department at Buffalo too, and he's going to live with the Kwakiutl Indians in Vancouver for his graduate work next year, while we form a tribe in the Huerfano. He wears an elaborately embroidered cloak and looks like a Confederate officer at a masquerade ball.

All of us in the circle have our arms over the shoulders of our neighbors and smile at one another. There's JB, a Gemini, released from the detox facility just in time for the wedding. He looks like some air's been let out of him, and he's thinner, but he's dressed in white and smiling. Hugh's next to him, a Cancer. Hugh's hair is cut fugitively short. There's a soft breeze, and it's looking more like rain, but I think it'll hold off until after the ceremony. Harton's standing straight across the way with the Scorpios—Harton, who rented a white donkey and kept it for a week in the basement squash court of Davenport College at Yale. Who went to the Mardi Gras party as Lady Godiva, dressed in a strategically stuffed body stocking and a long blond wig, astride the white donkey. Who was third generation at Yale. Who, the rumor went, chose Vietnam instead of disinheritance and came back alive. Who lives in a log cabin on his family's estate now. Who lost his frivolity and more in Vietnam. Whose eyes are different.

Jeff talks about restoring balance. All of us were affected by JB's breakdown, not to mention Nixon's expansion of the war and the daily casualty count of our contemporaries. The sun tries to break through the clouds, and Jeff says in his soft southern voice, "We live in a time when the earth is out of balance, when this country is horribly imbalanced, when it's hard for those who see the most to stay sane. We're gathered today, standing in astrological order, to honor the wedding of David and Roberta, exact astrological opposites, who've found a balance, who complete each other, who are in love." It's like a movie with the sound track turned down low. Jeff's mouth moves, and we answer, but somehow he seems far away. Then the white gold rings with the row of yin-yang symbols carved into them are on our fingers. David's face comes close and we kiss, and I wake from my trance like in a fairy tale. Everyone cheers, and he takes my hand and we walk to the edge of the river. I hear the water running over the rocks, and we take off our clothes and swim across the broad, cold, flowing water and stand nude on the other side under a small waterfall shooting down the limestone cliffs, and we kiss again. Our friends clap and hoot from the other shore, and the sun comes out as big raindrops pockmark the river.

When we swim back, my friend Linny meets me. "So much courage," she whispers, rubbing my back with a blanket and wrapping me in it. "You're forging ahead into a New World, and we're going there, too."

If the Vancouver commune idea doesn't play out, she and JB will go to India to live with Baba Ram Dass's guru, Neem Karoli Baba. Professor Chisolm walks up and kisses me on the cheek like a father as I shiver under my blanket, and he shakes David's hand again and walks slowly back up the trail with his hands in his pockets. I put on jeans and a thin Ukrainian shirt; David puts his wedding clothes back on, and we carve the geese, and people drink, eat, play music. It's *A Midsummer Night's Dream,* although it's May and a little cool. Some are too stoned to care about eating. A group of David's students sit in a circle in a clump of ash saplings and lean forward, pressing their foreheads together, crying and moaning happily. At least I think they're happy. At dark, a few Blades join the crowd as Henry and David play guitar around the fire, singing the blues tunes and early rock and roll songs they've played for years. Tommy the Dwarf sits sedately on a rock now. Hugh's smiling and listening, his small pack beside him, neatly tied up. He's ready for a fast exit on the off chance the state police might show up, and his eyes scout the darkness beyond the campfire circle.

Later it starts to drizzle, and the guitars have to be put away. Lots of people leave, but a few have pitched tents and are staying. Pam and Don are sleeping in their VW camper up on the road. Dr. Frank has pitched his mountaineering tent, and his camp stove and other equipment are set up neatly under a tarp. Doug, Ben, and Hugh are sleeping in an old Boy Scout tent. There are no stars. We forgot to bring a flashlight, so we borrow one from Frank.

Inside the tipi we stop short. The motorcycle gang lie in a heap like a bunch of sleeping walruses. Two of the guys are snoring. This isn't my idea of a nuptial chamber, and I look at David indignantly. David searches for Fuzzbo and pokes him gently with the flashlight.

"Fuzzbo," he whispers, "this is where we were going to spend our wedding night!"

Fuzzbo lifts his head groggily, gets up on his elbows, and burps. He rubs one eye and doesn't say anything, scowling and squinting into the flashlight. His leather headband is down over one eyebrow. "Cheyenne's gone, man," he says sleepily, burping again. "He's nowhere. And I promised Darlene I'd get him back to bury."

"Fuzzbo," David persists bravely, "*we just got married.*"

"Okay, okay," grumbles Fuzzbo. "Marge, get Lennie to move over."

"Fuckin' son of a bitch," Marge mutters. Lennie says "oomph" when Marge pokes him, swears and moves over a little, and starts snoring again.

Now a little strip of ground near the door is available. David steps over the bodies and valiantly pulls our blankets off them. He unrolls one foam pad. We don't undress, and we press together on the pad under the blankets. Rain drips down the tipi, and I squeeze back toward David. No ditch was dug around the tipi to keep the water out. Lennie and someone on the other side snore in syncopation. I smell the campfire smoke, the bodies, the tobacco and beer on their breath, and I stare at the tipi canvas, listening to the soft sound of raindrops between snores, sleeping fitfully.

At dawn, we're the first out of the tipi. Dr. Frank's outside his tent, dressed, shaved, and making coffee on his camping stove. It's bright, and there are only a few clouds, but the campground's muddy. We move a few food platters and sit around the plank table, sipping strong coffee in Dr. Frank's tin cups.

"I think I got one or two snaps with my Leica," he says. "I hope so, because Kevin was too wrecked to look through his viewfinder."

"Maybe it was too magical to be photographed," David says and smiles at me.

The sun gets higher, and the tipi gets hotter. The motorcycle gang stumble out like circus clowns spilling out of a Volkswagen Bug, but they're not smiling.

"Good morning!" David says. Only Fuzzbo and another guy grunt in reply. Marge's eye shadow is smeared and clownlike. Slowly they fan out and disappear into the trees, grunting and lurching up toward the road. Once in a while one of the men swears, and they break a lot of branches as they walk. Then we can't hear them anymore. Birds sing back and forth in the trees, flies buzz around the feast leftovers, and an indignant squirrel scolds us occasionally.

The morning sun's on the river dappling through spaces between the young leaves in the canopy above us. David and I are married now, and a marriage is more than the sum of its parts. We're the nucleus of our own family. Looking out over the river, I wonder if Cheyenne is on the bottom somewhere, sunk under the weight of his leathers, or still wrapped around his motorcycle, anchored underwater, pressing up against the strata of the limestone cliffs. Above the swimming water, the cliffs loom serene and timeless, just the way Thomas Cole or Asher Durand might have painted them. I take a slice of a pear David cuts and drink some more of Frank's coffee, gazing every once in a while at the ring on my left hand.

Later, we walk up to the car, stopping at Pam and Don's VW bus.

Tommy the Dwarf crashed on the front seat last night, and he's still sleeping like a child under Pam's Peruvian poncho. They say they'll drive him back to Buffalo. Pam stands outside, eating a chocolate bar and some granola from a bag, and Don smokes a cigarette. I take a handful of granola.

"Great wedding," says Pam. "But, you know, we don't believe in astrology."

I make a face at her. "Let me guess, another opiate of the people? You socialists, you're so predictable! What about magic, and the irrational, and *fun*?" She makes a face back at me, and we laugh and hug. "See you at the apartment. Thanks for taking care of Tommy," I say.

At the Chrysler, I kiss David good-bye. I'm driving Hugh to the border alone. It's safer that way. Cops don't stop me, even in the flamboyant Chrysler with California plates, because I'm so blond and normal looking, and I'm a woman. Hugh and David hug awkwardly on the road, and then Hugh and I get in the car and drive north to the border, the windows down, my hair blowing. We don't see any Blades on the road. We're lost in our thoughts, since the wind rushing in the windows makes it hard to have a conversation, but once I shout over the highway noise, "I'm thinking about our friends headed for Vancouver, and that Robert Frost poem about the road forking in the woods keeps running through my head, like a bad catchy song."

"Like 'To Sir with Love,' or 'Yummy, Yummy, Yummy, I've Got Love in My Tummy'?" I nod and laugh at him. "Your head's full of poems and movies and song lyrics, isn't it?" Hugh says, looking out the window.

Meanwhile, Frank, David, Doug, and the others stay behind to clean up the site and take down the tipi. They say later that they looked everywhere, but Chisolm's present was gone. They found lots of beer cans in the woods north of where our feast took place. The bikers guzzled all their beer before joining us. David and our friends picked up the bikers' empties too.

At the bridge, the border guards make us tense, although it isn't a problem for Hugh to get back into Canada. He grabs his pack, opens the door, and smiles at me. "You're happier now, now that you're married."

"Yes, I am. At least this much is certain," I say, looking into his different-colored eyes one last time. "Hugh, thanks. For being here." I try not to cry. The American and Canadian flags blow in the wind, their ropes and pulleys clanking against the metal flagpoles.

"Wouldn't have missed it for the world!" he says, and then he leans into the car, kisses me on the cheek, and whispers into my ear, "There are no borders!" He turns and walks slowly over the bridge. Below him, the Niagara's gray and murky. Who knows what chemicals they've dumped into it? I look past the ring on my left hand clenching the steering wheel, watching him walk away. If there are no borders, why am I so sure we'll never see him again? Hugh looks over his shoulder, smiles, and walks back out of his American life, and ours.

4 : Searching

It has taken David and me exactly a year to arrive at where we're headed. This June, we're packing the Chrysler and moving to Libre. Last summer, we packed a Corvair camper and toured southwestern communes. We sampled communes in Colorado and New Mexico like Goldilocks trying out the furniture and porridge at the Three Bears' house. With Leslie Fiedler's help, I got a faculty fund summer grant from the SUNY Buffalo English department to study new art and literature arising out of alternative lifestyles. No graduate student teaching fellow had ever applied for a grant before, but nothing in the fine print said I couldn't. It wasn't such a stretch to give me a little money to visit communes; one of my friends was writing his English doctoral thesis on the language of soap operas. With the grant money I bought a Pentax Spotmatic and some film. David got the Corvair camper and a kilo of marijuana. He thought the grass would make us welcome at communes, ordinarily suspicious of media and publicity. He was right.

So, one year ago, in June 1969, we headed west to the communities founded on peace and love, springing up in the same states where the government had hollowed out a mountain for NORAD, where the plutonium was piling up at Rocky Flats, where they'd dreamed up Little Boy and Fat Man on Otowi Creek, where the first atomic bomb exploded at White Sands. We drove straight through to Colorado, spending our first night on Pikes Peak, and the next day drove south past the Huerfano Valley without knowing it. We were headed for Drop City, near Trinidad. On the way south to Trinidad on Interstate 25, we stopped to see the site of the Ludlow massacre and stared at the photo of Mother Jones on display there. That was where saber-swinging Colorado National Guard had charged women and children during the Great Coalfield Wars at the beginning of the century, where striking coal miners and the Pinkerton detectives John D. Rockefeller Jr. had hired shot it out on the streets of Walsenburg and Trinidad. In comparison, the Chicago police bashing protesters' heads at the Democratic Convention in 1968 was mild. The mines were closed now, the company towns crumbling, and the area was too dry for decent ranching.

Drop City was situated on a few dusty acres too near the highway. It was the first geodesic commune, on its way to becoming the first hippie ghost town. I photographed the cluster of Buckminster Fuller—style domes, their wooden geodesic skeletons skinned with steel triangles blowtorched from the roofs and hoods of junkyard cars. A door on a small dome kept swinging open and slamming shut in the wind. There were only a few hangers-on in the main dome, standing around like they'd missed their train. Our footsteps echoed on the uneven two-by-four floor, and everyone's eyes looked up to meet ours. When David took out a joint, things perked up a little.

"Too many runaways and crazies came," explained Al, a sad-eyed older man. "There was a suicide here." I snapped more pictures of the domes and the people. The wind shaking the dome made me feel like we were at sea. A blond woman in a ripped Mexican blouse had chapped lips and a cracked, dry red face. David played guitar for a while with a guy who looked like a medieval serf. Outside the dome, a little blond girl with no underpants under her short dress held a baby goat and smiled at my camera. David filmed the domes and the goats tethered outside. We didn't stay.

As we left, Al said, "So, you're heading for New Buffalo, huh?" He looked like he wanted to go along.

"Yeah," said David, leaning out the window. "We thought we'd check it out."

"You ought to go up and see what they're doing at Libre, too," Al suggested.

"Where's that?" David asked.

"About two hours north, up past Walsenburg, in the Huerfano Valley," Al answered, picking up a tin can. A white goat had ripped the label off and was deftly rolling it into her mouth with her lips.

"Well, we just might do that, thanks, but first we're gonna check out the places around Taos." David smiled and turned the van onto the rutted road leading to the highway.

So we headed south to New Mexico for our second research opportunity. New Buffalo was nestled in Arroyo Hondo north of Taos. It was beautiful, but a little too far back in the past. I spent three days in the timeless adobe kitchen, helping the women cook and clean up three times a day. There were lots of toddlers and babies. The older kids played outside in the courtyard and ran inside and hid in their mothers' skirts. All the women wore long skirts and dirty Mexican blouses. I wore clean Levis and a T-shirt. On the third day, a big woman named Joyce wiped bread dough off her hands and rang the bell for lunch, and David and the men irrigating the corn field stabbed their shovels in the dirt and came in.

"How's it going?" David leaned over and asked me quietly after grace, as we sat on the long plank bench at the table.

"How's it going?" I answered under my breath. "*How's it going?* This is great what's happening here, it really is, but I'm getting dishpan hands. If I have to stay in the kitchen anymore, I'll have a nervous breakdown. *I went to Vassar, for God's sake.*"

"Okay, okay," David said soothingly. "You've got enough pictures, don't you? Let's leave after lunch."

As we packed up the camper that afternoon, we asked Buffalo Bob for directions to Lama Foundation, Reality Construction Company, and Morning Star Commune. Buffalo Bob told us, then smiled at us, took a big hit off a fat farewell joint David had rolled, and said, "I think you ought to go to Colorado and see Libre."

"Yeah," said David, "somebody else mentioned Libre to us."

On the mesa between Arroyo Hondo and Arroyo Seco, at Reality Construction Company and Morning Star Commune, they let us through the gate at the same time they turned away a CBS News crew and a *Newsweek* reporter. The landscape was beautiful, the mesa magical, and D. H. Lawrence's spirit was everywhere, but the women were in the kitchen again, nude or wearing long skirts, which bothered me, but probably wouldn't have bothered Lawrence. Of course, Lawrence enjoyed housework, while Frieda, a von Richtofen, shared my sentiments about cooking and cleaning. David offered to help some of the men make adobe bricks, and I tagged along to take pictures. I wasn't getting stuck in the kitchen again.

Max Finstein, a beatnik poet in his fifties, showed us around. He'd

Children at Reality Construction Company, men making adobes in the distance, summer 1969.

A bath at Morning Star, June 1969.

Strider at New Buffalo,
January 1970.

Peñasco, New Mexico, January 1970
(sign at lower right reads "United
States Army Recruiting Station").

been living at New Buffalo until his wife dumped him for another man. Max went east to the mesa and founded Reality Construction Company. He told us that when D. H. Lawrence got off the train in New Mexico for the first time he said, "I feel as if my eyes have been peeled!" Max asked me to make sure the men couldn't be recognized in my pictures. I didn't ask why, but took pictures of their backs and silhouettes against the sun. We spent the whole afternoon talking with Max, who'd spent time at Black Mountain in the fifties with most of the poets we'd studied in college. As the sun went down, Max said, "Why don't you go up and see Peter Rabbit at Libre in the Huerfano? I think you'd be interested in what they're doing there." He said Libre meant "free" in Spanish, and Huerfano meant "orphan."

Lama Foundation was our fourth stop, outside Questa, high on the mountain where Lawrence lived. The architecture was impressive, but it was hard to find anybody. They must all have been meditating. The main building was polished, serene, empty, and a lot more finished and elegant than at the other communes. We sat in the kitchen of the eight-sided adobe capped with a graceful wood dome and talked to a guy with an East Indian name, a Jewish face, and a Brooklyn accent. He shook his head when offered a joint, and when David started talking about Vietnam, he ran outside, shouting, *"I can't listen to this, I can't listen to this!"*

On the way north, David turned to me and said, "So, what did you think?"

"Oh, it's great what they're doing, and it's beautiful, but I'd go crazy if I lived anywhere we've been. I'd like something a little more Bloomsbury, a little more Dada, a little more Mabel Dodge Luhan, I dunno."

"You mean, you'd like to marry an Indian and pay members of his pueblo to build your house, like Mabel?" David asked.

"Well, you're part Indian," I said slyly.

He laughed. "I know what you mean. Shit, my hands are ruined from that adobe brick making. . . . I won't be able to play the guitar for days!"

Six hours later we drove up the dirt road off Highway 69 in the Huerfano Valley. The mountains loomed around the valley's edges, and my heart beat faster. I felt an inexplicable anticipation, enhanced by the exhilaration of seeing great distances. I hadn't been west before. My family always went east to vacation on Long Island or in Europe. When all my ancestors got off their boats in the New World, they stopped right there. No one lived farther west than the west bank of the

Hudson, except my dad's sister, Aunt Martha, who married a Texan and was considered nice but a little crazy. My grandmother always talked of California, her eyes shining. She bought a ticket west, but died unexpectedly, too young, before she could take her trip, bequeathing her western dreams to me. Likewise, David's European ancestors stayed in North Carolina, and his Cherokee forebears avoided the Trail of Tears and stayed east too. But he and Hugh took a drive-away car to Oregon one summer in college, so he knew what to expect more than I.

"This is it," he said, as we clumped over a cattle guard, the Corvair heaving with a fatal case of vehicular tuberculosis as my heart beat faster. On the open gate was a bright new sign proclaiming "LIBRE" in exuberant script. We coughed up the road to a spot across from a construction site under some ponderosa pines. It had rained, and the ground was muddy. The creek up ahead gushed under the pine trees. There was a little shed with a tarp for one wall. Parked near it was a wildly painted, hunchbacked 1946 Plymouth. There were stacks of adobe bricks covered with sheets of plastic, and a cement mixer. And the view! Out across the valley, more and more mountains traipsed across the horizon like the last herd of buffalo.

The tarp on the shed lifted, and a tall man came out. "Hello there," he said.

"Hello," said David. "Is this Libre?"

"Yes, it is," he answered, looking us over and puffing on his hand-rolled cigarette. When we first drove up to those places, it was like dogs meeting at the park, sniffing each other out.

"I'm David, and this is Roberta," said David. "Max and Buffalo Bob in New Mexico told us to come up and check you out."

"I'm Jim," he said, "and Sandy's in the lean-to there."

A *lean-to!* I'd only read about them, never seen one! In the Laura Ingalls Wilder books I read as a kid, Pa built a lean-to as soon as they got to a new place on the frontier. Here we were at Little House on the Commune! Jim, who had a beard like Laura's Pa, was our age, six foot two and lanky. He had crudely cut shoulder-length dark blond hair, dark eyebrows and beard, and Coke bottle—thick wire-rimmed glasses. His denim bell-bottoms sat low on his sharp hipbones and were patched with purple satin. The sleeves of his homemade shirt billowed, and the collar was large and pointy. The unbuttoned neck showed his black and blond chest hair. The shirt looked like Zorro's, except it was too gaudy, and reeked of patchouli.

"Well, we're from the University of Buffalo, and we're studying communes," David said ironically, then laughed softly. He looked Jim in the eyes. "Really, we're looking for a place to be." This was the first time either of us had said that.

"Yeah?" Jim puffed on his cigarette and looked us over again. I stepped forward and looped my arm through David's. "Sandy's cooking up rice and beans. Wanna come in and have some?"

"Yeah," David said, "that'd be great. We've got a bottle of wine, if you'd like it."

Jim grinned, "Bring it along. . . . Hey, is that a *Corvair* van?" Corvairs were a bad joke to anybody who knew anything about cars.

"Yeah," answered David sheepishly, and they laughed. David got the wine, and we walked past the small, square foundation with one row of adobe bricks laid on it already.

"How far can you see here, Jim?" I asked. I couldn't stop looking at the mountains. I was looking *down* at a cloud, which was drifting in the middle of the valley like a lost sheep.

"Oh, you can see just about as far as you want." Jim was right. At Libre, the feeling got stronger and stronger that we could see forever if we wanted to, that we could become anybody we wanted to be, that at Libre we had the opportunity to be—well, free.

5 : Libre

Inside Jim's lean-to were a Great Majestic wood cook-stove, a crude wood kitchen counter with three crowded shelves, a funky table, three chairs. And Sandy. Small and brunette with thin lips, she wore tinted granny glasses, a thick Mexican sweater, harem pants made from the same garish material as Jim's shirt, and Hopi moc-casins. She stood by the stove, smoking a hand-rolled cigarette with suave concentration, the way people smoke in French movies. She said "Hi" softly when Jim intro-duced us, exhaling smoke like the Cheshire cat and stir-ring a pot of beans. Above her, copper-bottomed French pots hung from hooks on a roof pole. Jim and Sandy had met in Austin at the university. His father was an air force colonel, and she was an upper-echelon army brat who'd lived in France. They'd been at Libre six weeks. While they built their house, they slept in the Hump-mobile, a '46 Plymouth Jim had modified, blowtorching the trunk and part of the roof out and welding a hump of metal onto it to make it into a camper. Jim painted mystical symbols on the Humpmobile, some traditional and some of his own invention.

We sat at the table while Sandy worked at the stove. On the wall behind Jim was his painting of a woman's profile. She was looking up, and in front of her was a tree, with a canyon behind it that ended in a geodesic dome which sat where the woman's lower brain should have been. Mountains bulged on her forehead, which had a third eye in the center, and in the background were sunset rays with arrow tips pointing at the setting sun. Sandy's knit-ting needles and yarn hung in a Mexican bag on the wall beside the painting. A glass kerosene lamp on the table

Sandy and the Humpmobile, June 1969.

was painted with more symbols, and a cup of dying wildflowers sat beside it.

Sandy dished aduki beans and rice into handmade bowls and pulled some bread out of the Great Majestic's oven. Jim lit the lamp and fat candles, and pulled up a large tin storage can as a fourth chair. David poured wine into crude clay mugs that matched the bowls. Libre was founded in 1968, they told us, three hundred and sixty acres, up against sixty-five miles of national forest that draped over the top of Greenhorn and down the other side. It was a nonprofit corporation, registered as a school because enough Libre people had postgraduate degrees to meet state requirements. There were few rules: you had to build your house out of sight of everyone else's, and you had to be a couple. Besides paying nominal dues to the corporation for group expenses, like taxes on the land or a pump for the spring box, you were on

your own. All the members had to agree to let you join. Two domes and a zome (a geodesic structure with separate rooms, not dome shaped) had been built the first year. That summer three more houses were being built, including Jim and Sandy's.

"How do you make money?" I asked, feeling a little crass.

Jim look at me and exhaled. "Oh, by hook or by crook. You don't need much. We get food stamps. We make art and sell it. We get gigs in cities in the winter. We got paid by the National Institutes of Health so they could study if we're able to communicate telepathically more than others." He laughed. "We can!"

David's and my eyes met in the candlelight after dinner. "This is far out," he said. Jim and Sandy smiled, accepting our admiration modestly. David rolled a joint.

The next morning, the clouds were gone. Jim walked us over the gushing creek to Dean and Linda's dome, which looked like the dome

Dean, Lia, and Linda, June 1969.

in Jim's painting. Inside, Dean and Linda were working at large tables on the perimeter. A Coltrane tape played loudly. There were two Morris chairs reupholstered with hand-painted canvas, a large bed platform made of logs and pine planks, and no other furniture. Dean's abstract, Rothko-like paintings hung on the one partition wall in the dome, which divided the kitchen and living space from the studio space. It was like a New York artist's loft, except the light was so bright coming in through the arc of triangular windows that tracked the Sangre de Cristo Range across the valley. Dean turned off the tape, a little reluctantly. Linda smiled—she resembled the woman in Jim's painting. A baby toddled beside her dragging two big rag dolls.

"Welcome," Dean said. He was broad chested, with white-blond hair and beard, and a little morose, like an Ingmar Bergman star. His muscular arms were deeply tanned. He had small, bright blue eyes with crow's feet around them, a beaklike nose, and thin lips. He was older.

Linda was twenty-three, like me; she'd been Dean's student at Carnegie Tech. She was my height, with long, rich red hair and shiny dark brown eyes. She wore jeans and a cowboy shirt she'd made from scraps of crazy but coordinating calicos. Their baby, Lia, stared and hovered near Linda. Lia was one, redheaded, with bright brown eyes. Her big nude rag dolls were anatomically correct. One had yellow yarn hair and stuffed fabric genitals, and the other had red yarn hair, stuffed fabric breasts, and red yarn cross-stitched over her crotch.

"Did you make the dolls?" I asked Linda.

"Yeah," she answered, laughing. "She drags them all over! Do you want some mint tea?"

"That would be great," I said. "Do you mind if I take some pictures?"

For four days we stayed with Jim and Sandy and walked around and met the rest of Libre. Each couple was different, and their visions were as varied as their houses. We walked with Jim over the back ridges to the waterfall on Turkey Creek. The water, crashing down the mountain, was too high to cross, swollen from recent rains. As David and I stood by the creek with Jim and watched the cold water gush past us, we knew we wanted to be part of what was going on at Libre.

On the shelf at Jim and Sandy's was a two-quart jar of little orange tabs. "Oh, Owsley sent that to us," Jim said one morning at breakfast. "It was a commune-warming gift, ha, ha."

"It spilled a month ago, and we spent a whole morning picking teensy orange pills out of the dirt floor," Sandy said laconically. "I still find some when I rake and sweep."

"Take a few for later," Jim suggested. "You might want to have some on hand on Santa Fe Baldy at that solstice celebration you're going to."

"Yeah, maybe that's a good idea," David grinned. "Kesey's going to be there, and they're supposed to have a school bus race with *Furthur* . . . man, we've got to see that! But they might not have enough acid for the hundreds of people who are supposed to show up . . ."

After breakfast, we walked over to Peter Rabbit's zome, west of Dean and Linda's meadow, through some piñons. Peter sat at his kitchen table sipping coffee with his wife, Judy, a lanky woman with large eyes and limp hair. We never found out much about her—Peter did most of the talking. Like Dean, Peter was ten years older than David and I; he was six foot three, but not handsome or strapping. He sat slumped over in his chair, his torso curving like the letter C, his chest caving in, his shoulders slouching, as if to protect his heart. He had thin, ginger-brown

hair pressed flat against his skull by the baseball cap he always wore outdoors. Below the cap line, his hair puffed out in thin clumps. He had
small, light brown eyes that squinted with laughter, or caginess, and a
sparse beard and mustache. He looked a little tired, as if he'd been explaining things to younger people a bit more than he liked. He was a
hippie with dentures, a world-weary patriarch, and his smile was sweet.
When younger, he could have played Ichabod Crane. He claimed he was
at Black Mountain, then came to Colorado in the sixties to start Drop
City. His paperback about his experience lay on his table. Libre was Peter's second try at utopia in the West. We smoked a joint and sipped coffee around the table, and Peter talked about Greenhorn Mountain.

"I thought this mountain was named after some eastern newcomer
who lived or died here," I said.

"No, no," Peter laughed. "It's named after Cuerno Verde, a great
Comanche chief. His headdress had one buffalo horn in it, painted
green. Three years after the Declaration of Independence was signed,
the governor of New Mexico, Juan Batista de Anza, and his men
ambushed and killed Greenhorn and his men on this mountain." He
stopped and sighed. Peter looked tired from repeating this story, but he
also liked to tell a tale. "You know," he continued, "Greenhorn and his
men were camped on the flank of this mountain, and some Ute scouts
took the Spaniards right to them." He swept his arm back toward the
mountain and raised his voice. "When the great chief saw the the
Spaniards, he yelled, 'Grandsons, it's a good day to die!' He died on
this mountain! Cuerno Verde was a great warrior and chief." Peter's fist
lingered in the air, and he shook his head sadly. Judy looked like she'd
heard the story a few times before. Peter lowered his outstretched arm
slowly. Since all the Comanches either were killed or escaped, and neither the Utes nor the Spaniards understood Comanche, and most
likely couldn't hear Greenhorn anyway, I wondered how Peter knew
Greenhorn's last words. Still, his story moved me.

After a reverent pause David said, "You know, we're thinking about
building here, if it works out. We thought we'd walk around and check
out sites."

"Only sites left are up on the ridge," Peter said. "There's no electricity like down here, and you'll have to haul your water. Someday,
though, we'll have a water system and tanks all over. There's a meadow,
straight up behind us, from when the piñons got the blight. It's closest
to the lower land. Check it out," Peter added with a wise look.

"Yeah," David said, "we will. Oh, and, by the way, do you have anything we could take these little pills with?" Judy Rabbit laughed and got some orange juice from the refrigerator.

By the time we reached the top of the ridge that day last June, we were feeling the acid. The edges and colors of everything were heightened and vibrating. Rocky Mountain bee plants, mountain asters, and Indian paintbrush dotted the meadow. Mounds of clustered cactus bore bright yellow buttery blooms in the center of their plump, spiked flesh. We smelled the pungent scent of sage we'd crushed with our footsteps. The bare skeletons of blighted piñons looked like something from the set of an old John Wayne movie. Hummingbirds zipped around like dive bombers, and the mountains across the valley shimmered. On the east side of the meadow was a huge boulder, about fourteen feet high—striated granite, spotted with chartreuse and orange lichen. We were immediately drawn to it. Gently running our fingers over the glowing, fuzzy lichen, looking up at it, we realized that we should build our house around it.

Or maybe it wasn't so clear where to build the house until Steve walked down the path and bumped into us. He was large and muscular, with big, blue eyes and leonine blond hair sticking out in electric waves. His leather shirt was loosely laced, and his chest muscles bulged under it. Nothing happens by accident, after all. We'd met Steve and Patricia earlier, and walked around the foundations of the hexagonal house they were building by Dry Creek, south of Dean and Linda's dome. Patricia was tall and ample, with reddish-blond hair, small, sky-blue eyes, creamy skin, and ruddy cheeks. They were stacking up reject railroad ties for walls, and were going to cover them with adobe. A huge tree trunk served as the central roof support for the lower level of the house, which would have a smaller room on the second story, surrounded by a deck. Talking with Steve and patting the rock like a pet elephant, we realized that the house asking to be built on the ridge was a lot like theirs. It would be an octagon, not a hexagon, but we would stack railroad ties for walls and plaster them with adobe. This huge boulder would be its center support instead of a tree trunk. It too would have a smaller second-story room and deck.

While Steve and David talked excitedly, I moved uphill to the back side of the rock. Because of the ridge's steep incline, it wasn't as tall there. There were enough cracks and ledges to grip and stick my feet into on this side, and I pulled myself up and sat on top of the rock and looked out at the Sangre de Cristo Range, which, in my hallucinatory state, I could hear rumble. I clenched my teeth and held onto the rock with my thighs, as if it might bolt. Were the mountains making that noise, or was it a cattle truck on Route 69, miles away in the middle of the valley? I couldn't tell, it didn't matter. The mountains pulsated with the energy that had forced them out of the ground sixty million years ago, when a new and greater uplifting of land started. I could see the Laramide Revolution Dean had told us about, the series of uplifts that had initiated a mountain-building process still slowly taking place. The mountain range undulated, it surged and rippled. The boulder I sat astride quivered with that same energy as I did. My blood surged, and my heart pulsated with the mountains.

Below, on the downhill side of the rock, David and Steve were talking about the house. Steve's part of the conversation grew as ideas sprang up in his head like the mountains pushing up in the Laramide Revolution, though he wasn't stoned on acid. He darted around the rock, describing rooms and windows, beams and doors. His big arms swept this way and that.

"You will build your house upon a rock," Steve said biblically, and we nodded. "This huge boulder will be your central support and your interior wall. The downhill half, with the kitchen and the dining room, will be tall ceilinged and spacious—maybe fifteen-foot ceilings! You could put in sleeping or meditation lofts above. The back, uphill from the rock, will be low and cavelike."

"With the fireplace back there, sort of kiva-like, with adobe bancos . . . ," David managed to interject enthusiastically.

Steve nodded, his arms frozen in the air as he listened to David. Then he moved them again, pointing expansively, explaining. "Above, a smaller octagonal house will be where you sleep. A deck around it for sitting, sunning, meditating, and getting high!" His arms swung around like helicopter blades. I giggled. He didn't notice and went on, mainly addressing David, anyway. "You can get your vigas on the mountain. There are plenty of felled trees the loggers left behind—too small for their purposes, just right for yours!"

"Yes," I said like Molly Bloom. "Yes . . . yes . . . yes." I was speaking to the mountains, but Steve thought I was agreeing with him. He couldn't tell I felt a rapture the saints must have felt, physical and overwhelming. When I went to Christ's Church as a kid, the people hung over from cocktails at the yacht club prayed and surreptitiously examined one another's outfits during the sermon. I read the entire Bible when I was twelve. Until LSD, however, I never felt that surge of wonder, the deep conviction that we are all God. I never understood that God was in me and everyone else, that life was infinitely precious, that the same divine energy pulsated through space, rocks, trees, everyone, everything, and that God was Love.

Taking acid is intense, and fun. You peel away like an onion to your core. Out the window goes who you think you are, your East Coast education, your history, your sex. I don't know how long I sat on the rock and stared at my hands, as variegated in color as the lichen on the rock. I couldn't tell where my hands on the rock stopped and the lichen began, and this was wondrous and overwhelming. The lichen twitched and rippled. I was on the edge of a new and profound understanding of the life force seeping through the lichen and me.

Starting down the path off the ridge, Steve stopped for a soliloquy. "It will be far out! Think of a visitor opening the door and staring at this huge rock in the middle of your house!" His voice jolted me out of my deep biological reverie, and he called over his shoulder as he headed down the ridge, "Why, you can build a stairway up the side of the rock to the sloped top and into your bedroom. There you can have windows, a skylight, too, so you can lie there and look at the stars and the moon rise and set. You'll see the Sangres bleed in the dawn . . ." We couldn't make out his words, and then we couldn't hear him at all, except for an occasional rock he'd kicked that would pop off the path down the slope. Then it was quiet.

There was a shriek above me, and I looked up at a falcon, swooping down from another ridge higher on Greenhorn. David was smoking, staring at a rotting piñon tree trunk as the blue smoke wisped up above his head. I knew what he was thinking—he couldn't tell where the decaying tree ended and the soil began, and the sensuality of decay was overwhelming.

"David, look up!" I whispered. The falcon turned, circling back to its craggy nest behind us. This was significant. To the Indians, big birds are spirits, messengers.

"'How do you know but ev'ry bird that cuts the airy way / Is an immense world of delight, closed by your senses five?'" David recited slowly. His face was pale and skull-like, his skin iridescent, his dark eyes boiling. Black wisps of hair around his face looked bluish-purple.

"Blake," I said, giggling. "'The Marriage of Heaven and Hell,'" and he grinned back. I sat a little longer on the rock, riding it into the future, and then climbed down and sat next to him, our backs resting against the west side of the boulder as we faced our destiny and the dining area. We laughed, got up, paced around the rock, our arms around each other, placing the stove here, pausing and planning what we would do there, where the doors and windows would be.

"Rock around the rock," David joked. He seemed happier at Libre. Also, he was stoned out of his mind, and he hadn't once thought of his draft status, or Nixon and Kissinger, or the baby-faced GIs, only pawns in their game, or the napalm. On the west side of the meadow we found a clearing big enough for our tipi and summer kitchen when we came back to build. We lay on our backs among the wildflowers in our meadow and watched clouds slide by like a stop-motion film. We held hands tight, too full for words for an eternity, and talked to each other through our skin. Later, we made love under the heaving sky, as our souls took root in the meadow. We walked back to the rock again to watch the sunset. Clouds flamed, light slanted, birds called, and the valley grew still as shadows crept across it.

"This is better than the seven o'clock news, and no commercials!" I thought, laughing, but I couldn't tell David. The words weren't there again. The sun dipped behind a mountain forty miles away, its final bolts of light shooting up, splitting the horizon. From this ridge in the Huerfano, we could look out forty, fifty miles anytime, and see inside ourselves further than that. The temperature dipped suddenly after sunset. At that altitude the air cools even when the sun goes behind a cloud for five minutes at mid-day. We'd been out all day, and we were overcome by cosmic shivers. I hadn't had anything to drink for hours. My mouth felt cottony and metallic, and my skin stretched across my skull. I could taste the aluminum in my fillings. My fingernails were dirty, and my hair had grass in it. David smelled of tobacco, piñon pitch, and faintly of human salt. We left the ridge at twilight, eager to sit by the stove and drink tea, to tell Jim and Sandy all our plans. As stars started to spatter the sky, the electric lights through Dean and Linda's dome windows answered. Trudging east across the creek, we smelled the piñon burning in Jim and Sandy's Great Majestic. Turning to look back up the ridge, for a split second I saw lamplight glow in the windows of our house around the rock. I can see it now.

The next day, we left and drove south to the solstice festival on Santa Fe Baldy, where hippies from all over the West converged on a parcel of

Ken Kesey and Furthur *before the solstice bus race, Santa Fe Baldy, 1969.*

land rented from Tesuque Pueblo for the weekend. David and I had connected with Libre, and I felt disconnected at the solstice gathering. We camped by a stream on the edge of things. It was fun, but a little beside the point—after seeing the Huerfano, we knew where we wanted to be and what we wanted to do. The weekend was half Fellini, half Be-In. Ken Kesey strode through the wildflowers in a short-legged, red polka-dot union suit, telling everyone the Beatles had given it to him. One afternoon under the aspens, a big yogi conducted a wedding of twenty couples at the same time. In the match between the Merry Prankster bus *Furthur* and another hippie school bus, both buses tilted dangerously as they careened around the course, tearing up the meadow. *Furthur* lost, handicapped by its fame. It was loaded down with far too many passengers, laughing, cheering, and hanging off its sides. Besides, Neal Cassady wasn't driving. He'd died the year before while counting railroad ties on a track between two Mexican towns.

We returned to Libre and New Mexico last January, six months after we'd taken acid on the ridge. I'd gotten another grant to study communes in the winter, and we headed to the Huerfano first. We wanted to make sure what we'd seen in the summer and what we'd dreamed about back in Buffalo was real. That January, SUNY Buffalo shut down when some students set fire to the ROTC building, so we extended our visit a few weeks longer than the two-week winter break we'd planned. Our downstairs neighbor Kevin mailed us our paychecks. In Jim and Sandy's little adobe, risen up from the foundations I'd photographed in the summer, we caught up with them as the snow clouds crept toward us over the Sangres. Libre was different. Dean was in Japan at Suwanose, the island commune where Gary Snyder and the Japanese poet Nanao lived. Nanao had stayed at Libre during the fall, in a cave up Dry Creek where we'd found some old arrowheads on a walk with Jim. The snow clouds crept into the valley as we chatted. When Jim and David went outside for firewood, Sandy talked over her shoulder as she cut up vegetables. At Thanksgiving dinner, she'd left for the cave with Nanao, and Linda left Dean and went off with Steve, who'd left his wife, Patricia. Peter Rabbit left Judy to sleep with Nancy, a friend of Jim and Sandy's we'd met last summer. Judy left Peter for good after that, and Nancy moved in with Peter. Nancy's husband returned to Austin alone.

I tried to nod casually as Sandy explained the splits and pairings. It sounded like a nuclear reaction, like a cross between an orgy and a screwed-up square dance, or a kindergarten game. Some cheeses were left standing alone. In the kitchen of their warm little adobe as the snow fell in a rapid slant outside, she told me only the bare facts, but I was preoccupied with odd details. Where did everyone sleep? Where did each couple have breakfast? How did they hook up with their toothbrushes? I didn't ask, sure I was working on the wrong level.

When Sandy said Nanao wouldn't be back, I asked, "What about you, Sandy?" as she chopped the tops off celery for the stir fry. The onions had made her eyes water.

"Me?" she laughed. "I'm here, aren't I?"

At dinner, Jim and Sandy told us that more people had come looking for land in the Huerfano. Friends who'd gone to high school together in Beverly Hills had just rented a house in Farisita. Some people from the Anonymous Artists of America, the Triple A, had rented a cabin by Gilbert Perino's ranch on this side of the valley. The Triple A was a California band that played at acid tests with the Grateful Dead, and they were looking for a big piece of land in the Huerfano. Some hippies from Boulder were going to buy the Ortiviz Farm on this side of the valley. The Huerfano was growing, and Libre was still going strong, despite cast changes.

I was a little uncomfortable during our January visit, walking into Dean and Linda's dome, talking to Steve and Linda as they sat cross-legged on the big bed and Lia played between them. David was the only person I'd ever slept with. It had just worked out that way. My parents had been married more than thirty years, and they still held hands while watching TV. I was an idealistic monogamist, but we'd talked about it some, David and I. We frowned on hypocrisy and the stifling repression of our parents' generation. You have to follow your heart, but it's dangerous, uncharted territory. Snuggling in our sleeping bags on Jim and Sandy's floor last winter, we talked over the Thanksgiving events. David didn't seem as bothered as I was, as usual.

"This is a consequence of freedom, and we need to support everyone," he said slowly.

"How do you support people with conflicting lusts?" I asked.

"These are frontiers we're facing," he explained, as if we were a New Age Lewis and Clark. "We have to love them all," he added sincerely, sounding like a groovy Jimmy Stewart. He kissed me, and we turned on our sides, his body turtling mine. When we got back to Buffalo after that second Libre trip, during long winter nights we'd gaze west at the light and dream, the same way Gatsby did watching the green light across his bay. Like Gatsby's, our dreams told as much about our past as our future. We wanted to leave a lot behind and go back, too. We wanted to leave the hypocrisy of this society, the way Byron left England for Greece. The way Hemingway, Fitzgerald, and Ezra Pound left America for Paris. The way Paul and Jane Bowles went to Morocco and Gauguin split for Tahiti. Like O'Keeffe, we decided to leave the gray, limited East, craving light, expanses, and sharp edges to our geography.

6 : The Way West

The Chrysler's long hood points west like a ship's prow as it heads into the plains. One year after the acid trip on Libre's ridge, the first summer of a new decade, we head to Colorado to start a new life. We've got lots of time to think about past Libre visits as we drive. Scraps of conversations, the look in someone's eyes, the Sangres at sunset come back like snippets of a vivid dream. Normally, the Chrysler cruises at sixty-five, but it's packed to its gills now, and it struggles to do sixty on a flat road. It moves more ponderously than the newer vehicles passing us, driving into the setting sun on Highway 40. It's our *Mayflower,* our Conestoga wagon, and we're the new pioneers. We're privileged, exiled, orphaned, as hopeful and as unprepared as most immigrants. We're leaving a decadent, evil society like the Pilgrims did. We're psychic frontiersman. Kerouac is our Columbus. We're the second wave, with domestic intentions.

We visited my parents just before we left. They're glad we're married, and they see how happy we are leaving for Libre. They know enough to keep their opinions to themselves. The Chrysler hums steadily west through the humid summer afternoon and evening. There's no air conditioning, but the vent tilts up on the cowl below the windshield. Unlike vents that take in hot air below, from the asphalt, this vent cools you off a bit. The Chrysler's heavy even when empty, and it steers like a boat. It's built of tank-weight metal left over from the war, genetically linked to the Chrysler tanks in World War II. Built when we were born, after the war, taking us and our belongings west to a new beginning.

We don't want to leave this country for a more tolerant foreign home, like the expatriate writers and artists who came before us, or like our Buffalo friends heading for Vancouver. Or Hugh, making his new life in Montreal. We want to create our own new, exotic American culture and traditions in the belly of the beast, taking cues from Native Americans, who were practically eliminated by the previous century's aspiring pioneers and their cavalries. We know My Lai is no different from Wounded Knee. We want peace, freedom, space to live in a new order. We want to be able to see at least fifty miles in every direction, to live in harmony on the earth.

We're leaving our bewildered nuclear families to become part of a tribe that's forming. Bob Dylan's our script writer. *He not busy being born is busy dying. . . To live outside the law you must be honest. . . She's got everything she needs, she's an artist, she don't look back.* We hear irresistible messages in the rock and roll melodies uniting us, though our parents hear nothing but noise. They remember reading "The Pied Piper" to us when we were little. Now we're Children of the Sixties, although we're legally adults. A decade has taken our parents' place.

David's profile is proud and romantic in the light from headlights of oncoming cars. He takes more time to decide, but he always seems more sure of his choices than I. It's easier for me to review our past visits to Libre than to try to envision our future there. I can look back and replay scenes of the last year easily, but I can't see the actual road behind us because of our belongings blocking the rearview mirror. The car's overloaded like the Joads' car in *The Grapes of Wrath.* It's packed solid with the big tipi and its liner, pots and pans, sleeping bags, suitcases, old Boy Scout camping gear, and a Coleman stove. Beside the crate of old tools Dad gave us there's a big box of books: *Whole Earth Catalogs,* the *I Ching, The Book of the Hopi, The Poems of William Blake, Black Elk Speaks,* Jung's *Memories, Dreams, and Reflections,* Castañeda's *Teachings of Don Juan*—Michelin guides for our journey.

And, although I can see clearly now the road glistening before us, I can't see our future so very well. We've known each other for five years, as students or graduate fellows, and we've been intellectual equals in academia, in eastern cities. How will living primitively on the side of a western mountain affect us? There's no other choice but to go to Libre, it's an irrevocable feeling in our hearts. But packed with our papers and journals is the recent draft board letter informing David he's losing his teaching deferment. The draft board says he's good army material. The war's spread into Cambodia, the sky is falling, the end is near. We have to follow our hearts, but I have no idea where that leads.

I guess we're solving our problems the way many others have—by heading west for salvation, escape, another life. We have two thousand five hundred dollars, the last of three grants we got from SUNY Buffalo to study communes in the Southwest. We have some cash wedding presents from confused relatives who didn't know what to give for a commune honeymoon. I have my camera and twenty rolls of film the American Studies department bought for us. David has his guitars. We have our books, our tools, and our tipi. We're running on faith, dreams, and hope. My doubts and uncertainty about the future are not very different from those of pioneer women bumping over the rutted Santa Fe Trail, although I'm more comfortable.

When I'm driving, David stirs in the seat beside me and picks up a conversation we had earlier about childhood TV shows. He grew up in Georgia; I grew up in Westchester County. Except for reading Faulkner, Eudora Welty, and Tennessee Williams, and watching television news reports full of sheriffs and German shepherds attacking civil rights marchers, I know nothing about the South. He's dark-eyed, strange, and a comparatively exotic person to meet in New Haven. But we share a childhood of *The Lone Ranger, Hopalong Cassidy, Roy Rogers,* and *The Cisco Kid.* None of them had parents who appeared in their weekly programs as we grew up. Now we're the good guys, living on the edges of the law, trying to do right, heading for the landscape of our TV heroes.

I say, "You know, eh, Kemosabe, I think that the second wave of people at Libre, building adobes and log cabins—for example, Jim and Sandy, Patricia and Steve—must have been into TV westerns as kids, and those who built geodesic domes and zomes the first year, like Dean and Linda or Peter and Judy—were more into *Buck Rogers, Captain Video,* and *Flash Gordon.*"

David nods. Like TV cowboys and most American heroes, the TV space pioneers of the fifties didn't have any family either. Now we're inner space explorers, with a new galaxy exploding deep inside us, in a new decade. We're taking off for Tomorrowland, Fantasyland, Frontierland, and Adventureland combined. That's the way it seems when we smoke a joint, intoxicated with low-grade marijuana, our youth, and possibility. We head toward the sun on the ribbon of highway, and above us is Woody Guthrie's endless skyway. Ours is a far more comfortable pilgrimage than Woody's, or the Joads', though they're predecessors anyway. We've got the Chrysler, and enough money to eat at truck stops whenever we want (although the closest thing to macrobiotic food is fatty beans, too sweet corn bread, and boiled coffee). We spell each other driving through warm nights and hot days, tuning in to powerful, faraway radio stations, as long as we can put up with the windshield wipers sweeping. Because of a wiring problem, the Chrysler's radio works only if the wipers are on. They sway hypnotically, to the beat of a Buddy Holly oldie, or the Byrds' harmonies, echoing in and out again on the rhythm of the radio waves.

We're not alone in our travels. Our Buffalo friends are packing for Vancouver right now. All over the country, Children of the Sixties are getting into revamped school buses, VW vans, Chevy trucks with campers, step vans, beat-up old Saabs, Peugeots, and slope-back Volvo 544s, heading west, north, up country, into the woods, the mountains, the desert, to the islands. Away. Outside St. Louis, the Gateway to the West, past the industrial sites dominating the fields by the river where the wagon trains once assembled, in farmland again, as the plains spread out, we actually need the windshield wipers for a while. They fight a brief but losing battle with a downpour, and the road is wavy as a mirage through the water pouring down the windshield. Then it's over, the fields soaked with late afternoon rain, and everything's as new as a beginning. A huge double rainbow arches in the lingering mist, curving over the greening plains. It glowingly points toward the Southwest, our destination.

I cry, "Oh, wow, *stop!*" but David's already slowing down. When we pull over, I grab my Pentax. We take snapshots of each other, to document the power behind our passage. Then we hop back in the car, heaving the heavy coupe doors shut, easing into the traffic. The windows are down now, and the tires of passing cars hiss on the wet highway. The rainbow's single now, less distinct, but still there. David looks at me and smiles knowingly, pushing down the accelerator.

This was a sign, an omen. It's so clear. We're on the right path. This is the way.

David and rainbow on the road west, June 1970.

7 : Libre Again

June 4, 1970

As we turn off Interstate 25 onto Highway 69 two days later, I'm driving, my cheeks flushed from fatigue. David rolls a joint to celebrate, leaning back, one foot on the dash, and we climb into the valley, passing Badito Cone on our right. On the left, the Sangre de Cristo Mountains pop up. New, jagged, and exuberant, they stretch along the southern horizon—Black Mountain, Silver Mountain, Little and Big Sheep Mountains, Slide Mountain, Blanca Peak, Kit Carson Peak, Crestone Peak, and the pointy Crestone Needles strut across the curve of the world. This range in the Rockies is called "Blood of Christ" for its vivid colors at sunrise. It's geography we'll look out at every morning—the mountains will be as familiar as friends. Greenhorn and the Wet Mountains, on our right, are older mountains, more worn.

The Chrysler's carburetor is calibrated for sea level, and its flathead six engine heats up. Although I waved away the joint, I swear I hear another sound besides the heaving engine. It's a choir, the white noise of wind at the top of the mountains, the roar of the sea covering the valley sixty million years ago. This is our new home, this is where we will die. At the dirt road for Libre, there are weathered wood signs for the McNabb and Hudson ranches, but nothing to let you know that Libre's at the end of the road. No Coors ads will be shot here—the cows have used up the land. There are a few scraggly piñons, some cholla cacti, and brown grass. Any real green is up the mountain.

I hit the gas on the washboard road. "What about the shocks?" I ask, clenching my teeth.

"Just keep up the momentum." David says with conviction, *Mr. Smith Goes to Washington*–style. *"Mr. Smith Drops Out,"* I think, and grin. The dust swirls out behind us,

Jim and Sandy's house.

past Johnny Bucci's modest ranch house and small, tin-roofed barn, past Max Valdez's Easter pink adobe, past the McNabb turn, past the small Valdez cemetery and its faded plastic flowers, past the shuttered Penitente adobe, then past the Vialpandos' scruffy adobe shacks in the scrub oaks at Maes Creek. Past the gate for the Hudsons' ranch ("Bob Hudson and Son," in chuck wagon print), the heat gauge soaring, we clunk over cattle guards that rattle our teeth. Finally, we pull in next to the Humpmobile in the parking lot, but don't dare turn the car off. It heaves and shudders, and we sit and look at each other.

"Here we are," says David, a master of understatement, as the Chrysler chokes for breath. Across the arroyo, Jim and Sandy come out of their house. We don't get out yet. I feel shy, like a mail order bride. They knew we were coming, and we stayed with them on two earlier visits, but it's different now. We're throwing our lot in with theirs, joining the family.

"Well, hello," calls Jim. "You're here." Another master of understatement. Meaningful understatement, as used by mountain men, gurus, and Indian scouts like Tonto, is very popular these days. Jim's

Jim (right) and Bill Keidel in the Libre garden, summer 1970.

bell-bottoms have more satin patches than before. He leans back a little as he walks toward us, like R. Crumb's "Keep on Truckin'" character. We stand in front of their house in the rosy sunset light among the dismantled truck engines and jacked-up vehicles Jim and his buddy Dallas have been working on. To the southeast, beyond Walsenburg, are the two Huajatollas, alone on the edge of the plains. The Anglos called them Spanish Peaks, but we like the Ute name, which means "Breasts of the World." Like Greenhorn, the Huajatollas are older than the Rockies and smoothly sloped—majestic, rocky bosoms. They're different from the other mountains, and look as if they might lift off for outer space. Aztec priests traveled from Mexico to the Huajatollas for gold—for religious, not commercial, purposes. They're magic mountains.

Texaco, the German shepherd a guy at a Trinidad Texaco station gave

Jim, wags her tail and trots over. David relights the joint, and soon we're all talking at once. We tell them about the long road here and the rainbow, then move inside and sit around the table in the cozy, low-ceilinged kitchen by the Great Majestic, on which food cooks and bubbles in copper pots. Over salad, rice, aduki beans, and tahini sauce, we catch up. Behind Jim, the woman with the dome growing out of her head in his hallucinatory painting seems to listen too.

"A group from L.A. bought the Red Rock Canyon down the road," Jim tells us, "lower on Greenhorn, on the road by the Valdez cemetery." He smiles. "Two years ago, the Libre winter tour stayed with some of them in New York, and they came out and decided to build. First they had a council at Libre. They wanted to build a huge dome that all their friends from L.A. could come and live in with them, because they'd all promised each other that if they ever found the end of the rainbow, they'd let everybody else know. We told them that wasn't what Libre was about, but we liked them, and suggested they look around the Huerfano for another piece of land. Johnny Bucci sold them a couple of hundred acres, his red rock canyon. They call themselves the Red Rockers, after the canyon and their politics. They're communists, in the old sense of the word. Share and share alike. They're gonna build a sixty-foot dome for all of them to live in. Some of them went to Beverly Hills High together."

"Some of them went to *nursery school* together," Sandy smiles wryly. "Besides them, the Triple A"—the Anonymous Artists of America, a group from Berserkely—"are looking at land near Redwing on the other side of the valley." Sandy rolls another Bugler expertly, licking the paper like a cat, holding it palms up, and deftly rolling it against her fingers with her thumbs to seal it. The tips of her fingers are brown. "Some of them met six of us from Libre at the Alloy Conference in New Mexico. Three of them have been living in that little adobe on the middle Gardner road, by Gilbert Perino's ranch. They got together with the Triple A band, who played at Kesey's acid tests. Oh, and a guy just bought the land bordering Libre on the west near the waterfall on Turkey Creek. First, he wanted to buy more land and add it to Libre. We encouraged it, introducing him to the Thatches, who were our realtors, but after he bought land through the Thatches and signed the papers, he decided after all that it would be better to own it himself. A guy named Clark Dimond is going to help pay off the Ortiviz upper land. More people rented houses in Gardner and Redwing, in the center of the valley."

Gardner and Redwing are towns up from Farisita on Route 69 on the

way to Westcliffe. When we visited last summer, Libre was the only out-
post here. Rick Klein from Taos, who'd put up the money for New Buffalo, helped pay for Libre. Two winters ago, after their first summer
here, Peter and Judy, Dean, Linda, and baby Lia, and the third couple
there that first summer, Tony and Marilynn, drove around the country
in Peter's red Chevy van, talking anywhere someone would pay them, to
raise money for building materials. They showed slides and, like tent
preachers, they spoke of a promised land, a chance at redemption.
Some Red Rockers met them in New York. Some Triple A people met
them at Alloy. Across the country, congregations were already con-
verted—they just needed details and directions.

After dinner I help Sandy wash the dishes with hot water from a big
black kettle on the Great Majestic. One enamel metal basin is full of
soapy water, and one's full of rinse water, with a little vinegar to cut the
soap. She washes the cleanest dishes first. There's something oriental
and minimalist about her. During our earlier visits, she read the *I Ching*
and Tarot cards, trying to figure out how the universe worked, while
outside in her front yard Jim and Dallas puzzled over why one internal
combustion engine after another was busted. She has less than others
here, but some of her stuff, like her French copper pots, costs a lot.

She speaks softly in clipped sentences. "Linda and Lia left for Japan
to join Dean at Suwanose. Steve and Patricia are back together, and Patricia's pregnant. The baby's due in August, and they're adding on to
their house. Three others are building on the ridge. There's Richard,
a jeweler from Missouri, and his family; Bill Keidel, a soldier of fortune; and Gary and Kathy Okie and their baby, some real Okies—no
kidding. He's a sculptor."

"When do you think we should call our council?" I ask.

"The sooner the better," Jim says. "Dean and Linda left their prox-
ies. Hey, do you remember Goat John?" Jim asks, chuckling as he tokes
on the joint David rolled. David nods, holding in the sweet smoke. We'd
met Goat John, wandering around with his goats, annoying the ranchers, dressed in goatskins like an anemic John the Baptist. He smelled
like an overripe French cheese, not so much because he doesn't wash
but because of his billy goat. Stand next to a billy goat for a few minutes
and your clothes reek for weeks.

"Well," Jim exhales, "he was pasturing his herd on upper Turkey
Creek last week and got attacked by a mountain lion. The lion didn't
realize he was jumping on a man, what with the smell and goatskins and

all. It peeled John's scalp back off his forehead, and then I guess it was kinda shocked to find John wasn't a goat, and it split pretty quick. He's okay. Old Doc White in Gardner stitched him up. Now he wants to be called 'Clawed'—C-L-A-W-E-D."

We laugh. Eccentrics are tolerated here. Why shouldn't Goat John—Clawed—live out his weird dream in the Huerfano? Nick Carraway says early in *Gatsby* that reserving judgment is a matter of infinite hope, and that rings true. We're sleepy from our trip, the wine, and the joints, but before we climb into our sleeping bags, Sandy gets her *I Ching* and throws out the forty-nine yarrow stalks. We get Number 4, "Youthful Folly." David and I look at each other.

"This is far out," I tell Jim and Sandy. "We got this the night before we left Buffalo!"

"Hmm . . . why not?" Sandy says. She reads out loud: "The Image. A spring wells up at the foot of a mountain. / The image of youth. / Thus the superior man fosters his character / By thoroughness in all that he does." The commentary reads:

> *In this hexagram we are reminded of youth and folly in two different ways. ["Fool" and "folly" in this hexagram should be understood to mean the immaturity of youth and its consequent lack of wisdom, rather than mere stupidity.] The image of the upper trigram, Ken, is the mountain, that of the lower, K'an, is water; the spring rising at the foot of the mountain is the image of inexperienced youth. Keeping still is the attribute of the upper trigram; that of the lower is the abyss, danger. Stopping in perplexity on the brink of a dangerous abyss is a symbol of the folly of youth. However, the two trigrams also show the way of overcoming the follies of youth. Water is of necessity something that flows on. When the spring gushes forth, it does not know at first where it will go. But its steady flow fills up the deep place blocking its progress, and success is obtained.*

We're quiet with our new friends as the cookstove fire crackles in their house. Outside, Dry Creek rushes down, bringing the last spring melt. Sandy wraps up the *I Ching* and yarrow sticks neatly in a scrap of hot pink raw silk. She switches off the bare lightbulb that dangles from the low ceiling and goes off to bed abruptly, climbing the ladder to the loft. Jim soon follows her. In our sleeping bags, when I close my eyes and David's body turtles against mine, I see white lines blipping on the highway, like dismembered *I Ching* hexagrams. Outside, the ponderosa branches creak in the wind, Dry Creek gushes, and the night creatures call, but behind these sounds looms the quiet Huerfano night, a silence infinitely deep, filled with stars and space.

8 : Come Together

The next morning I lie quietly as David sleeps, thinking about the council we must get through in order to join Libre. On our past visits, everyone acted as if a council was a mere formality. We wanted to have a council last winter, but Peter Rabbit said that we should just show up in June ready to build and call a council then. Now there are people building here whom we've never met. Will that make it harder to get the council's okay?

After our oatmeal with nuts and raisins, Sandy says she'll clean up, that we should get an early start walking around to meet the new people and call the council. As soon as we step outside and feel the sun on our faces, I'm less anxious. Outside the house, Jim and Dallas, Libre's two selfless and unpaid mechanics, are bending over an engine block, while Texaco sits nearby, staring thoughtfully at the engine with her ears half down in a gesture of German shepherd solidarity. Fifty miles southeast, the west sides of the Huajatollas are still in shadow. In the center of the valley, Gardner Butte casts a small shadow that shrinks and creeps back toward the butte as the sun gets higher. The crumpled ridges of the blue and misty Sangres are also shaded on the west in the angled morning light. Behind us, smoke twirls out of the stovepipe on Jim and Sandy's little house, which looks more like Badger's house in *Wind in the Willows* today than the Hobbit house it usually reminds me of.

"Well, lookee who's up," Dallas says in his imitation cowboy twang, his eyes and dimples creasing. "How are you two? Here for good? How's that big old Chrysler?" Dallas has rich, curly chestnut hair and a big bushy Smith Brothers cough drop–type beard. He's good-looking, but not a flashy dresser. He never wears anything but

Dallas working on Steve and Patricia's house.

pale blue houndstooth cotton coveralls in a muted chevron pattern, accessorized with a tin camping cup hooked to a waist loop. In summer he wears flip-flops, and in winter, boots. Like Jim, he's the son of a career military man—navy this time.

"Dallas, good to see you, man," David says. "We're good, and the Chrysler's good, but we need to adjust the carburetor sometime. We're glad to be here." After some more automotive chitchat, David asks Dallas, "Can you come to our council tonight?"

"Council, huh?" Dallas says thoughtfully. "Yeah, fine. Good. I'll tell Stephanie. Where's it at?" Dallas holds a valve up in his greasy but delicate hands and squints at it.

"Dean and Linda's, I hope. Okay?" Stephanie and Dallas are staying in the dome while Dean and Linda are away in Japan. The dome's more comfortable than the military surplus tent at Dallas's hogan site. It takes more time to build an adobe hogan than to build a frame building or dome, and it takes a lot more time when you're also repairing trucks with Jim.

"I don't see why not," Dallas murmurs. "Sunset?" When we nod, he touches the broad brim of his hat, smiles, and says, "See you then!" Turning back to Jim, he asks, "So, why do you think this valve won't fit?" Jim is puffing thoughtfully on a Bugler cigarette, nursing his big clay mug of coffee and staring out into the valley. We don't hear his answer as we head across the creek and into Dean and Linda's meadow.

Stephanie's not there, so we go on to Peter Rabbit's meadow and zome, where Peter's sitting at his kitchen table sipping coffee with visitors. Nancy stands with her back to us at the sink doing dishes, just the way Judy, the wife she replaced, was standing the first time we visited. Peter's zome is centrally located, and he has lots of visitors. Most of the time he encourages them, serving up coffee, his hybrid Native American–hayseed wisdom, and low-grade marijuana. He sees himself as the patriarch here, but then maybe Dean, Steve, Jim, and Dallas see themselves that way, too. Libre is a tribe of chiefs.

Peter gestures at the visitors. "Roberta and David, these are some Red Rockers—Winnie, Larry, Anson, and Mary."

"Winnie's for Winston Churchill—he was Mumsy's contribution to the war effort," Mary says in an aside to us, and we laugh. Winnie has dark wavy hair past his shoulders. He's slim, medium height, and moves a little stiffly. Later I learn he had polio as a child. Larry, his younger brother, who is much taller and looser, with curlier hair, looks like Frank Zappa. He wears denim overalls with an underwear T-shirt and doesn't smile as much as Winnie. Anson has a big crown of wavy hair and pleasant blue eyes. Mary's long red-brown hair is pulled back behind a blue bandanna, but large unruly curls escape from it. She has big blue eyes, thin arched eyebrows, and her lips are a thick bow, like a twenties movie star's. She's wearing a work shirt, overalls and men's work boots and another little scarf tied jauntily around her neck. Through the window behind them we can see their red GMC pickup, its door painted with two R's mirroring each other on a rocking chair rocker, like a brand on the side of a cow. Underneath, in crude script, it says, *The Red Rockers, The Southwest's Most Elegant Commune.* We've interrupted Mary's story, and she continues, speaking loud, fast, dramatically. I think it's because we're a new audience, but I learn later that's the way she always talks.

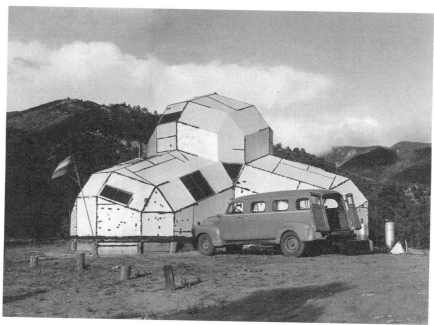

Peter and Nancy's zome.

Peter Rabbit on the windy summit of Greenhorn, 1970.

"So, there I was, dressed in my career clothes after work at *Harper's*, still wearing my fall, and when I saw the cops beating up the demonstrators at the Democratic Convention on TV, I picked up a chair and smashed it to smithereens . . . I'd never done anything like that before! The schizophrenia was too much . . . I'd sit at my desk at *Harper's* editing manuscripts all day and then we'd go to political meetings at night. My parents are old lefties—my father was blacklisted in Hollywood, and, sure, they're upset about the war, but not the way I am . . . Now that we're here, though, there's far less schizophrenia, just truck engines to fix and goats to milk and the dome to build. Now we are *living* it." Everyone around the table nods.

"We are the vanguard, and we have a job to do. We have to be an alternative, and we have to show the way," David says, looking around the table.

"Right on!" Everyone nods again.

"Did anyone ever tell you that you sound like Jimmy Stewart?" Mary asks. "I know his sons. Stepsons, actually."

"Yeah, yeah, it's been mentioned." David smiles.

"He's never figured out how to use it to his advantage," I add, but that's not exactly true.

We chat some more, and Winnie says, "Well, Mary, the immediate job for this *vanguard* is to get that carburetor from Jim and Dallas," as he grins across at us. I like the Red Rockers.

The door closes, and Peter giggles as he says, "Winnie and Larry have a sister at the Red Rocks, too. Their mother was the designer behind Cole of California when it got really famous—you know, all those velvet bathing suits in the forties. Anson has two brothers there, too—a set of twins. Mary and Winnie are the Red Rocker mechanics, and they may be a match for Jim and Dallas. Of course, the competition's not too stiff, heh, heh." Peter smiles, shifts his weight on his chair, and says, "Libre's too bourgeois for the Red Rockers. They pool their money and share everything. They just ordered new Herter winter boots for all twelve of them! They've pooled inheritances, savings, and proceeds from a lawsuit over a taxi accident."

"Hmph," Nancy says over her shoulder as she washes coffee cups. She's our age, tall and slim, and her smallish head balances on a long neck. She has long shiny blond hair, blue eyes that bulge a bit, and full lips. She's not quite beautiful, perhaps because she's so tense. Her parents live in Denver, and she's better dressed and more assured, the way people with money often are. Nancy's not ready to buy everyone at Libre new winter boots and is satisfied that her only group financial obligation here is the yearly Libre dues. She likes David and me, though. We met her last summer when she and her former husband drove up from Austin and visited Jim and Sandy. Now she sits down, wipes her hands on a dish towel, then folds it up neatly. She came for a visit and ended up changing husbands and her life. Her discomfort starting out here isn't the same as ours. "Did you guys know we're married?" she asks. "Peter and I got married the Navajo way, by stepping over a broom." The Navajos get divorced by stepping backwards over a broom, but I don't bring that up. There are some Navajo rugs around the dome that weren't here the last time, and we're drinking coffee from Dansk cups. Peter grins like a Cheshire cat, not particularly looking at Nancy.

"There's lots of building on the ridge going on now," Nancy says, accepting the joint David passes to her and taking a toke. "Richard's a jeweler from Missouri. He's really good at it, I've seen some of his stuff. He and Beth have two children, a boy and a girl. He's designed a house that looks kind of like four joined A-frames and says it's a model of a garnet crystal . . . *really* cool. And then Bill Keidel is building a frame house back on the next ridge from you, kind of a Colorado miner's cabin, only huge. He's *very* interesting, sort of a soldier of fortune—man, he smuggled marijuana in stuffed alligators from Colombia and hash molded and wrapped as Maja soaps from Spain! Gary and Kathy Okie are building down across the road from Bill. They're roofing over the space created by some giant standing rocks. Gary's a sculptor, and he and Kathy have a baby boy, Amon. They're . . . well, they're definitely Okies."

Peter laughs. "Oh yeah, no kidding—*they eat Spam and drink Coke!* And the Red Rockers—building a sixty-foot dome. Do you realize how big that is? They're crazy! First they rented a two-room adobe in Farisita, all eight of them. There was a little path between the feet of their sleeping bags in the bedroom. They spent days making an ornate gilded dinner invitation to us at Libre. Then they took some acid, and Mary and this guy Bad Eddy, a photographer and next door neighbor to Mary and her husband in New York, brought the invite to us by motorcycle. Then they went home and wallowed in the mud. When we got there, nobody had cooked anything, and they took hours to boil some spaghetti and put some ketchup on it."

"Johnny Bucci saw them coming," says Nancy. "He sold the land to them for a hundred and thirty-five dollars an acre, and there are no water rights or much water there." Two years ago Libre sold for thirty-five dollars an acre, and although Dry Creek runs through it on the east and Turkey Creek borders it on the west, there weren't any water rights either.

"Things are gathering momentum," David says. "Speaking of that, would it be okay with you if we had our council tonight?"

"Sure, the sooner the better," Peter says. "Where?"

"Dean and Linda's," I say, and Nancy hugs us both good-bye. We trek across Libre with Peter, meeting the strangers on the ridge who will be our future neighbors (if all goes well tonight) and visiting the houses on the lower land. We eat lunch late at Tony and Marilynn's dome on the lowest meadow. Tony's a British artist, and Marilynn's small, dark, and beautiful. Their dome is spacious and spare, more like a promising artist's loft in SoHo. At Jim and Sandy's, we take the tipi out of the Chrysler and spread it out in the parking lot. I want to paint a Van Gogh–like sun by its door. David will paint a crescent moon like a communist sickle on the other side, and there'll be dark green and red triangles along the bottom, like abstract mountains, a traditional design from the Laupins' book about tipis. The dark blue top will be dotted with yellow stars.

It's hot working on the white canvas in the afternoon sun. We shared a joint with our hosts almost everywhere we went. It doesn't take much to make me fuzzy-headed and confused. I switched to coffee after the first two stops, while David smoked on. He goes down to the creek bed to take a nap. The way I'm frantically slapping the canvas with paint has probably tired him out. Soon, working on the white canvas makes me hot and dizzy too, and I sit in the shade with my dripping paintbrush, thinking of being in our own kitchen in a house we make ourselves, eating food we raised, on plates we shaped and fired, sitting on furniture we made, wearing clothes I sewed, while I write poems and David composes songs. There will be paintings by our new family members, and everything will be new, original, creative! In Buffalo I copied a Blake quotation on the book of photographs of Libre. I know it by heart:

A Poet a Painter a Musician an Architect: the Man
Or Woman who is not one of these is not a Christian
You must leave Fathers & Mothers & Houses & Lands
  If they stand in the way of ART. . . .

It'll be tough sometimes, there are risks, but we'll be *alive*. Two years ago there was nothing but summer pasture here. The six houses now at Libre sprouted from dreams like ours.

9 : You Can Be in My Dream If I Can Be in Yours

June 5, 1970

The council's not going as I expected. People straggle into the dome around sunset, stand around chatting, and chug the jug wine we brought. The four oldest kids, two brother-and-sister pairs, each from a new family building here, orbit the dome. They run in and out, slamming the screen doors, yelling and laughing in the meadow. Nanda, a two-year-old boy Patricia and Steve adopted at birth, tries to follow the older kids, and even the Okies' baby Amon wants to scramble after the running, laughing pack. Tom Grow walks in holding a metal pail shot full of holes. He mumbles that Antonio Pando, the rancher who sold the land to Libre, shot at him this afternoon when Tom was getting water from Turkey Creek. Pando's a little crazy, and angry that the land he sold has become a New Jerusalem. He doesn't want us taking a single pail of Turkey Creek water because he didn't sell us any water rights. The holes in the pail are edged in sharp, asymmetrical star points flaring the way the bullets traveled. Tom seems half amused, half scared. He looks like an English serf, or a badly dressed fool in a second-rate court (I realize that he's the same man David played music with at Drop City last year). He's gaunt with a goatee, handsome underneath it all, and wears baggy, homemade canvas pants and a sleeveless shirt his lady Peggy made for him.

Peter laughs drily. "Oh, boy, it's the West, ain't it? Pando always has a dark cloud over his head!" Patricia, who doesn't look like she could get any more pregnant, though she still has two more months to go, laughs quietly and raises her fine blond eyebrows. Nancy rolls her big blue eyes, and all in all no one seems too upset, but it distracts the group and delays the start of our council. Dallas and Jim trail in at dark. They were using the last light to finish fixing an axle. Dallas unhooks his tin cup from his waist loop and pours some wine, and Jim's fingers are still black when he takes the joint David passes to him. Steve comes in last, shirtless, in leather pants, his blond waves sticking up wildly, making him look even taller and his head even bigger. He sits next to Patricia and Nanda, the boy they had adopted the year before Steve slept with Linda. Steve peers around the dome like a stranger. He has that deer in the headlights look that men with pregnant wives sometimes get. Nanda looks up at his dad and sucks on four fingers at once. The Dean and Linda rag dolls Linda made slump against each other by the wall, their large button eyes staring at me. I'd like to pull them into the council circle. I'm light-headed, my thoughts scattered, still tired—from the road trip, from trekking around, painting the tipi, and adjusting to the high altitude. I'd like to start.

David doesn't seem in a hurry, though. Peter and he are talking about Lewis and Clark. "The first image of the West is not the lone gunman," says Peter, sucking on a joint. "It's a group of thirty moving communally across the unknown. A black man and an Indian woman were with them, and when they took a vote about where to winter, everyone had one vote. There were about thirty people in many Indian groups traveling around this area, and I think that's just about the right size for us, too." David nods thoughtfully. I do a quick head count. Including Dean, Linda, and Lia and the new Libre families, there are twenty-three members. I'm relieved.

Suddenly, Jim calls the council into session, yelling, "Hey everyone, let's sit down!" and I'm more relieved. When we sit in a circle, however, Jim continues loudly, stopping any lingering conversations, saying, "It's summer, and the visitors are starting. Sandy and I have the first house here, and we get the brunt of it. We'd like to try a 'Visitors on Sunday Only' policy like they have down at the Lama Foundation. It's getting to be too much."

Everyone's quiet. I thought we were about to discuss our joining up, and I look down in frustration. We didn't arrive here on Sunday. David pats my arm.

"Jim, I know how you feel, I really do," says Steve, standing up. "But we're different from folks at Lama—man, our name is FREE. Do we want to be *so negative* to those who've traveled a long way up the road? Most of us came up that same road once, and probably not on Sunday."

Dean and Linda's dome.

"Free, oh Free, oh Free oh," sings Tom Grow in a sweet, melodic tenor, standing up. Peter calmly urges Steve and Tom to sit down. Tom squats, hugs his knees, and stares at the floor in the center of the circle, smiling and singing more quietly now. Does he act this way all the time, or did getting shot at shake him up? We haven't spent much time with him and Peggy. If they let Tom join, I can't see how there's going to be any problem with us.

"Listen, how can *we* be free if everybody and his cousin is sticking their head in the door, saying, 'OOOOOH, COOL . . . Is this where they eat? Is this where they paint? Can we stay with you, can we live with you?'" Tony, who lives with Marilynn in the dome down on the lowest part of the land, speaks abruptly, angrily mimicking a commune tourist in his Cockney accent. His hair has flecks of paint in it and stands up like James Dean's. He was a Park Place Gallery artist like Dean, and is more like an Angry Young Man than a New Age Aquarian.

"It's hard, you guys, very hard. We get the brunt of it after Jim and Sandy, and some days I can't get the dishes done because there are so many people traipsing through the zome looking for THE ANSWER," Nancy says, biting her lip. *But,* I think, *Peter likes giving answers.*

"We can't have so many interruptions that we can't do our art or whatever else we've come here to do," says Vesey, another Park Place painter. "That's crazy, man." Vesey's older, like Dean and Peter, and talks like a beatnik in a TV skit.

"Remember what happened to the Haight," says Patricia, who lived in Haight-Ashbury with Steve. She was eighteen when Steve's huge Day-Glo Last Supper painting bolted to the side of his van caught her attention as Steve was passing through her tiny Minnesota town. Then Steve caught her attention. She got into his van and got out in San Francisco.

"But this is not a city, like the Haight," says Dallas.

"We're a city of dreams," says Peter.

There are at least two camps, but lots of people change camps every time they open their mouths. It's bad to be inhospitable—that goes back to the Greeks. Everyone agrees with Peter when he points that out. But, it's a drag being interrupted all the time, especially by dorks with no dope, Peter adds, and Bill Keidel seconds that, although he's so far back on the land that he gets only the hardiest visitors with no dope or money, sent on by those down below.

The debate bogs down. Tom Grow asks, "Isn't everyone on earth just a visitor anyway?" We all pause for a second, and then the squabbling resumes.

"I can't take it any longer," says Sandy quietly. Everybody stops again. Nobody knows for sure what she can't take, and nobody asks.

"Let's put a sign up, you guys! We can make exceptions as we go along. It gives Jim and Sandy something to stand behind. Let's just try it awhile," says Patricia, looking at Sandy. "David and Roberta called this council for a different reason," she adds. I'm glad she points this out, because no one seems to remember us or what we called the council for.

"It's so uptight. The first thing is a bad vibe. I don't know," says Peter thoughtfully.

"Well, I could just direct everyone over to your house as soon as they drive up," Jim says.

"Peter, for God's sake, let's just try it," says Patricia. "Let's discuss David and Roberta. The kids are falling apart, let's get on with it."

There's no vote on this, but the discussion's over. David says, "Thanks, Patricia," and looks slowly around the circle, getting everyone's attention with a pause that's just long enough. He says, "Well, all of you know already that we want to build a house on the ridge, straight up from Peter's, in a meadow caused by the piñon tree blight, around that big rock, building with reject railroad ties and logs cut and left by the loggers on Greenhorn. We've traveled around the West a lot, looking for the right place to live, and this is it. The country's in crisis. We fought against the war, and were teargassed at the Pentagon and shot at by rednecks in Buffalo. I see now that Nixon and his cronies will fall of their own weight. We think what's happening here is a different kind of revolution. We're on the front lines, not of battle but of a changing consciousness for humanity. We want to live and work consciously and creatively—no more schizophrenia, no more hypocrisy. We'll win the battle with the way we wage our lives."

"Right on!" Peter and Steve say at the same time, along with general murmurs of approval. David's a born leader, and he knows how to work a crowd. When he was in high school, JFK was his hero. David won a prize with his urban planning project and was asked to talk to the Atlanta city council about it, and then he got a scholarship to Yale. Over his four years in New Haven, though, his role models changed, from the Kennedys to Jung, Rimbaud, T. E. Lawrence, Dylan, and Abbie Hoffman.

"Let's go around the circle," says Peter.

Decisions about new members must be unanimous, and everybody wants to say something. Tony looks at us warily and says, "That okay with you, Payter? You're nearest."

"More than okay." Peter turns to us and says, "Nancy and I welcome you as family."

"And you, Richard?" says Tony. "You're nearest on the ridge."

"We're happy to have them as neighbors," says Richard quietly. Beth smiles.

Dallas takes off his hat. He looks at the joint passed to him for a long time until Jim pokes him to pass it. He speaks slowly. "How're you going to get materials up the ridge?"

David looks at Dallas for a minute and says, "I guess we'll buy a truck."

Gary Okie, a chubby young gray-faced man in overalls, holds his fat blond baby Amon, while his ample blond wife snaps up the plastic pants around a fresh diaper. Peter was right—there were lots of empty Spam cans and Coke bottles at the Okies' site when we visited them today. "Kin you live without electricity?" Gary asks. "San Isabel Electric won't be runnin' lines up the ridge anytime soon." He sounds like L'il Abner and has sparse muttonchop sideburns.

"We want to live without electricity for a while. Lots of other humans have done fine without it in this valley," David answers.

"Can you get a house built in three months before the first snows?" asks Tony.

"I hope to God we can. We'll find out, won't we?" David inhales the roach that's come back around the circle.

"How're you going to get water up the ridge? Can you take hauling water on your backs if you have to?" asks Stephanie, who lives with Dallas, and consequently worries about vehicles breaking down. Since Dallas and Jim volunteer to fix them, that makes it hard for Stephanie to complain about Dallas not working on the hogan, and hard for the rest to complain about the speed or quality of their work. Stephanie has brown wavy hair, like a Breck girl's, and a little hair on her upper lip. You can barely tell she's built voluptuously under the full muslin blouse and long skirt she's got on. She was a student of Mark Di Suvero's, a big-time sculptor Dallas worked for, and left her studies to build a hogan with Dallas. Her bare feet are dusty, and the skin on her heels is cracked.

"We'll do what everyone else on the ridge does," David answers. "We'll haul water in trucks and carry it by hand when we have to."

"Someday we'll have storage tanks and pump water up there," Peter says, sure of his vision, like William Penn surveying the site of Philadelphia in an Edward Hicks painting.

"How will you make money?" Richard asks.

"The way all of us here do. By hook or by crook." David smiles.

Bill Keidel says, "There's a rich oil lawyer from Oklahoma who just bought land a couple of canyons over—Roger Randolph. He wants me to get a crew to help him and his wife build a cabin. He's about sixty or so, and is into Tibetan Buddhism. You can both be on my crew." Bill sounds like W. C. Fields. He's younger, heavier, more muscular than Fields was, and he has the provocative smile of the kid who's always getting sent to the principal's office. I smile at Bill, glad he's included me in the work crew. The council drags on, and everyone has a speech or a question, except Tom Grow, who still looks spaced-out. Peggy sits up straight beside him and looks at us. Her hair is thin and blond, her pale skin freckled and weathered, her eyes light blue. She was a concert pianist before Drop City, before Haight-Ashbury, but her freckled fingers look surprisingly short. Now that it's night, and the bats are flying around the meadow, her two blond kids, Lump and Lori, are inside the dome with Aaron and Aricia, the blond kids of our new neighbors Richard and Beth. Tom rocks on his heels and hums.

I'm impatient and can't pay attention anymore. I want to move on. I hated what seemed to me like long, aimless discussions at faculty meetings at Buffalo. I'm not as at ease as David is either. I miss our old friends the way the pioneer women missed their folk back east. I admire these people, and we share a vision of living harmoniously and creatively here, but we haven't spent as much time with them as you'd spend with members of a country club you were joining. We're adopting one another, in a way, so I guess it's natural to feel awkward at first.

"Railroad tie houses don't go up as quickly as domes." Vesey slugs some red wine and wipes his mouth. He's built a tiny, ramshackle A-frame attached to a small dome. "The winters come early at this altitude. You'll be slowed down with that ridge road and no electric tools."

David looks around the circle and sighs. "Look. Everyone says there's no more room on the lower part of the land. You have to build your house out of sight of everybody else here, right? We've got no choice but to build there. We'll borrow or buy a generator. We've chosen to do this, and it will work out."

"You know your plans seem a little, er, grandiose," says Vesey.

"So what?" says Steve, who helped make our plans.

"I'm for them becoming members," says Jim. "Let's get on with it!"

"Me too," says Sandy. It's the first time she's spoken since she said she couldn't take it.

"Is there any question that David and Roberta should be here?" Peter asks quietly.

"No!" says Steve, loudly, impatient to cut the discussion short. "And we should welcome them as part of this clan! Welcome!" Murmurs of congratulation and relief ricochet around the dome. Everyone stands up, except Tom Grow, who still squats in place and rocks on his heels. Nancy Rabbit detours around him to hug me, and then Tony's Marilynn, dark and petite, hugs me, then Bill Keidel robustly claps a big arm around me. One of the kids is crying, up too late. Over Bill's bulky shoulder, my eyes meet David's.

"Here we go!" David's eyes seem to say, and he shrugs his shoulders ever so slightly.

We've got three months or less until the first snow. It took three weeks since the council to get some building materials up the ridge and set up camp. I knew it would take an enormous amount of time to build our house, but in these last three weeks I've learned that even the simplest tasks take longer than expected. For example, the day after the council, we planned to take the Libre flatbed across the valley to Singing River Road beyond Redwing to cut lodgepole pines for our tipi. We needed to pitch the tipi and set up a summer kitchen to live comfortably, even during the usual two rainy seasons in summer. But the Libre flatbed developed carburetor problems, and Dallas had to go to Walsenburg to get a part. He couldn't get it there, so he had to go to Pueblo the next day, and the day after that Jim and he had some trouble putting the carburetor in the flatbed (some bolt broke). Four days after the council, we made it to Singing River. It took all day for David, Jim, Peter, and me to cut our twenty lodgepole pines, plus twenty more for Peter, who wanted to pitch his tipi for a solstice peyote meeting.

The tipi book said tipi poles should be skinned, and so the next day, David and I started stripping bark in the Libre parking lot. The long curls of bark mounded up under us as we pulled the drawknife down the slender pines, and globs of pine pitch stuck to our hair and clothes. The following day our shoulders ached, and we needed a break, so we went to town, did laundry, took showers, and bought Sandy groceries. We found a blue enamel Stewart cookstove in a junk store for fifty dollars, and a green '53 Chevy with four retread tires for two hundred fifty at Habib Tire.

What we're learning is new, and we have to make up

words as we hum along. For instance, we've learned you must change your plans to seize a vehicular opportunity. Since Richard was driving the flatbed to the valley lumber mill the next day and wasn't picking up a full load, we went along. We bought reject railroad ties, two-by-twelves, two-by-sixes, and two-by-fours. If the ties aren't perfectly square or if the boards have too many knots, are warped, or are too thick or too thin, they can't be sold as graded lumber. It cost five dollars for a regular truckload of reject lumber, ten for what we loaded on the flatbed after Richard had all he needed. The men at the mill thought we were crazy to build our houses with what they sold as firewood, while we couldn't get over the great deal it was. A lot can be built from the trash of the richest country in the world. The next day we drove the lumber up the ridge and unloaded and stacked it.

The flatbed's days were numbered. It clunked and coughed, then heaved and stalled. Seizing another opportunity, the next day we went along with Jim in the flatbed to Pueblo. We bought iron cook pots and pans at the junk stores on Union Street, groceries, rebar, and twenty-five bags of cement, a couple of ten-pound hammers, twenty-pound boxes of nails, and four used fifty-five-gallon coconut oil drums. We had lists of stuff to buy for five other households and didn't leave Pueblo till after dark, and then we had a flat tire on the way home and didn't get back until midnight. The next morning we stacked our bags of cement on boards on the ridge road above the site, covering them with thick sheets of plastic. We bought in on the truckload of sand that Richard and Bill ordered that would be delivered the next week. We cleaned out the drums in the creek, which was running a lot lower, and took them up to our campsite and the house site. Once a week, Dallas or Jim and some of the other men drive up the ridge in the flatbed or a visitor's new truck, hauling a three-hundred-gallon tank of water to fill all the coconut oil drums. We helped on the water run the following day. Bob Hudson, our rancher neighbor, diverted Dry Creek above Libre onto his land, which he has the right to do, so now there's only a trickle on Libre. We got water from Turkey Creek, making sure old Pando wasn't around.

Of course, we have to pace ourselves. The Pueblo trip was exhausting, so we took a day off and went swimming at Dr. Ferendelli's stock pond, which borders lower Libre. Then we went to Walsenburg because we'd forgotten to get stovepipe for the cookstove to set up our summer kitchen, and bought a box of "Jesus nails," the biggest nails you can get, to nail the railroad ties together as we stack up our walls. Any estimate of how long a job will take needs to be multiplied by two, at least. The following day, we spread the tipi canvas out in the parking lot and tried to finish painting it. We didn't want to pitch an unpainted tipi. We worked until sunset, got a lot done despite the fact that we'd put the canvas over a red ant colony, but we didn't finish. By then, Sandy was getting tired of having houseguests, and, even though we weren't completely ready, Jim insisted gently that we move up the ridge. So, early one morning during week three here, Dallas and Jim drove us up the ridge in the True Truck, the old army truck Dallas bought at an auction at the air force base in Colorado Springs. Dallas and Jim helped us unload our stuff and pitch the half-painted tipi, and then they drove back down the ridge.

It took two days to construct the summer kitchen. We leveled the cookstove, setting each of its four chromed feet on bricks and boards of different heights, and hooked up the stovepipe. We built a kitchen counter next to the stove with some of the wide planks from the reject pile at the sawmill, placing them bark side down. We tied a rope between some piñon branches and hung a tarp over it to make a canopy over the stove and counter to protect us from sun and rain. Under the shade of another piñon tree, we built a low table and benches from reject railroad ties. We slid our two Scotch coolers under one end of the railroad tie counter and moved a large, lidded plywood box holding other foodstuffs under another section, and then lined up the big, tightly sealed old food tins we found in Pueblo's secondhand stores. Using two large planks for shelves above the counter, we set out our pots, pans, plates, and silverware.

Inside the tipi, David made a four-by-four frame and nailed two-by-eight culls onto it to make a low bed platform opposite the door. We put a three-inch foam pad on the platform, and I made the bed. I threw our striped East Indian spread over the B. Altman orange wool blanket my mother had given us. David dug a shallow hole in the center of the dirt floor for the fire, and we ringed the fire hole with rocks. We dug a shallow trench from the door to the fire hole and buried a pipe in it to vent the fire, as our tipi book directed. It looked like we'd still be in the tipi for the early snows, so a good fire was important. To keep the dust down, we put the old oriental throw rugs from Buffalo estate sales around the tipi, along with the Navajo rug our friends Pam and Don had given us as a wedding present. Finally, we stood in the tipi and looked around.

Our clothes were hung on a horizontal pole lashed to two of the tipi poles, and our trunk was tucked under the foot of our bed. The rugs gave the space a slightly Arabian feel. The light through the canvas was soft and muted. It seemed like a long time since our wedding.

We soon realize that the house we envision can't be built by the two of us alone. We can't even lift one of the logs for uprights or beams to frame the basic octagon, much less put it in place. The only way we can get the house done is with others. Ever since our summer camp was set up, I've been looking down the Libre road whenever I hear a vehicle driving up, watching for our friends from back east, or David's brother, Doug. A lot of friends have said they'd visit us this summer, and a big work crew is our only hope. Doug and his high school friend finally arrive—the first reinforcements. They come with us on the flatbed run up Greenhorn with Jim, and we cut twenty-foot sections of trees left behind by the loggers and load them. They'll be the uprights in the eight corners of our house's octagon. We get ten more logs—not enough for the eight we'll need for the roof beams that will ray out from the rock, plus the eight beams that will rest on the eight uprights to make the outer rim of the octagon, but a start. We've been scraping bark off logs ever since. We take a break and mark off the perimeter of the house with stakes, then try to dig some holes for the upright logs. We hit rock less than three inches down. When I swing the pick with all my might, my spine and skull reverberate like a cartoon character's. Four of us work three hours to dig a hole twelve inches across and six inches deep. This job doesn't just take more time than expected—it's impossible.

We sit in the shade of the rock, aching, sweating and depressed, as Bill Keidel comes down the trail. He's wearing cutoff jeans that show off his tree trunk legs, rooted solidly in his work boots. I've never seen legs that big, and they're all muscle.

"Hey, I just figured out the difference between you and the Okies," Bill calls.

"What?" I say, wiping my face with my bandanna.

"Well," Bill grins, "the Okies are building a house *inside* some rocks—actually, just roofing over the space between some rocks. You guys, on the other hand, are building a house *outside* a rock!" Bill laughs. He's obviously been working on that one.

"That's *so very funny*, Bill." I grimace, standing up and trying to straighten out my back.

"Hold on, hold on—are you all actually trying to *dig* your post holes?" Bill asks incredulously, looking around the site and pushing his cowboy hat back off his brow.

"Well, yeah," David tells him, grinning apologetically. "How else are we gonna get it done?"

"Dynamite, boys—and girl," Bill says, winking at me, half older brother, half snake oil salesman. "Dynamite! Mr. Nobel's little invention is what you need!" he exclaims. "Why, I'm going to town tomorrow, and you can get everything at Unfug Hardware—dynamite, blasting caps, wire . . . I'll show you, and you'll get these post holes done in no time! *No time at all!*"

Things are looking up now that Bill has clued us in. We get the dynamite in Walsenburg, and Bill shows us how to blow out one of the post holes. First, he swings a maul powerfully, pounding a large iron rod deep into the rock, and places the stick of dynamite way down into the hole, where it will do the most damage. Next, he connects the dynamite with wire to the electric blasting cap, and runs the wire around to the other side of our rock, where he touches the wire to another wire running out of a nine-volt battery, which sets off the cap and explodes the dynamite. The echo of the blast thuds in my chest. We clear out the rubble, then pound the iron bar into the rock at the bottom of the hole, set up another charge, and blast it. If you do it right, two sticks make a hole three feet deep. Sixteen explosions and our house will take root.

With perfect synchronicity, our friends show up at last. Dr. Frank from Denver, where he's an intern, Mark and his blond girlfriend Debbie, on a road trip across the West before he goes to work on another family newspaper. Our old friend Henry, celebrating his 4-F status. Henry's blond hair is almost white from his time in Hawaii, and his skin's deeply tanned. He's taller and slimmer than David now. When they play guitars together by the campfire, they look like a photo and its negative. Danny, a friend of David's who's still at Yale, arrives with a friend of his, a big guy named John. Hugh's not here. He's somewhere in Canada, and people hear from Harton less and less since he got back from Vietnam. Still, there are enough old friends that we're happy. Fresh troops! Now we can really get things done! Including David, Doug, and Doug's buddy, with our new visitors there's a crew of eight men. I reevaluate everyone according to his musculature, endurance, and day labor skills. Our spirits are buoyed, and we work and sweat all day and laugh and talk around the fire at night. It's like sleep-away

David and Bill Keidel move a post with a little help from our friends.

camp! The mountains provide a grand backdrop, the blazing sunset and then the campfire illuminate old friends' faces. The moon rises over our laughter and the music of David's and Henry's guitars.

This morning, Debbie and I cleaned up after breakfast when the men left for the site. The brown rice for lunch is done now, and the beans are bubbling on the cookstove. We've rolled out about twenty-five tortillas. They're not as good as the ones old Mrs. Vargas, the valley midwife, made when she showed me how to do it, but they're good enough. After I put the bread in the oven, we take a break to go over to the site. I drop a few pieces of wood into the cookstove's firebox to keep the oven just hot enough for the bread, shake the crank so the ashes will fall into the ash drawer, and then Debbie and I walk across the flowered meadow. A squad of hummingbirds zips drunkenly across our path, whirring from blossom to blossom.

"Will I ever get tired of just looking around this place?" I ask Debbie. She shrugs.

They're working on the third hole. They finished pounding the big metal rod into the ground, but they forgot to twist it as they pounded, and now it's stuck. It takes Big John, the Yalie visiting with David's friend Danny, to loosen it. Big John's flaming red frizzy hair and pale, massive body quiver with his effort. He falls backwards almost onto Debbie when the rod comes loose, but Danny breaks his fall, diving and pushing with both hands against John's back like he's a big volleyball. Everyone cheers when the rod comes out, not noticing that Debbie narrowly escaped squishing. Dr. Frank and David set up the electric fuse.

"Everybody to the other side of the rock," David yells, unrolling the wires quickly as he backs up the incline and behind the rock. It's cub reporter Mark's turn to set it off. Maybe he'll write an article about this for the Lifestyle section of his newspaper. Frank lights his hash pipe and passes it around the circle so that Mark will be the last one to get it. "What a blast this is!" David says as he sucks on the pipe, and everyone groans.

"I'm certainly getting a bang out of it," says Henry, in his deep baritone. More groans.

When the pipe gets to Mark, he sucks at it and passes it to Frank, connects the two wires, and says, "Frank, man, I gotta tell you, this hash is really . . . *DYNAMITE.*" The blast and the noise of the flying rocks drown out our reaction. I crouch down. It's World War II, and we're holding off a German patrol. Debbie's beside me, genuinely frightened, and I hold her hand, but David and the guys roll on the ground laughing. We stand up when we hear the last large chunk of bedrock hit far below us, and then we walk down to check the hole. It's more than a foot and a half deep, full of chunks of shattered bedrock. The guys stand around like soldiers in a battlefield, passing around a water bottle, discussing the second charge. Big John swings a pick at the rubble around the hole, and Danny scrapes the chunks of rock out with a shovel.

Peter charges up the path, out of breath. "What the . . . fuck are . . . you doing?" he shouts hoarsely between gasps.

"What do you mean?" David asks.

"Man, pieces of rock almost hit my zome! They could break the skylights, and Nancy's wigged out of her mind! You can't do this!" The group gets very quiet. I've never seen Peter angry like this.

"Listen, man, we're really sorry," says David contritely. "We had no idea, really! Are you sure it could go that far? We're just about to finish the three lower holes, anyway, and the others won't even go in the zome's direction. We'll bury this next charge extra deep. Really, we're sorry. Let's sit down and smoke some of this hash."

Peter's still angry, but good hash is rare in these parts and comes only as hostess gifts. "Just be careful, for Chrissakes," he mutters, as his eyes widen while Frank pares off some hashish from a big, oily green chunk with his Swiss Army knife. Frank places the slice delicately into the pipe's tiny bowl, lights up, and hands the pipe to Peter. Peter almost smiles when he takes it and puffs. Debbie and I return to the summer kitchen. The bread's almost done, and I put the tortillas on the cooler side of the stove. We shift the water for the lunch dishes onto the hot part, nearest the firebox. Debbie looks sidelong at me as we heft the black kettle. She's pretty skinny and isn't too strong. "Ever think of paper plates?" she asks, grimacing with effort. A little water sloshes out of the kettle and hisses on the stove top.

"Sure, but think of the trees we save by not buying them," I grunt as we shove the kettle into place, and then I add some more piñon to the firebox. The next dynamite charge goes off, and we flinch.

"After I leave here, I'm sending you some rubber gloves," says Debbie. Our hands are chapped and dry from dishwashing, and she's broken three of her long, perfectly shaped nails since she's been here. "That's okay, ecologically speaking, isn't it?" she asks.

"As far as I know," I say, turning some tortillas. "You know, I'm not the domestic type. At New Buffalo last summer, I freaked after two days in the kitchen with the women. But these guys are making big progress. I couldn't keep up with them."

Yesterday, Dr. Frank saw I wasn't thrilled to stay behind and do dishes while they went back to work, laughing and joking. He said consolingly, "You know, your loaves of bread are building the house!" I pull four loaves out of the oven and lay them on their sides on the counter to cool. The tortillas are toasted and wrapped in a towel keeping warm on the open oven door. Debbie finishes the salad and then slathers on more hand cream, saying, "You need an IV of hand and face cream in this place!" She walks over to get the crew, while I grate a big hunk of Longhorn cheese for the burritos. Our new Siamese cat, Kachina, snarfs up the flecks of cheese that drop on the ground as I grate recklessly, and Sinbad, the orphan tabby kitten, muscles in beside her. Two piñon jays flit into the trees, ready to clean crumbs off the table after lunch. I stir the pinto beans and the green chile and wipe my hands on my jeans. The dishwater's starting to boil, and I wipe the sweat off my face with my sleeve. This is what it means to slave over a hot stove. I hear our friends heading back from work, meandering across the meadow like the Seven Dwarfs, but I'm no Snow White.

July 1, 1970

We're running out of time *and* money. Our friends stayed a week, worked and played hard, and we fed them well. We drank a lot of Coors during and after the hot, dry days of construction work. We've spent most of our nest egg on provisions, gas, building materials, auto repairs, other necessities. Even if we work on Bill Keidel's crew building the vacation cabin two canyons over for the Buddhist oil and gas lawyer, our wages will have to go for more building materials. Cement, sand, lumber, nails, tar paper, roofing paper, windows, hardware, propane—the list is endless. We're in a race with time for shelter before the first snow, and we can't make enough money for food as well as building materials in the two months left.

I went over these calculations several times on the drive to Walsenburg and the Huerfano County Health and Human Services Office, but I'm still uncomfortable. I squirm as I sit in the metal chair. I don't like applying for food stamps, but there's no question we need them. Mrs. Lenzotti's not amused. She purses her lips and looks over our application. Her eyes stop at the space where we wrote that David and I each have eighteen years of schooling. She doesn't pay much attention to Doug's application—he hasn't finished high school, and she probably views him as a mere child being led astray. Her head's down, looking over the forms, and her hair's thinning a bit on the crown, probably due to bad diet and too many sessions under the dryers at the Mane Attraction on Seventh Street. She tap, tap, taps the paper with the eraser end of her pencil.

"Think of it as a kind of NEA grant, to fund this important experiment in living," David said before we walked into Mrs. Lenzotti's office. She looks up at us now, unsmiling. Nobody's ever seen her smile. Why couldn't we have someone like the woman who runs the food stamp program in Taos, an old Roosevelt Democrat who happily okays food stamps for everyone on the communes there? My guess is Mrs. Lenzotti's a Republican.

She clears her throat. "So . . . Roberta. You've listed yourself at the Employment Bureau as a teacher, editor, journalist, and freelance writer. Do you have a certificate to teach in Colorado public schools?" she asks.

"No, Mrs. Lenzotti, but I think I'd qualify to do substitute work. I don't know all the rules, but Libre is a nonprofit corporation under Colorado law, and because so many members finished college and have a few years of graduate work, we've gotten Libre classified as a school. I'll be teaching reading there this fall."

"Hmmph," Mrs. Lenzotti says, looking down at her papers. "That's beside the point." She's right. I'm nervous and defensive. "And you, David," Mrs. Lenzotti continues, "you're a writer-scholar-journalist too?"

"Yes, ma'am," says David, sounding more southern than usual. At least we've been accurate. No job is likely to turn up for us in Huerfano County, where unemployment is rampant, but this is not as absurd as Bill Keidel's approach. He's at the bottom of the job pool, having signed up at the Employment Bureau as a scuba diver, although we're a thousand miles from the closest ocean. The high mountain lakes and the artificial trout pond for tourists south of Walsenburg aren't very deep, and even if they were, no one's likely to hire Bill to dive in them.

"Well," Mrs. Lenzotti says, tapping her papers on the desk to get them stacked up neatly, "everything seems to be . . . in order. It should take about a week for you to be processed." She makes it sound like we're canned ham.

"Thank you, Mrs. Lenzotti," we say, getting up and backing out of the tiny, windowless office with no pictures on the walls. She's looking down at the next pile of papers and doesn't answer. It's a relief to be on the street. As we leave, a truckload of Archuletaville hippies pull up and pile into the office. Old Dan Archuleta let them fix up his animal sheds and shacks to live in at his shabby ranch over in Redwing. It's the Huerfano version of Tobacco Road. I can't help feeling sorry for Mrs. Lenzotti. Her day's about to go from bad to worse.

"*Twenty years of schooling and they put me on the day shift . . . ,*" David sings, looking sideways at Doug and me. Doug smiles a little, but I'm not laughing. I'm wondering how many Vassar and Yale graduates have applied for food stamps. Peter's been telling us to apply ever since we arrived, but we've resisted, and he's chided us for our pride. Everybody else at Libre, including Nancy, who has *some* money, although no one knows how much, gets food stamps. The Red Rockers get them too. No doubt they've exhausted whatever modest trust fund or inheritance was there. They can't get by on occasional holiday caviar care packages from L.A.

"I wish there were another way," says David, as we empty our clothes from six washers at the Spanish Peaks Wash-a-Mat. He dumps a mound of wet towels and sheets into a dryer and continues, "But the government should be supporting people like us! One hundred and twenty three dollars a month isn't much. We're artists and thinkers, exploring new frontiers."

Libre's first three couples—Dean and Linda, Peter and the long-gone Judy, and Tony and Marilynn—got money from the National Institutes of Health their first winter here. NIH was intrigued by their level of mental telepathy, since they were twice as telepathic as the average groups tested. The institutes paid them a small stipend and conducted more telepathy tests. Being artists, they had a lot more experience than us scamming money. No one's offering David and me any more grants. Walsenburg's in a slump. The population of the Huerfano was much larger when the Colorado Fuel and Iron mines were running. Ranching in the arid plains doesn't pay off, and the young people are leaving in droves to find jobs in Denver or L.A. Hippies and a few Texas tourists are the only influx. There are lots of closed businesses in Walsenburg, and more bars than any other business in the center of town. Main Street hasn't changed much since the days when the Pinkerton detectives were gunning down striking miners.

"Well, someday when we're growing more food and stuff, I hope we don't have to do this," I say, putting dimes in the slots of the three dryers.

"Yeah," says David, "but really, what we're trying to do is so important, it's a small investment for the government. And it's worth it to them to get the troublemakers out of the cities and subsidize us on commune/reservations in the middle of nowhere." We head down to Main Street and the Central Bar to meet Doug, who was buying more nails at Unfug's. I haven't gotten over our friends' departure. To them, their week in the valley was an amusing adventure during their summer vacation, but it's our life now. They left after setting the eight posts, feeling like they'd accomplished something, but we have at least three hundred more tasks to do before the house is livable—setting the eight roof beams, linking the posts with eight beams around the perimeter, laying the foundations, building the railroad tie walls of the first story, setting the windows and doors. We definitely won't get to the second-story deck and small bedroom this year. The three of us are all that's left from last week's happy, raucous band. We're like the last of the Mohicans.

"We gotta get more honey," I say. Three days ago, I found our visitor Big John in the summer kitchen eating a quart of honey. Later he snuck over there again and ate a pot of beans I'd cooked for the entire crew. When I caught him scraping out the pot, he dropped his spoon and stared down at me with his blank, watery blue eyes. Some beans were smeared on one corner of his mouth.

"How did he get here?" I asked David that night in the tipi.

"I don't know . . . Danny knew him. I never met him at Yale," David said. Big John went over to the Red Rockers with Henry the day after the honey incident. Henry decided to visit the Red Rocks when the ratio of hashish to hard work changed for the worse. He made up for deserting us by taking Big John with him.

On Main Street we look up at the cut stone Huerfano County Courthouse, where Mother Jones was briefly jailed in the basement. Her cell had one high window, so she could see people's shoes as they walked by. She said later that she could easily tell their status by their shoes. I wonder what she'd think if she could see our new work boots.

We step into the Central Bar and wait for our eyes to adjust, feeling the cool, stale air. The Central's long and narrow, half a block deep, and just wide enough for the big, dark walnut bar on one side, a line of booths on the other, and an aisle in between. The few old-timer regulars are sitting at the bar near the door, and they don't turn their heads to look at us when we walk in. They're a permanent barroom frieze, in the same positions every time we come in. They don't talk to one another, much less take notice of anyone else. They seem stuffed, like the moth-eaten deer heads and the mountain lion crouching over the bar. Benny Archuleta pours beers under a Coors clock set into a molded plastic Rocky Mountains vista with a 3-D stag in the foreground. When our eyes get used to the dark, we walk to the back, to where the food's served, our feet echoing on the plank floor. Benny's the owner-bartender, and his wife, Shirley, cooks. You can get a frosted mug of beer and a plate of red or green enchiladas, rice, and beans for two twenty-five. We're almost out of money, but lunch at the Central is a basic necessity.

In one booth in the back some of the Red Rockers are sitting with two people we don't know. Mary, Larry, and Winnie Red Rocker are squeezed on one side. Across from them is a short, heavyset woman with thick eyeglasses and short, black frizzy hair. She has an anchor tattoo on her forearm. Beside her is a brown-haired man with perfect features, perfect white teeth, deeply tanned skin, and magazine model dimples.

"Oh, the Robertah and Daveed!" Mary Red Rocker greets us. "Say, are you two Hungarian, by any chance? My dad says that if you have a Hungarian for a friend you don't need an enemy."

"Eh-hem, Mary, are you forgetting that Larry, my sister, and I are all of Hungarian persuasion?" Winnie Red Rocker says, raising one eyebrow like a character in a screwball comedy. They grew up with family and friends who made those comedies, and their dialogue sounds like a hippie Preston Sturges wrote it.

"How could I forget?" says Mary, slamming down her beer mug and acting as if she's talking to Winnie, though she's keenly aware of her larger audience. "However—these guys have sent us Henry and Crazy [formerly Big] John," she says, waving her hand in our direction. "Unfortunately, the lovely Vicki, *your sister, your flesh and blood,* Winston, has dumped that sweet but spaced-out drummer and taken up with Henry, so we can't kick Henry out. The good news is we lost a drummer. Are all musicians lazy *and* crazy? And Yalies—I've always wondered about them." Mary has turned to us now, giving up all pretense of talking to Winnie alone. "Today Kelly woke up at dawn, and Crazy John was standing over her. He'd been there for God knows how long. *He drank two pints of maple syrup yesterday!* We asked him to leave this morning . . . there is something very wrong with that boy. Oh, yeah—by any chance, is Clawed, aka Goat John, a friend of yours?" There's no time to answer Mary, and she doesn't seem interested in our answers anyway. "Did you know his herd ate our garden last week? I—"

"Mary, I'm sorry, but we didn't really send Henry there," David interrupts, laughing. "And Goat—er, Clawed—has no connection to us! Big John, or Crazy John, has little or no connection to us either. I didn't know him at Yale, and we didn't know what to do. We thought a change of scene might help him."

"Whatever is wrong with Crazy John cannot be helped by the scenery," pronounces Mary, glowering, but not really mad. Waving her hand

*Adrienne working
on a motor
at the Triple A.*

across the table, she says, "This is Adrienne and Lars, of the Triple A, the Anonymous Artists of America, by the way. Adrienne is an excellent mechanic, and Lars is an unmelancholy Dane if there ever was one. Lars, Adrienne, this is Roberta, David, and David's brother, Doug."

"Pleased to meetcha," says Adrienne, her cigarette bobbing in one corner of her mouth as she speaks. Turning to Mary and squinting from the smoke of her cigarette, she grins and says, "I got an idear, Mary, why don't you build a gatehouse and have a shrink who's tired of L.A. come out an' screen all your visitors? Only trouble is, half the people at the Red Rocks wouldn't get through the screening either, har, har, har."

"Shuddup you little dyke!" Mary shouts. You can tell she likes Adrienne.

"Oh, Adrienne, you are *soooo* crass! And you are no better, my dear Mary." Lars smiles conspiratorially at me. "Honestly, can't you two behave around people of breeding?"

"Breeding? That's the last thing you're interested in," says Mary. Lars ignores Mary and flashes a white smile at us. He wears a fringed, home-made doeskin shirt and pants he sewed himself, and his light brown hair is in two short braids. His deep tan makes him look Indian, sort of. I sit down next to him and ask David to order for me in the next booth.

Lars is somebody you feel you've known before—or is it that you would have liked to have known him before? I could have known him, it turns out. As a kid, I visited the home of a Danish Mobil Oil executive in Jutland. It turns out he lived next door to Lars's family. "The Dugdales," Lars chuckles, his dimples punctuating his cheeks. "Dearie, what a small world it is. You played with Irene and her pony while I was over the wall with my brother on our grounds, and now we're eating en-chiladas in Walsenburg, Colorado," he says with a slight, Scandanavian lilt. Lars's father is some kind of minor Danish royal, Mary explains later, and Lars's mother was an American. Lars went to Stanford, where he met Trixie, and they rented Richard Alpert's California house when Alpert left for India to become Baba Ram Dass. Alpert, who was in his psychedelic Johnny Appleseed stage, left ten thousand hits of acid on the mantel for them, and that's how the Triple A band came to be, Lars tells us. He's one of the lead singers.

"We're signing for our land in the next few weeks—eleven hundred acres north of Redwing, on Slide Mountain. We're giving a party. Are you coming?" From the ridge at Libre, you can look straight across the valley at Slide Mountain, which has two big crevasses running down from the peak like a Fu Manchu mustache.

I say we'll be at the party and ask Lars, "And are you coming to the waterfall party on the Fourth?" He nods back, his brown eyes twinkling, exuding Nordic well-being, looking more like Gunnar the Great than Sitting Bull.

Larry Red Rocker sips his beer thoughtfully, and his brother Winnie grins.

"Larry, you should enter the Frank Zappa lookalike contest," I say, smiling at him.

"Are there any Frank Zappa lookalike contests?" Larry asks, a little sardonically. He got more of the Hungarian melancholy gene than Winnie did. My enchilada special and iced mug of Coors arrive at the next booth, so I move back. I like Mary, Adrienne, Winnie, Lars, and Larry. We scarf up our enchiladas, washing them down with chilled Coors. I'm a cheap drunk and can't finish my beer, so David and Doug help. They don't show their liquor, although Doug gets slightly more talkative. We take turns at the pay phone calling our families. I call my mom and report on the progress of the house and catch up on family news. My brother's at Price Waterhouse now, and my father's in Australia on a business trip. Mobil calls him out of retirement for sensitive jobs.

It's a needed respite, and we're having fun in the dark, cool Central with the overhead fans spinning above us. Three Patsy Cline tunes spin for a quarter in the jukebox while our clean clothes are spinning in the dryers at the Wash-a-Mat. The Chrysler's full of groceries for the next week, and we're drinking beer in mugs sheeted with frost and eating greasy enchiladas. But we look at the clock, figure our clothes must be dry by now, and say we've got to go. The Red Rockers leave, too, to fill some propane tanks at Ludvik's. We wave to Benny, who nods as he dries glasses, and we say good-bye to Adrienne and Lars, who are waiting for the rest of the Triple A town trip to show up.

On the way out of town, we stop at the Lenczes' Shamrock Station. Danny's red-faced, drunk most afternoons, and you can't understand what he's mumbling, but Janie's always friendly. Her orange-blond hair is pulled back tight, and she wears big tortoiseshell glasses on her Doris Day nose. She always has a sample of something for us—banana bread, wild horseradish, wild asparagus, or chanterelle mushrooms she's gathered, or maybe some tomatoes from her garden. She gives us a jar of watermelon rind pickles today, and promises to show us where there's a lot of watercress, and where boletus mushrooms come out on Greenhorn in August after the rains. The Lenczes live in a small apartment connected to the service station—liquor store. A bell buzzes in their apartment when a car drives over a cable by the pumps, and Janie goes out to pump gas while we drink her chicory coffee and try her new coffee cake covered with piñon nuts she gathered last fall. She smokes Kents, even when she's at the pumps. We buy a six-pack from Walter, the genteel Lithuanian refugee who works behind the counter and is in love with Janie. Walter deftly counts out change with the hand that's missing three fingers he lost in an oil rig accident in Texas. Danny stands sullenly behind him, and when we pull out and wave to Janie, she runs after us.

"Here's some venison sausage, too," she says, smiling. As usual, we don't tell her we're on a macrobiotic diet, except for the occasional enchilada at the Central. On the way back, we stop at the abandoned company town on the north side of Route 69. In the ruins of the big dance hall, we move a lot of trash, parts of the fallen roof, and tumbleweeds to check out the floor. It's tongue-and-groove oak, still in good enough shape for flooring and counters. I look for traces of the drunken payday joy stomped into them fifty years ago when John D. Rockefeller Jr. danced with the miner's wife when he bravely came here to investigate after the Ludlow massacre. At the old CFI mine farther up the road, we look at the three-foot-wide iron wheel with a six-inch rim Dallas told us about, part of the mine's vent system. We'll put it on top of our rock like a crown and rest the notched vigas on it as they fan out like wheel spokes to the eight upright logs along the perimeter of the house.

"We need to come back here with Dallas and the blow torch," David mutters, kicking at the big steel wheel as hard as he can, but it doesn't move a bit. At Farisita, we stop at Abe and Ersie's. We smell refried beans, and over the counter we can see the table where they and their two kids are eating dinner. Abe gets up to give us the Libre mail and our Snickers bars, which don't really fit into a macrobiotic diet either, but in our situation you must make adjustments. How many macrobiotic eaters are high-altitude, ten-hour-day laborers?

On the dirt road after the Farisita turnoff, we pull up beside the Red Rocker pickup. Winnie looks at the Chrysler, grins, and says, "*Nice car to drive after a war.*"

"What're you guys doing?" I ask.

"Stopping at Johnny Bucci's. Saw you in the rearview. Wanna come?"

Johnny Bucci's drive is no different from his yard, just dust and dirt, overgrazed right up to his door. His house is a small, pitched-roof, pale green stucco rectangle, with absolutely no plants or trees around it. His wife, Alta May, is in Walsenburg working at the five-and-dime, and Johnny stands alone at the open door as we drive up, smiling his big gap-toothed smile. "Color TV! Why lookee what the cat drug in! Color TV!" he says in his reedy voice. "Why, it's Mayree and Winston! And Larry. But—who are these strangers?" He looks at me and grins some more. "I'm Johnny Bucci," he says, pronouncing it "Byew-sigh." He's medium height, and his gray ten-gallon hat is on crooked, worn and stained with old sweat. He's got brown eyes and a pot belly that bursts the snaps of his plaid cowboy shirt.

"Hiya, Johnny," Winnie says, slamming the truck door. "This is Roberta, David, and his brother Doug. They're building on the ridge at Libre."

"Pleased to meetcher!" Johnny laughs, inviting us in. "Say, is that ol' Linda back yet from Japan? She's a red-headed Italian gal—something else!" Alta May has left the kitchen spare and clean. Johnny lights the gas underneath a chipped white enamel coffeepot. His parents were part of the wave of Italian, German, and Slavic immigrants who came here to work the mines at the turn of the century. His pastureland is poor, always overgrazed, and his cows are skinny, but his life is better than his parents' was. He enjoys company.

We chat and drink stale cowboy coffee, and the men roll Bugler cigarettes, and Mary says, "Johnny, *paisano*, we think our garden was eaten by Clawed's goats. But it could have been one of your cows. We've fixed the fence, but could you make sure your cows aren't getting in anywhere else?"

"Why, sure, Mary, I'll do that," Johnny says. "I just don't think it was one of my cows, though," he says sincerely, sounding slightly hurt. He doesn't explain why it wasn't his cow, and changes the subject quickly, "Sure wish it would rain! We could sure use it. If it doesn't start soon, we're all in big trouble. Say, how is that Clawed guy? I heard his wife was going to have a baby."

"Clawed's moved over to Archuletaville now, but he's trying to rent an adobe in Gardner," says Winnie.

We chat on, until I get impatient and say, "Boy, I forgot, we've got to get going! We've got groceries and blocks of ice in the car, and we need to get them up the ridge." I think we have to put a little less energy into building our community and a little more into building a roof over our heads, but I've always been less sociable than David. Maybe it's the difference between our northern and southern backgrounds. We step out of Johnny's kitchen into the hot afternoon sunlight.

Walking to our car, Johnny looks over his shoulder at me and exclaims once again, "Color TV! Look at them mountains!" He pauses, looking up at the sky. "I know why you people are here, you know." He pauses and then stretches out his arm like an opera singer. "You know that kind of freedom there is, like when the eagle soars? You don't see that kind of freedom much anymore."

"Yes," I say. "I know." Johnny looks at me out of the corner of his eye, his face still lifted up toward the sky, and then adjusts the brim of his hat.

"You've put your finger on it, Johnny," David says laughing. We stand around Johnny's yard, looking out at the mountains, thinking of freedom.

"Say, you know, you sound like some old movie star or other," Johnny says to David.

"Jimmy Stewart," Doug, the Red Rockers, and I say in unison.

We say good-bye, and Johnny smiles and says, "Be seein' ya!" We stir up clouds of dust as we drive out, and Johnny stands in his yard, touching the brim of his hat. I like Johnny, the Lenczes, genteel Lithuanian Walter, Benny Archuleta, the helpful salesmen at Unfug Hardware, the Red Rockers. I'm tired, aching, and sunburnt most days, and the creek's gone dry, and I don't like Mrs. Lenzotti much and hated applying for food stamps. But David's got a point, it's not a bad way for our government to spend its money. It's such a small amount anyway, compared to what it pays Dow and DuPont for Mace and napalm. It's just a month since we drove up this road in the Chrysler with our belongings, but it's starting to feel like coming home.

12 : Water, Cool Water

In the Huerfano you live at the mercy of the sky. Dry Creek's been dry for two weeks, and the spring box didn't refill last night. The wildflowers fade and curl, and when the hot wind blows, dust flies up in the meadows. We could see the ribs on the dead cow by the road down at Johnny Bucci's yesterday, which looked skinny even though it was bloated. The hours of daylight stretch out over the long summer days, and the sun shines relentlessly. We can't work in the middle of the day, so we take restless siestas. The tipi's too hot for afternoon naps, so we put a pad outdoors in the shade of some piñons, which isn't much cooler. The sunset's just one more fire in the sky. Libre looks completely different from the wet, lush place we first drove up to last year in early June.

We took the truck down to Turkey Creek to get water for mixing cement for the foundations. Doug, David, and I filled two fifty-five-gallon drums, passing pails down our short line. My hands and face are parched all the time, and my hair breaks off and moves up my back. At night I embroider a Van Gogh–style sun on a muslin shirt I'm making. Sinbad the kitten went berserk in my embroidery basket, and all the threads got tangled.

"The rains usually come on the Fourth of July," Peter says calmly, sitting in his rocking chair, although he wasn't calm yesterday when he and Bill Keidel almost got into a fistfight down at the spring box. Nobody's asking why. Two nights ago I waited at Jim and Sandy's to take a shower in the outdoor shower behind their house, but Peggy Grow and her two kids took long showers before me, and the water ran out. As I walked home, hot and dusty, I heard Peter and Nancy yelling at each other, so I veered around their zome. Even Doug sounded irritated yesterday when David dropped one end of a log they were moving. Richard and Beth look grim. People flare up the way wildfires do when it's dry, at the slightest spark. David's been playing a bluesy version of "Water, Cool Water" at night. Growing up in the East, where a drought means that the golf courses get a little brown and you can't water your lawn every day, I was oblivious. Now I'm afraid.

We went to a peyote meeting for water at the Triple A last week. Lars was road man, and as the tobacco traveled around the circle of flickering faces in the tipi, we prayed for the oceans, rains, relief. It clouded up a little the next day, but it didn't rain. At our Sunday community dinner the tone was subdued, and Libre faces have taken on a Dust Bowl look. Our Independence Day party's at the waterfall on Turkey Creek today. The Red Rockers, Libre, and the Triple A each buy a keg of beer from the Lenczes, and everyone brings a salad, dessert, or something to barbecue. Doug takes my cherry cobbler over in the True Truck with Dallas and Stephanie, and David and I walk over the back ridges to the waterfall. The little spring in the canyon between Bill's ridge and the next ridge is dried up, and the meadows on top of the ridges are parched. There are a few clouds to the far west, but I'm sick of false hopes.

The gushing waterfall is diminished to a splash dropping over the rocks. Still, the sound of the moving water soothes us, and there's a pool deep enough to keep the kegs cold, and the kids splash in and out of the deepest pool. David and I walk up the hill to the ruins of a log cabin built by a family called Graham in the last century. They thought they could grow potatoes here, but failed. There are smooth-edged pieces of glass from old colored bottles in the trash heap—frosted dusty blues, faded greens, golden root beer browns.

"David," I almost say, "I feel a little confused and lost, like Dorothy in *The Wizard of Oz*. I don't want to go back to Kansas, I just want to go back to the way I felt before this drought. David, I don't know if we can make it." But I don't say that, even to myself, much less to David, because the better part of me knows we'll overcome these hardships, and that this hard time will make our accomplishments more savory. Because David and I are the leads in our own movie, and we have to stick to our lines.

"We'll get through this," David answers the words I haven't spoken. It's half prediction, half promise. "'Difficulty at the Beginning,' just like the *I Ching* said," he reminds me. Can yarrow sticks be loaded like dice? Lately we get "Youthful Folly" or "Difficulty at the Beginning" nine times out of ten when we throw the sticks, even though there are sixty-two other hexagrams. "Just look around you at the people here, we'll make it," David reassures me as we listen to Turkey Creek gurgle. At the moment, I'm watching Tom Grow roll in the dirt and smear dust on himself, like a cat taking a dust bath, while behind him, closer to the waterfall, Bill's pumping beer into a big pitcher. Old Dan Archuleta is still standing up by the kegs. When he has a little more beer, he bends over like someone touching his toes and doesn't stand back up. He spends the rest of the party staring at the curled-up tips of his cowboy boots, although, for some reason, his huge cowboy hat never falls off. Clawed's wife is so pregnant she looks as if she might split open like an overripe melon. She's in the shade comparing notes with Patricia, who's almost as big. Lars is into his summer Cochise look, wearing only a chamois loincloth for the party. Adrienne's dressed in bunchy jeans and a T-shirt as usual, and she puffs on her cigarette, talking to Lars, who's waving her smoke out of his face and smiling. David and I walk over, arm in arm.

"Well, it's the Duke and Duchess, out for a stroll!" Lars says, smiling more widely. "Hello. Is it true that Dean and Linda are headed back from Japan?"

"That's what Peter says," David answers.

"Hmm, then it may not be true," Lars says cattily. Over his shoulder, we see the Red Rockers get out of their trucks. Their spring's dried up, and they're hauling their water from Gardner. Mary's husband, Terry, has left for New Mexico, and Mary's sitting next to Bad Eddy, and Larry and Kelly are expecting a baby. Farther back up on the road, two cowboy trucks are parked. The cowboys sit in the cabs with their radios on and drink beer, hoping they can catch a glimpse of hippie chicks skinny-dipping.

The *I Ching* commentary for "Difficulty at the Beginning" says that it's very important not to remain alone at such times. The sound of the water loosens the tightness inside me that's been building with the drought, and the laughter of new friends washes over me. Even though the pool above the waterfall is low, it's deep enough to dip into, and the water's still mountain cold. We lie on the rocks and air dry. We eat salads and tempeh burgers, and David and Doug eat some of Janie Lencz's homemade pork sausages that Adrienne brought. We drink cold beer and smoke the stray joint that comes by. David and Henry play and sing,

Sangre de Cristos from the ridge, rain cloud approaching, summer 1970.

and we laugh some more. Their version of "Water, Cool Water" is half send-up, half sincere. We look into one another's faces, and our backs and shoulders get a day's rest, and we relax.

Late in the afternoon, David and I walk back over the ridges. On the first ridge from the waterfall, we look back at the party, still going strong. Even a crowd looks sparse in this much space. Above us, the clouds to the west have multiplied and move slowly across the valley. We don't say anything about it. On the next ridge, the clouds have moved closer, and a breeze comes up and cools the sweat off our faces, but we still don't mention it. By the third and last ridge, the wind's picked up, and the sun's partially covered, and I grin at David. When we pass Bill Keidel's site, a few big drops plop on us, and by the time we've walked around the road to our site, it's raining angrily, and the wind whips the raindrops into our faces. The thunder cracks like the report of a gun, and our hair lifts with the electricity of the storm. We open our mouths, stick out our tongues, and stretch our arms out like Elmer Gantry as we run to the tipi site. We're drenched, cool at last in the wet wind that's blowing the rainstorm across the valley. In the tipi we towel off and fall on the bed and make love as the raindrops pelt the canvas. David gets up, naked like a savage, and closes the tipi flaps so that the rain doesn't pour in on us. His lanky body glistens from the rain when he steps back in. When the rain stops, we walk out into our meadow. The flowers are resurrected, the grass is green, and the air smells sharply of sage. A wet sheen makes the meadow sparkle and the rocks shine. It's still cloudy, although the storm has moved on. When sunlight breaks through in the west, a small double rainbow arches precisely over the site of our house against the gray sky.

"Another rainbow," David says. "*Clouds and thunder.* Do you remember what it said?"

"What?" I say, turning back to the tipi to get my Pentax.

"The *I Ching,*" he answers, following me into the tipi and grabbing the book. While I'm crouching in the damp meadow, snapping up all angles of the rainbow over the beginnings of our house, he reads:

Clouds and thunder are represented by definite decorative lines; this means that in the chaos of difficulty at the beginning, order is already implicit. So too the superior man has to arrange and organize the inchoate profusion of such times of beginning, just as one sorts out silk threads from a knotted tangle and binds them into skeins. In order to find one's place in the infinity of being, one must be able both to separate and unite.

13 : The Time Capsule

I haven't talked about David much. He's a given, like the clear air here, which I don't mention much either. We're together almost all the time. Working on the house, building, digging, hammering, carrying, sawing, mixing cement. In five years we'll log more time together than the average commuter husband and wife who've been married twenty-five years. We began with a conversation about Ezra Pound one night freshman year. His beard's longer now, and his hair falls to his shoulders. He's nut brown from the sun, and his muscles are harder. The sex isn't as frequent as it used to be, naturally—we're both always so exhausted—but that's just for now. He's my co-star, audience, co-conspirator, sidekick—my brother, my father, my child.

We've been here long enough for me to realize he's not going about things in the most organized way. He won't work on the house if the vibes aren't right, or if he doesn't have a clear vision. I think more about time running out, and I don't see why he has to have a vision every morning, but if I get anxious, he slows down, so I do my best not to appear anxious. But he knows anyway and slows down in reaction. He and Doug smoke a joint in the morning to get in the right frame of mind to work on the house. Sometimes I wish that he'd think less about gaining the right perspective and worry more about getting the job done. Some days I feel I'm here almost by accident, as if I just happened to marry the choices and life of my husband, the way wives have done for years, not questioning, putting the best face on it. I could just as easily have married a young liberal politician, I think, and be suffering through a Garden Club lunch. But that's on bad days, and I know it's not true even then. I'd

David's brother Doug with Peggy Grow.

look down on anyone who was not an artist, who didn't challenge me, who wasn't a truly creative thinker, and when David picks up his guitar at night by the fire and sings a sweet song, I gaze into the quivering blue at the base of the flames and know how good, how true this is. Across the fire sits Doug. He's not a dreamer or an intellectual, but despite his youth, he's calm, practical, helpful, self-possessed. He's a true brother, and we wouldn't have a chance of getting things done without him.

Chugga chugga chugga. The cement mixer interrupts my thoughts. Its motor is cousin to outboards and lawn mowers of our childhood. One part Portland cement, two parts sand, some small rocks, moisten with water. David dips the bucket into the fifty-five-gallon drum and carefully pours water into the mix. First it's the texture of wet sand near the sea, then it's damper and clumps up, then it's too wet for sand castles. As it circles around to the top of the mixer, it falls in one big, satisfying lump and starts its circular ascent again. I poke it with a broken pick handle to help mix it up. Doug, David, and I frown critically into the spinning drum.

"More water?" Doug yells over the motor.

"We don't want to get it too wet," David says, cautiously splashing in a bit more. The rebar is staked in the ground inside the plywood forms for the foundations. The four foundation forms we built are three feet deep and run between the five posts that mark the bottom half of the house. We'll be lucky to get the bottom half of the first floor of the house done before the snows. The bottoms of the forms are wider than the tops. When we fill them, we'll set big screws head-first in the cement so we can bolt the first row of railroad ties onto the screws. When Vesey walked by yesterday on his way up to see Bill, he laughed drily and said that the foundations would be "Egyptian and mammoth." What we're doing must look monumental compared to Vesey's small and ramshackle A-frame and dome, which were, however, completed in one summer and before the first snow last year. David wants a solid foundation, but maybe it's overkill and unnecessary. I simply don't know.

Dallas walked by earlier today, on the way to see Richard and Beth. Dallas didn't say anything about the size of the foundations, which is unusual, but he's pretty glum. The sandbags on the roof of Dallas and Stephanie's hogan got soaked when the rainy season started, and the roof caved in. Their relationship collapsed at the same time. Lately Stephanie's been hanging out with Benjo Red Rocker, one of Anson's twin brothers there. Stephanie and Benjo have become serious devotees of the Native American Church. Hippie men who convert to the Native American Church are even more rectitudinous and serious than Dallas can be.

That's odd, since the Indian roadmen who've run peyote meetings here aren't as serious as the hippie converts are. When John Pedro told me he'd lost his leg in World War II, and I said, "How horrible!" he smiled at me and said, "Heck, no, it wasn't horrible! They took me to Germany and fed me good and gave me a rifle and told me to shoot at white men. It was *great!*" When Frank Zamora, the hero of *The Man Who Killed the Deer,* leaned over to pass Linda the pipe in the last peyote meeting here, he stuck his tongue in her ear and whispered, "Do you want me to give you a little brown baby?" The male hippie devotees have none of this humor or lasciviousness. They walk around as sober as cigar store Indians and talk like Chief Dan George. Although David has more Native American blood than any of them, he hasn't been tempted to sign up for the Peyote Church. One reason the new members are so

Cement mixer at the rock house site, August 1970.

sober is that they have to give up alcohol and dope and just about everything else to eat peyote at Saturday night meetings, and this trade-off doesn't work for David.

Chugga chugga chugga. David's shirt is off, and his torso's tanned and dark. He's wearing a twisted bandanna as a headband to keep his hair out of his eyes, and, except for his mustache and beard, right now he does look a lot like Cochise in a B movie. Doug's plaid cowboy shirt is splattered with cement drops, but still tucked in. He stays cooler than David, and he steps away as he rolls a Bugler. I pick up the empty bag of cement, fold it up, put it on the pile of empty bags, and stick another rock on them to keep them from blowing away. We'll burn them in the campfire and cookstove tonight.

When the cement mixture's just right, it's the consistency of chocolate chip cookie dough. David stops the mixer, and we tip it over so the cement plops like cow pies into the forms. A load covers only about half the bottom with a couple of inches of cement. This is the southeastern wall, the first wall of eight, the wall of our kitchen.

"How many more loads do you think?" I ask as David and Doug smooth cement into the corners and level it with their trowels.

"Maybe fifteen," David says, sighing. The cement work's ruining his guitar fingers. I walk up to the road to get another bag of cement from the stack there, carefully tucking the plastic sheet back around the remaining bags. In one afternoon's rain, the exposed stack could become a monument to my carelessness. I stop to catch my breath and stare out over the valley, wiping my hands together to get the globs of cement off my gloves. At the end of the day there are tiny flecks of cement on my face, like too many gray beauty marks. I helped my dad mix cement when he built the foundation for our sun porch under the birches. He used an electric mixer, but I never knew the recipe. If you'd asked me last year if I knew how to mix cement, I would have stared at you blankly. What takes seconds to build in your dreams takes weeks to make here on earth. But we're doing it, we're making it. I pick up the fifty-five-pound bag of cement, balance it against my pelvis, and walk stiff-legged down the hill like Conan the Barbarian. David and Doug grin up at me.

David says, "Look at that, Doug—the china blue eyes, the rosy cheeks, the flaxen hair, the . . . bulging biceps!" They guffaw. I like lugging bags of cement half my weight down the steep trail. I dump the bag on its end at David's feet. He slits the top with a knife, and Doug starts the mixer and dumps the sand in, and then David and I hoist the bag to pour the cement into the rotating drum. I hold my breath and look away to avoid breathing the cement dust puffing up out of the mixer that will coat my hair and face anyway.

We stare into the drum again as it twirls. The mixer sounds like the Little Engine that Could. "I think I can, I think I can," it chugs. Peering into the spinning drum, I remember the paper I wrote in high school about Yeats and his widening gyre. Yeats lived in a little cabin at the foot of Ben Bulben, but he didn't build it himself. He was no dummy.

"Hey," I shout over the motor, "let's do a time capsule or something and stick it in here!"

"Good idea!" says David, and Doug nods. I run back to the summer kitchen, tear a page from the June 1970 issue of *Rolling Stone* with a picture of Bob Dylan on it, and sit at the railroad tie table in the shade of the tarp, biting the plastic pen. The cats are sleeping on the cool dirt in the shade and only half open their eyes. Once they're sure I'm not doing anything involving food, they shut their eyes and go back to sleep.

"*David and Roberta & Doug, August 1970,*" I write. Then "*The Rock House at Libre.*" Then that line from Jim Morrison—"*The West is the Best.*" David would probably stick in something about the revolution, but I'm leery of bravura or predictions in a time capsule. Who will find it? Where will

I be? Long gone? What kind of world will it be opened in? Will Steve and Patricia's baby, who will be born any day now in the tipi pitched by their house, still be around? I need something more, a line from a song, maybe—*"The times they are a changin'"*? Too hokey. *"In my life, I loved you more"*? Too sappy. *"We've got to get ourselves back to the garden"*? Likewise. *"Freedom's just another word for nothing left to lose"*? Not hopeful enough. The motor stops. They're dumping the next load, I should get back, so I scrawl, *"You can be in my dream if I can be in yours"* from "Talking World War III Blues."

I get a scrap of black two-inch PVC pipe and some duct tape and run back across the meadow. David puts a joint and two tiny tabs of acid folded in an empty Zig Zag rolling paper package, folds it up, and stuffs it down the PVC tube along with the page from *Rolling Stone* and my message. We seal both ends with the tape. He pushes the tube lengthwise into the wet cement. How long does newspaper last? How long before LSD breaks down? Where's the nearest time capsule? There probably aren't any time capsules in the Huerfano Valley. No one's done more to memorialize his place in history than to carve his initials in an aspen or ponderosa pine. This might be an unexpected find for some anthropologist or American Studies professor, if he bothers to have his student assistants chip up the foundation.

We know this is half a joke. Our time capsule nestles in the soggy cement. Its destiny slowly solidifies around it even now, the way ours congeals around us. I should have included a quote from Yeats, the last romantic. Doug pours gas into the mixer, then pulls the starter cord with a jerk and falls backward. The engine gives a few syncopated coughs and starts chugging again. We wipe our foreheads in unison, notice we're doing the same thing, then laugh and shake our heads as we get back to work.

September 2, 1970

Our most recent visitor, Jean Claude, has stayed with us for a week. He's a thin, frail French student who's been traveling around the American West. Jean Claude gets up very early in the morning, and before we can stop him, he uses half a pound of coffee to make a pot that is so strong David and I can't drink it. Jean Claude drinks it all himself at breakfast, and then goes back to bed with severe stomach pains for a few hours. In the afternoon, he staggers over in his espadrilles to help us at the site, but he bends about half the nails he hammers, and we have to pull them out, which takes much longer than hammering them in without his help. He shakes so much from drinking coffee and chain-smoking Gauloises that there's little chance he can hammer a nail in straight. He drops his end of each log at least once when we're moving it. Late in the day, he collapses against a rock and regards the mountain ranges, exclaiming, "*Ah, c'est magnifique!*" By then we're happy he's not trying to help.

The *I Ching* says that to overcome the chaos of new beginnings it's very important not to be alone, that you need helpers. I don't question this, but lately I've been wondering about the kinds of helpers who show up. Since Doug left to finish his last year of high school, we're a bit desperate for help, and we don't have a big selection. The saner, stronger, well-heeled visitors, the ones who drive up the road in new four-wheel drives, are snagged by those on the lower part of the land. It's the factory seconds who get up the ridge, like Jean Claude.

We didn't mind him at first. David and I love Godard. The fact that Jean Claude is French made him sophisticated, attractive, and though it was clear he was no John Henry (or, Jean Henri), we hoped he'd catch on after a while. It's wonderful that a stranger who grew up eight thousand miles away can walk up to our summer kitchen and we'll automatically welcome him. The message needs to spread across the world. He's young and inquisitive, and he's taken the trouble to get here. His hair's long, and he smokes dope. That's all he needs to be a member of the worldwide secret society of youth that's bigger than anything before, bigger than the Mafia, the Masons, the Communist Party, the Underground Railroad.

Jean Claude, however, has cast doubt on his membership standing in the new movement and outlasted the benefit of our doubts. I'm not so sure he's really one of us. He has no interest in making a significant contribution to our cause. Another problem is that his English isn't very good, and it gets a lot worse when you ask him to work. Even if you pantomime that you want him to go get a bag of cement or wash the dishes, he doesn't get it. Yesterday morning I screwed up my courage and said, "Jean Claude, um, when are you going to, uh, *move on?*" He didn't understand, so I raised my voice, out of the embarrassing American conviction that foreigners understand you better when you yell, but also in exasperation. "*WHEN ARE YOU GOING TO LEAVE? QUAND DÉPARTEZ-VOUS?*" So much for hands across the ocean.

He ignored my French, although my accent's pretty good, and said, "OOOhhhh—I would like to leeve here forever!" Last night, we hid the coffee. This morning, as Jean Claude stumbled around the summer kitchen groggily looking for it, I screwed up my courage and told him over and over he had to go, in English *and* French. "GO, GET OUT— *ALLEZ! VA T'EN!*" He was horribly insulted and suffering from massive caffeine withdrawal. He ran around yelling in French too fast for me to understand, almost crying, gathering up his books and belongings, and flopped down the hill in his torn espadrilles. I had to hold myself back from stopping him and apologizing. I felt horrible. Why do I have to be the one to evict these guys? David hates confrontations and never seems to mind these losers as much as I do.

The German TV crew were a better sort of European visitor. They didn't work much, but when Peter suggested they buy a few kegs of beer in exchange for filming us for their documentary about communes in the States, they quickly agreed, got directions to Janie and Danny Lencz's, and took off in their new rental van. Later that afternoon, we drank the beer on Dean and Linda's front porch and explained what we were doing in the Huerfano. The sun set as we washed down our words with more beer. I don't know if the film will give an accurate picture of what we're doing, but it was great to have free cold beer after work.

We live in a bizarre, repressed, intolerant society. There are self-sufficient and helpful visitors, of course. Stewart Brand, the founder of *The Whole Earth Catalog,* drives up towing his Airstream trailer, parks in Dean and Linda's meadow, and sits out on his lawn chair and chats. Dr. Frank, who just happens to be visiting us shortly after Patricia has her baby, probably saves Patricia's life by diagnosing an infection and immediately driving her and the infant up to a Denver hospital. But for every visitor who contributes to our endeavor, there are fifty who suck us dry. We're the destination of hopeless, crazy youth, the last stop before a mental institution for some. First there was Crazy John, who was big and strong and helped for a while, but lost it and started mumbling to himself and sneaking back to the summer kitchen and eating everything. Over at the Red Rocks, he busted the lock on the kitchen trailer one night and ate and ate. Some hunger deep inside him couldn't be satisfied. When the Red Rockers kicked him out, he went home, and the next time he came through, we noticed his underwear on the clothes-line had a state institution stamp. He was more subdued, but not better off. Then there was Marty Maya (nobody knows his real name), a seventeen-year-old high school dropout who arrived here during the driest part of the summer, before the first rainy season. The day Dean got back from Japan, he smelled smoke and ran up the ridge to find Marty feeding a big fire under a semicircle of five tinder-dry dead piñons. Dean barely got the fire out, frantically kicking it apart and throwing dirt on it, while Marty stood around protesting that it was an altar to the sun goddess he'd been ordered to build.

"What about the rain goddess?" Dean asked. *"We don't need any more sun!"*

We think Richard and Beth's quiet visitor, Joel, shot at us last week when we were working. Something pinged off the rock very near us a few times before David and I realized it was a bullet and ducked behind the boulder like the Lone Ranger and Tonto in an ambush. When we went up to confront him, Richard explained that Joel was shooting at a target behind Richard and Beth's site on the cliffs, but that didn't make sense. The bullets couldn't possibly have ricocheted from there to our house site. There was no trajectory that could get a bullet from the cliffs to our house. Richard took Joel's gun away.

Ben and Chipita came up from New Mexico. Ben was a member of the Motherfuckers, a street kid from New York's Lower East Side, and he and Chipita got together back then. They have six horses and a tipi now and were riding north to Canada from New Mexico, but the Huerfano was as far as they got before Ben came down with dysentery, so they pitched their tipi on the lowest part of the land near Tony and Marilynn's dome, where Ben lay on animal skins and entertained visitors, and Chipita ran around hunting, cooking, cleaning, chopping wood, feeding and shoeing the horses. She'd be a great visitor to have around. I invited them up to the ridge, but right after that, their horses got into the Libre garden a second time, and Ben got religion at one of John Pedro's peyote meetings, so they moved to the upper land of the Ortiviz Farm.

One guy came from California and stayed for two weeks, smoking cigarettes angrily as he worked, keeping to himself, not saying much. When he left, he told us Libre was hopelessly bourgeois, but he asked lots of questions about where we got our dynamite. After him, there was Carl, a graduate school friend of mine now dealing rare books in London. He was a bit overweight, with pale skin, no muscle tone, and a frizzy Afro, but he meant well. He helped David carry some five-gallon water cans up the ridge, sweating profusely.

"Roberta," Carl said, panting like a bulldog, "I've figured it out!"

"What?" I asked, wondering how young a person could be and still have a heart attack. I was trying to recall the techniques I'd learned when I got my Senior Lifesaver badge at camp. I said, "You know, Carl, it's nine thousand feet higher here than it is in New York or London. You really ought to take it easy."

"You . . . were a . . . princess in a past life . . . or maybe a sultan's favorite daughter . . . with thousands of servants, incredibly rich . . . clothes, silks . . . jewels, like what they took for the English crown jewels. . . . Now . . . in this lifetime . . . you're working off . . . karma . . . on this mountain, living this . . . hard life . . . to make up for the luxuries and decadence of . . . your past lives," Carl said, between deep, sucking gasps. He was a funny shade of pink, with a lot of blue in it.

"Do you think there's any way I could switch back to that previous life?" I cracked. I'm skeptical about past lives. Everyone's had a royal one; no one was a servant or slave or an average peasant. "Maybe I'm just working off my privileged life in this lifetime," I said to Carl, but didn't go on. He needed to save his breath. Bonnie, Carl's girlfriend, who was at graduate school with us at Buffalo too (she wrote on Jane Austen), was a good visitor, until the afternoon she found a field mouse Kachina had murdered and left for me on a shelf in the summer kitchen.

Bonnie screamed, *"IT'S THE MIDDLE AGES!"* and wasn't interested when I explained about the loyalty of Siamese cats, that the mouse carcass was a gift, Kachina's way of demonstrating her love for me, or maybe her concern that I'm not getting enough to eat. Bonnie and Carl left the next day, and it's probably for the best. They missed going to Gardner with us to visit Clawed, his wife, and their newborn. Clawed made a boeuf bourguignonne—type stew out of the placenta. He said some tribe or other believed that eating it brought great good fortune. After he told us what was in the stew, David pushed it around his plate diplomatically, but I went outside and threw up.

15 : Heart Failure

For the last three months we've seen Richard, our closest neighbor, almost every day. His face is familiar now. It doesn't change much and has no dramatic features: intelligent hazel eyes, long brown hair, a thin straight mouth, simple wire-rimmed glasses. He's quiet and calm, a good neighbor. Tonight, though, Richard isn't calm. His face is grayish white, and his eyes are red. He sits on a rocker in Peter's zome and chain-smokes while we wait for the sheriff. Peter's uncharacteristically quiet, and his shoulders slump more than usual. He walks around the zome as if there were weights tied to his big feet.

Nancy chats in a fake, buoyant tone that she must have picked up in Texas. "Well, he just chose to check out, and that was his choice. All we can do is wish him well on his journey. The Indians thought differently about it, didn't they, Peter?"

"I guess. I dunno," Peter says, sighing. "It wasn't a sin."

Richard's friend Joel, who shot at us two weeks ago, helped Richard and Beth and their kids move into their house today. Then he rolled up his sleeping bag and straightened up his camp underneath the platform of the new house, stacked up his esoteric book collection, leaned up against a supporting post, and swallowed thirty-five capsules of Seconal. When he didn't show up for dinner, Richard went down to check on him. Joel was slumped over sideways in the dark, dead.

"Do your kids know?" I ask.

"Nope." Richard bites his lips.

Beth's up the ridge tucking Aaron and Aricia into the new beds Richard made with Joel's help, while Joel's stiffening underneath the kitchen floor. It's been a long wait. Nancy made mint tea from Turkey Creek mint we gathered this week, and I gave Richard a big steaming cup with lots of honey in it, but he hasn't drunk any. David sits at the kitchen table shaking his head sadly, his mouth tight. With each new death we face old ones. His father died two years ago, but I haven't had to face a death like that. All my grandparents died more or less naturally. The accidental deaths in my life were only acquaintances. In fourth grade a classmate was electrocuted standing in a puddle in his garage working on his boxcar racer. When I was sixteen, another boy died when he crashed his father's XKE. I don't know anything about Joel, except that he was Richard and Beth's friend, that he shot at us, and that he seemed a little weird. Nancy puts out a plate of *Diet for a Small Planet* peanut butter cookies. No one's had dinner. She says Joel's spirit knew it was time to move on and we should wish him well on his journey. Once she stops talking, our chewing seems loud. Richard doesn't eat or drink, and hardly remembers to puff on his cigarettes, but he rolls one nervously every time the last one burns down.

When we heard the news it was dark, but we were still at the house site, using a big Coleman flashlight to give us enough light to slam in the last railroad tie on one of the kitchen walls. We heard Richard's footsteps on the path, and he paused after we greeted him, then sucked in his breath weirdly. "Joel's dead. Under the house. He's dead," Richard said simply. We put down our hammers carefully. Richard said, "He was so . . . troubled. In a bad way. Worrying about the draft started it, or made it worse. That's why he left St. Louis and came out here. We thought being with us here in the mountains, he would break out of it, calm down, feel better. He had these demons . . . he heard voices. We didn't know how to help any more than we did. He ate a bunch of pills he must have brought with him. He's dead."

There's a knock, and Dean steps into the zome. He's wearing only the garish orange pants Linda made him and a T-shirt, even though it's got to be forty degrees outside and it snowed lightly two days ago. His bright blond hair and orange pants seem too bright.

"What's going on?" he asks, stopping just inside the door.

"Richard's friend Joel ate a bunch of pills and died," Peter says.

"Oh shit," Dean mutters.

"Yeah." Peter says.

"Is Benedict coming?" Dean asks, sitting down at the kitchen table next to David.

Richard works on his floor with a friend, summer 1970.

Richard and Beth's house, fall 1970.

"Yeah." Peter sighs. "We called him on Hudson's phone over at the big ranch house."

"Oh, man," Dean says, holding his head and staring down at the table.

"Yeah," Peter repeats. No one says anything more, and we wait. After I don't know how long, we hear a truck climbing into Libre, and then we make out the sound of a distinctly new, powerful engine as it lumbers across Dean and Linda's meadow toward the zome. Our eyes meet and then look away again.

"Well, here they are," Peter says grimly when the motor shuts off. He's worried about the headlines in the *Huerfano World* or the *Pueblo Chieftain,* or maybe even the *Rocky Mountain News.* Will there be an investigation? Will the men in the Pueblo FBI field office come down and make life miserable? A suicide at Drop City was the beginning of its end. The truck doors slam, and Peter goes out to meet them. He walks back in with Sheriff Benedict Montoya and another man. Sheriff Montoya is about thirty, compact and round-stomached, with thick black hair. He's a friend, but he's all business tonight.

"Hi," Benedict says quietly. "This is Sam Dotmeyer, the Walsenburg coroner." Sam's middle aged, medium-sized, with short, thinning brown hair. He wears a cheap, dark business suit, a thin western tie, and cowboy boots. His rimless glasses have a dark plastic strip across the top. He hands us a card—he's the director of the local mortuary and the coroner.

Peter says, "Men, this is Richard, Joel's friend. Joel's the dead man." Richard winces when Peter says that. "You know Dean, of course, and my wife, Nancy," Peter goes on, ever the good host, "and this is David and Roberta—they're the nearest neighbors on the ridge. Want some coffee?" he asks wearily.

"Thanks, Peter, but no, we should go up and check things out," Benedict says quietly.

Richard puts out his cigarette slowly in a tuna can ashtray and says, "I'll take you up."

Peter says, "I'll go with you too," and grabs his jacket off the hook.

We sit in the zome and listen to the truck drive down the hill in front of Peter's and then curve around past Tom and Peggy Grow's house, the Grow Hole. Does Sam the coroner see the Grow Hole dug into a side of the ridge, where Tom and Peggy bent lodgepole pines to curve out from the ridge and make a roof? There's a south-facing glass wall slanting up to the roof, which looks like a big glass eye staring out at the road.

It's not finished. Does Sam see the two holes outside that Tom bored into the ridge for Lump and Lori's sleeping bags, burrows where the kids climb in, feet first, to sleep at night until the house is finished? I keep busy asking these questions so I won't think of Joel's body slumped under Richard's new house, of Aaron's and Aricia's faces in the Rembrandt light of the kerosene lamp, their pale, fine hair lit up like halos, as Beth reads to them and the men talk quietly and bump under the house.

I help Nancy clean up. With fall, new dangers have crept into the air. Last week, when we drove the flatbed up the mountain to get more logs, David and I walked down the mountain while the rest of the crew took the flatbed full of logs down the national forest road. No one has a watch, and we weren't used to the sun setting so early and abruptly as the equinox approached. We thought we had lots of time, but we ended up bumbling down Greenhorn in the dark of the moon. We stumbled on the edge of canyon cliffs through an ominous, silent darkness, struggling through tangled clumps of scrub oak and mountain mahogany that scratched our faces and arms. Oh, the mountain had a lesson for us that night. Who's the greenhorn? What's the lesson tonight, and why was it taking them so long? Was it like that for Joel, making his way through a hideous, unending darkness? I was frightened as we made our way down the mountain like the peasants in the Hieronymus Bosch painting of the blind leading the blind, but at least I had a companion. David almost fell off the cliff when a rock gave way. We were bruised and scratched, but we made it. As soon as we got down the mountain, the experience became a parable. It's all new. There's no choreography, no maps, and we're making so much up as we go along. Slowly but surely, we'll make it—we really don't have a choice. It was two days after we'd gotten lost that Joel shot at us and Richard took his gun away. Lately, whenever Sandy read the Tarot, The Tower kept appearing. The lightning on the tower, the figure free-falling. We should have known.

As we finish the dishes, we hear the truck crawling back up the hill past the Grow Hole. The four men enter the dome with a blast of cold air, and Sam Dotmeyer sits down awkwardly in one of Peter's rockers, trying not to rock. He clasps his hands and looks at the floor. His cowboy boots are dirty and wet from the snow and the mud. Nancy controls herself and doesn't ask him to take off his boots.

"Well," he says. We all lean toward him.

"Well," Sam says again, pushing his glasses back up his nose and looking up at us. "I think that your friend, er, Joel, he must have had a *very, very bad* heart condition. People don't talk about these things, especially young men. It's very sad. But there it is—these things happen. High altitude probably didn't help. His heart just—failed." We stand around in stunned silence.

"Well, Sam," Peter says, sagging and sighing, "it's clear to me it was a failure of heart, too. As you say, we'll never really know what happened. I didn't know Joel, and he certainly didn't confide in me. Did he say anything to you, Richard?" Richard shakes his head without emotion. He may be in shock.

"Well," says Sam, standing up, looking around the circle, "We need to take the deceased into town. We've got all the information, and we'll contact his family to see what they want done." He sounds more like an undertaker than a coroner now.

"Yes, that makes sense." David says.

Sam looks at Richard and says professionally, "I'm sorry for your loss." Richard nods. Benedict and Sam say good-bye and get in the truck. Joel's body's in the back, wrapped in his mummy sleeping bag, and the truck bumps down the road.

Peter shakes his head and says, "Heart failure!" He tries to laugh but can't.

"Did anybody hide the pill bottle?" Dean asks. Richard and Peter shake their heads. "Did they just not see it?" Dean asks. Richard and Peter shrug.

Richard gets up awkwardly and mutters, "I've got to get back to Beth and the kids."

Dean, David, and I leave with him. Dean hugs me and then Richard, as if he could pass some of his robust strength through the circle of his arms, and heads east back to his dome, moving through the piñons like a sullen bear. We trudge up the ridge path in silence. At a small clearing halfway up, we stop and look at the vast sky. The stars are crisper than they are in summer. A coyote from central casting howls over by Turkey Creek. I can't think what to say, and David's not doing any better. We trudge past our site up to the ridge road with Richard. Up the road we see the two triangles of Richard's windows, glowing golden from the light of kerosene lamps inside.

"Richard, man, don't let this spoil it. Remember your joy," David says. "You have a beautiful house and a beautiful family. This shouldn't spoil what you've done."

"Yeah, shouldn't," Richard mumbles. "Thanks for your help." He looks at us for a second, decides not to say anything more, then turns. His boots crunch in the patches of snow, then hit the steps and pound hollowly on the deck around the house, the edges of the platform under which Joel swallowed pills with mad resolve. He clumps across the icy deck to the front door, facing the ghostly and luminous Huajatollas, so far away. The door opens and shuts quietly, and then it's silent and chilly as death. I grab David's hand and try not to think of Joel's bumpy ride in the back of the sheriff's pickup, cutting through the valley under a cold dome of stars.

16 : The Libra Birthday Party

The snowflakes started mid-morning, silent and slow. Each one is big, wet, and individual, and they fall at a slant under the tarp as I work at the stove. They dissolve instantly when they hit the cake batter, but that's okay, because you're supposed to add more liquid at high altitudes. The eggbeater's a problem, though—its gears seize up in the cold, so I can't crank it very fast. I'm making the cake on the right side of the cookstove, away from the firebox. This side's not too hot, just warm enough to keep the ingredients at "room temperature" as I cook outside in a snow flurry in our summer kitchen. It could be that the beater is too far from the heat. I tap it on the edge of the bowl to get the batter off and hold it horizontally over the hottest burners of the stove until my fingers can't take the heat. A few drops of remaining batter fall onto the iron stove top and cook like miniature pancakes.

The cats, who usually wrap themselves around my legs when I'm cooking, have deserted me today. They're in the tipi with David, enjoying the fire, nestled together on top of our goose down bags. I don't blame them. They'll be here alone when we go down the ridge to Peter's for the Libra birthday party. I don't have to bake a cake in a snowstorm. I could make my excuses, but I promised I'd bake a German chocolate cake a few days ago, when it was sunny and warm, and it's not impossible. We can't do any work on the house in this weather, and I prefer baking outside to being stuck in the tipi until the party. David comes out regularly to offer encouragement and make sure I have enough dry wood. It's not like we're the Donner Party—we have choices. We could

quit, go back east—or to Denver, work in the city for the winter, and then come back and finish the house next spring. But we don't want to give up and return to the city.

David's in the tipi now, throwing the *I Ching*. He had one of his intergalactic travel dreams last night, which usually involve some kind of puzzling interaction with aliens, or a frightening speed-of-light trajectory through space that's hard to interpret. In contrast, my dreams are usually down-to-earth and ordinary, not worth describing. They involve misplacing the big three-foot mortar level, or running out of eggs. The extra heat did the trick, and now the eggbeater spins reasonably well. I mix the dry and wet ingredients, dump the batter into two greased and floured pans, and pop them into the oven. I hold the oven door open for a minute to let some heat out, because it felt hotter than three hundred and fifty degrees, and then I slam it shut. Nothing to do but check the fire every once in awhile and wait. I stack the dirty bowls and implements where the snow will fall on them and go inside the tipi. The fire's burning well, and the air's not too smoky. The tipi liner we put up two weeks ago helps with the ventilation and makes it warmer. The smells are familiar now—piñon smoke, wet canvas, damp earth. The cats lie on the bed like Chinese statues, their paws tucked compactly under their bodies, their eyes half closed and staring at the flames. Beside them are David's guitar and the yarrow sticks. He's been staring at the fire too, but he looks up at me as I walk over to the bed, and he passes the *I Ching* to me.

Number 3, "Chun/Difficulty at the Beginning" again. The Judgment is: "DIFFICULTY AT THE BEGINNING *works supreme success, / Furthering through perseverance. / Nothing should be undertaken. / It furthers one to appoint helpers.*" It seems right on the mark, but for how long should we undertake nothing? If it's just for today, it makes sense—it's snowing, and we're going to a birthday party for all the Libras. Libra's the cardinal air sign, the sign of the diplomat, the artist, and Libre's full of them—David, Peter, both Linda and Dean, and two of the kids, Aaron and Nanda. We have one big party for all, although this year's party happens to fall on Peter's birthday. It doesn't make sense to work on the house in a snowstorm anyway, but autumn in the Rockies has a split personality. In two days it'll be sunny and warm, and all the snow will melt, except for a few patches on the north sides of the ridges.

The commentary under the Judgment explains:

> *Times of growth are beset with difficulties. They resemble a first birth. But these difficulties arise from the very profusion of all that is struggling to attain form. Everything is in motion: therefore if one perseveres there is a prospect of great success, in spite of the existing danger. When it is man's fate to undertake such new beginnings, everything is still unformed, dark. Hence he must hold back, because any premature move might bring disaster. Likewise, it is very important not to remain alone; in order to overcome the chaos he needs helpers. This is not to say, however, that he himself should look passively at what is happening. He must lend his hand and participate with inspiration and guidance.*

There's no question we need as many helpers as we can get, but they're few and far between since summer ended. When Dean and Linda got back from Japan, they spent one long day with us, digging out the dirt and leveling the floor in the kitchen and dining area. Everyone else has projects to get done before the real winter sets in.

Since the days are so much shorter, I've been getting more and more exasperated at David's pace. He takes his time in the morning, working up to work. He was never a morning person, and he has to have a pot of coffee, several Bugler cigarettes, and at least one joint before he's ready to go. I tend to act quickly, perhaps prematurely. I charge into things, and sometimes working in haste can result in mistakes, which make more work, if not disaster. The snows came early this year, and as the days get shorter, it's getting colder, and David's preparations seem to take even longer. After the first snow last month, he bought some Martell's brandy at Lenczs' for our morning coffee, reasoning that we should have what the Saint Bernards carry to those stuck in the snow in the Alps, because no Saint Bernard was going to find us. Last week our five-gallon water containers were frozen solid in the morning *inside* the tipi. After we put them by the fire to melt enough water to make coffee, David sipped Martell's straight from the bottle. Now he keeps the Martell's behind his pillow so he can have a nip on cold mornings before getting out of bed.

Once he gets going, though, he accomplishes a lot more than I do. The *I Ching*'s advice is actually perfect for both of us. I should remember that acting prematurely courts disaster, and he shouldn't remain passive but should lend his hand and participate with inspiration and guidance. He's looking more like a mountain man and less like a scholar lately, with a longer, straggly beard and bulkier muscles. I suppose I'm different too. My hair's sun bleached, and my cheeks are ruddy from the sun and cold. Those are the obvious differences.

The snowflakes are smaller and fall faster by the time we walk down the ridge with the cake in the afternoon. Libre's up inside the snow clouds, so it's darker than usual. Inside Peter's zome, everyone's sitting on the living area carpet, bathed in electric light, and a record's playing loud—Janis Joplin belting out the last chorus of "Me and Bobby McGee." It's a jolt to cross into the world of electricity from our tipi world. Peter pours us some homemade chokecherry wine and shouts in our ears, "Wow! Look at that cake!" while I make room for it on the kitchen table between the perfect sprout salad I recognize as Beth's and the fifth of whisky I'm sure Bill Keidel brought. Peter clinks his enamel cup of wine with David's and says, "Happy Birthday to us, David!" He looks at the record player, and smiles ruefully, "And Janis, you stupid bitch, good-bye!"

"*Time keeps movin' on, / Friends they turn away, / I keep movin' on, / But I never found out why / I keep pushing so hard the dream . . . ,*" Janis sings, and Nancy asks,

"Did you hear?" as she hugs me. "Janis died of an overdose. Some Red Rockers told Dallas at Farisita when he was picking up the mail."

"Last month Jimi Hendrix, and now her," I say. We're outlasting the authors of our anthems, making our way through the battlefield like a platoon whose leaders are getting picked off. It's nothing new—the "best minds are still destroyed by madness, looking for an angry fix at dawn," as Ginsberg says. Our artists have been killing themselves with dope or motorcycles or choking on their own vomit—nothing new, even if the methodology is more rapid and efficient than that of previous generations. Kerouac took time burning a hole in his stomach with booze. Fitzgerald killed himself and his talent with alcohol, too, and Hemingway tried, but finally had to resort to a bullet. Sitting around with our friends, snow falling softly in muffled silence outside, we listen to Janis's rich, raw, Southern Comfort voice. Fueled by her anthems, shell-shocked by Nixon's death march, we're on another path, a quasi-utopian, extra-suburban pioneer mission.

The *I Ching* said, "It is very important not to remain alone." There are no visitors here tonight. All summer at least one stranger was at each community dinner. Joel was the last one. It's good to have Dean, Linda, and Lia back. There's a Far Eastern lilt in the way Dean and Linda talk since they've returned, and all three of them have eyes that look a little Japanese now—even Dean, although his eyes are ice blue. Linda laughs at something David says and turns to me. "Don't forget, I'm switching my school day next week with Marilynn." I nod, and as Peggy passes homemade blue corn chips around, Linda says, "We brought some blue corn to plant in Suwanose. It popped up in a minute, like time-lapse photography. It grew a foot a day in Japan, no kidding. Then it stormed, and all the plants were blown over!" Patricia laughs. Steve's holding Tawa, their little daughter. Dean looks around without smiling, but his hulking presence adds weight to our little group. Linda's red hair and clear, piercing brown eyes add vibrancy. Lia boldly hugs me from behind in her footed onesies, and her solid little body glows with heat. She smells of talcum powder and old milk. Everyone's in the circle now, chatting and laughing. David opens a birthday present from Peter. It's a brandy glass.

Peter says, "Martell's is too good to drink straight from the bottle, even if it's first thing in the morning!" and everyone laughs. The first time it snowed, Peter came up the ridge to see if we were all right because he didn't see smoke coming from the tipi. He laughed when he found us still under our down bags, putting off dealing with the weather. We sit around in the zome joking with each other and smiling while our separate memories of the first time we heard Janis sing her raw young heart out play in our heads. Nancy's in a good mood tonight and doesn't seem worried about people spilling wine on the carpet. This is how we celebrate the births among us, and Janis's life, late into the night, the zome toasty with the heat of the big space heater, the bright light courtesy of San Isabel Electric Company, the heartrending music courtesy of Big Brother and the Holding Company. Behind us, the kids stand around the kitchen table, boldly poking their fingers into the soft sides of my German chocolate cake, oblivious to Janis's life or death, to Earth spinning out another year, to history and the complications the adults wash down with tart chokecherry wine.

17 : School Days

Libre school is held at a different house each day. Not ours, because we don't even have a roof yet, much less a house, although the two kitchen walls are high in the section we'll enclose with temporary walls for winter. There's no school at Dallas's hogan either—its roof caved in during the rainy season, and it isn't fixed yet. With every rain or snow, the hogan walls dissolve a little more. Each morning I walk with the kids to one of the other houses, unfold the cardboard strip of perfect alphabet letters Beth made, and spend an hour teaching them to read, right after they've had math with Marilynn, who was an elementary school teacher in New York. My only experience teaching is two years of freshman English at Buffalo, but teaching is teaching, and I'm the only one willing to do it.

The kids run around outside, letting off steam between math and reading, while Marilynn and I have a cup of coffee and shoot the breeze with the school hosts. The rest of the day, the hosts plan the activities and make lunch and snacks for the kids. We have a varied curriculum and menu. At Richard and Beth's the kids make tiny Navajo looms before sitting down to a buckwheat groat casserole and carob-flavored soy drink. At Patricia's they spin and dye wool for the rugs they'll weave on the looms they made, learn how to change diapers and hold baby Tawa, then have quesadilla snacks and burritos for lunch. At Peter and Nancy's zome they write poems, and Peter tells Indian legends and reads them Walt Whitman before Nancy serves grilled cheese. Down at the Grow Hole, Tom and Peggy teach them to play the recorder. Tom once showed them how to skin a rabbit. Much to Beth and Richard's dismay, the kids had rabbit stew for lunch. At Dean and Linda's they're painting a mural and making clay sculptures, and little Lia paints and sculpts alongside the big kids. They eat sardines and crackers, bananas and apples—healthy foods that don't require preparation, which is a distraction from Art. At Jim and Sandy's, they learn about Tarot cards and engines, and eat aduki beans and Tassajara bread and drink iced lemon-mint tea. They used to clean engine parts with Jim and Dallas until the mothers complained about the kids' clothes getting ruined by motor oil. Up the ridge at Bill Keidel's, they learn rudimentary carpentry and how to brew beer (sort of a science experiment), before liverwurst or bologna sandwiches and Cokes, again to Richard and Beth's dismay.

Today I gathered up pencils at Bill's (the boys tend to use them as weapons if they're left lying around), packed up the workbooks, and folded up the alphabet as Bill said in his best W. C. Fields style, "Okay, kids, come on over here for a . . . whatchamacallit, story hour." The kids straggled over. Lori and Aricia arrived first and carefully sat down among the two-by-four scraps and sawdust on Bill's partially finished floor. Four-year-old Aricia had on a new dress with appliquéd ribbons Beth had made, and five-year-old Lori helped her straighten out the skirt and stroked one of the shiny ribbons with two fingers. Aricia smiled to herself and looked serenely at Bill. Lori's brother, seven-year-old Lump, wandered over with Aricia's six-year-old brother, Aaron. Two of Pabla's sons, five and six years old, followed. Pabla and her sons are up here from Taos visiting Patricia and Nanda. Two years ago, Pabla gave birth to Nanda at Libre and gave him to Patricia and Steve to adopt. Pabla had three kids before Nanda. I had spent most of the reading period keeping Jason, one of Pabla's sons, and Lump from stabbing each other's eyes out with pencils.

Bill sat on a ten-gallon can of roofing tar, his massive legs splayed out, one elbow on each leg. He held a book in his pudgy but nimble hands, and cleared his throat. "Okay, kids, more readings from *Revolution for the Hell of It*—by whom, by the way?" The boys looked at him as if he were speaking Swahili. Lori bit her lip.

"Abbie Hoffman," said Aricia quietly, looking down demurely at her dress.

"Right!" said Bill, frowning at Jason, who was leaning over and whispering something revolutionary to Lump and Aaron. Jason stopped mid-sentence when he noticed Bill's stare, and Lump grinned at Bill in his best Huckleberry Finn manner. "Okay, remember last time, reading about the Exorcism at the Pentagon?" Bill gave another warning look over the book and read:

Many wild happenings are planned in preparation: circling of Washington Monument, Empire State Building (vertically), Make Love Day orgy leading up to October 21st. On Columbus Day a mighty caravan of wagons will roll east out of San Francisco to rediscover America complete with real live Indian scouts, compliments of Chief Rolling Thunder of the Shoshone. Junk cars, stolen buses, motorcycles, rock bands, flower banners, dope, incense, and enough food for the long journey. Wagon train East. Yahoo! We will dye the Potomac red, burn the cherry trees, panhandle embassies, attack with water pistols, marbles, bubble gum wrappers, bazookas, girls will run naked and piss on the Pentagon walls, sorcerers, swamis, witches, voodoo, warlocks, medicine men, and speed freaks will hurl their magic at the faded brown walls. Rock bands will bomb out with "Joshua fit the battle of Jericho." We will dance and chant the mighty OM. We will fuck on the grass and beat ourselves against the doors. Everyone will scream "VOTE FOR ME."

I realized it was Columbus Day as I walked away, listening to Abbie's words. It was an appropriate reading, but I doubted the kids were following it. They probably perked up and listened to the stuff about running naked and pissing on the Pentagon, and the parts about water pistols, bubble gum, and bazookas. It was as good as the stories of the *Niña, Pinta,* and *Santa Maria* read in my grade school around Columbus Day, when no one mentioned what Columbus did to the natives.

A year ago David and I were protesting at the Pentagon a second time. It wasn't as festive as the October 1967 march Bill was reading about, when Abbie Hoffman and Allen Ginsberg chanted "Om" as girls stuck flowers in soldiers' rifles and MacNamara watched the crowds. That first time in Washington we believed the war would be over soon. Just look at the crowds! Everyone would see! Instead, it got worse, with more troops, more bombing missions, more deaths. At the second big Washington protest last year, the Bread and Puppet Theater's huge papier-mâché heads of Nixon, Agnew, and John Mitchell teetered on poles, a cartoonish French Revolution image. Eugene McCarthy spoke about the great harm caused by political leaders who based their actions on the people's loyalty. He urged Nixon to note the history of the Caesars and Napoleon. Nixon wasn't listening. He sat in the White House and watched the Ohio State—Purdue football game. Soldiers were lined up at the Washington Monument, the Treasury Department, all along the Mall. When the troops started gassing us, David fell down like he'd been shot, and I ran to him against the panicked crowd, bending down over him as other protesters knocked against me. I was Jackie in the Dallas limousine, I was Ethel bending over Bobby on the floor of the Commodore Hotel kitchen in Los Angeles. I was being overdramatic. He'd only been hit with a tear gas canister. It lay on the ground beside him, spewing fumes. Doug and I and two Good Samaritans picked David up and helped him run. Our eyes burned; there was smoke and screaming all around us, people coughing and gasping.

By the reflecting pool, a man and a woman handed out rags and strips of cloth soaked in water, and we wiped our scalded eyes and faces, and I cried until I was out of tears. A medic put some drops in my eyes and cleaned the contusion on David's head. The sun went down fast, and a boy rocked on the edge of the pool and yelled, "*Those fuckers, those fuckers,*" over and over. The protest was over. At the apartment one of my Vassar friends shared with other classmates who worked on the Hill, empty for the weekend, we stripped off our clothes, took long showers, put on fresh clothing. We stuffed our clothes in the washing machine and washed them twice. We put ice packs on our eyes. Later we watched the TV coverage, which naturally got it all wrong, didn't mention any gassing, and underestimated the crowds. David didn't say much, his lips in a tight line.

I called my parents to tell them we hadn't gotten arrested. "They gassed us!" I told my mother indignantly.

"Oh, too bad," she said, sounding as if I'd said the homecoming game had been rained out.

I took David to a crowded French restaurant in Georgetown, thinking it might cheer him up, but he stood in line looking as sadly resigned and out of place as Geronimo in the Cadillac he was driven around in at the end of his life. Soon people in line sniffed and curled their lips. When they started to suspect that the teargas smell came from us, I asked the maitre d' to *please* take our name off the list, we couldn't *stand* the odor, and we left. "Pfew!" I sniffed, and walked out in a huff, and outside we doubled over in laughter and headed for a White Castle. At least I'd made him laugh.

The first night we were back in our apartment in Buffalo, David stared out the window at the streetlights on Arlington Park and strummed an old Dylan song he'd never played before. My face was raw and burned, peeling from the gas. Snow was falling softly, and the flakes swirled like confetti in the cones of light from the street lamps.

He sang bitterly, *"The answer, my friend, is blowing in the wind, The answer is blowing in the wind,"* and there was no doubt after that weekend what was blowing or what the answer was. That fall in Buffalo, Abbie Hoffman visited us. He was the founder of the Yippies and the most flamboyant of the Chicago Seven on trial that year. Abbie sat in our living room in the same chair Dr. Spock had sat in a few weeks before, when Spock had been in Buffalo for an antiwar protest. Abbie sat on the edge of the chair, always moving, scruffy in jeans and an old denim shirt with an upside down American flag on its pocket. When Spock had visited, he'd leaned back in the same seat, crossing his long legs, tall and elegant in a pin-striped suit. Though their styles differed, they shared similar sentiments about Vietnam.

Hoffman was visiting Buffalo with his lawyer, Bill Kunstler, and our friend Buddy, who clerked for Kunstler. The following week, back at the Chicago Seven trial, Abbie was jailed for contempt for appearing in court dressed up as the judge. Abbie told us he'd been influenced by W. C. Fields, Ernie Kovacs, Che Guevara, Antonin Artaud, Alfred Hitchcock, Lenny Bruce, the Marx Brothers, and the Beatles. He said the Beatles were the new family group, organized around their communal creation of art. They were a horizontal family unit, instead of a vertical one across generations. Abbie smiled and said, "If you want to begin to understand our culture, start by comparing Frank Sinatra and the Beatles. It's not perfect, but it's a good beginning. Music is always a good place to start!" Now Paul McCartney's announced the Beatles have broken up, and I'm not sure of Abbie's analogy. Families are supposed to last. In the Huerfano, our horizontal family group is getting vertical with all the kids I'm teaching to read.

I jerk myself back to the present and hurry down the path to the site. It's miraculously warm and sunny. If the scrub oak leaves hadn't been killed in the last snow, you'd think it was summer. The weather here changes abruptly, the way scenes change suddenly in dreams. David's working on the triangular sleeping loft over the kitchen which we improvised when we saw we'd be lucky if we could wall in one quarter of the bottom octagon for winter.

"Hi," I say to him. The loft is made from two-by-twelve planks attached eight feet up the railroad tie walls. The planks are sandwiched between two courses of railroad ties like a piece of bologna between slices of bread and nailed at their other ends to a log we angled between the two adjacent kitchen walls. "Bill's just been reading to the kids from *Revolution for the Hell of It.* It made me think about the Moratorium in Washington last year."

"Hmm," says David, preoccupied with the jagged two-by-twelves sticking out beyond the log above us. "Well, past is prologue, I guess. You're just in time to draw the curvy edge on the loft. I went and borrowed Steve's chain saw to cut these planks." I'm holding the funnel so David can pour gas into the chain saw just as Bill strides down the path, the kids strung out behind him, skipping every once in a while to keep up.

"Field trip!" Bill says, wiping his face with his bandanna. "I thought I'd blow your outhouse hole for you like I promised, and show the kids how to use dynamite at the same time. Exactly where's the hole you started? Downhill from the house, of course . . ." I run over to the tipi to get some dynamite. We store it behind our pillows in the tipi to keep it safe and dry. David takes Bill and the kids down to see the outhouse hole we started. Abbie Hoffman would laugh at this school outing, but I'm not sure Dr. Spock would entirely approve.

When I run back with the sticks of dynamite, Bill announces in a booming voice, "Okay, kids, every good revolutionary should know about dynamite! First we stick the dynamite down in the hole David and Roberta made in the ground. Now, look at this, kids, you see how I attached these wires to the stick of dynamite? That's for the blasting caps, because we're gonna set the dynamite off *electrically.* Remember our discussion of electricity last week, when the lightning burned the tree over by the cliffs?" We move up the hillside, Bill lecturing and trailing wire. He puts the nine-volt battery on the sawhorse inside our future kitchen. "Okay, okay, who wants to set this off?" he asks.

Lump and Jason are the loudest and oldest. Bill says Lump can do the first charge and Jason can do the second. The boys have never been so interested in school before. They jostle each other, their eyes gleaming, circling around Bill and the dynamite, and the younger boys enviously eye Lump as Bill explains what to do. "So, when I say so, you just put this wire here so it touches this point and the other wire here so it touches this other point. You got me?" Lump, the Chosen One, nods and grins at the other boys. Aaron acts as if he doesn't care. The girls squat, their eyes shut and their hands over their ears, like two hear-no-evil, see-no-evil monkeys.

"Okay, do it!" shouts Bill, like Patton commanding a one-star general. Lump makes the connection the first time, and there's a shattering KABOOM! then chunks of rock rain down for what seems like minutes. The windows in our kitchen walls rattle but survive the blast. "Okay, right on!" Bill shouts. Lump grins. The girls look at Lump with new respect. "Okay now, let's see what we've done!" Bill yells, and the kids scamper down the trail after him. David and I grab a pick and shovel, the maul, and a big iron rod to pound a hole for the next charge. As we start down, Peter comes up the ridge path, fists clenched, eyes blazing.

"Oh shit!" says David. I'm glad Bill's here.

Bill stands his ground, hands on his hips, waiting for Peter. "Kids," he mutters, "class dismissed!" Lori and Aricia leave, but the boys hang out in the piñons about ten feet away, a little scared, secretly hoping there'll be a fight.

18 : Pearl Harbor Day

It's Pearl Harbor Day. The draft board won't give David any more deferments, and he's got to appear for a physical in New York City in January. My parents are visiting. The sky is steel gray, the mountains stark and wintry, and Dallas drives us up the ridge in the True Truck. I'd hoped the sun would come out for my parents' visit. I'd hoped David could get another extension from the draft board. Instead, we lurch over the rocky ridge road on a gray day, and I think about our dwindling options as we look down at dead winter fields and up at the ominous sky. I bet my mother's knuckles are white under her black kid gloves, even though Dallas is driving over the big rocks in the road extra carefully. She sits in the back seat in her fur coat like Queen Elizabeth at a minor stop on a tour of a third world country. Dad's more unassuming in his black cashmere topcoat, more like an ambassador who has some grip on the local situation, and I'm as nervous and eager to please as any colonial bureaucrat who's showing around visiting royalty.

When we drove into town yesterday to meet them at the Marlboro Inn, the draft board letter was waiting at Abe and Ersie's in Farisita. I don't know why we were shocked. For weeks we'd been expecting Kevin to forward it from Buffalo. David read it and handed it to me and didn't say much during the drive into town. I held the letter, read it over and over, and tried to think of something to say. I made some half-assed suggestions, and he shook his head and kept looking at the road, driving too fast. We got to the Marlboro Inn in the morning, long before my parents were scheduled to arrive, and took thirty-minute showers and saunas and did laundry in the motel machines in an orgy of cleanliness. I'm so clean that my skin hurts when the cold air hits it as we drive up the ridge. I feel like a snake that's shed its skin.

My parents arrived yesterday afternoon after a leisurely drive down from the Broadmoor in Colorado Springs in their beige diesel Mercedes. We had dinner at the Marlboro, the new motel outside town built by Joe Faris, a big rancher in the valley. Joe knows that ranching won't last, so he's moving into other markets. The Marlboro is sprawled around an artificial lake he built. He's sort of a Lebanese Ben Cartwright, but more entrepreneurial. He has seven children around our age, most of whom work for him in one business or another. We ate steaks from Joe's steers at the Marlboro under a huge blowup of the three Faris boys on horseback silhouetted against a western sunset. It's hard to put anything over on my mother. She knew something was bothering us at dinner, but the last thing we wanted to do was get into a discussion of the draft and Vietnam on their one day here. In our room at the Marlboro last night, David watched TV and didn't want to talk about the draft. He changed the channels when there was a news report about Vietnam.

As we drive down the road from Peter's, my parents pretend not to see the upside-down station wagon, junked engine parts, torn mattresses, cans, bottles, and other unburnable garbage in the arroyo opposite the Grow Hole. I explain that this junk will block the arroyo and prevent more erosion, but I'm not sure they hear over the engine, even though they both nod at me agreeably. They don't ask about the Grow Hole—they probably think it's a primitive greenhouse, not the home of a family of four. As we round the curve and start the climb up the ridge, and the Grow Hole is out of view, I say a silent thank you that Lump and Lori weren't crawling out of their sleeping bag holes in the side of the hill like prairie dogs. When the True Truck finally grinds to a merciful halt above our house, Dallas pops out and offers my mother his arm, putting his finger to his hat brim and giving her one of his big, dimpled smiles through his luxuriant beard as he dips in a courtly bow. I cross my eyes at him behind her back.

When we got the postcard announcing my parents' tour of the American West, we moved fast. We slapped up the temporary walls, moved the cookstove over from the outdoor kitchen, set up some four-by-fours and slabs as a kitchen counter, and installed the stainless steel sink, draining it with black PVC pipe into the compost pile down the hill. We bought an ornate chromed railroad station potbelly stove in Pueblo and put it near the western temporary wall. The roofing over the kitchen isn't finished, but we decided to move out of the tipi before they came. Unless it snows or blows, they won't notice the thin gaps of daylight in the ceiling. We also finished the outhouse hidden in the trees below us. David set opaque amber swirling glass in a side window for privacy. The door has a clear window, however, through which you can contemplate the mountains across the valley as you sit on the new, natural wood toilet seat we splurged on at Unfug's. It must be the best view from an outhouse in the state, at least.

This is my parents' first big trip west of the Hudson River. They've gone to Europe many times. My mom accompanies my father only on trips to northern Europe—even Spain and Italy are a little iffy in her book. She didn't go on his trips to Africa, Australia, or the Far East, either, and you can tell she's not so sure about southern Colorado. At the Marlboro this morning, we looked through an open doorway on our hall and saw a little calf in the bathroom of an unoccupied room, eating toilet paper off the roll. The calf eyed us calmly out of the corner of its big brown eyes as it unwound the toilet paper deftly with its tongue and kept swallowing. When we told Joy Faris at the front desk that there was a calf in Room 46, she looked mildly exasperated, rolled her eyes, and then smiled and said in her booming cowgirl voice, "Oh, I just don't know what we're gonna do about that little guy! He's an orphan, and he just loves toilet paper!"

My mother nodded sympathetically, as if she'd come up against this problem before, even though she grew up in Manhattan, and the closest she's been to a steer is when she's ordering steaks in the butcher department at her favorite A&P in Scarsdale. Now, after Dallas kills the True Truck engine on the road above our house, she holds onto her small red hat with one hand and Dallas's arm with the other and picks her way in her low heels down the steep, rocky path from the road to the house site. The jaunty feather sticking out from the front of her hat bobs as she makes her way down. My father looks out across the valley and stops to take a picture with his Rolleiflex. He's traveled all over the world on business. He grew up on a farm and has dined in sheiks' tents. I don't worry about his reaction to our dirt floor, and I'll explain quickly to Mom that the tongue-and-groove oak salvaged from the dance hall will go in next year. I've raked and damped the dirt down to make it as presentable as possible.

Dean with one of his paintings.

We spent a long time in lower Libre, visiting the more established and civilized houses. Everyone was on their best behavior. Linda explained to my parents how Libre was registered as a nonprofit school in Colorado and raved about my teaching the kids here to read. My parents acted politely impressed with the school and my dedication, but I know my mother was secretly thinking, "This is a girl who worked for the London *Vogue,* who could do anything!" Her mouth was set in a thin smile like Lady Bird Johnson's at a ceremony where antiwar protesters were acting up outside.

Dean showed my parents his crazy abstract paintings. My mother's partial to Winslow Homer, but I could tell she thought Dean was intriguing, in a Kirk Douglas–Burt Lancaster way. She was politely noncommittal about his work. Lia was the biggest hit, smiling and watching my parents with her impish, wise eyes. My mother pretended not to see the anatomically correct Dean rag doll with the yellow yarn pubic beard, which wasn't easy, since Lia was dragging the doll around by the penis. At Peter's zome, Nancy served the cold cuts that I'd bought for her to give us for lunch. She knows how to talk to my parents—hers aren't too different. Peter sat around and smiled at them a lot, looking like a geriatric Tom Sawyer having tea with Aunt Polly. After lunch, David ran up the ridge to start the fires in the stoves at our "house," while I rode up with my parents and Dallas.

Hearing us arrive, David comes out of the house and walks slowly up the path to meet us. We stand above the house and tell them that, eventually, it will be an eight-sided structure, and that we've put up temporary walls to enclose the kitchen wedge for the winter. We describe the low-ceilinged living room and fireplace that we'll build on the back side of the rock. I say that the smaller octagonal bedroom will be on the second story with a surrounding deck. David adds details, like the eight-sided, star-shaped skylight in the roof of the second-story room. My parents nod their heads as we gesture and explain, but they don't see what we see.

We get to the terrace we've built up with stone walls outside the kitchen door, or, actually, the kitchen tarp (there wasn't enough time to build a door before they came). David pulls back the tarp, and Dallas holds my mother's hand as she steps in gingerly. Inside, you can smell the dirt floor, and you can hear the fires crackling in the blue cookstove and the potbelly, but you still feel the chill from the rock. My mother stares at the boulder in the center of the house and carefully descends into the kitchen on the pine steps David finished yesterday. She sits on the Navajo rug on the banco under the rock in the kitchen area. The rock towers behind her. Kachina and Sinbad sneak up and cautiously smell her fur coat, then wrinkle their noses. The lichen are bright chartreuse and gray. I sprayed them with water to perk them up before we left for town yesterday.

My father sits next to my mom, crosses his legs as he gets his pipe out, and begins stuffing it with tobacco. "We had a cookstove like that on the farm," he says. He was born in 1908, the youngest of six children on a farm in New Rochelle, New York. The potbelly, the old iron pots, and the waffle iron I bought on Union Avenue in Pueblo must look familiar to him.

"We drove up Pikes Peak. It was wonderful," says my mother. "So much space!"

"The *London Times* is doing a story on Libre and is using my photographs," I say.

"That's very nice," she murmurs. I pour her tea and she looks quizzically at Dallas, who unhooks the tin cup from his waist loop and cleans it out with his bandanna before holding it out for his tea. Everyone except Dallas is tired from maintaining this polite veneer and trying not to talk about what's on our minds. My mother can't ask why I'm throwing my life away. I can't tell her why, or talk about Vietnam, Nixon's depravity, the rich getting richer and the poor getting poorer, the government's hypocrisy, the dull sterility of suburban life, the ruination of the earth. David can't talk about the revolution of consciousness or, even if he wanted to talk about it, his date with the draft board. We sip our tea and clink our spoons noisily. Despite it all, I'm happy they're here, like a kid whose parents are visiting her classroom.

Dallas, never much of a conversationalist, makes a gallant effort and says, "My dad has decided to retire in San Diego after looking around, like you two are doing."

"Oh, that's good," says my mom, taking some Walker's shortbread Nancy got for me on her last visit to Denver. It's Mom's favorite brand. Dallas spends a long time selecting which shape of shortbread he wants while I hold the tin in front of him like a good hostess. "I love San Diego, but it's damp, and that's not good for my arthritis," my mother continues. "The day Roberta graduated from high school, I was on a stool getting some fancy glasses down for her godparents, her aunt Mabel and uncle Carl, while she was at the prom. I twisted my knee getting down and developed arthritis. Never had it before that."

"Hmm," says Dallas sympathetically. "What a shame. How unfortunate." I'd like to brain him with the shortbread tin, but instead I make small talk and struggle to control myself. David's got to show up for his draft physical, or we'll have to leave the country, or hide in the hills here or somewhere else. His life's hanging by a thread, out of our control, and my mother's detailing her aches and pains. I slam the shortbread tin down on the counter too hard, and she pauses and raises her eyebrow a little.

Awhile later my dad glances through the window and says, "Looks like it might snow a lot soon." It's no surprise he can read the sky.

"We'd better get you down the hill to your car so that you can drive out while it's still light!" David says. I gather up the tea things and stack them in the sink, relieved they're leaving without noticing the faucet doesn't work. My parents scratch Kachina's and Sinbad's heads and stand up. They never took off their coats. David holds the tarp open, and we exit like we're leaving a sideshow at the state fair, and then we make our way slowly up the steep path to the True Truck. David gives my mother his arm. Dad and I are last in line. He stops and knocks his pipe out halfway up to the road, his deep blue eyes gazing out over the valley. The cats follow us and twirl around his legs. He stares thoughtfully at the stacks of lumber, the crated window glass propped up against a dead piñon tree, the black roofing paper rolls, the bags of cement covered with plastic sheets like corpses. Our jerry-built winter quarters would make a shanty look classy.

He says quietly, "This is very ambitious, Berta," as he puts his pipe in his coat pocket, "very ambitious." He's not the sarcastic type, and he doesn't criticize. I hold his arm like we're climbing the Ramble in Central Park, like he's walking me up the aisle. The sun's lower, and a chill breeze comes up. Mom and David stand by the road as Dallas turns the True Truck around.

"*Ambitious?*" I stop and smile, but he looks at me guilelessly with his clear blue eyes, and I know he's not joking. We start walking slowly up the path again, and I hook my arm closer to his, saying, "I guess you're right about that, Dad. I guess you're right about that."

19 : The Physical

In mid-December we pointed the Chrysler east and re-traced last June's journey across the plains. Most immigrants or pioneers don't get to return to their points of origin so easily. We came back for Christmas with my family and David's draft physical. When we left Buffalo and David lost his graduate school deferment, he wangled two three-month postponements. But then the letter came, denying further extensions and setting the date and place of the physical, in downtown New York City at Whitehall today. We've kept a New York address in case things go badly—we don't want them to know where we are.

After spending Christmas with my family, we came to the city a few days ago. We're staying with my friend Pam's older brother Ed, his wife, and baby. Ed wakes us up at 5:30 before he runs in the park, and I get out the bag of beauty aids I bought at Woolworth's on Lexington Avenue.

First I use the jagged-tooth comb to rat David's dark, shoulder-length hair so it stands out at all angles, and then I apply hair spray to give it volume and keep the lift. I put on foundation quite a bit paler than his natural skin tone, using my fingertips to work it in. After that, I line his eyes subtly with sable eyeliner. He stares out the bathroom window at Park Avenue before dawn, like an actor getting ready for his big scene. I stay quiet, except for terse requests like "Chin up!" or "Please, don't blink." It's hard to curl his eyelashes. I've never used much makeup, so I'm not the best to begin with. I'm out of practice, too—it's not like I put on Cover Girl to chop wood and haul water. When I brush the powder on his lids before applying black Maybelline mascara, he grimaces in distaste.

I'm going for the Charles Manson look. Manson's trial for murder in California has been front-page national news, and his crazed face appears regularly on the television evening news. I use some white to highlight the area under David's brows and use a paler than natural lip color, kind of a Julie Christie look. Nothing too obvious—no blush, nothing to diminish the pallor from the foundation. He's sitting on the toilet seat, and I back up to the edge of the tub across the bathroom and squint at him. He looks sexually ambivalent, demented, and I'm quite pleased with my handiwork. He wears jeans, ordinary cowboy boots, and a nondescript yellow shirt. Dressing like a hippie wouldn't help. The draft board has seen everything by now, and we wouldn't get anywhere if they typed him as a peacenik hippie. Many peacenik hippies are now reluctant soldiers in Vietnam, shooting first before they're shot. A bisexual psychopath with delusions of grandeur is more likely to get their attention.

I don't know what he plans to do at the physical. He hasn't talked much about it. During the last twenty-four hours he's gotten quieter and quieter. Ed and his wife were sympathetic and understanding last night at dinner, even though Ed's in the Marine Reserves. They and I carried on a pleasant enough conversation about F. Scott Fitzgerald and Hemingway, Kerouac and Ginsberg, Vassar and Yale, my family and theirs, while David ate quietly and stared at his plate.

Jack Kerouac was dismissed from the navy on psychological grounds in 1948. I don't know all the details. More recently, Joe, a friend from Yale got out of the draft by meditating and getting his blood pressure down below the minimum. Danny smoked cigarettes and drank so much coffee in the twenty-four hours before his physical that his blood pressure twitched above the maximum. Tom, who's six feet tall, fasted, lost fifty pounds, and got his weight down below the minimum for his height, one hundred and thirty four, for two different physicals. The second time, they said, "You're not going to go, are you?" Archer got FUCK YOU tattooed on the side of his right hand, the part that faces out when he salutes, and they didn't want him, though after that another guy got his hand tattooed the same way and was drafted. A guy from Harvard acted crazy and got himself chased into the bathroom, where he secretly slipped two unwrapped Baby Ruths into the toilet bowl. When they caught up with him and tried to restrain him, he scooped up the candy bars, which were sitting in the toilet like turds, and ate them. I've heard that some men drink egg whites, hoping they'll increase the albumin level in their urine and get classified 4-F for diabetes. Todd didn't go to his physical, and he's somewhere in the Sierras in Northern California the last we heard. Brian didn't go to his either. He's probably in Mexico. A friend from Columbia took three tabs of White Lightning the morning of his physical. He hallucinated and yelled gibberish throughout his processing, but he got inducted anyway. A friend of a friend at Buffalo shot off his big toe the night before his physical, like a wolf that gnaws off his paw to get out of a trap.

I hug David at the door of the apartment, a parody of an Upper East Side wife kissing her banker husband as he leaves for work. "Good luck," I say. "I love you."

"Yeah," he says, as the elevator door closes. He's got a few things to say about the new women's movement, sexual equality, and the fact that women aren't drafted and don't have to go through this. I know him so well, and we've talked about this so often, that I know what he's thinking, and my imagination works overtime. I close the door quietly, but I see him walking down to Lexington Avenue and Eighty-sixth to get the IRT express downtown, wearing his grandfather's old tweed overcoat, thinking of his grandfather, who died at fifty-nine from the mustard gas and shrapnel from World War I. Thinking of his father, zigzagging safely through Japanese antiaircraft fire in World War II night after night, then dying two decades later in a corporate jet, safe in home territory, before he and David could finish their argument about Vietnam. Thinking of watching Hugh burn his draft card in the bonfire on the Yale quad, and losing Hugh to Canada. Thinking of losing Harton to the war. Harton, back from Vietnam and visiting in Buffalo, staying up late with David, smoking sticky black opium brought back from 'Nam in a regulation duffel. Dry-eyed, telling stories David wouldn't repeat to me.

As David heads downtown, I bet most of the other men in the early morning commute are brokers, bankers, and lawyers traveling to work in their pin-striped suits and London Fogs, peering over their *Wall Street Journal*s at the tall, lean, dark-eyed man who's their contemporary, standing in the corner of the subway car. I bet he's not reading a paper, his hands are in the pockets of the vintage overcoat, and he's staring angrily back at them. He'll get out at Bowling Green and walk the block to Whitehall, hands still in his pockets, looking straight ahead. No one will meet his gaze.

At the apartment I put the makeup and hair spray back in the Woolworth bag and stuff it in the trash can in the kitchen. I have breakfast with Ed and his wife and baby before they leave for the day. I stack the breakfast dishes in the sink, go back to bed, and pull the covers over my head, then give up trying to sleep around ten. I dress and walk out in the pale gray that passes for morning light here. I walk without thinking to the Met and head for Arms and Armor and stare at the helmets, chain mail, heraldic flags, the swords, knives, lances. I examine the maces and spiked metal balls chained to a wooden handle, lethal lariats you swing over your head before sticking it to the enemy. There are saddles and armor for the horses, and drawings of winches and cranes used to lower the armored knights onto their mounts. There are paintings of the Crusades in the Holy Land, in which the medieval equivalents of gooks lie on the battlefields in the swath cut by the Christians.

I don't realize I'm crying until the line of third-graders pushing around me stop and stare, so I head south through the entrance hall to the corridors where I can sit and look at the cool marble bodies of the Roman boys. Then I leave and walk down Fifth Avenue, watching people pushing their baby strollers, lugging their shopping bags, walking their dogs, chatting and laughing with companions, hailing cabs. They rush down the sidewalks to shop, work, lunch, all of them on their errands without a care for the war across the world from them, the burning villages, the body bags.

I cut into the park and walk down past the Armory, where I worked the summer of '68 after graduation, in the Department of Cultural Affairs—my reward for campaigning for John Lindsay. There was nothing much for me to do at my job, and after a while I gave up pestering my supervisor for an assignment. He was a short, nervous history professor from Hunter College. I sat at my desk defiantly reading *Magic Mountain* the rest of the summer, hoping somebody would say something. Nobody did. Early that summer David was mugged at eleven one morning by three strung-out kids as he crossed Morningside Park to get some draft counseling at Columbia. After he gave them his money, he made the mistake of turning his back to bend over and pick up the "Law and Order" postage stamps that had fluttered out of his wallet, and one kid stabbed him in the lower back, just missing his liver. He stumbled out of the park, and the first five people skittered away when he asked for help. A graduate student in psychology found him lying on the sidewalk, took him by cab to Saint Luke's, and called me at work from the emergency room.

When he was released from the hospital and was well enough to get

around, I got David a job in the city bookmobile through my connections in Cultural Affairs. He drove around Harlem and Bedford-
Stuyvesant playing his guitar and leading sing-alongs, driving a big
school bus and towing a generator through rush hour traffic. He
showed *The Living Desert* to the children in the air-conditioned bus. They
ran their popsicle fingers through his soft, straight hair and sat on his
lap. Already familiar with battles for survival, they always rooted for the
scorpion in the Disney movie. When we left for graduate school in Buffalo after our summer in New York, we were already facing west.

I walk up across the park and back again, sniffing the marijuana smoke
on the east side of Bethesda Fountain. New York City is where I came of
age, where Pam and I would go down to Café Figaro when we were sixteen, dressed in black turtlenecks and ironed jeans, looking for Allen
Ginsberg and other middle-aged beatniks or the young Bob Dylan. But
it doesn't feel like home anymore, and when I close my eyes, I see the
blinding winter whiteness of the Sangre de Cristo Range. I walk up
Madison Avenue, where the women striding down the sidewalk think
they're Someone, then back to the apartment, where I sit in the living room in the dark afternoon with my feet up and the lights off. If
he doesn't get out, would we be safe in the Rockies, or should we go
to Canada? If we left Libre, we'd be leaving not just our future in
America but our vision for America's future. Am I ready? I'd be able to
go back and forth across the border without him, but how could I?
What would it be like to have family, friends, home over a border he
can't cross?

When he comes in, he looks at me sadly. I can't tell what happened,
so I say, "Tell me, for God's sake!"

He says quietly, "I'm not going." I'm happy and hug him, but he
says, "There's nothing to celebrate." He's spent the day with young men
not privileged, selfish, scared, angry, or clever enough to try to get out
of being sent to Vietnam. I rest my forehead against his. In the kitchen
I make tea, and he smokes cigarette after cigarette nervously, describing scenes out of Kafka, the line of youths humbled and holding their
clothes. How when some of the answers on his questionnaire, such as
that he was a lifelong bed wetter, caught someone's attention, he was
taken to a room to discuss his answers and his attitude. He counted to
ten before answering any question the captain asked, to suggest that
maybe he wasn't a good candidate for following orders promptly, but
he was getting nowhere until he played his last card.

"What makes you think you're unsuitable for Vietnam?" sneered the captain, looking across his desk at David in his underwear.

"I think I'd have a tendency to shoot my officers in the back, sir," David said. Harton had told David stories he'd heard that hadn't made it to the evening news. It was the look in David's eyes that did the trick. For generations, his kin and the Feds were enemies. His eyes had the look of the eastern Cherokees who outsmarted the army, avoiding capture and the Trail of Tears. He had the stare of mountain men with nothing left to lose, two steps ahead of the T-men, careening down mountain roads in North Carolina with shotguns under the seat, headlights off, jugs in the back of the truck sloshing moonshine. On top of that, there was his crazed visionary poet look, one of his eyes gazing slightly beyond the captain at the future, or something behind the officer's back.

For years the draft and Vietnam have hung over us, changing our futures and choices in a sickening government-sponsored roulette game that caused persistent apprehension. Now it's over, but we can't feel happy. Lying in bed at night, listening to the traffic, when he puts his face against my shoulder, his lashes are wet. This relief diminishes a proud man and is a bitter, shameful thing to feel.

20 : Sinbad

While we were back east, Dallas's younger brother Billy took care of our cats. He'd been crashing around, and by agreeing to feed our cats, he got a place to stay if nothing better came along. People often go away in winter, so other more comfortable places were frequently available. Richard, Beth, and the kids went to St. Louis for Christmas, so Billy stayed in their house, which was far cozier than ours. He walked down and fed Kachina and Sinbad at our place twice a day. Then Billy moved down the ridge to zome-sit for Peter and Nancy while they were at her parents' in Denver. The zome was likewise a lot more livable than the bottom quarter of our house, with our two thin, uninsulated temporary walls and the temporary roof. Billy fed the cats at the zome while he was there. When Peter and Nancy returned, Billy came back up the ridge, but the cats lingered. Kachina went back up the first night she wasn't fed at the zome, but Sinbad, younger and less resourceful, stayed and yowled outside. Sinbad's crying drove Peter and Nancy crazy, and so Peter grabbed his rifle and shot him.

The night we returned, Kachina met us on the path, howling her Siamese cat story of indignities she'd suffered, a litany of our wrongs. We called and called for Sinbad but couldn't find him. It was late, we were exhausted, worried. We saw a light at Richard and Beth's and walked up. The kids were asleep. Richard was reading and smoking, and Beth was carding some wool by the light of one kerosene lamp. We greeted them warmly but skipped the small talk and asked if they'd seen Sinbad. Richard's lips tightened, and he looked at Beth. She looked down at the wild wool on her lap. There was the familiar pause before bad news, when your stomach tightens. Richard stared out the window, his cigarette burning down almost to his fingers.

Beth said quietly, "Peter shot Sinbad."

"What?" we said. "*What?*" We stood up quickly, confused and angry, and left immediately to go down the ridge. Beth called softly, so as not to wake the kids, "Sorry . . . we're so sorry!" as we shut the door.

When we'd stopped by the zome earlier, Peter and Nancy had hugged us, but Peter didn't offer us a joint, a drink, or a cup of coffee. We knew something wasn't right. They listened as we told about David's draft physical and our city adventures, but they seemed nervous, preoccupied, and didn't look us in the eye. We thought we'd interrupted one of their low-grade fights, and we were also tired from the trip, so we left. When we got to the zome the second time that night, their lights were out, but we banged on the door anyway. I stood on their doorstep and tried to catch my breath, to slow my heart. David had walked down so fast on his long legs that I'd had to jog to keep up, and I was out of breath from running in the snow. When a light came on inside, we opened the door ourselves.

"Peter," David stepped in, "what's this about, man? You shot Sinbad? What the fuck?"

Peter was halfway down the ladder in his socks and nightshirt, moving like an old ape, and he waited until he was on the floor to answer. His hair was flat and wispy, and he looked funny without his glasses. "Yeah. Yeah, I did," he said. He sounded so calm.

"How could you do that?" I asked, my voice shaking more than I wanted it to. I was still breathing hard from crashing down the ridge in eight inches of old snow.

"How could I do it?" Peter's eyes looked small without his glasses, and he had a funny, twisted grin without his dentures. "I'll tell you how I could do it," he said coldly. "He was yowling around the house, and I shooed him away, but he kept coming back, and he was driving us crazy, so I shot him."

"Oh man, Peter, oh man," David said sadly.

"Look, you guys." Nancy came down the ladder barefoot in her white flannel nightgown, her long blond hair loose on her shoulders. "I am sorry, I am sorry, but he was driving us crazy, and it just happened, okay?" She bit her lip and looked at Peter.

"You just don't shoot people's pets. *Your friends' pets.*" My voice wouldn't stop shaking. "I will never forgive you, you stupid, gun-crazed fuckhead."

"I'm sorry, I'm sorry," Nancy said again, and her voice shook too.

"You can't tell a hunter not to hunt!" Peter said.

"WHAT? Peter, Peter, man . . . ," said David again, shaking his head.

"*A hunter not to hunt?* Are you kidding? We're talking about a kitty cat!" I spit out the words. Peter, our wise man, who always shored us up with a joint, a cup of coffee, some venison stew, a laugh. When you had a bad day and the chain saw busted, or your truck threw a rod, he listened and told a great story, and you ended up sitting at his table, laughing. He told visitors how he'd had a vision that was Libre. That night his hair was matted, his eyes narrow, his lips thin, his teeth out, and I didn't recognize the man standing by the stairs. In the Huerfano, more than dreams get free rein.

"I'm sorry, you guys. Can't you hear me?" Nancy cried.

"Well, I'll tell you," Peter interrupted, stepping back, then whirling around as if he was surrounded. "I'm not sorry. *I'm glad.* I hate pussycats, I hate them. I'm glad to be rid of him. I shot him, then put him on the compost, and I'm glad!" I don't know if he was smiling or sneering.

David turned around and left. I followed, but I couldn't maintain his dignified silence, and I muttered, "You asshole, you asshole."

Nancy came up the ridge and said she was sorry some more and cried, and David soothed her and said it was okay. He forgave her, and I said I forgave her, though I didn't mean it as much as David. I said it because I wanted her out of the house so we could go to sleep. It had been such a long trip back to the valley. The Chrysler needed a valve job, and we had to use 10W-40 and STP in it, which was incredibly thick. We had trouble starting it in the cold, so we had to park it on a hill. It wasn't easy finding hills in Kansas.

Sinbad was just a kitten, but he meant a lot to us. We're building a house up the hill from a man who shot our cat. People have fights that change their marriage forever and still stay married. I guess we'll make it here despite this unforeseen "difficulty at the beginning," although I'm not sure the *I Ching* was prophesying anything like Sinbad's murder.

At the Ground Hog Day party at Bill's, the Red Rockers and the Triple A made it up the ridge despite the snowstorm, which gave us another reason to celebrate. David and Henry were going to play some new songs. Lars and the Triple A band would play too. Bill hadn't yet covered the pink wall insulation, which gave his big cabin a frivolous Vegas feel. Mary Red Rocker walked over to me and asked quietly, "Did Peter *really* shoot your cat?" When I nodded and bit my lip, she said, "I'm so sorry. That's outrageously wrong, so totally stupid and cruel."

I said, "He was just a kitten. Pets are substitute children, and it's silly to care so much—"

"Oh, shuddup," Mary interrupted kindly. "He meant a lot to you, right? Peter's a total and complete asshole. Don Pedro, my eye." Lars nodded in agreement, tucking his Rolling Stones T-shirt in tight, getting ready to sing. The guitars were tuning up, and some kids in pajamas beat the bass drum erratically.

"Just go on, Roberta, just go on," Lars said, sticking his chin up a little. I stuck my chin up courageously too, and he smiled. "He'll get his, don't you worry. He'll get his without your having to do anything about it. It may not be instant, but it's karma. Take the high road."

I didn't see Adrienne behind him because she was bending over the amp wires running to the gas generator outside, but she poked her curly head out from behind Lars's molded torso and chimed in, "High? Did someone say high? Reberter, come 'ere and have some of this hash someone from Boulder left us."

Mary put her arm around my shoulder. Linda stepped over and draped her arm over my shoulder, too, over Mary's arm. Across the room Nancy smiled at me, and I smiled back weakly. Peter had his back to me. He was telling a story to some Ortiviz Farmers, gesturing dramatically. They smiled and looked up at him, hanging on his every word.

Two weeks later, I'm sitting in the loft reading Baby Doe Tabor's last diary entry, in March, 1935, thinking it's probably not the best thing to be reading just now. Baby Doe wrote:

> *Went down to Leadville from Matchless—the snow so terrible, I had to go on my hands and knees and creep from my cabin door to 7th Street. Mr. Zaitz driver drove me to our get off place and he helped pull me to the cabin, I kept falling deep down through the snow every minute. God bless him.*

Later, neighbors found her frozen body in her shack by the Matchless Mine after they hadn't seen any smoke coming from her stovepipe for a week. Baby Doe had her difficulties in the end, as well as the beginning. She'd left Denver and lived in an old storage shack by the Matchless for thirty-six years, ever since Horace Tabor's death. It was just a myth that Horace told his faithful wife on his deathbed, "Don't give up the Matchless!" In fact, he was in a coma for many days before his death,

First quarter of the rock house in winter, 1971.

and he'd already lost the Matchless to creditors. The new owners let Baby Doe squat in the shack near the mine entrance. Why she lived there after Horace died is unclear. She was a staunch Catholic repenting the sins of her colorful early life in Leadville. She refused handouts and wrapped her legs and shredded boots with gunnysacks tied with twine and called on her old Denver society friends to raise capital to repurchase the Matchless.

In her 1883 wedding picture, when Horace Tabor was a United States senator and worth over nine million dollars, she's wearing an ermine-trimmed dress and train. Fellow senators bold enough to attend the extravagant wedding dinner smile in the background at the Washington hotel, but their wives wouldn't come because of the scandal of Horace's divorce from his first wife to marry Baby Doe. Horace died sixteen years later without a dime, still believing the silver market would come back, that he'd make another fortune. Thirty-six years after he died, Baby Doe still held onto his dream. I put the book down and pick up *Six Racy Colorado Madams.* The life stories of six top entrepreneurs in early Colorado are more upbeat.

The low temperature every day for a week since we got back has been almost fifty below zero. Alamosa, on the other side of Mount Blanca, sixty miles south and a few thousand feet lower, has been the coldest town in the country. Who knows how cold it is at Libre? Nobody has a thermometer that goes down that far. Alamosa's record-breaking temperature, fifty-one below zero, has made the national news. Our temporary walls are two-by-twelves with roofing paper stapled to the outside. On balance, Baby Doe's shack looks more comfortable. Although we burn as much wood as we can in the two stoves, the house doesn't hold the heat. Rings of decreasing temperature swirl around the stoves like planetary orbits. If you get too close to the potbelly stove (Mercury), your pants burn up, especially if they're corduroy. If you have to leave to get a book on a shelf far away (Pluto), it's close to freezing.

Our theory is that once the rock is enclosed, it will absorb the heat and warm up the house at night, like a brick in a bed. It's just a theory now, although the converse is true: with less than a quarter of it enclosed, the rock never gets warm and chills the house constantly. Since heat rises, the sleeping loft is the best place to be, day or night. We sit on the bed, smelling piñon smoke, beans cooking or bread baking, and the fresh pine scent of the railroad tie walls. David and I are the Gold Dust Twins. We read or write. When our fingers are warm enough, I knit, and David plays the guitar, and we take turns going down the ladder to stoke the two stoves. The kitchen is the engine room where we feed the fires and ourselves, but we return to the loft to navigate through winter. We sleep fifteen hours a night under our goose down bags and don't get up until the late-rising winter sun shines in the window of the loft. Our house is like a really neat playhouse or fort, only there's nowhere to go home to when we're through playing. We don't visit Peter and Nancy much anymore, and Dean and Linda are in New York. Patricia's in Taos, and Jim and Sandy are visiting Jim's parents in Austin. We can visit Richard and Beth only so often. I expected winters in the beginning here to be difficult, but I hadn't expected the house to be so unfinished and flimsy. This time, however, when we throw the *I Ching*, we don't get "Difficulty at the Beginning." We get Number 33, "Tun/Retreat," nine at the top, explained as:

Nine at the top means:
Cheerful retreat. Everything serves to further.

The situation is unequivocal. Inner detachment has become an established fact, and we are at liberty to depart. When one sees the way ahead thus clearly, free of all doubt, a cheerful mood sets in, and one chooses what is right without further thought. Such a clear path ahead always leads to the good.

The *I Ching* is right again. We know without further thought that we should retreat to Jamaica. David has been reading about new music there, not to mention the great dope. Our clear path leads to the Caribbean, and our cheerful mood sets in as soon as we decide to go. We've got enough money for round-trip air tickets from Miami to Kingston, plus some extra for inexpensive hotels. It's tough to roll and jump-start the Chrysler across a thousand miles of plains. We'll hitchhike to Florida, staying in motels along the way.

Ten days later, we're ready to go. Richard and Beth will feed Kachina. I don't think she'll go down the ridge or that Peter will shoot her. There's a small community dinner at Patricia and Steve's when they get back from Taos the night before we leave. We eat sitting on the bancos by the adobe fireplace, watching the logs fall and flare, like prehistoric families huddled in their winter caves, like the kids we were, watching *Howdy Doody* on a flickering TV on snowy evenings. Peter gives David the names of Florida communes where we can stay.

"Thanks, Peter," David says sincerely. I don't say anything.

21 : Miami

In retrospect, hitchhiking to Florida was a little like being Dorothy in *The Wizard of Oz*, picked up by a tornado and lifted off the farm. Instead of Oz, however, I landed in the Miami Colosseum, leaning over the rail of the biggest boat there, a sixty-five foot Chris Craft yacht. In slow moments during the Miami Boat Show, I go back over our trip, connecting the dots.

We didn't travel at tornado speed. The day we left, we almost couldn't get out of Libre. It had been so cold for so long that Libre's ordinarily marginally working vehicles refused to start. Jim and Dallas messed with them a bit, but it was too cold to work on cars for long. We just about gave up when the Red Rockers' all wheel drive truck appeared, weaving and lumbering up the snow packed road. It was Winnie, Anson, and a guy named Mumford, who'd moved to the Red Rocks to be with the mother of Larry's baby. (She'd recently split up with Larry, who was a new item now with a woman from the Ortiviz who'd also moved up to the Red Rocks. This is one version of our commune student exchange program.) Two fifty-five gallon drums tied onto the bed of the truck were still making sloshing noises.

Mumford got into the back, unfastened the top of one drum, peered down into it, and yelled, "I think they're ready, guys!"

"What are you doing?" I asked, squinting up at them and into the sun.

"Well," Winnie grinned and explained, "we're experimenting! It's too cold to wash diapers in the washing machine outside, plus the gears on the wringer don't work well if at all in the cold, so we filled one of those fifty-five gallon drums in the back with soapy water, put the dirty diapers in, clamped the lid, and then drove around to agitate them. Now we'll dump the water out, switch the diapers to the rinse water drum, and drive around some more. I think we'll end up driving about two or three miles per diaper. Bumpy roads are better, of course."

"Do you think you could take us down to Farisita for your rinse cycle?" David asked.

They laughed and agreed. We rode in the back down to Farisita as the diapers and rinse water churned in one drum, and then we got a short ride with the manager of Bob Hudson's ranch to Colorado Highway 87, where we caught our first long ride with a mother and three kids moving to Dallas from Salt Lake. Everyone in the family was pear-shaped, with pale blue eyes and thin blond hair, a family of rabbit people. We rode with the older son, Darrell, who was driving one of the two family Fords alone. He'd just gotten out of the army in Fort Carson and had stayed up for three days straight. Up in the front seat with Darrell, forty-five miles of small talk and companionable silence later, David said, "Would you like to try some marijuana?"

David believes if you're old enough to die for your country, you're old enough to smoke a joint. He thinks smoking dope is the first step toward an independent and revolutionary point of view, to seeing what a mess the world is in, to understanding we need a new way of thinking and acting. I was stuck on the practicalities again in the backseat. I'd heard that giving marijuana to a minor carried the death penalty in Texas, which we'd just entered. Who knows what Texas would do to you if you turned on a soldier, or an ex-soldier. I glared at the back of David's head and cleared my throat loudly, but he was messianically rolling a doobie and ignoring me. As soon as Darrell smoked it, he pulled over, saying he felt dizzy and was going to pass out. We quickly loaded Darrell into the backseat, and I ran back on the highway to tell his mom that poor Darrell was resting with a headache and that David would be glad to drive. We drove straight through to Dallas, except for short gas station stops, during which I assured Darrell's mom that Darrell was fine but still sleeping. Darrell opened one pink-rimmed eye a few times and smiled. He smiled again with his eyes closed when I scolded David for giving him a joint. He recovered completely outside Dallas. He should have just asked us to drive.

Lee, the truck driver who picked us up next, leered at me occasionally, but I behaved like a debutante, and he was too embarrassed or confused to suggest anything untoward in front of David as we drove through the Louisiana night. We sped through to northern Florida, David sitting on the other side of me, listening to Lee's life story and commenting in his sincere Jimmy Stewart voice. I slept on the bed in the back of the cab while they talked. Lee had been married three times, but he lived in his truck now and was a lonely man. He cried a little telling his story but never slowed down. When he dropped us off outside Cook's Hammock, Florida, on a Sunday morning, a large young black woman in a pink suit and matching flowered hat picked us up after church. She opened the trunk of the car for our bags and moved a wreath over carefully. I sat in the front seat of her immaculate three-year-old Chevy and asked where she was headed.

She said, "Taking that wreath to my Daddy's grave in Fanning Springs." After she left us off on Route 27, we caught uneventful rides with traveling salesmen or college students, and I sat in backseats ignoring David's questions and the drivers' monosyllabic answers as we streamed south through the Florida peninsula the conquistadors had raged through around the time their brothers across the continent were tracking down and killing Chief Cuerno Verde on Greenhorn Mountain.

At the Coral Gables commune Peter told us about, a lot of members were psychiatrists and therapists. They'd leased an old, slightly neglected Mediterranean Art Deco mansion on the canals. It was different from the Huerfano communes. It didn't have a name, and all they debated at the after-dinner meeting on the first night we arrived was what temperature the water in the indoor swimming pool should be. David's eyes met mine as a gray-haired shrink was arguing for a lower temperature. I thought of our frozen five-gallon water cans in the tipi and laughed out loud. The shrink paused until I told him to go on, it was nothing. After the meeting, Candy, the woman I happened to sit beside, invited us to stay at her place, the mansion's old boathouse, right on the canal. She was going to Nassau with her new boyfriend to visit his family. They owned a big chain of hardware stores in the Caribbean. The next morning she stopped by to pick up some clothes, and we sat on the boathouse balcony and chatted lazily and easily in the sun.

David came out on the balcony and said, "You two act as if you'd known each other in grade school or something!" Candy and I laughed, slightly embarrassed. She told us we could stay in the boathouse when we came back from Jamaica, and offered me a job she'd taken as a hostess on a Chris Craft yacht at the Miami Boat Show that week. It paid one hundred and fifty dollars a day for five days. I couldn't refuse. I'd be doing Candy a favor, because she really wanted to go to Nassau to meet her boyfriend's family, but she'd made a commitment to Chris Craft. She even arranged how I'd get downtown by calling her friend Brenda, who lived in Coral Gables and was one of the other women working for Chris Craft at the boat show too. Candy said Brenda would be glad to give me a ride.

So, just like that, for the past three days since we got back from Jamaica, I've been commuting to the Miami Colosseum with Brenda every morning at eight thirty in her little Triumph convertible. David and I have fresh orange juice, toast, and coffee on the upstairs porch of the narrow, two-story stucco boathouse. We sit in the morning sun, read the *Miami Herald,* and watch the birds flit over the canal. When Brenda toots, I kiss David good-bye, and later he leaves for the job he found through the want ads, hanging wallpaper in a condo that's being built on spec in Coral Gables on the grounds of another old mansion, recently demolished. Poof—we're Mr. and Mrs. Suburban, sort of.

Dressed in my Chris Craft uniform—white slacks, navy blue crew neck sweater, and nautical rope belt cinched neatly around my waist— standing on the bow of a sixty-foot yacht indoors, with an ocean of humanity lapping around its sides, I keep my grip by going over how I got here, starting with reading Baby Doe Tabor, who could have been a Chris Craft girl if she'd been born a century later. After our solitary winter months on the mountain, so many people and so much change is mind-altering. Brenda and some of the other girls go to a storeroom to smoke a joint during breaks, but I couldn't cope.

Our time at sea level on the island of Jamaica was such a radical change from living at nine thousand feet in the Rockies in January that the whole week was an altered state. There's nothing new to say about tropical paradises. The draft, Peter and Sinbad, the frozen short days and long nights in our loft didn't seem real, but neither did Jamaica. Mrs. Merle Stephenson, a beautiful middle-aged Jamaican woman, appeared out of nowhere at the airport tourist desk when David and I found out we didn't have enough money for a week in any hotel during high season. In her lilting, cultured Jamaican tones, she asked, "Why don't you come back to my house on the north of the island? You can stay for thirty-five dollars a week with meals." Merle's large, slightly dilapidated house in the hills was filled with young Jamaican soccer players and fledgling career people sitting around the pool, and every day she planned something for David and me to do. She arranged for us to visit a friend on the empty beaches of Negril and to see the carnival in Brown's Town. We finally got warm when we smoked some really strong ganja and had some rum drinks Merle's friend made us at his thatched-roof bar without walls in Negril. We would have finished our house before winter if we'd been building in Jamaica. We sat on the beach, and I saw that the sun was my father and couldn't hurt me, and we lay on the sand for hours, dipping in the warm, clear Caribbean to cool off. I would have gotten third-degree burns if I'd realized my solar paternity any earlier. It's lucky I have dark skin for a blonde. Now it's just the right shade for a Chris Craft gal.

If I'm not quite right in the head now, it's because I'm on sensory overload on a yacht dry-docked in the Miami Colosseum, cut off from all natural light, as tides of visitors ebb and flow through the building. We're in Republican heaven. There aren't too many revolutionaries shopping for yachts here. Some of these people probably dined with Bebe Rebozo last night. What's happened? I'd thought that when David's draft status was resolved, we would feel freer, not adrift. I'm buying makeup at Woolworth's again, smiling sweetly, and saying "Step up" all day to fat white-haired men who, I suspect in my unbalanced and intolerant state of mind, probably made their money manufacturing napalm and selling "America—Love It or Leave It!" bumper stickers. The model condo David's wallpapering epitomizes the kind of tasteless, greedy development we hate. All I have to do is stand in various spots on the yacht and smile, reminding people to step up as they pass between rooms, and making sure no one unscrews any brass fixtures, but it's getting harder and harder. David and I talk late in the warm Miami winter night, and I know we're converting the Chris Craft money into something good, that our life in the Huerfano is the end justifying these means, but the edges are fraying on our Miami days.

Yesterday David mildly electrocuted himself at work. He was putting a strip of wallpaper on the ceiling of the bathroom when he accidentally stuck his head in the exposed wire box for the overhead light. The charge knocked him off the ladder, and the gooey wallpaper wrapped around him like a cocoon as he fell. The other workers ripped it to bits to get to him and revive him. The boss wasn't happy about the wasted wallpaper and time, and didn't seem to care that David could have been killed. I tried to sympathize when I got back from an eight-hour shift on the yacht, but I've asked him not to smoke dope on the job, and it might have contributed to the accident. David resents doing manual labor for five and a quarter an hour while I stand around in a yachting outfit and make much more money. Since the electrocution scare, he's actually seemed angry at me, as if it we're my fault. But my work takes its toll too. Today some Chris Craft bigwigs and their guests drove inside the Colosseum right up to the boat in two Cadillac limousines. When one gray-haired fat cat too many leered and asked me, "Do you come with the boat?" I tried to stay in control, but couldn't help smiling back at him and saying sweetly, "Only when it rocks." I'd run out of the breathy laughs and "You devil" looks I'd used the last twenty times some old fart asked me that. I wasn't one of the girls asked to lunch with the top brass, and that's probably just as well.

By the time Brenda drops me off on a humid, smoggy afternoon, I'm ready to leave Miami. My mood improves when I see Candy, just back from the Bahamas, and we sit on the upstairs porch and drink piña coladas. I don't drink much, but they taste like tart ice cream sodas, not booze. I tell her the "Only when it rocks" story, and she laughs. She's leggy, tanned, brunette, and beautiful. Her laugh's husky, and I feel I've known her a long time.

When David gets home, we ask him to join us upstairs. "No thanks," he calls, "I celebrated with the guys." He says they were fired for hanging the wallpaper throughout the demo condo upside down. It had an abstract fleur-de-lis pattern, and upside down it looked like a swarm of dive-bombing angry wasps. He's always had a highly developed sense of the absurd, but he sounds bummed out. "I guess this is good-bye, Candy," he says, walking inside.

"Visionaries shouldn't hang wallpaper," I say to her, and we both shrug. In solidarity with David, Candy tells how she quit Merrill Lynch two years ago. "Wait a minute," I interrupt, "my brother works for Merrill Lynch!"

"What's his name?" asks Candy, delicately licking a piña colada foam mustache off her lip. When I tell her, she says, "No kidding, that's your maiden name? That's *my* last name! Everybody knows your brother, he's the youngest VP there! What a guy!" Candy's a Virginia Price, and we might be distant cousins. Is this why she gave us her house and me her job, and why I took them? We're *family!* We laugh and chat as the sun slips hazily behind the palm fronds, not at all like the stark dive it takes behind the sharp edges of the mountains at home. The pitcher of piña coladas is gone, and Candy has to go soon, too. She won't be back before we leave, and we won't see each other again. She'll never come to the Huerfano—she's not the type—but I don't mind. Tonight it feels as if I've found a small, missing puzzle piece. Leaning over the porch wall, I draw circles in the air with the stem of my empty glass over the soupy canal. Is it the piña coladas that help me see more clearly how, since we moved to the Huerfano, we've been living a charmed life, how everyone's connected, and family's wherever we go?

We're back on the ridge a week after the equinox. The days are longer now, the sun shines more strongly on our faces and sets farther west along the rims of the Sangre de Cristos. Wild crocuses push up through the remaining patches of snow on the north side of the ridge. In seven years, all the cells in your body have changed, but more than one-seventh of us has changed this past year. We've adjusted to marriage and mountain life, we know a lot more about construction, and we're connected to the Libre family. This year we can get a lot more done on the house. We'll start in May instead of July, for one thing. Even though the last freak snows can fall in June, there will be plenty of warm days to work and bring building materials up here. When we got back from Florida, there was a short card from Doug, typically terse—"Hello! Coming back in June for good!" he scratched neatly. We're glad. With his help, we'll finish the upper house and deck and move the temporary wall around the rock, enclosing more of the lower octagon. We might even get the whole bottom finished, if we're lucky.

"*Little darling, it's been a long cold lonely winter / Little darling, it seems like years since it's been here . . . ,*" David picks out the familiar George Harrison tune. It means more now that we live in the mountains. David starts work like this, warming up his fingers and his voice. He's down on the banco under the rock, with pencils and pad, putting the finishing touches on a new song after our eggs and toast. He's gotten more interested in music since he's been here, and he and Henry are putting a band together called the Dog Brothers. It'll take time away from building the house, but, as David says, it's equally important to live creatively, and they might make some money, too.

I'm in the loft, knitting socks for David. My needles are tiny, and the wool's thin as thread. The cable pattern's a bitch, but the second one's almost finished. Kachina lies in the sun at my feet, kittens growing in her belly.

Even though I don't know for sure what everyone else at Libre is doing right now, I feel as if I know what's going on all over the land, which is a sign of settling in here too, I guess. When I go outside, I hear Jim playing Big Brother and the Holding Company at top volume down below. I bet he's working on the Fool, a card in the Tarot set he's been drawing and coloring all winter. Jim says the Fool is the unnumbered Tarot card, central to the whole deck. Jim's card, like most traditional Fool cards, shows an androgynous person, a prince or princess of the world, setting out on a journey on a sunny morning in the mountains. The Fool carries all his belongings in little bag hanging from a stick and holds a flower in his left hand. He's looking up, though it looks like he's close to stepping off a cliff. Jim says that the Fool's not about being stupid or silly, but about having the courage to trust your inner instincts as you begin your journey to wisdom. It's the card of infinite possibilities. Jim likes to work with rock and roll playing at infinitely loud levels. I bet Sandy's walked far up the creek to meditate at her favorite spot, where the ice is broken and the creek gurgling down the mountain blots out Big Brother.

Outside, we can often hear Steve's chain saw at his and Patricia's house across Dry Creek. I can see Steve unloading a truck full of lumber with his brother Monty, who's been visiting. There's a study in genetics for you. Steve and Monty are both large, blond-haired men, but Monty got the Noël Coward gene and Steve got the Grizzly Adams one. Steve's often on some new purification diet—macrobiotic, vegetarian, wheat grass juice fasts, and so on, whereas Monty usually has a cigarette in the corner of his mouth and sips black coffee, a vodka martini, or a brandy while thumbing through Julia Child for a recipe for sweetbreads. Steve's putting the finishing touches on the room they added last summer when they were waiting for Tawa to be born. Patricia's probably inside weaving at her floor loom, throwing the shuttle and clack-clacking the pedals speedily, working on a bright rainbow-striped weaving she's going to line with flannel for a baby bunting fastened with Navajo silver buttons. She made one for Tawa, and this one will be for Larry Red Rocker and his wife's baby. It's more complicated visualizing what's happening at Dean and Linda's dome. In breaks between Big

160 : HERE COMES THE SUN

Brother and Steve's chain saw, we can hear Dean playing Coltrane out on his deck while he works on his current series of big black and white abstracts. He's been walking by our house a lot lately on his way to the retreat house he's constructing on the back of the land. Steve and Linda have been helping Dean build a Zen shack on the last ridge before the Turkey Creek waterfall. They're the reason Dean's retreating. Patricia usually watches Lia while Steve and Linda help Dean build a place where he can be far enough away not to see Linda and Steve together. Today it sounds like Dean's taking the day to paint at the dome, though. Most likely, in their uneasy peace, Linda's finishing up that crazy flowered shirt for Lia, who's usually watching her mom sew as she works on her own Fauvist series of crayon drawings. Next week, Dean, Linda, and Lia will all go over to the Triple A to paint the Triple A school bus. The sketches for it depict a muscular, cartoonlike chain of the Sangres in brilliant hues across both sides of the bus. The Triple A wants "*Life's Music is Best*" scrawled across the side, and "*Life's Music is Beth's*" on the front.

Peter's probably at his kitchen table in the zome this morning, writing. There's no music playing, and Nancy's most likely in the alcove, cutting out a cowboy shirt she's making for him. They've been getting along pretty well lately, and she doesn't seem too uptight these days, and chances are Peter's thinking maybe he can get her upstairs for an afternoon in bed, even though he paid a lot of attention to a woman visiting from California at a party two weeks ago.

On the lower land, although I can't hear it, ten to one Tony, Libre's slightly older version of the Angry Young Man, is playing Brubeck while he works on some new acrylics for his New York gallery, and dark and gorgeous Marilynn's making venison stew from a deer Peter shot last fall. The stew's for the community dinner at Tony and Marilynn's this Sunday. When I taught reading yesterday at school at Marilynn and Tony's, Marilynn told me that a bottle of fennel fell off the spice rack into the stew, so she's calling the dish fennel deer.

Vesey, the other old Park Place artist here with Tony and Dean, is probably in his A-frame with his new lady, who just found out she's pregnant. Vesey's ex-wife is visiting, along with his ex-girlfriend. Vesey's current lady, his ex-wife, and his old girlfriend resemble one another—they're small, with long, dark wavy hair and slightly aquiline noses. Some men go for the same type over and over. His A-frame's pretty small, but the three women have been getting along well so far. Just as I'm thinking of him, I see Vesey walking up the ridge road, on

Tom Grow and a piano painted by Linda.

his way to see his old pal Bill and spend the afternoon in some masculine company. Bill's got a visitor—a dark, good-looking, tough-talking guy named Joey Machine, who Bill says had to get out of New York for "health reasons." Vesey's probably got a hunch that Joey Machine brought whiskey, beer, and who knows what else.

Down the road from Peter's zome toward Turkey Creek, Tom's probably in the Grow Hole working on that one-stringed instrument he's making out of balsa wood, using who knows what kind of gut that he's cured for the string. It's about time for Peggy to fix lunch for the kids before she goes over to Tony's dome this afternoon to practice with the Dog Brothers. Peggy plays electric piano, Tony plays drums, Jim plays bass. Henry and David sing, with Henry on lead guitar and David on rhythm. Henry's coming over from the Red Rockers to practice. He and David have each written new songs the band needs to learn.

When I was at Richard and Beth's earlier, Richard was about to go to work at his jewelry bench. He showed me the pieces of delicate silver earrings he's making for his gallery in St. Louis. The kids are probably still outside playing, getting used to the mountain again after their recent visit to family in Missouri. After she cleans up in the morning, Beth usually weaves on the Navajo loom Richard made for her, using the soft brown and gray wool she spun this winter. Richard's going to Trinidad with us and others next week to tear up another old tongue-and-groove dance hall floor for materials. When Doug gets here, we're going to start on the next quarter of the house. Richard, Beth, David, and I plan to build a goat house up on the road between our houses and keep goats this summer. Patricia, Peter, and Nancy have ordered fifty chickens. We'll trade our yogurt for their eggs. This year, the Triple A, the Red Rockers, and Libre are going to help the people at Ortiviz Farm work their land, because it actually has fields, pasture, and irrigation rights. We'll grow amber fields of grain.

Dallas was supposed to go up to Pueblo today to get more materials for the garage we're building in front of Sandy and Jim's house so Jim and Dallas will be able to work inside in bad weather. This fall we used our neighboring rancher Bob Hudson's backhoe to dig a real mechanic's pit for it. I heard the flatbed leave the parking lot early this morning. It's almost time to put down my knitting and punch down the donut dough on the kitchen counter. I've had a craving for donuts lately, and you can't just pop out to the corner bakery when you get cravings here. I'll work as quietly as possible, because David's busy humming and scribbling a new song. It'll be great to have more space next winter. Maybe Henry will come up after practice tonight and have a donut. More likely, he and David will prefer the last of the aged Jamaican rum we brought back. I'll probably have a tiny glass too, and, after I put some lentil soup on the cookstove and one of the loaves I made yesterday in the warming oven, we'll sit by the potbelly, sipping rich, dark rum, talking about plans, and all the new things to come.

Little darling, the smile's returning to the faces
Little darling, it seems like years since it's been here . . .
Sun, sun, sun, here it comes.

23 : The Nature of Time

It's May—time to think about gardens. This year, all the communes in the Huerfano are undergoing some loose centralization. We're going to farm collectively at the Ortiviz, and have school there for all our kids. We've agreed about the group farm and school. We've agreed to chip in what we can, and to work as much as we can down there, but that's about as specific as we've gotten. There's a range of sharing in the Huerfano. The Red Rockers, with a core of two sets of siblings and old friends who met in kindergarten, share the most and are most committed to a socialist ideal. They're true social revolutionaries. The population of Libre, many of whom didn't know one another very well before, if at all, is more bourgeois— intellectuals and artists, I suppose. We agree to the minimum, to pay dues to the Libre fund for taxes and general expenses like the pump. If anyone has a windfall, he or she can pay for something that will benefit all, and I suppose there's some community pressure to do so, but that's strictly up to the individual. The Triple A, many of whom were friends in college, is somewhere in between. They live in separate houses that are closer together than the ones at Libre. Who knows if there's any organization at Archuletaville? At the Ortiviz Farm, there's New Buffalo-style agrarian communal sharing of income and work.

Despite the fact that we're centralizing our agricultural efforts, Libre will still have a small vegetable garden in the sloping meadow in front of Jim and Sandy's house, south of the half-built garage. In the meadow south of Jim's house, actually. In April, Crosby drove up in his new Toyota Land Cruiser, looking for land. He was a Buddhist, like a lot of rich hippies, and he stayed with Jim and Sandy. Sandy took him over to see some acreage for sale on Turkey

Stephanie in the Libre garden, Huajatollas in the distance.

Creek. Then Crosby and Sandy drove around the Huerfano with the Thatches for a couple of days. The Thatches, the realtors for Libre's land, are developing a sub-specialty selling to hippies. They didn't have any luck with Crosby—he decided to look for land in Arizona. His spirit wanted more desert. Sandy's spirit wanted more Crosby. I think Crosby's serious interest in Buddhism and his serious bank account were an irresistible combination. Sandy took her Tarot cards and her *I Ching*, but she left her copper pots. She can afford to replace them, but Jim can't.

Successful gardening at over eight thousand feet is a challenge. No Early Boy tomato is early enough, but if the Incas could do it, why can't we? No one knows if the Incas grew much besides potatoes. First, we must improve the soil. It's a claylike dirt called caliche, full of big rocks. We dig, terrace, and pry out rocks for days. Our garden has the best view we've ever seen—from the Huajatollas around to Sheep Mountain in the Sangre de Cristo Range, across the sweep of the rest of the Sangres, and up behind us to the rounded slate blue summit of Greenhorn, a three hundred and sixty—degree mountain diorama. Since we stand around staring at the views at least as much as we work in the garden, the views are important.

Today we'll haul manure. Seven of us with pitchforks and shovels climb in the back of Libre's '51 Chevy flatbed, and Jim drives four miles down the road to Mick Montaño's place. The spring winds have been blowing all week. Linda and I are the only women along, and we're dressed in turtlenecks, long underwear, overalls, scarves, hats, and work gloves, with kerchiefs over our faces and Ray-Bans on our noses. We're more covered up than women in purdah. Linda tells me that a few years ago, when she and Dean lived in the Purgatory Valley near Trinidad, an old rancher's wife asked her to tea. The woman poured tea and advised Linda kindly, "My dear, you must nevah, nevah go out without hat and gloves!" She'd approve of our outfits today, if not their style.

After Dean dropped Lia off to play with Nanda, he picked up the new issue of *China Reconstructs* from the Libre mailbox. We don't know who gave us a subscription to *China Reconstructs,* an English-language propaganda monthly put out by the Communist Chinese. It's formatted like *Life,* but the photographs are inferior and look like old Technicolor movie stills. There are pictures of happy factory workers and happy farmers, their lips touched up with an orange-red peculiar to that publication. This issue has an article about enriching the soil, plus English translations of songs workers sing while carrying manure up the mountain.

"Hey," Dean says. "How could we forget? It's International Workers' Day!"

"Wow!" we say.

"I'd rather think of it as May Day and have a maypole, and some May wine," says Steve's brother Monty blithely. His bandanna is tied like an ascot. But in a gesture of solidarity, as the truck lurches down the road, we try to sing one of the work songs printed in *China Reconstructs.* This doesn't work for a variety of reasons. First, no melody is given, the translation is goofy, and the lyrics awkward. Second, there's only one copy of the magazine, and most of us can't see the words. Third, we're trying to sing while passing a joint and struggling to stay in the flatbed as it lurches and jolts down the road in twenty-mile-an-hour winds. Nevertheless, we give it a try, expressing unity with workers around the world, although nobody believes the propaganda in *China Reconstructs.* We wouldn't last a day in a Chinese commune—we'd be congenitally unable to submerge our egos in furtherance of the revolution. We couldn't take being bossed around by the captain of our cadre, and we'd be shipped off for hard labor with all the other artists, effete bourgeois intellectuals, and aberrant personalities. Or worse. Next we try Sam Cooke's the "Chain Gang," but that doesn't work either, because even David can't remember many of the lyrics, and all we end up doing pretty well is the background "*Oooof. . . Whup*'s" of prisoners swinging picks at rocks.

Dean gets out to open the gate at Mick Montaño's. It's a low stucco house with a few small windows and a low pitched roof in a hollow by Turkey Creek, the only house in the valley I know of that has no views whatsoever. Mick lives with his sister Guadalupe, whom no one's ever met. She's kind of a hermit, although she lives with him. Smoke blows horizontally out of their stovepipe in the wind. Mick comes out, hunched against the wind, thumbs tucked in his front pants pockets. He's heard us coming for a while. He's middle-aged, maybe ten years younger than my father. His eyes are squinty and brown, his hair matted gray and black. There's a yellow tobacco stain on his scraggly beard, running from one corner of his mouth at the same slant the Rio Grande cuts along the south Texas border. He's short, bony, and gnarled, with the gray face men get in these parts from cigarettes, cowboy coffee, western diet, and dirt.

There are no trees around Mick's house, nothing green. Cows and sheep have eaten everything up to the door. Only a few dried cow pies and some listing posts punctuate the dirt in his yard. One window looks at us like an eyeball without a lid. It's too dark inside to see anything in there. Is Guadalupe inside, frozen in her tracks, peering out? There's a hand-operated water pump downhill from the house, and the pig pen's uphill from the house and pump. Mick tilts his head toward the old pens north of the house when Jim asks where to go. Mick's laconicism is legendary. Jim nods and then backs the flatbed up to a pen with a broken fence on one side, and we hop out and start shoveling old caked pig manure into the flatbed. It breaks into clumps, and the air is full of shit dust. Strands of hair get loose from my scarf and blow in my face. I wish the girls from the Miami Boat Show could see me now. Community relations are just as important as manual labor, so I walk down to the pump where Mick's standing.

"Some wind, eh?" I try for an opener.

"Yep," says Mick.

"Thanks for letting us have this manure."

"Yep." Different intonation. Mick and Guadalupe probably don't talk much.

I look at the layout of Mick's place, and, after a particularly long pause, I lose the game of conversational chicken. "Mick, why don't you have your pig pens *downhill* from your pump? It sure would be a lot easier that way," I blurt out helpfully.

Mick looks uphill at his four black pigs, clumped in their pen, butts to the wind, and then down at the pump. He looks at me, standing in front of him with a bandanna over my face like a bad guy in a western. He looks at the rest of us, shoveling petrified pig shit in a dance that looks like it's been choreographed by the Three Stooges. He looks at the truck that might not make it back up to Libre. He spits tobacco in a delicate stream, away from me, and downwind.

"You could save a lot of time, you know, getting water to your pigs that way," I explain.

Another long pause. I'm trying to get used to it. Mick wipes his lips with the back of his hand thoughtfully, and then he says softly, *"What's time to a pig?"*

Suddenly I'm a Zen student, scared to tell the Roshi I don't get it. Mick smiles at me. "Yeah, you're right," I mutter after a while, lying into the wind, and going back to shoveling. As we rumble back up the road, the road dust swirls up into the manure dust blowing off the truck, and I feel like Lawrence of Arabia in a sandstorm. My teeth grind on grit and dirt—at least, I hope it's dirt. I tell David what Mick Montaño said, and David tells Peter, whom David's speaking to these days, although I'm still not. I'll never forgive him for shooting Sinbad, even though Sinbad was driving Nancy berserk—a short drive in the best of times. Peter laughs, his hands clutching the slatted sides of the flatbed as it swerves to avoid big rocks in the road.

"Hee, hee, hee, *'WHAT'S TIME TO A PIG?'*" Peter shouts. We all double over, clinging to the flatbed sides, our eyes tearing from laughter, blowing dust and shit, and the wind itself, and we keep laughing as we spread pig manure in the terraces. Linda leaves to pick up Lia. We break for lunch, and David and I don't go back in the afternoon. Too much wind can make you crazy. Let the people with finished houses complete the job! Jim and Dallas will be busy trying to repair the Ortiviz Farm's rototiller, which busted soon after we borrowed it.

What did Mick Montaño mean? Did he misunderstand me? Did I hear wrong? Or is all the wisdom of the ages here in the Huerfano whenever we need it?

Rainbow on the road west, June 1970. Photo by David Perkins.

Red Rocker dome going up, September 1970.

*Larry Red Rocker at a
Triple A party, May 1971.*

*Libre School
(Lori, Aaron, Aricia
in the center, Travis and
Jason, visiting from Taos,
on left and right),
October 1970.*

Early rock house construction, Peter's zome below, September 1970.

David and Big John setting a viga, September 1970.

Upper bedroom of the rock house under construction, October 1972.

Rock house in winter, December 1972

(opposite)
Rock house kitchen with
Kachina, September 1972.
(above)
Marilynn and Tony
in their dome, June 1969.
(left)
Aricia by a space heater in
Richard and Beth's house,
November 1972.

Peter Orlovsky, August 1977.

*Sangre de Cristo Range
from the Ridge*

It wasn't easy for Dean and Linda this spring. A couple of weeks ago, Dean went to the Ortiviz Farm to give Linda some space. A few days later, Linda walked Lia down there so Lia could be with Dean for a while. Lia was playing with some farm kids on the upper land while Dean cleared out nearby ditches with the Ortiviz men. It was a glorious day in May, and they were getting a lot done when little Joe-Joe ran up to Dean and said, "Lia's playing in the pond, but she's not moving." Lia was almost three. No one knows how she could have drowned at the pond. When asked about it afterwards, Joe-Joe and the other children looked at the ground and said they didn't know. Joe-Joe's big brown eyes widened, and he bit his lip. I don't think any of them saw what happened. We'll never know.

The morning we buried Lia, truck after truck drove up the Libre road. David and I dressed in our best clothes, but we couldn't move very fast. Doug, who'd arrived a few nights before, said he'd stay up on the ridge and take care of the goats. Doug was fifteen when their father died, and he didn't need another funeral. When we finally got down the ridge, everyone in the Huerfano was sitting in a circle in the meadow by Dean and Linda's dome. They'd wrapped Lia in a blanket and buried her to the east of their dome before we got there.

I wished there had been more of a ceremony, and things to read, and beautiful music to help Dean and Linda through. But we weren't prepared for death, and no one could think up any rituals now. Your rituals should be in place before tragedy or loss. The circle was silent, and on the faces you could see the tracks of their tears. We all looked like we'd been kicked in the stomach.

Dallas had his hat off, and the top of his forehead was ghostly white. Nanda, Lump, Lori, Aaron, and Aricia sat clumped behind their parents, all of them with their fingers in their mouths. Across the circle, Dean and Linda sat cross-legged, close but not touching, next to the small mound of fresh earth. Dean had just finished speaking when we got there, and the wind was whipping up unkindly out of Dry Creek Canyon. The silence was almost unbearable.

Orphan is a word for a child whose parents are dead, but there's no word for parents who've lost a child, and ever since Lia's funeral I've wondered about this inadequacy in our language. Sitting beside the new grave, Dean and Linda were pale, disheveled, and red-eyed, and they looked suddenly frail. Linda didn't seem to see anyone, her eyes focused on some middle distance. Across the circle, Lars sat erect and never took his eyes off her face. Adrienne slumped beside Lars, tears escaping from under the rims of her thick glasses and running down her puffy cheeks. She didn't bother to wipe them off. Earlier this year, in California, she'd been in a car wreck in which her lover had been killed. Her hair frizzed out in all directions. She finally took a bandanna out from behind her suspenders and blew her nose hard. The Red Rockers sat close together, staring at the same point on the ground in front of them, as if there was a message on the rocks poking out of the grass.

Linda spoke dully above the wind. "We walked down to the Ortiviz Farm two days ago. We passed a dead cat in a puddle on the road, and I told Lia the cat had died. But she said, 'No, Mommy, the cat has broken through the glass and is happy!'" Linda's voice wavered on the word "happy." She had a blanket over her shoulders. It wasn't very cold, but she was shivering. The circle broke up, and we gathered in front of Dean and Linda to hug them, but they didn't get up. One after another, we crouched down to touch them, to tell them how sorry. When I hugged Linda she felt limp, and all I could think to say was, "I'm so sorry, I love you." She put her head on my shoulder for a second, and I smelled the fresh dirt. I couldn't think of anything to say to Dean, and he held on to me too hard, as if he was drowning. I was kneeling on a rock, and it dug sharply into my knee—a sharp but limited pain.

There was nothing to do after the ceremony. It was a strange valley gathering, with no food, drink, or music. I hugged Mary Red Rocker and Nancy Rabbit, and I hugged Patricia as she held Tawa tightly. Steve was on the perimeter of the crowd, pacing around in the dirt. Linda stood up, and Lars hugged her and rocked her in his arms. Adrienne talked to Dean, who got up and swayed slightly, as if it was hard to keep his balance. I didn't understand anything. Dean and Linda were more caring and conscientious than any parents around. Lia was special, you could see it in her eyes. David and I don't have any children. I can't know Dean and Linda's loss. It's a frontier I don't want to explore, ever.

"I don't get why this happened," I said to David as we stopped to catch our breath, halfway back up the ridge after the funeral.

"Me neither," David said. "But in all societies there are births, and inexplicable, tragic deaths, and struggles, and unendurable pain and joy. This is a test for Dean and Linda and for us, and we will have to try to love each other and help each other more than ever." He was right, of course. We hugged numbly and solemnly, and then walked up to the house holding hands. Later I saw how Lia's death bound us here more than any party or peyote meeting.

I haven't seen much of Dean and Linda since Lia's funeral. I walk by their dome not knowing whether I should stop in, so half the time I do, half the time I don't. The Dean and Linda rag dolls are out of sight. I don't think it matters to Dean and Linda either way whether I visit. They didn't come to the equinox peyote meeting. Mary Red Rocker told me some peyote people said that the reason Lia died was that Linda had been a roadman for a meeting over at the Triple A and that women weren't supposed to be roadmen. That's it for me and the peyote people for a while. I'm only twenty-five, with no experience of death, really. Lia's is the first funeral I've been to. My parents thought I was too young to go to my grandparents' funerals. Nevertheless, I know Lia's death is way beyond blame.

This morning I'm down the ridge at Jim's, asking if he'll have any time to look at the Chrysler. He's leaning over the hood of the flatbed in front of the garage we built of barky slab lumber, poking at the spark plugs in a desultory way. I stand around giving him moral support, inspecting the dill growing in the Libre garden—almost the only crop thriving there, as it turns out. I'm not sure our household has worked in the garden enough so that we can pick some chard for dinner tonight.

"Got your temporary wall moved over, I heard," Jim says, standing up and wiping his hands on a rag.

"Yep. We'll be in half the bottom part of the house, and maybe the shell of the upper house will be finished by the end of summer, too."

"I gotta take a break and come up there one of these days and see what you've been up to," Jim says, turning, leaning back on his elbows on the flatbed and looking out into the valley.

"Yeah, come for dinner anytime." There's a clop, clop, clop behind us, and we turn our heads to watch Linda ride up on the little bay mare Johnny Bucci gave her two weeks after the funeral. Linda's made some saddlebags out of old Mexican blankets. They bulge and wobble on either side of the mare, and Linda's sleeping bag is tied to the back of her saddle.

"Hey, you guys! This is Pokey," she smiles. Linda's eyes are small and puffy.

"Where're you headed?" I ask. Linda's legs stick out too far from Pokey's fat sides, but this isn't the time to give her riding tips.

"Over to the Triple A, but I might stop in Gardner on the way," Linda says. Her face is pale, and her cheeks are unusually flushed.

"Hmm," I say, "that's about thirty miles, isn't it? You're going to be a little sore." Maybe I shouldn't say anything so negative.

"Don't worry, Roberta, this is an adventure, and I'll be fine."

One thing Linda doesn't seem is fine, but I smile back. "Good luck on your, uh, quest, and don't forget to write." She leans down and hugs me. Theoretically, Pokey could notice Linda's vulnerable as she leans over and could easily lose her balance if Pokey gave Linda a little toss, but there's no real danger of this happening. Pokey's snoozing standing up; she's done a cost-benefit analysis and decided it's not worth it to buck.

Jim and I watch Linda bounce down the road, her legs scissoring out as Pokey actually breaks into a bumpy trot near Maes Creek, where the aspens are fully greened out now. "That was nice of Johnny Bucci to bring Pokey up for her, wasn't it? I wonder why he did it," I say.

"I dunno. What makes Johnny Bucci do anything?" Jim's been hanging out with Dallas so much that he's picked up Dallas's irritating Zen habit of answering questions with questions. When you ask a question about your carburetor, you don't want to get a riddle back. I won't answer Jim's question out of principle.

"How did he know she wanted a horse?" I repeat instead.

"I dunno. What makes Johnny do anything?" Jim repeats. "Maybe he gets psychic messages through his TV."

At the Central in Walsenburg the following week, I see Mary Red Rocker and Adrienne, eating lunch with Adrienne's cousin Stewart, who's decided to move to the Triple A. Mary's just found out she's pregnant with Bad Eddy's baby, and she's staying over at the Triple A for a few days. She says Linda and Pokey made it over to the other side of the valley in three days. Picking at her enchilada, Mary says, "Last night I walked by Lars's tipi and stuck my head in to say hello, and Linda was all tucked up neatly in her sleeping bag. God—the inside of that tipi is so spare and Scandanavian, the floor's brushed, everything's in its place, what a trip! Gay men know how to keep house, or tipi, you know!"

"Yeah, he's got that shelf hanging from rawhide strips with his stainless steel espresso pot and all those Medaglia d'Oro cans in a row," I say, laughing.

"Whatever," says Mary, whose heritage, personality, and living situation at the Red Rockers' makes her less obsessed with order. "So, there he was," she continues, "sitting on Linda's sleeping bag, reading this book to her in Danish. I asked him what it was, and they both said, 'Icelandic fairy tales!'" Listening to Mary, I can see Lars's smile in the light of the Coleman lamp, the perfect white teeth, and the deep dimples in his tanned face. "So," Mary continues, "I asked, 'Linda, do you know any Danish?' and she whispers, 'Not a word!' When I left them to go back to Adrienne's, he started reading again!"

Sitting in the booth next to Mary, peering into my frosty mug, I hear Lars reading soothingly in the language of his childhood, and I see Linda, her sleeping bag zipped up to her chin, listening intently to Lars's calm, steady voice, and staring at the fire. She doesn't ask what the words mean, and he doesn't tell her. I see Mary moving away in the darkness until their voices are absorbed by stars.

Adrienne takes a big drag on her cigarette, then swigs her beer. She plunks her mug down loudly, and the sound brings me abruptly back to the table. Then she wipes her mouth on the back of her sleeve and says, "Yep! He reads those goddamn fairy tales to her every night!"

25 : Change in Seasons

Mount Blanca across the valley is the highest mountain in the Sangre de Cristo Range. It's over fourteen thousand feet, one of the fifty-four "Fourteeners" in the Rockies, and it's dusted with new snow already, a sign that summer's ending, but I'm not thinking much of the change of seasons. I always stop on the road after milking the goats in the morning and look across the valley for a while, listening to Little Egypt, Trinity, and Johanna behind me, munching and snorting contentedly on the new alfalfa I've put in their feeder. Then I check out signs of life here at Libre. I'll hear Bill slamming his screen door back on the next ridge, going out for his early morning bathroom break, and, on a few chill mornings, there's been smoke coming from Peter and Nancy's stovepipe. Sometimes I see Dean walking outside his dome, moving the hose around. Earlier this summer he planted three apricot trees around Lia's grave. He stands outside the dome in the cool of the morning or evening watering the little fruit trees, staring out at Mount Blanca.

One day in late June he called to us as we passed and asked if we'd come down to the Ortiviz Farm with him the next day to help plant two hundred trees. We were about to pour another foundation, but we couldn't refuse. He'd gotten Libre to contribute the money for the trees, and he and Jim had taken the flatbed to Pueblo to buy them. We all wanted to help with Dean's Arbor Day, and there weren't too many ways we could, so we jumped at this opportunity. David, Doug, and I drove down to the Ortiviz with our shovels and dug holes in a field where Dean placed sticks at measured intervals for fruit trees. We planted seedling poplars where he indicated, along the alfalfa fields on the ditches for a windbreak. Mary,

Anson, and Larry Red Rocker were there too, and some others from the Triple A. Even in the kinder soil at the Ortiviz, it was hard work.

When we broke for lunch and tromped back to the old adobe farmhouse, it reminded me of New Buffalo. It wasn't just that the personnel were the same (some people we'd met in Arroyo Hondo years ago had moved up to the Ortiviz), and it wasn't the sight of barefoot women with long skirts cooking in the low-ceilinged kitchen. It was how serious and silent they were at lunch. Maybe it was because they were so tired from working the fields day after day. Even when we're tired, though, we have enough energy left to laugh. We're the grasshoppers, too busy playing our fiddles to store food away for winter, and they're the ants.

Fortunately, there were other grasshoppers at the Ortiviz that day. While we dug the holes for the trees, I talked to Anson Red Rocker about Godard, and we discovered we had mutual friends at Harvard. Anson has a rich deep voice, and he seems thoughtful and faintly amused at the same time. I talked to Mary Red Rocker about her job at *Harper's*. She recalled the girl at the next desk, Linda Eastman, who came in one day and cleared her desk out and said good-bye, she was going to London to marry Paul McCartney. Anson, Mary, and I discussed the rumor that Kissinger had engineered the breakdown of the Vietnamese peace talks so Nixon could get elected. We talked with Elaine Baker from the Triple A about her civil rights work in Mississippi in the early sixties.

Dean and Linda went about their grief in different ways. He looked older, sterner, and he planted the trees until the last light, while we shrugged tiredly at one another behind his back and kept working too. Linda wasn't there. I didn't see her much in the early summer—she was "flitting around the valley," according to Dean. She and Lars hung out together a lot over at the Triple A. A week after tree planting at the Ortiviz, I bumped into her in Farisita at Abe and Ersie's, and we leaned against the bumper of our truck outside and drank a Coke.

"Guess what?" she giggled. When I raised my eyebrows as I sipped the Coke, she went on, "I made it with Lars last week!"

"Huh?" I said, as some Coke fizzed back up my nose. "But, he's not, he's . . ."

"Shh," Linda giggled, as a local rancher drove his pickup to the pumps and nodded at us, and Abe ambled out to give him some gas. She said in a low voice, "You know how Lars always had the hots for Coba?" I nodded. Coba is a dark, handsome piano player playing with the Triple A band this summer. Who didn't have the hots for Coba? Coba and his

Linda and Lars.

wife, a successful artist from the Bay Area, had rented the old one-room schoolhouse on Pass Creek Road for her studio. Coba was a great piano player, with heavy-lidded bedroom eyes. Now I was really interested. "One night," Linda went on, "after a gig outside of Trinidad, Lars and Coba and I slept in the back of Coba's station wagon, and you know how Coba has always flirted with me, and so we just had a threesome."

"*So you just had a threesome?* Well, I guess, where there's a will, there's a way, as my mother always says," I told her, and we both laughed so hard that the rancher turned around and looked at us curiously. Lars isn't about to go straight, but this was a triumph of love, of sorts.

Linda didn't come to the party on the upper land of the Ortiviz a month later. I don't think she'll ever go near the place where Lia drowned. Clark Dimond had put up the last of the money to pay for the upper land, and so the whole valley was celebrating, even though, by this time, the plan for a centralized farm in the Huerfano wasn't working that well. Dean was at the party, and by the end of the evening he was stumbling like a dancing bear around the circle of drummers, who beat their drums frantically and stared into the fire. Others fed the fire with big branches and logs, and it grew bigger as the flames leaped high up into the moonless night.

David drank a lot of wine too that night, and drummed for a long time, but when it got late, I just wanted to go home. Doug had left earlier with Steve's brother Monty. I couldn't catch David's eye—he was staring into the fire—and I figured that I was going to have to sit it out. I was so tired. We'd put up some beams for the roof deck on the next section of the house that day. The drummers were beating their drums maniacally, and a dark-haired woman named Bella, who was living in an Airstream trailer purchased for her by her wealthy parents, though she'd immediately torn out all the custom-built wood cabinets inside because they looked too "bourgeois," had taken her blouse off, as she usually does at parties. She grabbed Dean's hands, and they stumbled around the outside of the circle, knocking over a jug of wine here, listing against Mary Red Rocker and Eddy there, stepping on little Lori's foot and making her cry, moving around the circle and into the dark, where I gave up tracking their collisions. I walked over to the circle and touched David's shoulder. When he looked up, still drumming, he didn't seem to recognize me at first. He stood up reluctantly and stepped unsteadily out into the darkness.

"Do you think we could go?" I asked. "I'm beat."

"Sure, sure," he said. "Man, *that was incredible,* did you see that?" he asked, putting his hand to his head. "I really got *lost.* That reminded me of when Jung went to dances in the African bush, and he started dancing with that tribe all night and said he had to stop because he realized he was going to lose himself, remember?"

"Yeah, but he wasn't drunk, and neither were the natives!" I couldn't stop myself from pointing out. David frowned at me. "And who are the natives here, anyway?" I went on. "Strider, from the Southern California Biker Tribe?" I should try to control myself when I'm tired and cranky. I knew I was being a drag, but I couldn't stop.

"We're all na-tiffs here," David said, slurring his words a little.

August has slipped into September. It feels like fall now every morning, and the summer's clearly over. The Ortiviz Farm dream is over, too. No one's talking about valley-wide communal farming at Ortiviz next year. We walk by the dome and stop to visit with Dean and talk about his next big journey. Two of his friends drove up the road recently in their new, super-outfitted Land Rover, with gas cans for extra fuel bolted to its sides. The three of them are going to drive from here to the tip of South America later this fall. They spend their days taking equipment out of the Land Rover and repacking it, checking over their lists one more time, and going on buying trips for last-minute necessities in Pueblo or Denver. But this afternoon they're taking a break, sitting on the deck in the late summer sun. Linda's inside, working on the design for her Halloween costume early this year. She's going as a peyote button, and she's having trouble figuring out how to stuff her outfit so that she replicates the plump, tufted sections of the green peyote fruit.

"She's going as Button Huay-nay," Dean smiles. "Huay nay" are words used repeatedly in peyote songs. Now that he's going to put another continent between them, it's easier for them to be around each other.

"Who'll take care of all those trees we planted down at the Ortiviz when you go?" I ask.

Dean can pierce you with his sky-blue eyes. "Those trees are already dead," he says. I'd heard that the oats we planted in the Ortiviz fields this spring were choked out by weeds and stunted from lack of water, but I hadn't heard about Dean's trees. We haven't been down there for a while. There's too much to do on our house.

"I'm sorry," I say. "I wish we could have worked down there more. As it is, it's going to be hard to get the deck insulated and shingled, or just covered with tarpaper before the snows." I look at the trinity of apricot trees by Lia's grave. The dirt of her grave has relaxed more into the meadow with the summer rains. "Those trees look like they're going strong, anyway," I add.

"Yeah," says Dean. He stares at the trees. His shoulders are slightly more sloped. After a long pause he straightens and turns to David and says, "Hey, David, you were asking about the route, and we're just looking at the map, do you want to see?" As he points down at the map of the Americas, David asks Dean and his friends how long it will take, how long they will stay in different countries, where they think they will be when, how long their fuel will last, other masculine questions. They point to places on the maps and talk seriously and earnestly among themselves. Their voices get more excited as they pronounce names of cities and stops: Tehuantepec, Riobamba, Ayacucho, Laguna Blanca . . . A journey might be helpful. Just like Linda, Dean's doing the best he can, but he'll never get far enough away from this spot.

Looking at the crowd at the first Thanksgiving dinner in the Red Rockers' sixty-foot dome, I feel as if David and I are practically a Norman Rockwell holiday couple. Compared to most Huerfano duos, we're devoted to each other, but our romance has changed a little too. Not just that we're old marrieds, or that building a house is the most challenging, frustrating, and tiring thing either of us has ever done. My feelings for David are deeper but more suffused with my feelings about the house, Doug, the cats, the goats, Libre, the entire valley, and, above all, our vision. In Buffalo it felt sometimes as if it was us two against the world, but now we have grown roots that are entwined with others and tenacious.

In the year and a half we've been here, there's been a lot of bed-hopping among our comrades. There were those cataclysmic switches at the first Thanksgiving at Libre in 1969, between our first and second visits, even before we moved west—when Peter's wife, Judy, left Peter after he went off with Nancy at the Thanksgiving dinner, and Nancy's husband went back to Austin, and she moved in with Peter and stepped over a broom and got married to him. Linda left Dean that Thanksgiving and went off with Steve, who left Patricia. That's all over now, but none of these four can return to what they had before.

Once we settled here, the square dance continued ("Your partner swings!" instead of "Swing your part-ner!"), and there were more cast changes. At Libre, old Vesey and his first wife split up, although both she and an old girlfriend of Vesey's stayed with him and his new wife down at his tiny A-frame. Steve left Patricia several times. He's building a small house in the creek bed not far from the house he and Patricia built so he can be near

Nanda and Tawa. Two bachelors—Steve's brother Monty and a guy named Minnesota, a sandy-haired, kind, and quiet man from Patricia's home state—live with Patricia now, helping her with the house, kids, and two hundred chickens in her and Peter Rabbit's joint egg venture. Last spring, Sandy left Jim for Crosby, and now she's pregnant, living on a ranch straddling the Arizona-Mexico border. This fall, Dean left on his road trip to Patagonia, and Linda made love to Lars last summer in a threesome with Coba. Now Lars is in New York, getting ready for a trip to Africa. Most of the Triple A band has moved up to Denver for the winter. Back at Libre, Stephanie left Dallas for Benjo Red Rocker, and Stephanie and Benjo are Peyote Church converts now. They're expecting a baby in January, around the same time Mary Red Rocker and Bad Eddy are having their baby. Mary's soon to be ex-husband came back from a long trip to New Mexico with a woman I worked with in the New Buffalo kitchen two years ago—I can't remember whom she was with back then, maybe the father of her two kids. After Larry Red Rocker's wife had her baby, she left him and paired with Mumford, who'd moved over from the Ortiviz, and now she and her new man and Larry and his new woman, also from the Ortiviz, and the baby live at the Red Rocks. The summer before last, Winnie's and Larry's sister Vicki dumped the drummer she was hanging out with for our old friend Henry after he went over to the Red Rockers with our problem visitor, Crazy John. Vicki and Henry are an on-again off-again pair.

At Libre, Tony and Marilynn have been remarkably stable. They didn't partake in the orgy at the first Thanksgiving two years ago. Recently, however, Tony decided that he should be a monk. He walked to the waterfall at the back of Libre and had a long talk with the guy who'd purchased the neighboring piece of land, where he lived alone. It was a package deal. Tony shaved his head, got an orange robe, and built a retreat house on the neighbor's land and Marilynn moved in with the neighbor. Getting left for the path to enlightenment must be easier to take. Now, a legal aid lawyer working in Pueblo and his wife are considering moving into Tony and Marilynn's dome. Beth and Richard have been pretty stable, too, but last week I saw Beth talking to Dallas's brother Billy up by the goat house, and it looked like there was a little spark between them. I don't have a full grip on the latest switches or couplings at Archuletaville or the Triple A, where the lead guitarist and

Trixie, the bass player, have moved to Denver, and the guitarist's wife and kids remain in the valley.

Today, at this first valleywide Thanksgiving at the Red Rocks, it's hard to remember all the results of this low-grade fission, especially among the couples we don't see often. I watch who's standing with whom and who isn't talking to whom for cues, since we sometimes miss the recent gossip up on the ridge. So far, it doesn't seem as if any couple is holding up too well against free love, and fission wins over fusion every time. David's more curious about the experiments than I, maybe because he's a guy, or because he's always been more of a revolutionary thinker. I'm learning to share him now—not with somebody else but with the entire valley. At parties like this, the musicians get lots of attention. David's preoccupied and nervous before he performs. When we arrived, he went off with Henry to mess with the amplifiers and smoke everything offered to him, even though he and Henry won't play until after we eat. I have to accept David's preoccupation with his art. I'm gratified that I live with someone so many love to listen to, and my role as muse is flattering. At parties, though, I'm by myself a lot.

But I'm not alone amidst our new family. We swarm inside the big dome, where it's warm, loud, colorful, and full of cooking smells. I dump my coat on the pile of jackets and ponchos piled up behind the kitchen, checking first for infants—they're often put on top of coat piles at parties. I survey the crowd and see Mai Ting, a doctor from San Francisco who recently rode into the valley on horseback with her husband. She's standing near Tom Grow's parents from Arkansas. Mai has a lovely wide Chinese face and long straight black hair. Tom's dad, Chester, is a chiropractor who looks like a fat Gabby Hayes. He and his wife parked their camper by the Gardner dump this summer. While he worked on me outdoors on his leather table in August, the dump's squad of vultures circled overhead. Janie and Danny Lencz from the Shamrock station are talking with Mai and Chester. As usual, Danny looks three sheets to the wind, while Janie holds the zucchini relish she brought, and Walter the Lithuanian lurks behind her, watching her in his lovesick, middle European way. Tiny Mrs. Vargas, the midwife, and Mr. Vargas, a water witch, are here with their son, a cowboy. Johnny Bucci talks to Mary Red Rocker. The weathered old rancher Dan Archuleta is already in his party pose, bent over the beer keg as if he were trying to touch his toes, hands dangling.

Dan Archuleta in the Red Rocker dome, Thanksgiving 1971.

I jam my goat cheese and corn bread into a small space on one of the serving tables, then hug Bill Keidel, our stout ridge neighbor. He has his own huge beer stein—no paper cups for Bill! I hug Nancy, avoid Peter, get some homemade peach wine in a plastic cup, and sit on an overstuffed chair with the lovely dark-haired Marilynn and the lovely redheaded Linda. Only one blond, one redhead, and one brunette per chair, we joke. We try to talk, but *Beggars Banquet* is playing too loud. Linda shows me a postcard from Dean and allows that she might join him in Ecuador this winter. Johnny Bucci brushes past us, grins, and tips his beat-up hat. In the big sleeping loft upstairs, a pack of kids bounces from bed to bed raucously.

"There must be more than a hundred of us 'gathering together,'" I yell. Marilynn and Linda nod affably in the din. Comfortable chairs are scarce, so one of us stays in the chair whenever the other two make wine and hors d'oeuvres forays. We sit close together, leaning back against each other, laughing as life goes by. David passes, bends down, and kisses me absentmindedly. Henry stops and kisses each of us. Then they confer worriedly—there's a problem, a mike cord's missing.

Someone pulls the needle off the Ray Charles record with a loud scratch, and Mary and five other Red Rockers stand on the natural stage made by the steps to the sleeping loft and sing:

Going to the chapel, and we're
Gonna get ma-a-a-ried
Goin' to the Chapel of Love.

With her pregnant belly and long legs, Mary looks like a melting ice pop. Shoulder to shoulder, the Red Rocker sextet swings back and forth, and as they sing, Bill Keidel's brother Jimmy and his bride, Marsha, strut down the stairs. Jimmy and Marsha are building at the Triple A. She's tall, eight months pregnant, and wears a pink minidress that's more mini in front due to her big belly. Marsha holds a bouquet of dried wildflowers, and what looks like a scrap of lace curtain is pinned to her head. She has a slight overbite, and grins and laughs. All of us join in exuberantly:

"Goin' to the Chapel of Love . . ."

When they step onto the kitchen platform, Adrienne appears in a clean tuxedo shirt, bowtie, her usual suspenders, and clean black jeans. Standing next to the tall bride and groom, she looks like a Hobbit. Adrienne puts people together as well as engines—besides being the Triple A ace mechanic, she's also a Universal Life Church minister. She holds an R. Crumb comic book open in her hands decorously, and in deference to the occasion, she's not smoking. She waits for us to quiet down before she twists around to face the bride and groom.

"So, you guys wanna get married, izzat right?" she asks.

Jimmy and Marsha nod enthusiastically.

"Okay. Jimmy, do you wanna marry Marsha?"

"Yes!" says Jimmy, turning red.

"And Marsha. You wanna marry him?"

Marsha nods shyly, whispering, "Yes."

"Well, okay then. By the powers vested in me by the Universal Life Church, I hereby pernounce you man and wife. Congratulations!" Jimmy and Marsha grin at Adrienne. "Okay, *it's over,*" she says. "Kiss if you wanna!"

They embrace lustily, and we applaud. Adrienne lights up a cigarette immediately. Bill pops some champagne, and the crowd presses toward him, cheering. All things considered, this ceremony's more palatable than the Episcopal ceremony I grew up with, and better than the New Age rites David and I witnessed in the summer of 1969. Under the aspens at the June solstice celebration on Santa Fe Baldy after our first Libre visit, forty people were married that day in a ceremony conducted by Yogi Bhajan, a tall Sikh with a white turban and a curly black beard. He'd been a young East Indian postal worker in San Francisco who came across some stoned hippies in Golden Gate Park. They realized at once that he was their guru, and he took the idea and ran with it. At the solstice he had white robes and an entourage instead of his regulation Post Office shorts. The couples were ecstatic, sobbing and trembling with joy, all in white, and the big white-robed yogi towered above them and smiled beatifically, his arms open in a Christlike gesture. I couldn't hear what he was saying and looked away. David didn't believe in marriage at that point (too bourgeois), and even though I did, I didn't want to be part of this ceremony either. From the looks in the couples' adoring faces, it seemed as if they were getting married to the yogi as much as to each other. But they were part of something, swept away, and I wondered how that felt. How many of them, I wonder now, are still married? How many brides have slept with their yogi since a ceremony like that?

Have I always been so cynical? It's hard to remember who I was in 1969. Since then, we've designed our own wedding and our home in the West. We've lived in a tipi till December, mixed a hundred yards of cement, sawed and stripped logs, dug holes, hauled hundreds of gallons of water. I've baked bread in a woodstove and taught reading, worked on Bill Keidel's crew roofing a vacation cabin, milked goats and made cheeses. David's written a dozen songs and formed a band. We've memorized sunsets and hitchhiked to Florida and back. We applied for food stamps and slept outside to watch meteor showers spraying the August skies. This summer I saw a woman who was passing through Libre give birth. For better or worse, we've settled in.

Marilynn pokes me from my reverie, offering champagne. Linda's smiling at someone across the dome, I can't tell who. I prefer a Marx Brothers wedding to mass delusion and a diluted Eastern rite. It's warm in the big dome from bodies, cookstoves, and space heaters, all stoked to capacity. The bride's flushed, her hand resting lightly on her swollen belly, and the groom drinks straight from a champagne bottle. Bill Keidel pops another one. With another scratch, "All You Need Is Love" starts up. In the swirling dramas and our veneration of honest passion, just how and where does permanence fit in?

27 : Consciousness Raising

It's April Fool's Day, but this foolishness isn't funny.

By winter we'd walled in the bottom half of the house. One temporary wall had moved west around the rock like the hand of a clock to mark the passage of 1971, while the other temporary wall stayed put. We framed and shelled the small octagonal room on top, and built the deck above the half of the house that's finished. We could have moved our bedroom upstairs last fall if the Indian summer had lasted a few more weeks. Instead, we didn't move our bed up there till last week. The roof of the top room isn't insulated yet, and we don't have any insulation under the half that's above the unfinished part of the house. As soon as we moved upstairs, the weather turned, and there were some late spring snows. The wind whipped over the snowy ridges and under the floor of the upper bedroom. My parents' old oriental rug kept some of the cold out, but it's just a rug. Doug built a little tower at the tipi site last fall—a two-storied, ten-by-ten frame building. He roofed and insulated it and slept there most of the winter. Frame buildings go up so quickly.

It's been cold sometimes up in the bedroom—but the view, always the view! We can sit up in bed and see the whole mountain range rimming Earth on the other side of the Huerfano. The mountains sparkle with late spring snow. The physical discomfort is offset by the psychic charge of living in a space we conceived and built ourselves with our own hands. We've read about Jung building his tower-like round house on Lake Zürich and his spiritual development there. He was right. We're more complete now, more rooted, more whole.

We continue to underestimate the time it will take to do a job, and the detail work always slows us down. Over the past year we had to choose between making the existing living space more livable or enlarging it. We put in the tongue-and-groove oak floors in the kitchen and dining areas with wood we salvaged from the dance hall. It was hard working with the old boards, which were twisted and warped, or would split just as we hammered the last nail in, so we'd have to tear the splintered board out and start over. As we stacked up the railroad ties for the dining area walls, we decided to add another loft in this section too. The walls are thirteen feet high in this downhill area because of the steep slope of the ridge—high enough so we could put planks for another triangular loft between the ties about eight feet up. Heat rises, and the two lofts were comfortable to work or read in during winter, although we couldn't stand up in either of them. On the two dining room walls we built bancos under the windows where a kidney-shaped table I designed will go. It took a great deal more time than we estimated to build and install the Dutch door in the fourth wall, but we wanted a door that would let air in and keep goats out. When winter finally set in, it took lots of time to haul and chop wood to heat our enlarged and not fully insulated space. We had to haul water or melt snow, get provisions, cook, clean, take care of the goats—all the usual time-consuming daily chores. The business of mountain living took most of the daylight hours in the short winter days.

Things got derailed when I came down with a bad case of Asian flu in late January. One day David stoked the fires and left me with a thermos of tea to go down the ridge for an important band practice. Doug was back in Ohio visiting his mom. Even the cats deserted me in the loft to sit by the stoves. Then Steve came up to visit. He knocked on the kitchen door, didn't hear my faint answer, but stepped inside anyway. When I moaned quietly up in the loft, he climbed the ladder and sat cross-legged at the foot of the bed and asked what was wrong.

"Flu," I mumbled. "Bad flu, I guess." He didn't say he was sorry or ask about my symptoms—Steve doesn't spend much time on preliminaries. He cleared his throat to get my attention and put one big hand gently on my right foot. I opened my eyes a little and looked at him through the slits.

"You know, Roberta," he said gently but firmly, "sickness is really *only in your head*. It's your spirit making your body sick! It's as simple as that. Think about it, you'll see I'm right. *You need to meditate more.*" Steve spoke sincerely, his leonine head bobbing as he talked, and in my delirious state, his frizzled gold hair seemed like an extension of his brain waves.

So much energy made me faint. "I am meditating, Steve," I thought feverishly. "I'm meditating on getting enough strength to grab the flashlight and hit you upside the head, and then tell you that the pain is *only in your head.*" I was too weak to do anything like that, but I enjoyed my joke and laughed a little. He frowned, so I sobered up and nodded to him. He smiled, reassured I'd got the message. At least as he left he put some more wood in the stoves.

When I was better, I took up my brother's offer of a ticket east. It was a small betrayal, a retreat. I was weak from being sick, and I wanted to go back to my parents' centrally heated house and be comfortable. I wanted a break from the hard work of keeping our life going. I wanted to visit an old friend from Vassar at a commune in Vermont. I also planned on calling Jonsie in Vermont, and I suppose this was another sort of betrayal. Jonsie was a Vermont Yankee, a gentleman farmer who played the twelve-string guitar. He was an old friend of Dr. Frank's who passed through Libre this fall. There was a little spark between Jonsie and me, and I hitched a ride with him down to New Mexico to see my friend Pam and her husband, Don. Jonsie and I got along really well on the trip, and he stayed for a couple of days at Pam and Don's. It was fun traveling, seeing old friends, being a guest and not the hostess. Oh, I suppose we kissed once or twice—nothing serious, it was just a little escape—but I was curious whether that spark between Jonsie and me would flame up back east, although I didn't really put it in so many words.

Of course, as soon as Jonsie learned that I was in his neck of the woods and wanted to see him, he backed off big-time. I was less attracted to him, too, and I don't know what I would have done if he'd been more interested. Maybe I secretly wanted to be whisked out of my hard pioneer life and set up at his Revolutionary War–era Vermont farm, which had electricity and running hot and cold water, and was quaint and rustic only up to a point. Anyway, nothing happened. It seemed Jonsie was more attracted to me when I belonged to someone else in the West. In Vermont, he may have been worried I'd stay.

Here's the thing: David never objected to my jaunt to New Mexico with Jonsie last fall. He never asked whether I was going to see Jonsie when I left. He was too proud to say anything, but I knew he was upset. Would it have been better for him to tell me he minded? I have to remind myself of my betrayals so as not to lose perspective on the situation

I found when I returned. David welcomed me with open arms and was genuinely happy to see me, but I sensed something was up. Two days after I got back, he finished the dishes, rolled himself a cigarette, and said casually, "Well, I guess I should tell you before someone else does . . . I had an affair with Patricia while you were gone." He tried to sound laid back, but he didn't quite pull it off.

"Oh," I said. There was a hole in my stomach. The center of me had disappeared in an instant. "Humh," I said, placing one hand where my stomach had been.

"It doesn't mean I love you less, you know," David said. "We're capable of loving people in different ways at different times, and we shouldn't repress these feelings. Patricia's a single mom with two young children, and she's had a hard time with Steve. We have to overcome possessiveness and jealousy so that we can explore all the possibilities. If we love each other, we'll give each other this freedom."

"Oh," I said again. I couldn't tell if what had happened was a reaction to my flirtation with Jonsie, or whether David was saying this to persuade me to stay with him even though I might be attracted to others. I lacked perspective. He reminded me of Steve talking about how to get over a fever. I jerked into action and started straightening up the books and magazines on the banco. "So," I said, slapping the magazines into stacks, "you slept with her because you felt sorry for her? It was *charity?*"

It's easier to be sarcastic than to talk about pain. I was in a double bind. David's opinion of me would change if I acted angry, possessive, and jealous. I wanted to be the ideal he envisioned, and to act the way he thought people should act. Jung wrote that men are naturally polygamous. There were a lot of people in the Huerfano who shared David's vision. Mostly they were people who wanted to make love to someone else instead of or in addition to their partner. I couldn't stop being hurt and angry, though, and whenever I got low, I suspected he was putting something over on me. I tried to take the middle road, and focused on the fact that he hadn't told me about Patricia as soon as I got back. I was humiliated that everyone at Libre had known and for two days I didn't. I focused on his dishonesty. It was still bad to be dishonest, so I could be legitimately upset about that. I admit, considering what happened—or what could have happened—with Jonsie, I was being unfair. But fairness has nothing to do with blame. Besides, I felt it was much more thoughtful of me to have a dalliance with a stranger, not someone we saw every day at Libre.

We yelled. I cried. He stormed out. I stormed out. We didn't speak to each other. We talked calmly and then started arguing again. David said he wasn't going to continue his relationship with Patricia. That wasn't enough for me. We didn't touch some nights in bed. It went on for a week or two like this, until my old friend Pam in New Mexico came to the rescue and offered to pay for our tickets to Martinique from Miami so we could meet her and Don there.

We packed and hitched to Florida again. You can escape for a while. Martinique was hot, French, and tropical. We toured the island and ate big French meals with our old friends. In the pool of a big guest house outside Marigot, we swam and laughed. Other guests, three slightly older couples from Australia, were getting drunk by the pool. One woman, plump and deeply tanned, looked at David and me and asked us how long we'd been married.

"Two years," I said, my arms around David's neck because it was too deep for me to stand in that part of the pool.

"Hmm," she said. "The honeymoon isn't over yet!" I wanted to tell her it was.

Now we're back at Libre, with the geese flying north, the crocuses poking up through the old snow on the north side of the ridge, and the women's movement taking root. Annie, a Texas friend visiting Nancy Rabbit, hit it off with our neighbor Bill Keidel and moved in with him on the ridge while we were away. All the women at Libre are having a women's meeting at Annie and Bill's house this weekend. We pass around *The Female Eunuch* and *The Second Sex*. Linda borrowed copies of *The Feminine Mystique* and *Diary of a Prom Queen* from the Red Rockers. My anger's got a more acceptable venue now. The problem's not David and me—it's our society and culture, and the revolution's in our homes. Sisterhood is powerful.

This afternoon, when I walk back to the house, David sits on a pile of two-by-fours by the road and looks a little whipped. I almost feel sorry for him, but mostly I'm still mad.

"Hi," I say. "I've got to get some more clothes. How're the goats doing?"

"Fine," he says, watching me out of the corner of his eye, as if I might pounce. "Looks like they're going to pop, especially Trinity. She may have triplets. How's the meeting?"

"Fine. Oh, yeah, last night Beth mentioned you two had a little flirtation last year."

"Oh yeah?" David says, sounding uninterested, and not successfully hiding his exasperation at the way things are going. Maybe he's disappointed in Beth, too, but she volunteered that information to help me remember that David wasn't Patricia's victim, and that seduction is a two-way street. I go inside, grab a sweater from the trunk upstairs, take a pack of tortillas from the shelf in the kitchen, and then head back to Bill Keidel's. David's still sitting on the two-by-fours, staring out at the valley. Doug's over at the tower. Since he got back, he's been staying out of our way.

"Have you seen that hand mirror?" I ask.

"No," he says. Then he grins a little. "What for, are you putting on makeup?"

"Actually, we're going to look at our vaginas. Men see their sexual organs all the time, and it's, well, empowering for women to see theirs," I say awkwardly, feeling as if I'm parroting the words from *Our Bodies, Ourselves,* a book the Berkeley Women's Health Collective sent to our doctor, Mai Ting.

"Hmm," he says, grinning a little. "Sounds like fun!"

"See you later," I call. I'm not going to laugh, and I don't feel like kissing him.

"Yeah, later," he calls back.

By the time we got back from Martinique, David and Patricia were definitely over. I wasn't seriously threatened. I never thought David would leave me, but that didn't stop the pain. I haven't felt warm and fuzzy toward Patricia since, but she wants to discuss everything at the women's meeting. What David said, the dinner party they had, the story he told her about Harton at the Mardi Gras at Yale. I don't want to know the details, and I mind that he shared the stories of our friends and past along with his body. I believe some things are better left unsaid, but Patricia's not of that school.

"Listen, I really understand, I know just how you feel, I felt like that when Steve was with Linda, and I know what you're going through," she says to me as her baby, Tawa, grabs her tit. I think Steve was crazy in love with Linda and might have left Patricia if Linda hadn't vacillated, and he eventually left Patricia anyway. I'm mad she equates what I view as David's dalliance with Steve's passion. Maybe I mind that she has a baby and I don't. I can't say for sure why I think these cruel thoughts. She's got two little kids and has been making a go of it pretty much alone since Tawa was born. Monty and Minnesota help out, but she doesn't have a

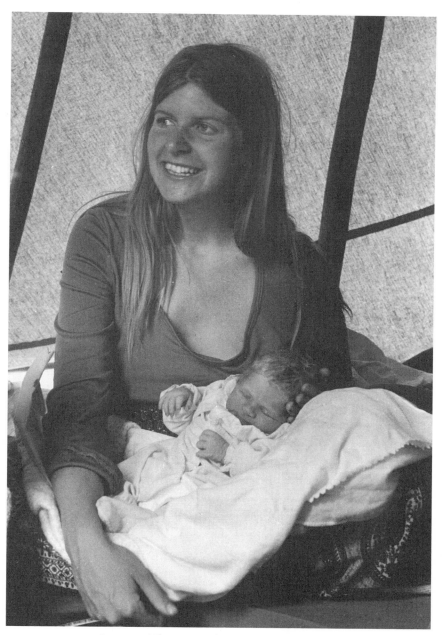

Patricia and Tawa the day Tawa was born, August 1970.

mate, and her kids don't have a father around all the time. I grit my teeth and nod as Patricia explains more. Her cheeks are red. Reliving her time with David and sharing it with me and everyone else excites her. The other women seem a little tired of listening to both of us.

I tell myself that the fact that she's been in love with Steve for years should make me sympathetic. I think of Steve patting my foot and telling me so surely that my sickness was the result of wrong thinking. Vicki and Mary Red Rocker are here tonight, so there are new things to talk about besides Patricia's blow-by-blow account of her affair with David. They've already had a women's meeting at the Red Rocks, but Mary doesn't like to miss an opportunity to mix things up some more. The Red Rockers are more on the cutting edge, as usual. The men had a men's meeting, and they paired off and slept together, although they all kept their underpants on. I try to imagine Peter sleeping in the same bed as Bill Keidel and laugh out loud.

"You see," Mary says, "we're the proletariat, and the wealth is our bodies, which we don't control in our society. *We must seize control of our bodies from the male ruling class.*" Compared to what I hear about Steve and our old friend Henry, David doesn't seem that bad. Vicki tells how Henry pulled her IUD out because he wanted to have a baby and she couldn't make up her mind. She's going to have the baby in September. We sit on our sleeping bags as she talks, exclaiming, "That fucker!" She says Henry is opposed to washing dishes with commercial dish liquids and insisted that she wash the dishes in the stream with sand. We can't believe how crazy that is, or how crazy Vicki is to go along. She and Henry moved out of the dome last year to live in a tipi up the canyon from the dome. I remember something about Dr. Mai chasing Henry around the dome with a butcher knife, and I think that had to do with washing dishes, or not washing dishes, too.

After Mary's talk, I rise to the occasion. I'm sick of being the reactionary. I tell them that Mary McCarthy wrote in her journals she'd slept with three different men in twenty-four hours and didn't feel promiscuous. Of course, she wasn't married then, so it was probably less complicated, I point out to my sisters. I describe the scene when Robinson Jeffers and his wife came to Taos to visit Frieda Lawrence after D. H. Lawence died. When Jeffers's wife saw that Jeffers was attracted to a Swedish friend of Frieda's, she tried to shoot herself but didn't succeed—either she didn't really want to, or else she didn't have a good aim. Frieda nursed her back to health. "At least we're a little less dramatic here," I say, looking around and laughing drily.

There's no question about it. Despite my discomfort at Patricia's eager description of her every interaction with David, this meeting has been good for the women here. Things are going to change. I've already told David and Doug that we need to share equally in the cooking, dishwashing, laundry, housekeeping, goat chores. They looked down and then across the table at each other and agreed. What else could they do? I have to chop as much wood as they do, but it's spring, and we don't need that much wood, and by next winter I'll have the hang of it. Doug showed me how to split logs with a wedge and a maul last week, and it's actually kind of fun. I'm already pretty good at it. Last week when I paid our bill in full for the goat feed at Sig Sporleder's, I asked him if women who paid their bills also got a shot of the tequila he kept in his desk drawer for such occasions. Sig raised his bushy gray brows and shrugged, then took out the José Cuervo. I didn't really want a shot of tequila in the middle of my shopping day, but I needed to educate Sig about women's rights. At the Central Bar later, I called Ms. magazine and offered to write a piece about women on the communes. The editors seemed interested.

There's a perpetual knot in my stomach, more than an ache in my heart. I see now how Jonsie's and my interaction was a product of the sexism we've grown up with. Jonsie was interested in a woman possessed by another man. I see that my desire for him to rescue me is also a product of that same sexism. And my resentment at David for not getting the house finished quicker is due to the same thing. No doubt about it, I understand more now. I know that when your mate sleeps with someone else, you're in a force field with her whether you like it or not. I know that love is never free, and that it's so much easier to understand and forgive your own transgressions. I'm disgusted with myself for being secretly ready to escape into someone else's arms when things got tough. Being with strong women here over the weekend has been good. We've been stuck in our individual homes too much. Sisterhood is powerful—we can't forget that. We've agreed to meet once a week or so, to keep on track.

When I get back to Bill Keidel's, Nancy hugs me. Annie, our new hostess, moves around Bill's kitchen like she's been there forever. She's petite, with bushy eyebrows, generous lips and tits, and hairy legs. Bill's at the Triple A, visiting his brother Jimmy, Marsha, and his new baby niece while we have the women's meeting.

"Shall we make the quesadillas now?" Nancy asks the group, her arm still around me.

"Yeah," smiles Patricia, looking up from a game of hearts with Mary, Vicki, and Marilynn on a jumble of sleeping bags. "Want some help?"

Nancy looks at me and smiles, and I nod. "Sure," Nancy says, "you can grate the cheese while we chop the onions and tomatoes." Patricia jumps up. I grab the block of longhorn cheese from Bill's propane refrigerator and hand it to her, and she smiles at me happily.

28 : Easter

April 8, 1972

Halfway across the world, Vietnamization is almost complete. Most U.S. troops have been withdrawn, and the intelligence structure has been dismantled. The communist Easter offensive began last week. In Paris, Kissinger's hinting that the U.S. might respond by nuking Hanoi, but the breaking Huerfano news is that Trinity just had triplets, two does and a buck, and something's not right. I found them in a motionless pile in the corner of the goat house this morning when I came up to milk Johanna and Little Egypt. Trinity stared at me blankly and hovered as I poked them with my finger. They're dark like her, but their tiny noses are pink, their lashes white. Usually newborn kids pop up and wobble around immediately. An hour later, they're bopping around like crazy. These kids are motionless, eyes shut. Their pulse is faint, and their breathing's imperceptible.

The knot in my stomach's getting bigger. I'd like to cry, but my eyes are dry. I sit by them for a while, then get up to milk and feed Johanna and Little Egypt, give their kids some milk, and go back to the house with the rest of the milk to make yogurt. As I heat the milk on the stove, I flip through the *Goat Husbandry* pamphlet from the Colorado Agricultural Extension Service, which isn't helpful. David's out early chopping wood. It's his day, and we're almost out. I hear the *thwunk* of the maul hitting the wedge, splitting the big piñon logs. Doug's still asleep at the tower. I don't feel like breakfast. They're so new and soft when they're born . . .

I'm afraid to go up again. It's bitter cold today—the warm spell last week was just a ruse. I put another log in the cookstove. I should tell Beth and Richard, and I hope Aaron and Aricia aren't around when I do. Then a truck engine strains up the ridge, getting louder as it approaches. I look out and see Johnny Bucci's Ford, newer than a hippie vehicle but older and more beat up than the Faris Ranch or rich Texans' trucks. Johnny slams his door, turns around, puts his hands on his lower back, and stretches, taking in the view.

When I go up to greet him, he says, "Hey, Rowberta! Color TV! Mighty purdy up here, ain't it? But it turned cold today, didn't it?" He gives his crooked-toothed grin, touching his hat.

"Hi, Johnny," I answer. "It's really cold. You picked a great day to come up the ridge for the first time. It is your first time, right?"

"First time up on the ridge since you guys been here, yes, I guess that's right . . ." Then he looks in my eyes and asks, "What's the matter with you? What's wrong?"

"Sorry, Johnny," I wipe my eyes with the sleeve of my long underwear top. "Our goat Trinity had kids early this morning, but they're not moving, and I don't think they'll make it."

"Goats? Hmm, aw gee," says Johnny, rubbing his chin stubble. "Let's go look at them." He checks them out and looks up quizzically at the remnant of the Doors at the Avalon Ballroom poster David nailed on the goat house wall when we finished it. David put the poster high up, and we don't know how the goats managed to tear it down and eat most of it the first night unless they stood on each other's shoulders. We're sure the old battle-ax Johanna was the ringleader, though.

"Well," Johnny says slowly, "I think you should put them in your oven."

"What? What do you mean?" I ask.

"That's what my daddy always did with newborn lambs like this, and that's what I've done too. They need to get warmed up a bit."

"*In* the oven? You're saying put them *inside the oven* and shut the door?" I ask.

"Yessiree, that's what I'd do if I were you. Warm 'em up. Worth a try," he says, coaxing me a little and looking down at the three lifeless kids.

I say, "Well, okay . . ." doubtfully. Johnny picks up two gently, and I get the other one, and we walk carefully down the path to the house. Trinity doesn't seem to mind that we're taking them. David's inside, stacking wood by the potbelly. He looks up and says, "Hey! What a surprise, man. Johnny, how's it going? What brings you to the ridge?"

"Oh, nothin' perticular. I was jist out and about 'n' always wanted to stop by," he says.

Johnny Bucci.

David notices the limp kids in our arms. "What's up with Trinity's kids?" he asks.

"They're not opening their eyes or anything. Johnny says we need to heat them in the oven."

"No kidding," David says, pouring Johnny a cup of coffee.

We line a shallow wood box with old towels and tuck the kids inside. Johnny checks his watch and says, "Gosh, look at the time! I gotta go take Alta May to Walsenburg!" and chugs his coffee. He says, "Don't worry!" and winks. We hear his truck turn around and head slowly down the ridge. Kachina and her near-grown kitten, Fritz, appear out of nowhere, the way cats do, and smell the box of goats as if it were full of Limburger cheese. Kachina looks at me in disgust.

"So, are you going to do it?" David asks, as we stare at them.

"I don't know. I can't just put them in like a pot roast. The stove's been going awhile, and the oven's so hot. What if I just open the oven door and rest them on it?"

"What do you have to lose?" David asks. The box is pretty heavy for the open oven door, so David props a log under the door to protect the hinges. I add another log to the fire, check the milk to see if it's heated up enough to add the yogurt culture, find it's too hot, move it over to cool, and then sit down on a banco. David hugs me and sighs, then leaves to split more wood. I get William Blake down and try to stop thinking about them. "Little Lamb" is the obvious choice: *"Little Lamb who made thee / Dost thou know who made thee / Gave thee life and bid thee feed / By the stream and o'er the mead . . . ,"* I read to the baby goats, feeling stupid. The cats prick up their ears, then realize there's nothing in it for them, and go back to licking each other under the rock. The fire crackles in the cookstove, and I wonder if Johnny knows what he's talking about. Maybe I'm cooking them. I smell warm, or maybe singed, goat hair. I flip through Blake and try for something more attention grabbing. I stare at the Laocoön engraving and read, *"The Whole Business of Man is The Arts & All Things Common / Christianity is Art & not Money / Money is its Curse . . ."* Blake, a spiritual forefather. No one understood his visions, and he died lonely and crazed. He'd have been less lonely with us. He'd enjoy Jim's paintings, which look like they were painted by Blake on acid, with his left hand. *"A Poet a Painter a Musician an Architect: the Man / Or Woman who is not one of these is not a Christian / You must leave Fathers & Mothers & Houses & Lands / If they stand in the way of ART . . ."* It's hopeless. I stare at the rock. Should we bury them? Put them in the compost? Peter'd probably like to feed them to his two pigs. *Thwunk, thwunk,* goes David's ax. Then Kachina shoots past my legs, and there's a staccato tap on the kitchen floor. One kid's jumped out of the box and stands in the kitchen, his legs splayed out from his body like a broken tripod. One sister struggles to stand up in the box, stepping on the head of the other, who looks dazed, like a drunk beaned by a cop.

I run to the front door and shout, "David, David, they're alive!" He's walking up the path with an armful of wood, and Doug's behind him, looking sleepy. Back inside, all three kids are standing on the kitchen floor, staring around at their new world. They get more and more chipper, and one actually *baas* softly. We each pick one up and take them to the goat pen. My kid's heart beats wildly as I hold it against my chest. We expect Trinity to act like Lassie and rejoice at their reunion, but she stares at us indignantly when we try to stick them near her. We follow her around the goat pen trying to get them to nurse. Eventually, one gets the idea and tries to suck, but Trinity kicks at it, catching Doug in the arm. She runs around the alfalfa feeder and takes a big bite of hay, looking back at us resentfully.

"Maybe she's the one who ate the copy of *The Female Eunuch,*" Doug says, rubbing his arm. David guffaws until I frown at him. Johanna and Little Egypt eat as fast as they can and stare at us quizzically. Their older kids nibble a little alfalfa, dropping more than they chew.

"I guess we have to feed them by hand," I say, holding the kid Trinity tried to kick.

"Huh," says David. "Maybe we should just leave them alone with her for a while." He doesn't like the idea of extra goat hassles, and he's still mad about his vintage Doors poster, but I know he's glad they're alive.

"I bet she knows they're hers, but she figures she can get out of a whole lot of work by putting this over on us," says Doug, rubbing his arm. Trinity looks at him indignantly, as if he's talking nonsense. Goats are experts at credible deniability. I run down to the house and bring up some warmed milk, stick my fingers in it, and shove them at the kids' mouths. In a few minutes they're sucking my fingers till they hurt.

"We'll get some old baby bottles from Patricia or somebody," I say. Just then Beth and Richard walk up, and Beth says Aricia has some toy baby bottles and goes back to get them.

Richard stares down at the triplets, thoughtfully smoking his first cigarette of the day. "Wonder why Johnny came up the ridge," he says. "He's never been up here before, has he?"

"Just a lucky coincidence, I guess. Ol' Johnny-on-the-spot," I say. "I'll have to stop by his house and thank him. He saved the day." The kids cavort, resurrected, so glad to be alive, even if they're practically orphaned. The knot in my stomach loosens a little.

29 : Brotherly Love

Dallas's bare feet look Gothic and delicate sticking out from under my brother's rental car in the Libre parking lot. They look like Christ's feet in a van der Weyden altarpiece, but not as pale. My brother Jimmy paces at the rear of the car, carefully stepping over Dallas's feet, and Jimmy's companion, Penny, looks at them bemusedly. She's not as worried as Jimmy about being marooned here. Maybe she's studied van der Weyden. She's from California and is quite beautiful. Dallas's feet flip over like pancakes, and he crawls out from under the car, stands, and slowly and carefully brushes grass and dirt off his coveralls.

"Well?" says my brother, trying not to sound impatient.

"Well . . . ," says Dallas slowly, picking some small twigs out of his hair and beard, "I think you must have zigged when you should have zagged on that rocky spot just below the Hudson turn, or something like that, and you've got a hole in your gas tank."

My big brother doesn't panic, he's in control. He planned to visit me for part of the weekend, and he and Penny drove down from the Broadmoor in Colorado Springs this morning. They can stick it out here for one night. Before his *Rebel Without a Cause* period in high school, Jimmy was an Eagle Scout. He had some Merrill Lynch business in Denver this summer, and he decided to add a family visit. Getting stuck on a hippie commune isn't acceptable. He hasn't taken the suitcases out of the trunk yet. I don't look at David because I don't want to giggle at Jimmy's predicament, like a bratty younger sister.

"So, what should we do?" Jimmy asks Dallas.

"Oh . . . it's not a problem, nothing a little bubble gum won't fix," grins Dallas.

"Bubble gum?" asks Penny. She has a soft, melodic voice, like you'd expect.

Dallas grins at her, showing his attractive dimples, and explains, "We just chew up a big wad of bubble gum so that it's nice and flexible, and then we stick it over the hole and let it dry there. Bubble gum and baling wire are the most useful automobile repair tools in these parts."

My brother frowns. Since Jim, Libre's only other mechanic, is at the Triple A working on Dr. Gonzo, a big hippie school bus, with Adrienne, Dallas is the only available authority. Dallas's plan is risky but plausible. Jimmy's dressed for the commune in ironed jeans, ironed polo shirt, and sneakers. He smells of aftershave and talcum powder. He stands between David and Dallas, who look like runners up in the Charles Manson lookalike contest. Penny's tight denim bell-bottoms hang low on her slim hips, and she's wearing a clean Grateful Dead T-shirt that almost hides her delightful breasts. Her wavy strawberry blond hair is pulled back in a soft pony tail, and her complexion is flawless. She has no makeup on and doesn't need any.

"Well, okay, I'd very much appreciate it if you could do that," Jimmy says decisively, as if he's talking to the garage attendant at his apartment in New York. He's used to being decisive.

"I'd be glad to," drawls Dallas, still staring at Penny with a goofy grin, as if she's the one talking to him. Penny smiles back, showing her small, perfect white teeth.

On the way up the ridge, we don't stop by Patricia's. Must I introduce my brother to the woman who slept with my husband, just to show how evolved I am? Instead, we stop at Peter's zome to visit with the guy who shot our cat. I've got to learn to forgive in order to make it here. Peter offers us a joint like the bad boy he is, which rattles my brother, but Penny takes a toke expertly. On the bumpy ride up the ridge, when Jimmy is in the bed of the truck, she giggles and tells me that when she smokes joints in my brother's hotel rooms, he rolls up towels and pushes them up against the crack under the door to the hallway.

My brother's seven years older than I, and he missed the hippie thing entirely. Maybe he would have missed the hippie thing even if he were my age. Still, he's my brother. He was always a lot heavier and had the advantage in our fights, but he never let anybody else in the neighborhood mess with me. He talked my parents into sending me to private school instead of White Plains High. He's always been more like a third, hipper parent. Now, we've switched places. In high school, I was the good girl and got straight As, while he wasn't so good and got disappointing marks. Some of his friends were minor juvenile delinquents. Once the police stopped by to ask about them and missing hubcaps, and the principal called about cherry bombs in the high school toilets. Now he's the youngest vice president of Merrill Lynch, and I'm only slightly less of a problem to my family than Patty Hearst is to hers. We love each other, even though each of us has always suspected the other doesn't get it. I'm glad he's here, and I'm nervous, too. I want him to understand what we're doing. It's good Dr. Frank's also visiting us this weekend. He's almost a doctor, and graduated first in his class at the University of Chicago Medical School, even though he and a classmate smoked hash daily as a scientific experiment. Frank can't seem that flaky and may add credibility to what we're doing.

In the afternoon, David, Doug, Frank, and Jimmy drive over to the ridge at the back of the land overlooking the waterfall to set up our tipi there for retreats and peyote meetings. Doug's little tower is at the old tipi site, so we need to put the tipi somewhere else. I stay home to make dumplings to go with the chickens from Peter and Patricia's flock that we're having for dinner. Penny's walking around Libre. After I've cleaned up the kitchen, I go up on the deck to take a breather. Penny's meandering across Dean and Linda's meadow down below, a string of single men following her like ducklings. Dallas is first in line.

At dinner the guys are flushed from their adventure with the tipi. They got the whole thing up, although they were stumped over how to hook the smoke flaps over the tipi poles, until Jimmy kneeled down and told Frank to stand on his shoulders and they got it done. David plays the guitar after dinner, and Dallas, Peter, and Nancy stop by and visit. Nancy, who's been having an affair with Doug all spring, plays footsie with him under the table. Dallas ogles Penny. Jimmy doesn't notice. He's talking about the Easter offensive with Frank.

"You've got to admit," he says, "the North Vietnamese don't look so good invading as soon as we pull out." I stay out of it and clean the dishes. The next day, Sunday, Jimmy and Penny are going to the community dinner with us and then taking off. I'm glad they're seeing how Libre works. Peter brings a venison stew, and even though we never plan what we're going to bring ahead of time, it's one of those dinners where just enough people bring just the right dishes. After dinner, there's a short meeting.

"Can we get the flatbed running for a hay run?" Peter asks Jim and Dallas.

"I don't know," they say in unison. "You see," Dallas continues, "there's a problem. There are no working vehicles here now, and we've got to get someone with a truck big enough to tow it into Walsenburg and get the axle fixed." The True Truck would be perfect for towing the flatbed, except Dallas dismantled it. He's never explained why. It was running fine. I think he couldn't stand seeing it being run into the ground. Only he knows where all the parts are now.

"The Ortiviz truck could do it," suggests Peter.

"Yeah . . . ," say Dallas and Jim at the same time.

"Anybody asked them?" says Monty. Dallas and Jim look at each other.

"We need to get the first cutting of alfalfa at Badito before it rains, so we have to have a flatbed," says Peter. "We could borrow Dr. Gonzo from the Triple A, but I don't know if we could fit all those bales on a school bus."

"Hmm," say Dallas and Jim in unison. They've been working together too long.

"Okay, look," my brother stands up, like Field Marshal Montgomery. I look down.

"Whozzat?" Peggy Grow, who came late, whispers to Patricia.

"Roberta's big brother," whispers Patricia, and Jimmy waits until she stops and he has everyone's complete attention.

"We're leaving right after this dinner," Jimmy says. "We could drop somebody off at the, what is it, Ortovise, and you could borrow their truck and drive it back here and tow the flatbed into town tomorrow morning. How about that?" Jimmy looks around the circle.

Dallas and Jim look dumbfounded. They understood Jimmy, although he talks twice as fast as anyone here, except me when I'm excited. It's the rapid course of action that stuns them. The whole circle's silent. Finally, Jim looks at Dallas and says, "I don't know why not." Dallas nods. If one of us had suggested this, Dallas would have given a hundred Lao-tzu answers, but he's too polite, or doesn't have the nerve to try any on my brother. After dinner we walk to the parking lot, and I hug Jimmy. I hug Penny too. Dallas hops in the backseat of the rental car. My brother's happy that Dallas is along for part of the trip, in case Dallas has to chew some more bubble gum and crawl under the car to plug the hole in the gas tank. Dallas is happy to be with Penny awhile longer.

"Take care, Roberta. And call Mom!" my brother shouts out the car window. I watch him go with tears in my eyes, feeling like I'm at camp and visitors' weekend is over.

"Do you think he'll settle down with Penny?" David asks hopefully, his arm around me.

"Uhh-uh," I sniffle. "She's his hippie commune date." As always, Jimmy's arrived, confirmed his suspicion that everyone's less competent, taken charge, and moved on. Despite all experience, each time I hope it'll be different, that he'll stop, look around, then look me deep in the eyes, and say, "Oh, *now* I see!" This undimmed hope is one of the true mysteries of family.

30 : Woodstock Revisited

We've done a lot in our third summer. We poured the foundation for the fifth wall, adding another eighth to the house on the west, and we finished the insulated deck over this new section. The enclosed part of the house has turned the corner and moved uphill around the rock. Because of the twelve-foot difference in floor levels between the downhill part and the unfinished back, this transitional section has two stories. On the lower level, even with the dining area, is a root cellar—pantry which we dug about six feet into the side of the ridge. A big rock sticks up through the dirt floor in back—it was too hard to take out. The propane refrigerator's in front, and the back has shelves for canning jars, boxes of root vegetables packed in straw, and our cheesecloth-wrapped Parmesans, which must age in a cool place four to six months. We put in big tins of grains and flour, and hung a heavy tarp and blankets over the front. Sometimes David pulls the tarp aside and exits like Rudolph Valentino leaving his tent in *The Sheik,* except he carries a butternut squash instead of a scimitar.

The upper story of the new section, almost level with the unfinished back part of the house, has a two-by-six floor over the root cellar. A plywood worktable stands against the wall under a line of windows looking out at the Sangres. The old treadle Singer sewing machine is there too. Now I have a place to cut and sew the crazy cowboy shirts I've been making. Custom cowboy shirts are a cottage industry in the valley, supplying rock bands and urban cowboys with the right look. The shirts are made of satin, or have velvet yokes and sleeves and bodies in different patterns of calico, and are selling well in cities. I usually sew on my electric machine at Dean and Linda's dome, but sometimes I don't. After Linda came back from visiting Dean in South America, she had an affair with Dallas. Now Dean's back.

We built stairs up around the rock to get to the sewing loft. They end abruptly in the temporary wall, which adds a Magritte touch to the interior. Someday these stairs will take us into the back room.

David, Doug, and I worked on Bill's crew this summer. He got several jobs building vacation cabins for Texans, and the income helped, although working elsewhere slowed progress here. Paydays slowed us down, too. One Friday after a week when David and Doug worked while I was home with the goats, they didn't get back until late. Monty, Libre's bon vivant, bought a bottle of Wolfschmidt's vodka, and the crew practiced Cossack dances, squatting and kicking in the back of the truck all the way home. They didn't do much the next day. David and Henry's band, the Dog Brothers, has gotten some paying gigs, but David's share is usually only twenty dollars a gig or less, not a living wage yet. David's exhausted and can't work much after a gig either.

We still have time before the first snows, but the work on the back section is daunting. We have to shovel the dirt from behind the rock to make a level, hollowed-out living area and pick into the ridge to install the big black metal Heatolator fireplace form. There's no other option now but to dig two tons of dirt and rocks out by hand. A backhoe can't get under the roof beams already in place over our low back room. I doubt a backhoe could make it down to the site anyway. We can't use dynamite—it would wreck what we've built so far. Plus, no one can buy dynamite easily anymore, ever since they traced the explosives that blew up the Santa Barbara Bank of America and found they were purchased at Unfug's Hardware. We should have thought more about the excavation issue before we started the house, but that's Monday morning quarterbacking.

Working on the house has helped repair some of the damage caused by the Patricia/David/me/Jonsie constellation. Building the house is building our future together. We didn't resolve any philosophical conflicts about free love, we just gave up talking about it. Our peace is a bit uneasy, but it's still peace. Today we dug about four wheelbarrows of dirt and rocks and broke for lunch. Neither of us wants to go back, and Doug's over at the tower, building a permanent ladder to his second-floor bedroom. David sits at the table as I do dishes—it's my day. There's a knock, and Peter steps in.

"Hi there," Peter says.

David working on the root cellar.

Rock house sewing loft under construction.

"Hi," I answer in a neutral tone. I've graduated from ignoring him totally to acknowledging him minimally.

"Hey, Peter, how's it going, man?" David says.

"Great!" Peter heads straight for the joint David just lit and takes a toke. "I came to tell you guys that *Woodstock*'s at the Walsenburg Drive-In. Some people from the Red Rocks and Triple A are going tonight, and we're taking some cars in. Wanna come?"

"*Woodstock*—no kidding! We gotta go!" David says. Drive-in movies have closed in most big cities, but the Walsenburg Drive-In, east of town on Highway 160, is still hanging on, much like the drugstore with its marble-topped fountain and tables on Main Street. It's not so much time travel as time layering here. Last fall, at Huerfano Pharmacy, Dallas, Jim, and I sat at a marble-top table and had ice cream sodas after a long town day, checking over lists to see if we'd gotten everything everyone wanted. Dallas's and Jim's hair and beards fall past their shoulders these days, and my hair's almost to my waist. They were dressed in their usual outfits—Jim in the satin-patched bell-bottoms that Sandy made long ago, which are a bit torn and threadbare now, and his Mexican woven vest, and Dallas in his regulation coveralls. Both of them were covered with a veneer of 10W-40 from working on the truck engine when it stalled this morning on the way to town on Route 69. I was in the tie-dyed velvet vest lined with fox fur given to me by a Berkeley woman passing through who said she was renouncing all vanities. At the table next to us, five teenage girls in ponytails and sweater sets sat sipping their sodas and giggling. Through the windows we watched the Walsenburg High School Band march by. It was Homecoming Weekend. In front, five baton twirlers high-stepped in short skirts and white fringed boots. Inside the drugstore, where the band music was slightly muffled, as if it were traveling from another decade, Mr. Leskey carried trays of sodas and sundaes between the tables as he's done for thirty years. If he noticed anything different about our group, he didn't let on.

Tonight, the Walsenburg Drive-In is a similar mix of eras. There are teenagers in pickups or convertibles and families in trucks or sedans. Janie Lencz and Walter the Lithuanian are here in her turquoise Chevy wagon. At the cement block concession stand, Shirley from the Central Bar and her sister order Frito pies. Two salesmen from Unfug Hardware and their families are here. The Huerfano contingent met in the Safeway parking lot and left some cars there. To save money getting in, all of us piled into three vans and the Libre flatbed. The Red Rocker van was the first to go through the line at the ticket booth. The owner looked at the fifteen adults and three kids stuffed inside the van and made a face when Winnie said, "Family ticket, please!" but we all got family admissions anyway.

We parked in the back row. The sound from the old metal speaker hooked over the driver's-side window is bad, and everyone talks and yells to other cars. I'm in the front seat of the Libre flatbed between Jim and David, with a pretty good view, despite the cracked windshield and the dead bugs on it. What I notice most in the movie is how much water there is, how green the meadows are where the stage goes up, how the kids' faces are moist with perspiration in that Hudson Valley humidity, how soft and supple their bodies are, and how young. Nobody looks like he could hold up his end of a log for long. When Richie Havens performs, his orange dashiki is soaked, his face is wet, and a drop of sweat hangs on the tip of his nose as he bends over his guitar. In the Huerfano, your sweat evaporates almost immediately. *"Freedom, Freedom, Freedom,"* Richie sings in his unmistakable, slightly hoarse voice. He thumps and strums his guitar with staccato power. *"Sometimes I feel like a motherless child, A long way from home. . . ."*

David and I had tickets to Woodstock, but we didn't make it. In late July 1969 we both came down with hepatitis A and flew home from California before we visited any communes there. We contracted it in New Mexico on our commune research tour—poor hygiene in the kitchen of Reality Construction, where, we found out later, a number of people got sick. David and I watched Woodstock on the evening news as we recuperated in our separate family homes and talked excitedly on the phone at night. It was like the June Solstice Celebration on Santa Fe Baldy that we had gone to earlier that summer, but the crowds at Woodstock and those on Santa Fe Baldy were in roughly the same ratio as the population of New York City to that of Tesuque Pueblo. Wavy Gravy and the Hog Farm and their brightly painted buses, who were at the Solstice Celebration in New Mexico, were at Woodstock too. They were older and more knowing than the concertgoers, like kind upperclassmen at freshman orientation at the University of Consciousness, offering crash courses on Getting through Bad Trips and Instant Rural Communal Living.

I look through the back window at the faces of our Woodstock Nation. Everyone's sprawled on the truck bed on blankets and mattresses, laughing, smoking, joking, passing jug wine. Is it me, or is there an ironic edge to our take on Woodstock? Is it to protect tender hopes? Woodstock was three years ago, and it feels a little different now. Compared to the faces onscreen, the faces of those sprawled in the back of the flatbed are weathered and older. The kids onscreen are on a lark, a late summer weekend, but we've come here for a life. Patricia passes a bag of homemade popcorn dusted with brewer's yeast into the cab. Doug hands in a can of Coors for me and David to share and gives another to Jim. The beer's not cold, but it tastes good after the popcorn. By the time Sly and the Family Stone are playing, Bella's outside between the cars, dancing in the dust with tall, toothless Strider and two other women from the Ortiviz. Peter grabs Bella's wrist when she starts to take her blouse off and says something to her. She keeps her blouse on and goes on dancing as Sly jumps ecstatically across the screen, the long white fringes on his shirt whipping around him.

When Jimi Hendrix bends his beautiful young face over his guitar and plays "The Star-Spangled Banner," the notes reverberate through our nervous systems again, and we laugh at his sweet, cosmic joke. I've had some jug wine, some of Adrienne's whisky, some strong dope a Texan brought, and some more Coors. It's dawn in Woodstock on the third day, and it's almost midnight three years later during the dog days in the Huerfano, and when Jim leaves the cab to go to the men's room, I lean against David and say, "David, I want to finish the house next year, and then maybe have a kid, I want to move on." David turns slowly. He smiles and starts to say something and then looks at me more. His gaze deflects off mine and traces the edges of my face. Suddenly, Triple A Chip sticks his head in the cab and grins broadly. The little gold star inlaid in Chip's left front tooth glints.

"Ladies and gentlemen," Chip says through his cupped hands, mimicking the Woodstock stage announcements, "you can do what you want, it's your trip, but some people are saying the orange Frito pies are bad, so stay away from them, only the *orange* Frito pies, now, stay away, or only eat half . . ." David hoots, and Chip grins at me, flashing his gold star some more, and I laugh with them. Jim comes back and unhitches the speaker from the window and hangs it on the post, gets in the flatbed, and starts it up. Nancy Rabbit squeezes in the cab for the short drive to the Safeway and the other cars.

I don't know what she's taken tonight. She asks excitedly, "Did you hear Richie Havens, what he was singing? FREEDOM—that's FREE . . . *LIBRE*, you see? FREEDOM, FREEDOM, FREEDOM, and then that next line, about the motherless child . . . that's an ORPHAN, get it? That's the *HUERFANO,* it was, like, a prediction, a direction, and he was in New York, and we were in Austin, and you guys were back east or somewhere, but his music was in the airwaves, and we *got it* on some level, and we're here . . ."

"Hmmm, right, that's funny," I say, unable to add more textual interpretation.

In the following days, David plays Joni Mitchell's "Woodstock" some evenings while we're on the deck looking for meteors. He sings it like an Appalachian ballad. "I came upon a child of God, / He was walking along the road . . ." We think of that young kid heading down the road for Yasgur's farm to join in a rock band and camp out on the land, going to try to let his soul free.

We are stardust
We are golden
We are caught in the Devil's bargain
And we've got to get ourselves
Back to the garden . . .

More than the movie, the song brings back what we felt then, what we still feel. In the deep, clear Huerfano night, Woodstock returns to us as meteors flame and fall like signal flares. When David sings about getting back to the garden, his version is more intense, and slightly more desperate.

At the end of the summer, at a party at the Red Rockers, we hear that the Walsenburg Drive-In has closed for good.

We made it through winter with nothing eventful happening. Nothing as eventful as what's happening at Bill Keidel and Annie's tonight. She's having their baby. She lies in a circle of kerosene lamps on a mattress Bill put in the living room. Dr. Mai pulls on her surgical gloves and kneels between Annie's splayed, hairy legs, waiting. Annie's been in labor for hours, it must be past two. It's cold tonight, so Bill lit a fire in the space heater. David and Peter are outside smoking a joint, and Bill's making hot toddies. Linda, Nancy, and I sit in a semi-circle to Annie's right, panting like a Greek chorus, doing Lamaze breathing with her. We're an odd trio. David and I haven't talked about having kids since that night at the drive-in last summer. Nancy had a miscarriage last fall, and Lia died two years ago this month. Christine, the eighteen-year-old daughter of crazy Mr. Calzone, the junkyard man in Walsenburg, sits next to Jim on the other side of Annie. She lives with Jim now, and their baby is due next fall. Jim's arm is wrapped around her, and his hand lies gently on her belly, and she watches Annie without expression. Patricia is sitting by Annie's head, wiping her forehead with a damp cloth.

Annie stiffens suddenly and says, "Here comes another one," between her teeth.

We exhale rapid Lamaze breaths like overheated dogs. We're the Supremes, and Annie's Diana Ross. The tight skin of her belly rolls like the surface of a calm sea when the baby moves. After the contraction I go out and look at the stars, brushing by Peter and David weaving back inside. David raises his eyebrows as if to ask if anything's changed, and I shake my head. The moon's set, so many more stars sparkle in the sky, and a pinprick satellite edges mechanically across the firmament. I spot the Big Dipper, the Little Dipper, Gemini, and the Milky Way spills over my head. When I saw the last two babies born, I got the same dizzy, oceanic feeling I get looking at the stars. Richard and Beth's house is dark and empty. They went back east for good this winter, when Beth returned to Libre after running away with Dallas's brother Billy for three weeks. I miss them. I'd like to tell Beth how my understanding grew this winter as Annie's baby grew inside her. David doesn't want to have a child right now, or maybe ever. The pull he feels is destiny, not biology. He thinks about raising man's consciousness, not raising a baby, and lately he can hardly stand the responsibility of a house cat. Milking the goats at sunrise and sunset doesn't fit his rock and roll existence, and building the house is just another chore. As for me, the more I've become rooted here, the more I've felt a pull working like gravity, although every issue of *Ms.* repeats that anatomy isn't destiny. Getting pregnant with an ambivalent father is unprincipled, not playing with a full deck.

If Beth were here, she might ask softly how we could raise a baby in our house, even if David wanted one. What about the triangular opening in the top room's floor and the fifteen-foot drop down to the kitchen? So far there are two sets of steps and four levels in the finished five-eighths of the lower part. David read about a study in which human babies put in a baboon habitat were much more agile than average babies, but it's just as likely that a baby in our house might break a lot of bones at best before getting the hang of it. I'd be a nervous wreck with a toddler teetering around inside, and the outdoors isn't so toddler friendly either. It'd be nice to talk to Beth. I don't talk to Linda about babies.

The kerosene lamps and candles light Bill's house gently. Mai's big flashlight sits ready to give her more light. Between contractions she leans down and measures Annie. "Three centimeters, Annie," Mai says softly. We congratulate Annie on the size of her cervix. The last two babies born here were perfect. If something goes wrong, Mai's truck is outside, but they couldn't get to the nearest hospital in Walsenburg in less than an hour. The jolting ride would be horrible, and probably not fast enough. This is the first birth Linda's been at since Lia died, when Linda rode into Walsenburg on a frantic truck ride holding Lia's body in a blanket.

I need to snap out of it, put good energy into the birth. Nothing will go wrong, everything's going to be perfect. Dean's off on a retreat. Linda and Dallas's affair is over. Linda went to Ecuador to see Dean this winter, and they came back together, but they separated shortly after their return. Dean's with Muffin now, a woman who visited and fell in love with life at Libre and stayed when her husband went back to New York. Lars came back from Africa but is living in New York. I grab Linda's hand, and she looks over and smiles. Lia was born in the old adobe they lived in the first summer at Libre, when the first six were building. Mai wasn't here, so Mrs. Vargas, the valley midwife, came over from Redwing, and old Dr. White came up too.

The next few contractions go fine. Annie flops around like a fish landed on the deck of a boat. Her legs are bent, and her feet dig into the mattress whenever she has a contraction. Her toes curl and spread like claws. She yells. We smooth the sheets and plump her pillows, and Patricia wipes her forehead in between. We pant louder, and when she stops and groans we say, "Come on, Annie, keep up with us, come on, won't be long now . . ." The wick of one of the kerosene lamps burns down and the light dims. Nancy gets up and blows out the lamp, takes the chimney off, and trims the wick efficiently. When she had a miscarriage last year, she and Peter seemed to take it pretty well. She wipes out the chimney, relights the wick, replaces the glass, and it grows brighter.

Bill wanders over with his hot toddy and says, "Thatta girl, Ann!" The men are peripheral, slightly embarrassed, with nothing to do. They talk in clumps quietly, like defendants waiting for a jury to bring in a verdict. Except Peter. He kneels down by Mai, stares at Annie's cunt, looks at her, and says, "Annie, tell me how it feels." Annie groans, averting her face.

"Not too many more now, Annie," says Mai in her clipped Chinese accent. How many babies did Mai deliver in California hospitals before she came here? She knows what could go wrong, but she's got a good track record in the valley so far. In two years she's successfully delivered three babies at the Red Rockers (including Mary's daughter Molly), two at Libre, three at the Triple A, two at the Ortiviz, and two elsewhere in the valley. After Annie's baby, three more wait in the wings this summer. She puts a stethoscope to Annie's belly and listens, her eyes narrowing. I wonder how long ago I looked at the stars. I'll have to milk this morning no matter how late I stay up. My back's stiff.

"Don't push until I tell you, Annie," orders Mai firmly. Annie doesn't look like she hears. She licks her lips and stares at the ceiling. Patricia holds a wet sponge for her to suck on.

"Bill, Bill," Annie turns her face and moans softly.

"Bill, get over here," orders Mai.

Bill sets his mug down and wipes his mustache. He strides over to Annie and kneels on one knee at her head. His jeans might split. His big arm wraps around her thin one at the elbow, they hold hands, and he looks down at her. I forget to pant until Linda pokes me. We lean forward toward Annie, here for the new life. The goats had kids two weeks ago. I'm never there when they're born, but I get there pretty soon after, and their newness, their perfect little hooves make my heart ache. In the article about commune women for *Ms.*, I'll write about Annie's baby too. Something like, "This spring, the pigs had their piglets, the goats had their kids, and Annie had her baby . . ." I lean on Linda's shoulder and close my eyes until Annie screams. Mai leans forward, all business, and everyone tells Annie to push, *push,* and she screams again, and the baby breaches and then slides like an otter into Mai's hands. Mai doesn't ask Bill to cut the cord—she moves quickly, wiping the baby, sucking the liquid out of its nose with a tiny bulb, cutting, swabbing, knotting the cord, and swaddling the baby girl, and we all lean forward waiting for her cry.

Her first sound is like a cough, and Mai clears her nose out again and holds her up, and the baby cries like a kitten, and Annie's crying, and Mai puts the baby in Annie's arms and says, "She's perfect, Annie," and we are crying, except Linda, who stares at the floor. Bill looks pleased with himself and grins around the room and then stares into the baby's tiny face and kisses Annie. Mai tells Annie to push, *push,* to get the placenta out, and the men come closer and stare down at the tiny baby whose eyes are half open and whose cries grow stronger. This is the way babies have come into the world forever. We've returned, ripping away the sterile curtains, we're connected again, elated. Bill holds the baby now. Tears well in the corners of Linda's eyes, and she stands up.

She says, "Congratulations, Annie. She's so beautiful, *so beautiful.*" Everyone agrees, and Linda's careful not to walk out the door too fast. I break away from David's arms, go to the window, and see her running down the path in the dawn, and I know she's crying even though I can't see her face.

On Kentucky Derby day a few days later, we're at Bill's drinking mint juleps and listening to the Derby on his radio. They still haven't thought of a name for the baby, who's sleeping in a sling hanging from Annie's neck. Annie's having a tiny mint julep. Secretariat wins the

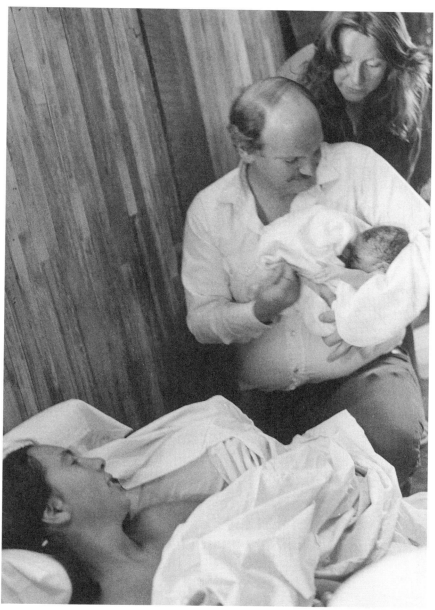

Julep's first minutes, May 1973.

Derby and sets a track record, under two minutes. We cheer and down our drinks.

On the second round, I look at the baby and say, "Hey, *how about Julep?*" and everyone says, "Yeah, that's it!"

"Yeah," says Bill, swaggering a bit. "I like it! *Julep!* Hey, little Julep." The baby opens one eye. "Whaddya think, Annie?"

Annie purses her plump lips for a minute and says, "Let's try it!"

As we walk home arm in arm, David smiles at me. "Julep," he sighs. "Another family member, another hope."

Two weeks later, Dean tromps by on his way back from the retreat house, gulps down a glass of water, shakes his head, and complains, "Jeesh, man, I could be wrong, but it sounded like Bill and Annie were throwing dishes at each other!"

32 : The Peach Run

The more the house gets built, the less progress we make.
The first year we put in all eight posts, set the eight roof
beams out from the rock and onto the posts, poured
four huge foundations, and built the bottom quarter.
The second year we finished the next quarter and closed
in the downhill half of the house, covered and insulated
the deck sections above it, and built and roofed the top
room. Last year we poured the fifth foundation and
added the eighth of the house that circles back uphill
around the rock. This summer we haven't added a new
section.

Not that we haven't accomplished anything. The existing space is more comfortable. We added a propane
wall lamp and stove, plus a fifty-five-gallon drum in the
loft above the kitchen sink, hooked up to the faucet, for
fifty-five gallons of "running water" at a time. We put in
gutters and rain barrels and terraced the area outside the
kitchen door and made a railroad tie table and benches
for a great morning coffee spot. We made kitchen counters with the remaining tongue-and-groove oak. David
made a narrow set of French doors with a red glass diamond window in one of them for the kitchen entrance.
I traded two cowboy shirts to a couple from Raton for a
stained glass unicorn window they custom-made for our
kitchen wall. We plastered both kitchen walls and caulked
the cracks in the tie walls in the dining area so there will be
no icy breezes on our backs at the table this winter. We put
bookshelves in the loft over the table, shelves in the sewing
loft, and a tall desk behind the bed upstairs. Last spring
David was away at a gig when a group of enthusiastic Japanese art students visited. I asked if they'd help insulate the
roof of the upper room, and when their translator told

them, they nodded furiously. I was proud I'd gotten something done, but when David came back, he was upset because they did a sloppy job. He's slow and a perfectionist. I'm neither.

Finishing the next three eighths to come full circle around the rock isn't on the horizon. We've got enough energy to refine our living space, but not enough to excavate two tons of dirt and enclose the back room. Summer's almost over. Doug left for North Carolina this spring, and David's practicing, playing gigs, and traveling. I've got to be realistic. We're in the difficult and amorphous middle of things, where so many novels and movies bog down. I don't know how long the middle will be, but I know the beginning is over.

One morning, after milking, when David's away at a gig, I take out the *I Ching* and the yarrow sticks, but before I throw the sticks, Monty knocks on the kitchen door and steps in.

"Roberta, my dear, good morning!" he says. "*Comment allez-vous, ma cherie?*"

"Okay, oh, ah, *bien*," I say, sighing and putting the *I Ching* aside. "Coffee?"

"No thanks. I had some espresso, and I'm twitching already!" Even though Monty and Steve have similar beefy physiques, they're so different that I often forget they're brothers—Steve the New Age Mountain Man and Monty the New Age Sophisticate. Steve's erect, intense, proud, primitive, and talks in staccato spurts when he gets excited, which is often. His blue eyes bulge and he can't sit still; his hair and beard explode in golden kinks around his face. Monty, however, always seems calm and relaxed, even a trifle bored. He slouches, as if he's wearing an imaginary satin smoking jacket, and his eyelids droop lazily over blue eyes almost the same shape and color as Steve's. His hair's smoothed back, and he's clean-shaven. He has a deep, slow, affected drawl, somewhere between Hud and Diana Vreeland.

Monty's real name is Peter, but he changed it awhile ago when he became our version of *The Fugitive*. After visiting Steve at Libre a few times, he dropped out of law school, and was waiting to pick up a big shipment of hashish in San Francisco when he didn't like the way things felt at Customs. So he ran. That's hardest to imagine—Monty moving so fast that a posse of federal agents couldn't catch him. I don't know how many were chasing him. Monty doesn't talk about it, but every time Peter Rabbit tells the story, more and more are in pursuit. Monty hid in a back alley Dumpster all night, then headed back to the Huerfano, changed

his first name, and has lived at Patricia's, his ex-sister-in-law's, ever since. He doesn't get food stamps. The FBI agent from Pueblo assigned to us visits every few months, but he's never asked about Monty. He's too busy looking for the Symbionese Liberation Army. Monty's my ally, my buddy. He, Minnesota, and Patricia are single, so it's easier to visit them on a lonely night. They're more ready for company than couples are.

"Listen," says Monty, pulling out a pack of Camels, which he wouldn't do in front of other smokers because they'd be on it like locusts. "We're going to make a run up to Paonia in Dr. Gonzo to get peaches for the whole valley. Winnie, Vicki, and Hickory from the Red Rockers. Stewart and Mary Anne from the Triple A. Strider from the Ortiviz Farm. I thought you and I could go as Libre delegates." Monty narrows his eyes as he puffs his Camel and smiles. "It would be a nice jaunt, don't you think? It's beautiful country, and a trip might be fun. Leave David to milk the goats for a change," he adds slyly. "What do you think? Come on, Roberta, remember, *'You're either on the bus or off the bus!'* Peach jam, peach wine . . ."

One week later, eight of us are in the Safeway parking lot in Salida, cooking dinner in Dr. Gonzo's kitchen. Highway 69 through Westcliffe is the shortest way to Montrose and Delta counties—up 69 to Cotopaxi, west on Highway 50 though Poncha Springs and over Monarch Pass (we hope), through Gunnison, then up 92 to Hotchkiss and Paonia. We didn't get far this first day. In Westcliffe, thirty miles west of Farisita, one of Dr. Gonzo's rear tires went flat, and the axle made a weird clunking noise. It took three hours for Winnie and Hickory, with the help of the local service station and a welder, to fix everything. The repairs went smoothly, with only minor screwups. Monty washed his hair in the bus's kitchen sink while we waited, and pulled the plug on his water when Hickory and Winnie were under the bus, directly below the drain. And for awhile we lost Strider. He took a walk past the varnished log cabins and well-tended white clapboard houses with dark green shutters in a town that has more money, more water, and fewer hippies than our end of the valley. He was dressed in black, as usual, tall and swarthy (or maybe just dirty) with black, stringy hair and beard. He's missing two front teeth and has a crumpled black hat that looks like the ones the Seven Dwarfs wore. We finally found him near the band shell just as the sheriff was asking him what he was doing sleeping on a bench.

We didn't want to try Monarch Pass at night, so we stopped at Salida. We bought pizza ingredients at the Safeway with our pooled food stamps and shoplifted smaller imported items, like anchovies, which you can't buy with stamps. A jar of capers and a small pepperoni appears out of the floppy sleeve of a Ukrainian blouse, and we have two cans of smoked oysters with crackers for hors d'oeuvres. Monty sips cheap Chianti and tosses the pizza dough around with increasing élan, dropping it half the time. When it's ready, Vicki and I smother it with tomato sauce, sliced mushrooms, pepperoni slices, anchovies, green pepper, and cheese and pop it into Dr. Gonzo's gas oven. Stewart and Mary Anne tear romaine leaves into a plastic tub that's the nearest thing to a salad bowl we find. Hickory and Winnie are resting.

Strider sits in a bus seat nearby telling stories. "So, the first time I tried amyl nitrate, I was home, and I put one popper in each nostril and let 'em rip, and it knocked me out, and my mother found me out cold on the kitchen floor with the poppers still in my nose, passed out in my underwear, har, har." My sympathies are with Strider's mother, even though I heard she was a Goldwater Republican. The first time Strider took acid in high school, she found him on the floor again, eating cat food from the dish with his cat.

The oven's not hot enough to make great pizza, and the salad greens don't compare to homegrown, but the jug wine gets more passable as the night goes on and we sit around the table in the back of the bus. We're an instant commune that works well together. When the bus broke down, there were no bad vibes. Is it because this group has no history? Or that we're on our good behavior, like a new couple? Or that we're away from our humdrum lives, like people on cruises who have shipboard romances? Or is it that, like all Americans, we have a hard time sitting still? We're on the road, like Kerouac, and on the bus, like the Pranksters. But we're on a round trip, not seeking nirvana on the highway, just a ton of peaches in Paonia. At twilight we light candles stuck in empty wine bottles, and Stewart plays a Taj Mahal tape, the only tape we have. *"Take a giant step outside yo' mind,"* Taj sings softly. The bus must look cozy with the lights glowing in its windows, but the Safeway shoppers don't park their cars and trucks too close. One or two bolder ones have stopped to look at Dean and Linda's mountain range, rainbows, and clouds on the sides of Dr. Gonzo, and to puzzle at the *"Life's Music is Best"* and *"Life's Music is Beth's"* slogans painted on the bus.

"So, I think we should clean up and drive out of town to set up for the night, then get an early start over the pass when it's still pretty cool, whaddya think?" Winnie asks, chewing on a piece of pizza on one side of his mouth and looking around the circle. We agree, and Winnie smiles. Beside him, Hickory cuts his slice of pizza into small pieces with his buck knife. I remember that I took his picture at Reality Construction Company in 1969. Before that, he says, he was at a commune in Georgia, but he doesn't say much about his past. He has thick, wavy strawberry blond hair that's pulled back neatly in a ponytail, and he's smooth-shaven, with light brown eyes. If he were a little less muscular, he could play Ashley Wilkes in the valley version of *Gone with the Wind*. His last name is Hicks, and I wonder if he's related to Edward Hicks, but don't ask. I had a print of Hicks's *Peaceable Kingdom* in my Vassar room opposite a copy of the Cloisters unicorn tapestry. Hickory listens carefully, smiling pleasantly as he eats.

"It's good Henry or Steve isn't along," I say to Vicki as we clean up.

"Nobody objects to paper plates!" Vicki smiles thinly. Everybody helps clean up except Strider, who's passed out, and we finish quickly and fill our water cans from a hose at a gas station. Outside the town limits, we pull off in a field to sleep. Vicki and I take our sleeping bags and climb up the welded ladder to the top of Dr. Gonzo to sleep on the plywood platform built to carry the band's musical equipment. We lie on our backs looking for shooting stars. I don't miss David or home. This is like a funky cruise vacation. I'm on deck staring at the stars, although our vessel's a 1954 GMC school bus that Adrienne bought at a Colorado Springs auction and Dean and Linda painted the spring Lia died. I'm tired but can't sleep—it's the excitement of travel, or the bus's aura.

"Hey, Vick," I say, "do you feel that pent-up energy coming up from the bus? You know, left over from all the school kids riding in it in its previous incarnation?" She smiles faintly, maybe thinking of her baby girl at the Red Rocks, or her school years in Beverly Hills. Across the land, all of us rode buses like this as children. Now some kids have hijacked the buses. It's just my overactive imagination that makes me feel the vintage, bottled-up school energy, seeping through me and dissipating in the clear Colorado night.

33 : Mr. Wagley's Peaches

The next day we're on the road early after a quick break-fast of granola and my goat milk yogurt, anxious to get over Monarch Pass. Winnie's shoulders and jaw jut forward as he drives. We lean forward, too, as if to help Dr. Gonzo motivate over the hill. Hickory grips the pole by the stairwell, listening to the engine. The guys checked the tires this morning again—a blowout could be fatal. Conversation stops completely when the engine starts heaving and the bus slows. Tourist families in big sedans and ranchers in pickups pass in a blur. We stare straight ahead, ignoring their exasperated looks. Dr. Gonzo is creeping at about five miles an hour by the time we crest the pass, but we make it. Hickory sighs with relief, and Monty says, "Hoorah, hoorah!" in his deep, blasé voice; Strider slept through the whole thing.

The peach season is almost over in Paonia, and no one's interested in hiring our crew, so we streamline our approach. When we stop, Winnie and I, the most conventional looking, who talk best to straight people, get out. I'm wearing jeans and a cowboy shirt, and Winnie's got on a plain white shirt over his jeans. He's clean-shaven, and his dark hair is tucked behind his ears. Even we two can't persuade any fruit farmer it's a good idea to hire a bunch of hippies hiding inside a garishly painted bus. They look at us suspiciously, and we speak more glibly and enthusiastically, and they act as if we're trying to put something over on them, like Elmer Gantry or some snake oil salesman. Returning to the Huerfano with no peaches isn't an option. At a gas station by the turn for Orchard City on Route 92 we stop and buy Cokes.

"Look, peaches are almost done with in Paonia, so

they could afford to be picky about pickers," Winnie reasons, looking around our circle. "Mr. Blaisdell back there said they were still coming in strong in Delta, so we'll find something." Everyone agrees, except Strider, who's pouting in reaction to Mary Anne's suggestion that he hide so no one can see him when we apply for the next job. We chug our Cokes, and I pull a bandanna out of my pack and tie it jauntily around my neck, trying to look western and professional. Up the road in Delta, we pull into the Wagley Ranch. Mr. Wagley's a small man with leathery skin, pale whiskers like peach fuzz, and small eyes that squint at Winnie and me. His peaches are ready just now—at last, there's someone as desperate for workers as we are desperate for work.

"Six dollars for every bushel picked, and you can have as many bushels of Grade B peaches as you want for two dollars each," he says. There's no dickering with Mr. Wagley, and, after a short consult, we agree. "You can pull that bus up behind the fruit shed by those trees," he says, indicating with a slight jerk of his head where to park. "There's a hand pump between there and the shed." He points to outhouses and showers for workers by the first field.

"Thank you, Mr. Wagley, thanks a lot. You'll see, we're going to pick a lot of peaches for you," I gush. Mr. Wagley smiles slightly—maybe. It's hard to tell. He walks away slowly.

"That was at least a hundred-watt smile, and you didn't get anything back," Winnie mutters. "Maybe he's on drugs, or a serial killer. Maybe an alien has taken over his body, and we'll be abducted. Maybe he belongs to the Ku Klux Klan. Is the Klan out here?" I shrug and smile. Our spirits are high as we cook dinner—Chico-San organic brown rice, cooked pinto beans Mary Anne brought, and hot tortillas topped with grated longhorn cheese. During dinner I sit next to Hickory and notice he's got his beans on exactly one half of the paper plate and his rice exactly on the other half, and he's using his buck knife to cut his whole wheat tortillas into fourths, then pushing beans or rice on each quarter precisely with the side of his knife.

"Are you by any chance a Virgo?" I ask.

He says slyly, "How'd you guess?" His brown eyes are flecked with amber and green.

"A *Virgo*?" Vicki laughs, "Haven't you noticed how he folds his overalls up at night?"

"Vicki, my dear," says Monty, chortling over a post-burrito cigarette, "I imagine orderliness is a welcome addition to the dome, and should be encouraged, don't you think?" At a certain blood alcohol level, Monty can sound snide.

But Vicki isn't offended and smiles her lovely smile. "Monty, I appreciate Hickory fully, I assure you," she says in her low, husky voice, "When he changes diapers, they're clean and on to stay." Everybody laughs, and Hickory looks down and smiles. His hair's pulled back in a ponytail low on his neck, sort of like a Revolutionary War soldier. Later, when Vicki and I get up on the bus with our sleeping bags, I look down under the trees where he's camping, and, sure enough, he's folding up his overalls, his lean body glowing ghostly in the moonlight.

Monty, Hickory, and I pick together the next day. Monty's in high spirits, despite a slight hangover, and we work on a musical about the Huerfano Peach Run. We start adapting "Officer Krupke" from *West Side Story* as a song about Mrs. Lenzotti, our food stamp lady—"Oh Mrs. Lenzotti, we're just misunderstood"—and then we move on to using "The Street Where You Live" from *My Fair Lady* for "The Ranch Where You Live," but we don't get far. Monty and I interrupt each other proposing lines and argue about whose is better, while Hickory laughs and steadily picks peaches. I feel more like singing "*Something's coming, something good*" from *West Side Story*, but keep that to myself. We have baskets hanging from our necks, into which we carefully place the peaches, and then we carefully put what we've picked into a larger basket that Mr. Wagley's boys pick up in a small tractor trailer. I think of Sal Paradise in *On the Road*, and Terry, his sad, wise Mexican girl, and her son, picking cotton in California.

Winnie walks over and interrupts: "Massa Wagley done said we can break for lunch, and sista Mary Anne has made a mess of quesadillas." By the second day, we've picked eighty-three bushels of peaches. At night at the shed where women grade the peaches, we pick enough Grade B's to fill the bus. We're into it, adding up our wages around the table at night, although the skin on the inside of my arms and face is red from the peach fuzz and whatever Mr. Wagley sprays on his crops, and even though I showered and wore gloves and long sleeves the second day, the rash is redder and really hurts.

Winnie, Monty, and I want to pick one more day, but the other five resist. "Are you crazy?" says Mary Anne. "I'm about to send all my money to César Chávez!"

"We won't get over the pass with any more peaches," says Hickory quietly, looking at me steadily, and I stop arguing. He's right. It's funny, he's the only other person I've met from the deep South besides David, but he's different, so self-contained and self-effacing. I can't imagine him mesmerizing a class of two hundred students the way David did at Buffalo.

"We haven't finished the musical," sighs Monty.

"We could pick a little more and just sell some before we get to Monarch Pass," Winnie suggests, only halfheartedly. Nobody responds. That's it. Our last night here in the orchard under the moon. Tomorrow we head back, and I'm surprised how sentimental I feel. We're an instant family within the larger Huerfano clan. We shared this mission, laughed a lot, got along well, were away from the routine of milking goats and getting enough money for the next truckload of lumber and the often tedious, endless process of building our dreams, or just maintaining them. I look at the faces in the candlelight as we smoke a joint and laugh. Strider's in the middle of a story about his transition from biker to New Buffalo farmer.

"Should I play Taj Mahal again?" Stewart asks as he's handed the joint.

"NO!" Everyone yells, and we laugh some more.

"I wish we'd brought someone who could play the guitar or something," Stewart says.

"Name a musician who'd pull his weight peach picking!" Monty snorts.

Winnie stands up and stretches. "Oh, my aching back! I'm turning in—we've got to get off early tomorrow." As we're getting our bedding out of the bus, Hickory stops beside me and asks if I mind if he sleeps on the top of the bus too. I say no, trying to sound casual and not looking at him. He grabs his bag and follows me up the metal ladder on the back of the bus. Vicki's disappeared, and we lie on the plywood platform and watch the shooting stars.

"You can see a lot more in the sky here than you can in Georgia," says Hickory.

"Yeah," I agree, although I've never been there. I lie awake listening to his breathing become more rhythmical. I'm close enough to see the tendrils of his wavy, strawberry blond hair. I'm tired but restless, the skin on my arms and face burns, and I can't get to sleep.

When we leave Wagley Ranch, we sense that the trip is ending and joke about who Mr. Wagley really is. "Did anyone see his wife? His 'sons' didn't look like him at all—they're four times his size," Mary Anne says.

"What does Mr. Wagley do at night when all the peaches are in their crates?" Monty wonders. No one answers. We can't imagine. Dr. Gonzo lumbers even more heavily with two tons of peaches stuffed inside and lashed on top. We stop at Belle's Stop 'n' Snack ("Best Pies this Side of the Continental Divide") before Monarch Pass, and Winnie and I go talk to Belle.

"We'll trade you a bushel of peaches for lunch for eight of us. They'll make great pies, just like your sign promises." Winnie grins at Belle.

"Two bushels," says Belle, not smiling, wiping her hands on her apron. We take up most of the counter and order meat loaf, liver and onions, chicken fried steak, chicken pot pies. I sit by Hickory—I feel closer to him after sharing the bus platform last night. Everyone orders strawberry pie à la mode for dessert.

Winnie says excitedly between bites, "We could just keep driving, trading peaches for gas, food, whatever, go to Las Vegas, trade peaches for poker chips, make a fortune and—"

"And rush back to the Huerfano and share our winnings!" Monty laughs drily.

That night we sleep outside Cotopaxi. Dr. Gonzo's so loaded down it doesn't go over forty on flat roads. We're wrung out from getting back over the pass. We thought we might have to dump some peaches on the side of the road to make it. Hickory doesn't ask if he can sleep on the platform tonight, he just grabs his gear and follows me up. We spread out our foam pads and sleeping bags. The smell of the peaches under the tarp in the back fills the night air.

"Well, the last night on the peach cruise!" I say nervously. He looks up as he smooths out his bag just right. He restraightens my foam pad, then shakes out my bag and smooths it gently with his hand. It's closer to his than it was last night. I kneel down on it, facing him. He rises up on his knees and looks at me, his eyes shining in the moonlight.

"So!" I say nervously.

"So," he says softly. It's not a question.

"So," I say, holding my breath, "is this a peachboard romance?" It's the best I can do under the circumstances—Stewart's joint was so strong. Hickory chuckles politely. He looks at me, then smooths my hair back gently with one hand. He places that hand lightly behind my neck, pulling my face toward his, putting his mouth on mine, softly and precisely.

My romance with Hickory isn't revolutionary or new, and the force that pulled me into his arms is actually very ordinary. I catalogue the brief passions of Neal Cassady and Jack Kerouac and their alter egos, Sal Paradise and Dean Moriarty, then I review the free love and changing romantic constellations in Bloomsbury or at Mabel Dodge Luhan's in Taos. To live creatively means taking risks and breaking barriers. That's not new either. Talking to myself this way proves my sophistication and detachment, and it's a diversion from my churning stomach, my shifting heart. My familiarity with cultural history and opera plots will insulate me and trivialize my feelings sufficiently to get me through.

David and I sit on the terrace outside the kitchen door, resting after carrying two bushels of peaches up the ridge. The kettle of water for dipping peaches to remove their skins is heating up on the cookstove, and a big canner full of water is heating up beside it. A change in the angle of the sunlight and a restless breeze suggest summer's end. The piñon smoke blows directly east out of the stovepipe. A piñon jay hops around the nearest tree, eyeing the peaches. When I tell him, David doesn't seem upset about Hickory and me. He looks out into the valley and says with a little smile, "I thought you'd end up with Winnie. You've always seemed to like him." He smiles more, assuring me everything's all right again. That he was speculating about whom I'd sleep with isn't comforting. Is this just a good front, or has he been waiting for this opportunity?

"So, you're not upset?" I ask slowly, looking down at my knees.

"No, no, this is natural, we can love each other *and*

others. We're beyond the petty bourgeois possessiveness that plagued our parents, aren't we?"

"We are?" I say, buying time. I can't be angry at David for not being angry at me for sleeping with Hickory. He's right, after all. I'm a product of bourgeois possessiveness, not prepared by anything but books for this situation. My parents have been devoted to each other through their seven-year engagement during the depression and their thirty-five-year marriage. I didn't know anybody whose parents were divorced until I was in seventh grade, and that was Penny's mom, who was remarried by then. Penny's real father was just a face in a photo in her bedroom. Nana was divorced, but who could blame her? My real grandfather abandoned her and my mother for the horses and the track. Much later he was found dead on a street with his winnings in his pocket. His lucky day. When Nana met Pop, the Swiss architect who wanted to marry her, she went to Philadelphia to get a divorce. There she met another man and wasn't sure she should marry Pop. Pop said, "If you want to marry him, Lil, you should do it." Nana married Pop after all, but when I overheard the story, my mother's voice suggested there was something wrong with Pop's response. Now I understand.

"Of course," David says, "it's hard, but we'll be able to do this." Maybe David's the more conservative of us two. His way, we can stay together. With mine, I might be headed for an Elizabeth Taylor add-a-marriage necklace, a life of serial monogamy. He says, "You know I'm not upset. We have the rest of our lives together. It would be ridiculous for us to cripple each other emotionally and prevent each other from experiencing love with other people. Our love is strong enough not to be threatened by the love of others." He talks about loving others, but I'm thinking about loving Hickory. I've heard this before. Open marriages bloom all around us, usually before the old marriages wither and die and newly passionate couples spring up. Oh, there was his fling with Patricia, and my near fling with Jonsie, and things probably happen when he's on the road with the band, but until now, we've been more spectators than players in Huerfano melodramas. Our eyes met over the heads of the spurned and betrayed as they sat despondently at our kitchen table. We laughed and shook our heads when Peter told us about a very pregnant woman from Archuletaville chasing her old man with a butcher knife.

"So, you don't mind if I see Hickory again?" I trace circles on my sunburned knees with my thumbnail.

"Of course not," David says, putting his arm around my shoulder.

I try not to shrink from his touch. I'm not very evolved. David and I are family, and we've shared so much. He's my intellectual twin. We gestated and arrived into this new life together. We're perfectly matched, equally good at convincing ourselves and each other what we should think. We've shared the work and the dream. But the one I want to touch right now is Hickory. Suddenly, I have a pleasant thought. I'd thought I could never be with Hickory again, and I was wrong about that too. We go inside, extra-considerate, almost formal with each other as we work on the peaches, as if we have something to prove. We're the most efficient canning team in the valley. I scald the peaches in the boiling water, then David and I peel off the limp skins, halve the fruit, remove the pits, and put the halves in quart jars. I pour hot sugar syrup over the peaches in each jar, then run a long, thin spatula around the inside of the jar to let any air bubbles escape, then wipe the rim of the jar with a clean cloth, then put on the rubberized lid. I screw the rims on tightly and put the eight jars in the wire holder, and slowly David and I lower the wobbling jars into the boiling water in the blue enamel canner. He puts the lid on the canner carefully, and I stuff as many chunks of piñon into the firebox as I can and slide the canner over the firebox, where it's hottest. The water chortles and rolls, and the jars clink softly against one another. To can peaches at this altitude, the jars must cook for forty-eight minutes. When the time's up, we lift the wire harness and gently place it on the counter. I take out each jar and put it gently on the back of the counter, and then we refill the harness with the eight jars of peaches we filled while this batch was canning. Our hands, arms, and thighs are sticky with fruit sugar.

When the scalding water is too funky with peach fuzz, we each grab a handle of the pot like Hansel and Gretel and carry it down from the house to the compost. We pour it over the pile, dumping the compost bucket full of peach pits and skins at the same time. While we work on another batch, we listen for the popping sounds of the lids on cooling jars that tell us the seal is good. Later, Monty stops by. He reports that Linda's back from her trip east and found out that Bill used her drawing table to slaughter and butcher a pig while she was away.

"How'd she find out?" I ask.

"There are a lot of hacks in it. The whole idea of a drawing table is to have a smooth surface," Monty says, grinning perversely. Although he's a diplomatic guy, he loves to see a good fight. We take a break, and Monty and I sing parts of the Mrs. Lenzotti version of "Officer Krupke" that we made up on the Peach Run. David laughs and shakes his head. Monty probably came up to see whether David and I were throwing peach pits at each other, but I don't care, I'm glad to see him. He was my companion on the Peach Run and reminds me of the fun we had. We eat the rest of a peach crumble I made.

"Gotta get back down," Monty sighs dramatically when he finishes his second piece. "I've been living with Patricia longer than Steve! How did this happen?" He gives a Maurice Chevalier shrug. "Well, back to the peach mines . . ." He waves jauntily and shuts the door.

The second day we don't halve or pit the peaches, we can them whole. The third day we cold-pack peaches in freezer bags and store thirty quarts in Peter and Nancy's freezer in their shed down the ridge. I make peach jam in pint jars and can it, and we use the last bushel to start some wine in the ten-gallon crock, saving enough for two pies for community dinner. We've canned and frozen two hundred quarts of peaches. I stand in the root cellar while David hands me cooled jars for the top shelf. They're still a little warm. I slide them tight against one another, a phalanx of peaches. The yolk-colored fruit hangs in the sugar syrup like specimens in a laboratory. Who will take out the last jar next year, and who will share it? I feel like I've invested in a foreign country about to default on its loans.

I brush my palms against each other, smile, and say to David, "'Another job well done!' as Mr. Natural says!" My voice sounds a little forced. Maybe I'll ask around at the community dinner to see if anybody's driving over to the Red Rocks soon. David smiles ruefully at me, as if he can read my thoughts.

35 : Cousin Carlene

Since the peaches, David and I don't talk about free love, Hickory, or our future. It's like putting unstable chemicals into a pot over a low flame and then trying to relax and forget about it. The pot's lid rattles occasionally, and it's just a matter of time before it boils over or explodes, but we're exhausted and pretend not to notice. A visit from one of my cousins five days later serves as a diversion. Cousin Carlene and her second husband show up for an afternoon visit on their grand tour of the West. She's the youngest of Aunt Mabel and Uncle Carl's three daughters. Since we've been at Libre, all three cousins have visited in descending order of age. First Frannie, the eldest, who lives in Houston, stopped by with her right-wing Texas oil company executive husband. They were on their way to Pagosa Springs to buy some land and build a cabin near Wolf Creek Ski Area. Peter has a bumper sticker that reads, "If God wanted Texans to ski, He would have given them mountains." I don't know if Frannie's husband saw it. They arrived the same day the FBI agents came down from Colorado Springs looking for Patricia Hearst. Peter wasn't in a good mood that day, and he had some problems with authority. He drove at the agents in his truck, yelling obscenities out the window, and they put their car in reverse and backed out of Libre recklessly, with Peter in hot pursuit, shaking his fist at them, yelling out his window.

Linda and I stood on her porch watching. "There goes all the goodwill he cultivated in coffee klatches with special agent Sam for the last five years!" I said. On his last visit, Sam told Peter he'd learned a lot from us and was taking early retirement. He'd decided to stop and smell the roses. Because Frannie arrived right after the

FBI agents left, and because her husband looked so uptight, many people thought he was another undercover agent. They stayed for just over an hour—maybe they picked up on the vibes.

Cousin Betty, a second-grade teacher at the army base in Hamburg who married Charley, a career army man, and adopted two German orphans with him, stopped by with her family when they returned to the States on their way to their new posting in Honolulu. The older boy had been sick with something not yet diagnosed. Although he weighed over a hundred pounds, Charley carried him over his shoulder up the ridge and then went back down again for their army tents and gear. They're the only ones who've spent the night, probably thanks to Charley's boot camp training. Their boys were named, coincidentally, David and Doug. Whenever Charley barked their names in his army captain style, my David or Doug would be so startled he'd drop his coffee cup or cigarette. They were both nervous wrecks by the time Betty and her family left.

This afternoon, Cousin Carlene tickles Kachina behind the ear, and Kachina flops on the banco beside her. Carlene has a way with animals like I do. She and her second husband, a doctor, live on a farm in New Hampshire and raise miniature donkeys and Great Danes. She supplies animals for TV commercials in the Boston area. My mother sent me a picture of her driving a team of ten tiny donkeys hitched to a miniature Budweiser wagon. Carlene sat up on the driver's seat holding the reins, looking like a giantess. The family affectionately calls her "Crazy Carlene." I don't know what they call me. She sits at the kidney-shaped dining room table Minnesota helped me build last winter and says, "What a great table! I'm impressed. This is all so *permanent!* I didn't expect it to be so *permanent!*" as she sips tea and looks out at the mountains.

"Did you think we'd be living in tents?" I'd like to ask. Instead I say modestly, "To be honest, Carlene, I designed the table, but Minnesota made it while I stood around our garage—wood shop this winter, trying to be helpful and stay warm. However, I sanded it *a lot.*" Carlene was named after Uncle Carl. I guess he and Aunt Mabel gave up trying for a son after the third time. Carlene's husband, Doc, is taking a bird-watching walk over the ridge with David.

"This would be a great place to have horses," says Carlene. She had an old white horse named Trigger when I was little. I was a strict constructionist and was troubled because the TV Trigger was a palomino and Carlene's Trigger was white. The Lone Ranger's horse, Silver, was white, and Hopalong Cassidy had a white horse named Topper. It was typical of her not to choose the right name for the right color. She was eight years older and a rebel of sorts. My mother has a yellowed article from the *Newburgh News* with a photo of my brother and Carlene, bare-back on Trigger, after they'd been kicked out of Newburgh High School one Saturday when they were caught riding him through the halls and up the stairs. It was on the society page. Jimmy's giving his best James Dean–Marlon Brando scowl behind Carlene, who's grinning impishly, if you can be big and still look impish. On Sunday visits to Uncle Carl and Aunt Mabel's, they'd let me ride Trigger around the backyard for hours while the grown-ups had cocktails.

"I'd like to get a horse soon," I say, cleaning the counter for the third time and tucking the baggie of marijuana farther back on the shelf, behind the herbal teas. "How's Aunt Mabel?"

Carlene looks into her teacup as if she's reading tea leaves. "She's okay," Carlene says. "She's a fighter. The doctor says she might have more than a year left."

"And she still doesn't know she has cancer?" I ask, not quite masking disbelief.

"Well, that's what Dad wants," says Carlene.

The kitchen door opens and Hickory steps in, skillfully shutting out our pretty little Nubian goat, Little Egypt, who protests bitterly on the other side of the door. My face flushes when I look up at him, shirtless in his overalls on the landing above the kitchen level. His face is red, and his shoulder muscles are shiny from sweat. "Oh, hello," I say as casually as possible. "Carlene, this is William Hicks, whom everyone calls Hickory. Hickory, this is my cousin Carlene, who's visiting." As if Hickory would think she was here to join the commune in her beige no-iron travel pantsuit.

"Hello," says Carlene, smiling pleasantly at Hickory and sitting up because she senses something's going on.

"Hello," says Hickory, twisting a stray hair that's come out from behind his headband and putting it back into place with one of his typical old maid gestures. He's obsessively neat and thorough, which is probably what makes him such a good mechanic and lover. Hickory clears his throat. "I came to get a truck part Jim said he had, but it turns out he doesn't. He thinks he gave it to Adrienne at the Triple A. I thought, while I was here, I'd just stop by." Meaning he thought he'd just run five hundred feet up a ridge while the other Red Rockers are down the hill smoking joints or drinking the beer Peter's invented, Cottontail

Ale—with the Hippity Hops, brewed from hops *and* marijuana. Hickory comes down into the kitchen level and stands too close while I pour him a glass of water. Carlene seems puzzled by his long explanation. He walks over to the dining area and sits down opposite her. I stay in the kitchen, cleaning the counter some more.

Just when I thought I couldn't feel more awkward, David and Doc come back. Little Egypt bursts in behind them, *baa*-ing indignantly like a society girl mistakenly barred from the 21 Club before the maitre d' recognized her. Her hooves staccato on the landing floorboards, and she swings her head around, showing off her neck and her delight at having outwitted David and Doc. A few pebble-sized goat turds pop out of Little Egypt's butt and bounce on the floorboards. I start to say she's staging a shit-in but then decide not to and shove her out the door as she protests loudly. I sweep up the goat pellets and dump them into the compost bucket.

"Well," says David, laughing a little too wryly, "what have we here? Hickory, ha-ha, how are you?"

"Fine," says Hickory, smiling, then pursing his lips a little, and after we introduce him to Doc, and Hickory explains where and what the Red Rockers are, and Doc tells Carlene about the falcons he saw on the back ridges, Hickory says he has to leave because the others must be waiting for him down at Peter's. I step out the kitchen door with him and we kiss quickly as the goats watch, but they don't care, and I go back inside to my cousin.

"I suppose we should be on our way, too," says Doc, finishing his glass of beer.

Carlene nods and stands up. She repeats, "I just never expected it to look like this. It's so permanent, so impressive. I'm going to tell everyone in the family how much you've done." I wonder if this endorsement will help.

We kiss good-bye. "Give Aunt Mabel my love, and tell her I'm going to call her," I say.

The last of my three cousins to travel to the Huerfano looks in my eyes but doesn't say much of anything. I wish I could talk frankly with her. She's been divorced. What could she tell me? Are passion and intimacy diminished by so much past and future? Is it because Hickory isn't preoccupied with the revolution or the new society that he can focus with such sweet vehemence on me? If I went with Hickory, how long would this vivid fleshiness spill over into our tomorrows? Did Carlene ever think that her love was free?

David will walk them down to the parking lot. It's almost time to milk. I hug him and whisper not to stop at Peter's, they're probably sitting around the table under a cloud of dope smoke, still sipping Cottontail Ale. Outside the goats stop grazing and look up as I hug everyone good-bye again. Last week at the community dinner I got the "Most Visited by Her Family" award. Why do they keep finding me? Is it curiosity or concern? I haven't taken the trouble to visit them—do they care more than I? What does blood mean these days? We'd be on the other side of the barricades from that fascist my cousin Frannie married, if it ever came to that. Could I plug him? I'd try to protect Frannie, and maybe get him sent off for reeducation, cleaning latrines or something like that. We'll stay at Frannie's in Houston if we hitchhike to Florida again, despite our differences. Carlene looks back one more time and disappears into the piñons. The goats were watching me like a crowd waiting for a speech, but now they go back to nibbling scrub oak.

One week later, on the morning of the fall equinox, David broke the Chemex coffeepot. I was at the table, reading my *Ms.* article about women on the communes. It was his dish day, and he was cleaning up after breakfast. He put the Chemex on the cookstove, waited for the coffee to heat, poured himself another cup, and threw the Chemex at the wall. It hit between the kitchen window and the plaster cast of the Tibetan calendar I bought in the West Village for my brother Jimmy years ago. Jimmy didn't like it and gave it back a year later. A friend from Vassar, now living on what's evolved into a gay-lesbian commune in Vermont, sent me a card that says, "*A Woman without a Man is like a Fish without a Bicycle,*" and I put it on the kitchen window ledge this morning. I don't think that's what made David snap.

I think it was when he hugged me this morning and patted my butt and felt my diaphragm in the back pocket of my jeans. I was going to head down the ridge later to see if there was anyone going over to the Red Rocks, and I've gotten into the habit of putting my diaphragm in my pocket on the off chance I'd see Hickory somewhere. It was a long shot, but I'm still a Girl Scout (Be Prepared). I'm not too interested in sex with anybody but Hickory these days, so this isn't turning out the way David expected. He expected there to be more people to share love with, including me—that there would be less repression and hypocrisy. Although he anticipated difficult moments, he expected a loosening, an evolution of understanding about love and physical intimacy. He saw a no-lose situation, because he's turned on by me and numerous other women at the same time. I'm not like that, and I know it's terribly bourgeois and counterrevolutionary of me, so very retro. The *Ms.* editors I talked to about my article would be disappointed. His vision is much more evolved and desirable, but I can't do much about my feelings.

I didn't say anything when he threw the Chemex. There was only a little coffee left, which dribbled down the wall, and most of the glass fell behind the potbelly and into the firewood crates. I looked up at him, but he didn't look at me, and without saying anything he slammed out the door. He must have walked up to the ridge road, because I heard the goats call as he passed. I picked up all the big pieces of glass and put them in the arroyo trash bucket and saved the wooden handles. I think you can reorder the glass part. People have accidents. Or maybe we should switch to a Melitta.

My heart was beating faster, even after all that tidying, and I couldn't go back to reading. I let the dishwater heat up really hot. Maybe I can joke about it later. "That was a heck of a way to get out of your dish day!" I'll say. I can stick my hands in hotter water than David or Doug can. I poured the water into the stainless steel sink and washed the breakfast dishes, dried them, and put them back on the shelf. I swept the floor and dumped what was in the dustpan into the potbelly. I added more wood to the potbelly and to the cookstove. I cleaned the wooden counter with a Brillo pad. I brought in some more wood that I'd split yesterday and spotted some more pieces of glass in the wood box. I felt more upset when I saw them than when he'd thrown the pot.

The first summer we were in the valley, the Triple A band had a gig in Walsenburg, and a woman from the Triple A hooked up with Mary Red Rocker's husband and went back to the Red Rockers to spend the night with him. Mary took this in stride. After all, she'd come from New York with her husband and their next-door neighbor Bad Eddy, whom she was a little in love with even then, so she hoped things would loosen up a bit. I don't know where Bad Eddy was, but Mary and Benjo Red Rocker went back to the Triple A and spent the night there. Anson Red Rocker went back to the Triple A with Lars and Running Deer, and they all spent the night in the barn the Triple A lived in while they were building their houses, and Adrienne got drunk and upset, and stumbled around in the dark asking, "What about me?" When I heard Peter tell this story, I didn't feel like I was missing anything, but David laughed.

I don't know how everyone split up and paired off that first Thanksgiving at Libre, when desire was so palpable. I'm not sure they even had dinner first. Sandy and Nanao left for his cave, but I don't know where Steve and Linda went, or Peter and Nancy. What did Dean and Judy Rabbit and Patricia do suddenly, orphaned by passion? Play Scrabble? Where was Lia? I haven't asked about these details even now.

David's known as the calm, easygoing one, and I have my flash points, I admit. I'm generally not as agreeable, but I've never broken anything. I let off steam regularly so it never builds up. He erupts suddenly and unexpectedly, like when he shattered the chair against the wall in Buffalo the night after the Kent State killings, or when he threw a glass on the floor after Larry Chisolm, the head of the American Studies department at Buffalo, told him a year living in a hippie commune in Colorado couldn't be considered a year outside American culture, a requirement for David's American Studies doctorate.

"You're mistaken if you think the communes aren't very much a part of our culture," said Chisolm wryly. David nodded, but back home he threw the glass. Once when David stayed up all night writing songs and I asked if he was going to milk the goats, he blew up too. That was my fault, really, and so is this. He's a proud man whose wife isn't too interested in him at the moment. I can't stay here. I wish he'd broken something less expensive, and I'm pissed even though I understand. I'll go to Monty and Minnesota's, which used to be Patricia's, too, but she's moving down into the valley. I'll burst in and tell Monty what happened. Minnesota is probably helping Patricia move her stuff down to Farisita Farm. Monty will put down his Graham Greene novel and laugh at this latest example of human folly, puffing on his cigarette with a flourish, and I'll feel better already. He'll fix tea and listen to me, smiling, making wry remarks, and our conversation will play out, turning to books, music, valley gossip. I'll sit by his fire reading and chatting all afternoon as he putters around the kitchen. He'll say, "Stay for dinner, why don't you?" and I'll say "I'd love to, why not?" David can stew in his own juices. It's not as if I've run over to the Red Rocks. Monty's house is a neutral zone in the war of the sexes. By sunset I'll come round to Monty's view—this isn't important, we're silly to get so self-involved.

"Have a glass of wine," Monty will say, "You'll enjoy this cassoulet, even though I had to improvise a bit." Then he'll grin mischievously and say, "What a shame Hickory and David aren't here to enjoy it with us," and I'll slap him on the arm. He'll laugh his deep smoker's laugh, and it'll be all right, at least for tonight.

36 : The Red Rocks

In the middle of the big round table in the Red Rock dome is a three-foot lazy Susan for condiments and platters. It spins like a roulette wheel at meals, then stops with a jerk when people grab and hold onto it while they're helping themselves. Tonight, Winnie heaves the restaurant-size pan of enchiladas onto the lazy Susan with a flourish, steps back like a gunslinger holding a scorched pot holder on each hip, and narrows his eyes. He waits until Stephanie and Benjo look up from their Peyote Church grace and says, "Two enchiladas each, and everybody can have as much salad as they want—the greenhouse lettuce is still going like gangbusters. No limit on tortillas!"

Some of the bigger men sigh loudly. There are guests tonight, so everyone's on good behavior, like the time when I asked a boy to dinner before a dance, and my family was extra-convivial and gracious. We rose to the occasion, laughing and smiling, eager to please and show my boyfriend what a happy, zany family we were. It's not so different here.

"Winnie, which ones have the rattlesnake meat in them?" asks Vicki. She's not sure she wants her baby to eat rattlesnake. You can tell from their stories that Vicki, Winnie, and Larry spent a little time being a zany Hungarian family in Beverly Hills, and they've got leading roles in the Red Rocks sequel. Hickory serves me some enchiladas, while a few of the Red Rocker women watch him, look at each other, and raise their eyebrows. I blush and look down, my hand touching Hickory's thigh under the table. He cuts my portion precisely.

"Oh, excuse me, Hickory, I don't think all the angles in that rectangle of enchiladas you're cutting for your gal are exactly ninety degrees! You'd better start again," says Mary, and Adrienne, another guest tonight, guffaws. Hickory blushes.

Winnie answers Vicki, "You know, I don't even know myself at this point which enchiladas are which! I think it's better we don't know which are of the poultry persuasion and which are of the serpent variety, don't you? It seems fairer." There wasn't enough chicken to go around after I showed up at the last minute with Adrienne and Stewart from the Triple A. Bad Eddy shot a big rattlesnake down on the road near Johnny Bucci's this afternoon, and the cooks improvised. Rattlesnake is supposed to taste a lot like chicken. I help myself to salad and smile at Hickory. The fresh snakeskin, about three feet long, is stretched and nailed on a board above a kitchen window. Libre's too high up for rattlesnakes, but it's lower here.

The Dog Brothers left this morning for a gig in Taos this weekend. The goats are at Beebe's goat farm in Purgatory Valley for their annual two-week vacation, having wild sex with Mr. Beebe's prize Nubian billy goat, who's sort of the Warren Beatty of goats. Following their lead, I got a ride with Stewart and Adrienne over to the Red Rocks to spend the night with Hickory. We've seen each other at parties and in town, and he's come over to Libre twice, but this is the first time we'll spend the night together since the Peach Run.

"Oh, I've definitely got a snake one," says Mary enthusiastically, "and it's good, just a little more delicate than chicken." Bad Eddy's dimples puncture his cheeks, and his blue eyes crinkle at Mary. If it's possible to swagger sitting down, Bad Eddy's doing it. I fork some enchilada and chew it carefully. The green chile is particularly sharp and flavorful this time of year, and there's so much melted Monterey Jack on top that I can't really taste the meat. A two-foot-long block of Monterey Jack sits on the kitchen counter, and a calico cat jumps up and stealthily approaches it, using pots and bowls on the counter as cover, darting between them toward the cheese like a cowboy in a gunfight. Larry Red Rocker looks over his shoulder at the counter, picks an apple from the bowl on the lazy Susan, and throws it at the cat, which jumps off the counter as the apple splashes into the pot of green chile on the stove. Some Red Rockers raise their eyebrows, but Larry doesn't get up to take the apple out.

"It'll probably improve the flavor," he mutters, concentrating on cutting his enchiladas. "We'll call it Tree of Knowledge chile. Get it? *Snake? Apple?*" Nobody responds.

Mostly Red Rockers at Triple A smoky campfire (from left: Vicki, Stephanie, Annie, Benjo, and Mary).

"So . . . Lars is back from Africa, right, in New York now?" I ask Adrienne.

"Yeah, he bought an apartment on West Seventy-fourth Street, between Columbus and Amsterdam Avenues. He's gotten some bit parts in soaps, that kinda thing," says Adrienne with her mouth full. I think about the picture I took at the Leo party this summer at the waterfall. Linda and Dean were nude, embracing and laughing in a pool. They'll be having another baby next spring, and Lars won't be back for a lot of reasons.

"He's got a boyfriend, too," says Adrienne, pouring another glass of dark, home-brewed beer from the pitcher on the lazy Susan, "and a guest room. It's small, but very Scandanavian, with a white birch double bunk bed above the desk."

"Surprise, surprise!" says Mary sarcastically.

"What's 'surprising'? The boyfriend or the white birch?" asks Dr. Mai.

"Both," says Mary, helping herself to more enchilada.

"Hey!" says Winnie.

"Winnie, I have a child to feed," Mary says.

"Yeah, but you're not nursing," laughs Vicki.

Their homemade beer is dark and strong, and my cheeks are red. After dinner, I help clear the table and clean up. It's Hickory's dish night, so I help scrape the dishes, but then leave it to Hickory and two other Red Rockers to wash them in the deep double sinks.

"So . . . how are you?" Mary asks confidentially, sliding up to me near one of the pillars of the sleeping loft at the edge of the kitchen.

"Oh, I don't know, I guess I'm okay," I say, caught off guard. A little concern in someone's voice brings tears to my eyes.

"But, I mean, what are you going to *do?*" Mary asks quietly, leaning toward me.

"I don't know," I say. "It's complicated."

"No doubt about that," Mary cracks, looking over at Hickory. "Or, maybe it isn't. How do you feel?" she tries again.

"I don't know," I say again, watching Hickory's back. He's talking and joking at the sink, but knows I'm watching.

We don't want to be the first to go to bed, so we sit on the ripped, overstuffed couches in the hot, dry dome trying to look like we're part of the conversation. All the time the side of my body next to Hickory's heats and glows, and the heat spreads over the rest of me, and when he brushes my arm or puts his hand on my knee, a wondrous desire uncoils like a snake deep inside me. Finally, Stephanie goes upstairs to put her toddler to bed, and we listen to *Goodnight Moon* and then count her footsteps over to her bed in the sleeping loft above us. After a suitable wait, Hickory stands up and says, "Well, I guess we'll turn in." I get up too fast, then try to look casual and say good night to everyone. In turn, they try to look uninterested, but when we're halfway up the stairs, there's a muffled laugh. It's a little like high school here. There are more high-spirited jokes, like Anson Red Rocker's framed summa cum laude Harvard degree hanging in the two-seater outhouse across the meadow from the dome.

Stephanie's bed and her little girl's crib are at the western end of the semicircle of double beds strung across the loft against the dome wall like beads on a big necklace. Hickory's bed is at the far eastern end. The loft smells of dust and dirt, of piñon smoke and dirty laundry. "I washed my sheets yesterday," Hickory says, reading my mind, as he slips out of his overalls like a snake shedding its skin. The candle he's lit flickers on his strawberry blond hair as he unbinds it, on his pale pinkish skin where the sun never hits it, on his slim butt, on the long muscles in his lean back. I take my clothes off quickly and jump under the covers. It's even warmer in the loft—heat rises. Hickory lifts the covers and slides in toward me. Our feelings compress into the present. They burst out and roll over us, as we lock ourselves in each other's arms, twisting and sliding out of time entirely into a sweetness that may only be novelty. Who knows? Hickory understands how my life's entangled with David's, twisting back through the end of our childhood, across the continent, and far into a mythical future. He knows I take David's acceptance as a betrayal, and recognizes the contradictions in my philosophy. He probably realizes before I do that I'll never be a regular in the Red Rockers' dormitory, that I'll never leave the house around the rock, and his knowing makes me want to please him tonight. We're not unaware how pleasure is heightened by impossibilities. I lie back on his foam mattress after making love. The dome darkens, and people trudge up the stairs to sleep, and we wait impatiently for everyone to fall asleep so we can make love again.

Late in the night I get up and pad down the stairs, cross the empty dome, and walk gingerly in my bare feet out into the meadow to take a pee. The smell of the sage mixes with the salty, acrid human odor I've brought with me into the last of the cold mountain night. I squat and watch the moon, about to set over the Sangres down through the crack of the canyon, an unfamiliar angle and a partial view of the range I see completely from up on the ridge. We don't sleep much, and just before dawn I want to make love again, but Hickory doesn't. He can't help being angry and hurt by my choices after all, even if he understands them. Hickory doesn't have a New Age view of sexual encounters, I guess. I'm glad to be in a crowd at breakfast, and Hickory and I don't talk to each other much at the table. Dr. Mai and her husband will give me a ride back to Libre on their way to Ortiviz Farm, where Mai wants to check on a sick baby. Hickory walks out behind me, and we hug and kiss good-bye as Mai busies herself checking her doctor bag again. Hickory's eyes are wet with tears, and so are mine when we step back from each other, and I turn quickly and get in the truck, and we drive slowly down the rutted road away from the dome. I look back through the cracked cab window at him. When our eyes meet, he turns slowly and walks back inside.

By November, Hickory's hooked up with a pretty redhead he met when he was in Taos for a month getting over me. I'm relieved, actually happy for him, and a little sad.

37 : Horse Dreams

One late October night after dinner David twisted the gear to lower the delicate mantle on an Aladdin kerosene lamp. If a mantle burns too high, it flames up, ruined, and they're expensive to replace. He took his cigarette out of his mouth, looked at it for a while, and said, "Henry and I want to go to Denver this winter to try to make it with our music—get gigs, and try to sell our songs. I'd like to raise some money for spring, you know?" He didn't ask me to come too. Of course, that was impossible, as I was teaching reading at the Ortiviz school, and there was no one to take care of the goats, the cats, the house and plants if we both went away. Bill Keidel was back in New York. Doug was in North Carolina. Annie and baby Julep were in Texas for a long family visit. From Texas, Annie and Julep were meeting Peter, Nancy, and Monty to go to Rum Cay for a Caribbean holiday later in the winter. Peter had scammed a boat there.

Dallas was on the ridge in the early winter, but he couldn't cover for me. His two kids from a former marriage had come back with him from California, and they were all staying in Richard and Beth's former house for a few weeks. I never even knew that Dallas had kids. He said their mother needed a break, and I saw what he meant. Richard and Beth's house lost its Zen feel pretty quickly. There were empty boxes of Froot Loops lying all over the place.

"Dallas," I yelled, as little Dallas beat frantically on his drums in the loft. "Why Froot Loops?"

"That's all they'll eat," he said, keeping his Zen demeanor against all odds. Dallas couldn't have covered for me if I'd gone to Denver with David and Henry. His hands were full. I didn't want to crash around at different houses in Denver this winter anyway.

"For every action, there's an equal and opposite reaction," I said to David that night.

"What does that mean?" he asked. "Look, no one will discover us on the side of a mountain. No one's going to buy rights to our songs in Gardner. We're almost broke, and we can't build in winter. This is my chance to see if we can make it!" I was becoming an obstacle to David's artistic freedom instead of an inspiration. I liked the role of muse better.

"Well, I'll miss you. It'll be hard without you," I said slowly.

"We'll make it down for visits in the week sometimes, even if we're working weekends," David said, standing up. "I'll do dishes tonight."

So, for most of this winter, I was the only person on the ridge. After Dallas and the kids left, there was an old-fashioned three-day Colorado blizzard, like the one Baby Doe Tabor froze to death in. To get up to the goat shed, I fell face down in the snow to tamp it into a walkable path. I thought of Baby Doe in Leadville, going through the same motions to get to her cabin by the Matchless Mine, but I got so short of breath I lost the extra energy to think about history or metaphors. I had to repeat the trip carrying up melted snow for the goats to drink. My legs got sore high-stepping through snow. I locked the goats in their coyote-proof shed. It was sealed and insulated, and they kept one another warm. They didn't want to go outside.

Once the snow started, I didn't have anyone to talk to except the cats and the goats. I had enough wood and food, and enough drinking water in the coconut oil drum in the sleeping loft above the kitchen sink. I melted snow and ice all day in the dish tubs on the stove for wash water and for the goats. I started *War and Peace* and didn't leave Tolstoy's world even when I stopped reading—the snow outside looked Russian. Sometimes I was so entranced by Tolstoy I'd forget to stoke the stoves until I started to shiver. I wrapped myself in a sleeping bag, wore gloves to hold the book, and read fourteen hours a day. The cats nestled on the down bag and complained when I moved. My eyes hurt from reading by kerosene lamp. I became constipated out of self-preservation, to avoid going down to the outhouse. The third day I had to go, and did the falling-face-first routine again. At the outhouse I hesitated, screwed up my courage, and slid my pants and long underwear down to sit on the cold seat. I opened the most recent *New Yorker* arbitrarily to a full-page ad: "*Mr. and Mrs. Elliott Detchon on their Third Trip to Bermuda*" was the caption under a picture of a couple smiling at each other as they waterskied. Inside the outhouse as the blizzard howled, I laughed. Tolstoy could do something with this, I thought. I had broken up with Elliott Detchon at Yale before I met David. I didn't want to be in Bermuda with him, but I appreciated the irony. Two days later, Minnesota came up the ridge on snowshoes to check on me. At first the words stuck inside my mouth like peanut butter, but Minnesota was patient and pretended not to notice, and eventually I got the hang of human conversation again.

By the time I meet David in Denver to fly east to see my family for Christmas, I'm ready for a break. I haven't told them he's living in Denver and I'm alone on the ridge. They don't notice we're any different, and this is reassuring. The man sitting across my parents' big Portuguese dining table is the boy I brought home for Thanksgiving my sophomore year of college. Others are around a lot, so David and I don't need to have long conversations, which don't come easy lately. We know just how to behave here. Only my mother is slightly suspicious because we're acting so normal, but she's too busy with holiday preparations to focus. The familiar tasks and traditions keep all of us occupied: buying the Christmas tree with my father two days before Christmas and lying to my mother about the price so she's not upset, switching the colored light bulbs when Mom points out two reds together, unwrapping her childhood ornaments and hearing how kids back then were *happy* to get an orange for Christmas.

After the Christ Church midnight service, where my dad's sung tenor solos for decades, my brother leaves for the city, and everyone goes upstairs to bed. I linger in the living room with just the Christmas tree lights on, soothed by old familiar objects and the customary clank and hiss of radiators. Do all our memories grow into childhood? On the wall is an old print in its heavy gold frame, an English country scene. I see each detail, more from memory than by the muted light from the Christmas tree bulbs and the streetlights reflecting off the snow outside. A white stucco farmhouse with a thick thatched roof is in the foreground on the left. Large trees shelter the house, and a woman in a long dark skirt, white blouse, and big head scarf stands in the shade in the yard, holding a basket on her hip. Three fat Guernsey cows stand in the middle of a summer afternoon, their front hooves in the wide, shallow river flowing by the house across the foreground of the picture. One cow's drinking, and the other two stare lazily past me into the living room, a world away from Johnny Bucci's scrawny brown steers. Tall grass waves in the wide meadow in the center of the print, and a few innocent clouds punctuate the sky. Some birds fly above the grass—you can't tell what kind. In the background to the right is another white house, and a small dirt lane weaves between the two houses. I know more about dirt roads now, not to mention building houses like that.

I used to get lost in the picture when I was little. My parents' house is built on the site of an old farmhouse. There's a large old linden tree in our front yard, one left from the pair in front of the farmhouse, torn down to build our house. Our home was new, postwar, first in the suburb named after the farm. My father grew up in a family of eight on a New Rochelle farm not far from here. My mother was an only child who grew up thirty-five miles south in Manhattan after Nana threw my grandfather out. My mother says that when her father left, she threw his clothes down the stairwell after him. He liked the horses too much, and died on the street with all that money in his pocket. In my family there were two children, me and Jimmy, who was seven years older. He told me we were a nuclear family, but never said what we had to do with the bomb.

The stories about my father's childhood were better than my mother's. His were closer to the books I loved—Laura Ingalls Wilder's *Little House in the Big Woods*, *Little House on the Prairie*, *By the Shores of Plum Creek*, *The Long Hard Winter*, stories of the pioneer family restlessly moving across the West, and Pa playing the fiddle by the stove during the long winter nights. Kate Seredy's *Good Master*, about the spoiled little Budapest girl visiting her uncle's farm, riding horses over the plains with her cousins and wearing layered skirts and shiny red boots on Easter Sunday. Walter Farley's novel *The Black Stallion*, with shipwrecked, orphaned Alec Ramsey and an Arabian stallion stranded on an island, galloping on the beach.

One night I had a dream that took place on the farm in the picture. My friends and I rode our horses up to the white farmhouse, hitched them to a post, and went inside to drink mugs of sweet, cold milk. After that, when I lay on the oriental rug and looked at the picture with half-closed eyes, I could go back to that dream and make things happen. I put my feet up on the piano bench, which was scratched from when Nana and I played horses and men and pretended the piano bench was a mesa. We hadn't noticed we were gouging the wood as we galloped our little plastic horses on top of it until my mother came into the room and scolded us.

First, my friend Leigh and I were cousins in the dream, and then there were more friends, six of us living in a kind of dormitory room in the eaves of the big white farmhouse. I had a boyfriend a little like Kate's in *The Good Master,* a little like Alec in *The Black Stallion,* but also like Trevor, the blond Swiss boy who lived down the hill from us with four brothers and a little sister. They didn't have a TV, so they watched *The Wonderful World of Disney* with us on Sunday nights. As time went on, I embellished my dream. No dream stands still. My boyfriend couldn't be in the same family, so his family lived in the other house in the print, up the lane and across the meadow, and his brothers had minor roles in my stories. I lay on the Persian rug with the front door open in the spring after school, and the songbirds in the linden tree outside flew through the screen door into the picture and landed in the thickets by the river and sang. My parents were there, kind and more distant than usual, though it was hard to imagine my mother in a long skirt and head scarf—she had short, wavy hair, and wore stockings with a black seam running down the back and high heels, even when she vacuumed. But my parents were only supporting actors. The real action was between me and my friends.

My dream was my own secret place. It made me feel the way I felt sitting on the big granite rock in the woods behind our house where Nana and I walked when I was little, and she stood on the path and picked pussy willows, and I climbed up the big rock, which was a gentle whale, an elephant, a fort—mine, all mine. My mother would say, "What are you doing lying around on the carpet on a beautiful day? Daydreaming again? Why don't you go outside and play?" Soon I didn't need to look at the picture to have my waking dream. I could have it anywhere, usually at night when I finished reading, when my parents kissed me, turned out the lights, and I circled into sleep. First my friends and I rode in the meadow, but soon we rode out of the picture, past my boyfriend's house all the way to the village, or we splashed into the stream and followed it beyond the gilded frame into a big grove of trees and then into wilder fields with rock walls we jumped over on our horses, laughing and calling to each other. Sometimes my horse was a sorrel, sometimes a bay, Leigh's was a pinto, and my boyfriend's horse was a deep gray.

I'm not sure when I stopped dreaming the dream—maybe it was when Trevor kissed my hand while no one was looking as we watched Davy Crockett in Frontierland, or after Nana died in the hospital in the city, or in seventh grade, when Pam became my best friend and we were always together. I mentioned my old dream, but Pam didn't like horses much and wasn't interested. We sat in her bedroom and played 45s of Chuck Berry and the Everly Brothers. As we grew older, our dreams took place in the city, where Scott and Zelda had splashed in the midnight fountain, where Kerouac and Ginsberg stood on the fire escape and read poetry, where Bob Dylan sang at Gerde's Folk City. The print stayed over the piano, like a picture of the family farm left behind to cross the waters, like a counterfeit postcard from the past.

On Christmas Eve the animals talk, but the Guernseys in the print don't say a word as the headlights of a passing car pan the living room wall and the tires swish slowly in the wet eastern snow. You've got more control projecting your dreams on inanimate objects, but even so, I can't go really back to this childhood waking dream. Was it replaced by the waking dream of Colorado? Was my first dream prophecy or practice? Tonight my Huerfano life seems not much more real than what happened in the print, but more complicated, and not so easy.

Underneath the Christmas tree are pillows I wove at Libre for my mom, the Parmesan cheese I made for Aunt Mabel and Uncle Carl, the cowboy shirts for Dad and Jimmy I made working next to Linda in her dome. She and I laughed and sewed and talked about everything, except her baby who was coming and her baby who was gone. The gifts prove that my Colorado story is real. We'll spend New Year's in New York with Lars and some Huerfano folks. Lars will be wearing a tuxedo now instead of his buckskins, but our laughter will testify to the valley and our dreams. After the holidays, we'll show slides to American Studies students at Yale—more proof. I turn out the lights and tiptoe upstairs to my old twin bed, next to the one David's sleeping in. Before I climb under the worn satin duvet, I kiss him on the forehead, but he doesn't wake. It's Christmas. On the wall at the foot of our beds is the lithograph of the baby burro and the print of the Triple Crown winners Nana gave me. In the electric twilight of the streetlights, Citation stares at me majestically.

All the time I thought my first real love was David. How could I forget it was horses?

38 : Biting the Bullet

David and Henry came back to the Huerfano a month ago. Over the winter they'd gotten gigs in Denver and surrounding ski resorts. A coked-out agent from L.A. heard them at Vail and gave them his card, but they didn't call him. They spent most of their earnings on living expenses. It's almost summer. For every action, there's an equal and opposite reaction. In this new, warming season, they're back, the goats had their kids, Dean and Linda had a another baby, and I had another affair. Then I made enough money working in a Holly-wood western to buy a horse.

Linda had a perfect baby boy this time, in the little geodesic dome she and Dean had connected to the big dome with a passageway. Only Dean and Dr. Mai were there, but I knew it was happening. I was outside taking a pee late at night when I saw Mai's truck drive up down below. The lights were on in the little dome, and I stood nude on the deck until I got chilled, hearing only the oc-casional whir of bat wings. He was born with the cord wound tightly around his neck, and Mai had to work hard. Linda told me that she lay in bed listening to a cricket while Mai worked. Later, once the baby was fine, asleep in his bassinet, and Linda was half dozing, she felt something on her arm and flicked it off. She woke up suddenly, checked the baby, and saw it was a black widow that had landed on him, and carefully removed it.

When I visited the next morning, Linda sat up in bed with the baby folded against her, his small mouth mov-ing as he slept. He had red hair—redder than his sister's hair, it seemed to me. Dean stood behind me and stared down, as if he needed to keep watching the baby or he'd disappear. Linda's face was tired but translucent. I sat on the edge of the bed, and she smiled at me as I pushed the flannel blanket back gently to see his face.

"What's his name?" I whispered.

"Luz," she said in a low voice. Luz means "light" in Spanish.

"Well, umm, so, a boy this time," I said. "It couldn't be any more different."

"No," she agreed, looking down at him, "it couldn't be." It seemed as if she hadn't smiled like that forever. Our first year here was darkened by Lia's death, and this year is illuminated by Luz's birth. I walked out into the morning sun past the fruit trees Dean had planted over Lia's grave. The hole in their life is counterbalanced, not filled in.

Against these facts of birth and death, my affair's hardly worth talking about. I don't know how it happened. Do things "happen" to you when you prefer not to take responsibility? David's and my marriage was at a fragile, tedious equilibrium. We were still familiar, polite, and perhaps a little numb. After the long, hard winter alone, I had to act up. I went to Taos in April with the head of the Ortiviz Farm school, Lynn, to back her up and ask the Lama Foundation for some money for the school. Lama had published Baba Ram Dass's *Be Here Now,* a bestseller, so we figured they had some extra money. Hippies sniff out extra money the way pigs find truffles. Daddy Dave Gordon, the drummer for the Dog Brothers, who'd lived in Taos for years before the Huerfano, drove down with us. He had many Taos friends he needed to see, and he wanted to set up gigs for the band, since David and Henry were returning soon. We stayed with my friend Brooke, a six-foot-tall blonde who looked like Virginia Woolf dressed in Peruvian textiles, and who lived in a house low on Lama Mountain. The first night there, Lynn and I sat at the kitchen table sipping mint tea with Brooke.

"Who's that big guy in the other room who keeps looking at me funny?" I asked.

"That's Paul. He's Danish. He rode his horse up into the mountains last year and lived in caves and meditated." Brooke flipped her hair out of her eyes and smiled. "Mountain man type—he doesn't talk much." Maybe my interest was piqued when I heard that Paul rode a horse all over the mountains. Maybe you fall in love to absorb another lifetime. Love and learn.

Lynn, Brooke, and I caught up on Huerfano and Taos news and drank two pots of tea. Bill Keidel was still in New York. Doug had been hired to paint a big house in North Carolina and fell in love with the woman of the house. After that, he took a lot longer to finish the paint job. She's the sister of our Buffalo friend Jeff Davis, and has three kids, and her husband's not taking it well, so Doug, she, and the kids might escape to the West. Peter and Nancy went to Rum Cay this spring with Monty, Annie, and her baby. Peter paired off with Annie, and Monty kept Nancy occupied.

"Monty's not a good bet for the long run," Brooke said, putting more honey in her tea.

"No kidding!" I said. "He backed off big-time when they got back, but Peter and Annie are still going strong."

"Oh-oh, Spaghetti-O," said Brooke. Paul must have heard me tell Brooke I'd forgotten my toothbrush that night. The next morning he bought a new one and dropped by the house with it. I was impressed with his thoughtfulness. Later that day, the Lama Foundation promised to give us some money for the school, though somewhat reluctantly, and it wasn't as much as we'd asked for.

They said, "You overestimate our royalties from Baba Ram Dass's book. We've spent a lot of those profits. Our well is running dry."

"At least you had a well," I said. To celebrate getting the school money, Daddy Dave organized a trip to the hot springs in Ranchos de Taos the next night. Lynn, Daddy Dave, Brooke's friend Star, and I squeezed into the cab of Daddy Dave's Chevy pickup. Star had just gotten a cast taken off her leg, and she wanted to go to the hot springs to heal it. She'd broken her leg on acid, when she jumped off a bridge in Arroyo Seco, convinced she could fly. Maybe Icarus was high on a hallucinogenic root. At the package store in Arroyo Hondo, we bumped into Paul and his buddy Chuck, who decided to tag along.

It was a cold, starry spring night, and there weren't many trucks on the main drag. We smoked a joint on the way to the hot springs, and I had a few sips of beer, but that doesn't explain what happened. When the truck turned off and we parked on the ridge above the hot springs, all of us felt the starry silence and stopped talking. We were outside time, walking down the path to springs that Indians used for centuries to heal their battle wounds, as if we'd walked through a door into a different world. Paul walked behind me, his step light for someone his size, and we all made our way fairly nimbly down the steep and narrow path to the springs. Even Daddy Dave, a perennial chatterbox who limps because of a childhood case of polio, wasn't making any noise. At the springs, steam rose off the pool in the pale starlight, and there was a moist, mineral smell. We undressed and put our clothes and shoes in precarious stacks on the large rocks around the springs to keep them dry. We slipped into the pool quickly, out of modesty, I suppose, and to warm up.

Neither Paul nor I spoke, but when he glided toward me in the water, I put my arms around his neck without thinking as we treaded water in the pool. I can't explain my actions. I was treading hot water with a quiet man who'd brought me a new toothbrush that morning. We were under a sliver moon and myriad stars, and I gave up trying to figure it out. It felt so natural—so what if it's a cliché? I thought of the hot springs scene in *Easy Rider,* and of Mary McCarthy writing that she didn't feel promiscuous, despite the evidence to the contrary. Daddy Dave and Lynn were in one corner, and Chuck and Star were in another. There were a few low words and some occasional soft laughter across the pool, and then little waves rippled across the surface and lapped against Paul and me with the undulations of their hips. Then Paul and I followed suit, and our hips pressed and swayed together, and the water got more agitated around us, leaping up and licking against our necks, splashing our hair as we moved faster. We clung to each other in the warm water, my cheek pressed into the side of his straining shoulder. The steam from the water made it hard to see the others, and above us the thin, pearly moon blurred. Our attitudes have changed so much from those of the repressed society in which we grew up. If you feel any affection or attraction for someone, it's downright rude and quite awkward not to make love if the opportunity comes along. It's not much more than a handshake to some. I know, for example, that the Tahitians have a more casual attitude toward sex, but I grew up in a different climate, and it's hard to change completely.

But I'm taking a more Continental, existential approach this time. There's the fact that David wants to accept an open marriage, while in my view, I'm unfaithful. There's the fact that Luz was born, and the fact that the Huerfano's my home, and the fact that David doesn't seem to want children anytime soon, or maybe ever. There's the fact that, viewed from the front, our house looks complete, like fake houses on western movie sets. But I'm not going to drive myself crazy trying to connect the dots like before, when I was so immature. I'm just going to try to *be,* like Jean Seberg in *Breathless.* Geography helps us keep our equilibrium—it's easier to *just be,* when I'm being with Paul in Taos and David's in the Huerfano.

In late July, when the Dog Brothers are on a long road trip, I get a ride down to Taos to see Paul. The first morning I'm there, we go over to New Buffalo with his buddy Chuck, who's looking for a guy who owes him money. The debtor's disappeared without a trace, as debtors often do, and we sit at the big kitchen table in the New Buffalo kitchen, drinking bitter cowboy coffee with two men passing through on their way to Nevada. When I chopped onions with the women at New Buffalo in 1969, the kitchen was bustling with domestic, feminine activity all day. There are still a few of the originals around here, Chuck says, but they're not in the kitchen right now, and it feels empty and tomblike inside the heavy adobe walls. The huge ceiling vigas have darkened, and the two big wood cookstoves are cold. They made coffee this morning in a six-cup pot on a Coleman stove.

As we sit around the table, tires crunch in the courtyard, and then car doors slam crisply. Four strangers walk into the kitchen, one woman and three short men dressed in new, ironed clothing, but they're not cops. She's got dark hair and wears makeup, and she moves quickly, like a bird searching out worms. She glances at us brightly and says, "Okay, we're looking for some male extras for a movie directed by Richard Brooks that's filming in Chama next week. Gene Hackman, Candace Bergen, James Coburn, and you! Fifty dollars a day plus meals! Anybody here interested?" One of the men with her uncaps his pen and opens a notebook.

Paul looks at Chuck, and Chuck smiles and says, "When do we start?"

"Next Monday up in Chama, seven A.M. for wardrobe and makeup. Expect to be there a week or two," the woman answers, sizing them up and smiling briefly. "Do you have any friends who might be interested? We need about fifty men."

"What about women?" I ask.

"We're looking for men, mostly," she says. "We need a few barmaids, but they have to look like they've been around."

"I been around," I say, trying to sound like Mae West.

She looks at me, frowns a little, then decides it's not worth arguing. "Okay," she says, "but we need lots of men." I'm glad I got the job, but then worry I'm losing my ingenue look.

"What's the movie?" Chuck asks, towering over the little guy with the notebook who's taking down our names. He doesn't answer, just looks over at the Hollywood minionette.

"Bite the Bullet," she calls over her shoulder, almost out the door, her job here done. "Got any ideas where I could find more guys?"

In Chama, a high mountain town near the Colorado border, they dress me in a tight-necked lace blouse and a long black skirt, and one of the hairdressers piles my hair on top of my head. I don't look like Miss Kitty in *Gunsmoke,* there's not enough décolletage, but it's their movie. They give Paul a fake leather vest and Chuck and Paul cowboy hats and tell them to put their wristwatches in their pockets during takes. In makeup, they pat me with powder and rouge and put on layers of mascara. They give Chuck a fake mustache that makes him look like Pancho Villa. They've turned the narrow-gauge railroad house into a bar, and all day long we run through the swinging doors of the saloon, whooping it up, ready for a good ol' time tonight. Each time Richard Brooks runs his bony fingers through his white crewcut and shouts "Action!" Paul picks me up and runs, and I wrap my arms around his neck and fling back my head and laugh wantonly, and we stampede inside with the other thirsty cowboys, racing at the camera.

This suits me fine. It's easier to just be when I'm away from the Huerfano, and David's got to be glad I'm making good money. Vicki Red Rocker, Monty, and Minnesota get jobs here too, so a small stream of Hollywood cash is diverted into the Huerfano. Paul and I have a room at the Elkhorn Hotel looking out over the narrow-gauge train and the set. Nothing's better for lovers than being orphaned like this, losing your history, escaping difficult situations, and starting life somewhere else. Presto! It's simple—most of the people here don't know anything about me, except that I'm with Paul. Change-o! We're not hippies anymore, we're extras in a big Hollywood film, paid to pretend we're from another century. I'm part of the fake Old West I fell in love with on our black and white TV or at the drive-ins, an eight-year-old swooning over Clayton Moore and Randolph Scott. Everything comes full circle.

There's at least an hour's wait between takes while Brooks, his cameraman, and the assistant director confer with the sound and light men. During breaks, most of the extras sneak down to the river and smoke joints. Consequently, the later takes are better, since the extras are more and more stoned and weave and stumble realistically through the saloon doors. The movie's about a cross-country horse race, and sleek Hollywood horses stand in the corrals under the aspens by the river. During the breaks I walk down to talk to them. They're bored and happy to see me, and lean over the fence so I can scratch their noses and straighten out their thick manes. When they've had enough primping, they stomp impatiently and flip their heads like peevish starlets. My girlhood love for horses was a cliché, but that's okay. I'll take my movie money and buy the horse I always wanted, ticking off my checklist of dreams one by one. But two weeks' salary may not be enough to buy a horse.

At the end of the second week, the assistant director stands on a table and says, "That was a good day! That's all we need you for now, but we'll do some more crowd scenes here in, oh, three weeks. Pick up a sheet of paper with instructions and the number to call from Cindy over there." Cindy, who recruited us at New Buffalo, sits on another table with a stack of papers in her arms. "Oh, yeah, before I forget," he adds, "is there a barmaid here who knows how to play blackjack?" I raise my hand quickly, and he glances over at Richard Brooks, who nods absentmind-edly, and then he says, "Okay, stay to talk to me afterwards." Cindy looks at me suspiciously.

I don't know how to play blackjack, but try to look confident as the assistant director explains they need a barmaid to deal blackjack in a critical scene between Gene Hackman, James Coburn, and a white-haired character actor who plays the sponsor of the movie horse race. "Same pay, now," the assistant director says, "no lines, or we get in trouble with the union. Be at makeup at seven to get your hair done each day. It's gotta be the same for continuity."

"Will you teach me how to play blackjack?" I ask Monty as we head back to the hotel.

"How did you end up a hippie?" Monty asks. "You go, but not ex-actly with the flow!"

The next three mornings, I sit in a makeup chair next to Gene Hack-man, who treats me like an equal, which makes me feel guilty that I lied about knowing blackjack. In contrast, Coburn and Bergen treat me like I'm no one, which is annoying. I deal cards to the stars in close-up for three days. We come back three weeks later and film the crowd scenes by the train, getting covered with soot and smoke each day. Paul's and my movie is drawing to a close, too. After Chama, he moves up to the Red Rocks, too close to home, breaking the rules. We don't have a future, and we've just about played out our present. Paul's sad but philosoph-ical, the way someone who's spent a year in a cave thinking about things can be, and besides, he's got a Scandinavian sophistication to begin with. It's too messy, too difficult, and I can't be with him in the Huer-fano. But I have nine hundred dollars, enough to buy a horse and make a getaway.

Back in L.A., the nice, white-haired character actor has a fatal heart attack before the movie wraps, and they have to cut his scenes and reshoot them in Hollywood. His scenes were my scenes. I tell my par-ents, but they go to the premiere at Radio City Music Hall anyway.

"You weren't in the movie much," my mother says, sighing.

"I told you, Mom, the guy died, and I ended up on the cutting room floor," I say.

"Oh, well," she sighs again.

"Look, that's Hollywood! I hope you haven't told a lot of people I'm in it," I sigh.

"Not that many," she sighs more. She'll always be better at sighing than I am. "Aunt Mabel and Uncle Carl, of course. They went with us to Radio City. They're your godparents, after all," she says.

"You don't need to remind me who they are! Look, what's good is that I have enough money to buy a horse," I say, hiding my exasperation.

"That's nice," she says. "I used to ride." After Nana married Pop, Mom rode in Central Park in the taupe wool jophurs that are still in the cedar trunk in her cellar. She'll probably mail her riding pants to me, imagining me in a similarly genteel scene. Despite my years in the wild Rockies, she can't help casting me in a different life. Last Christmas she walked in when I was taking a bath, looked at the muscles in my shoul-ders and arms, and cried, "You can never wear a formal gown again!" I sank down in the suds, not bothering to point out I wasn't going to any charity balls in the life I've chosen.

Likewise, I don't bother to contradict her now, saying, "Talk to you soon! Love you!" and hanging up. Why bother to correct her illusions? She's doing her best not to correct mine.

39 : Tricky Dick

Nancy gave Libre ten thousand dollars for a new water system this summer, and everyone's been working on it. In June, Mr. Vargas, the Huerfano water witch, came up with his willow dowsing stick to find the right spot to dig a well by Peter and Nancy's zome. Since Nancy gave the money, they get to have the well nearby. Peter and some other men here have dug down forty-five feet and there's no water yet. Peter hired Philbert Montez to trench the lower land to bury the pipes. Philbert's not trenching down to Patricia's house because of Peter and Patricia's fight over the water system. I don't know the details and don't want to find out. Since Patricia's down at Farasita Farm most of the time, I don't know how they managed to have a fight. Dallas, Monty, Minnesota, Patricia, and her new boyfriend, Vincie, are digging their trench by hand.

The ridge is too rocky and inaccessible for trenching, but Peter found a heavy old three-thousand-gallon steel railroad tank in Trinidad. To get it up the ridge, we got the county road grader to tow the flatbed backwards carrying the tank. David steered the flatbed blindly as it was pulled in reverse, and the big water tank slid back and teetered over him. We set it on a pedestal of railroad ties on the ridge road above the goat house. Dean, Linda, David, and I painted for short spurts inside the tank with Retardo, which had a skull and crossbones on the can. We probably lost some brain cells, but we've got running water on the ridge, at least in summer. In winter we'll fill the fifty-five-gallon drum in the loft above the kitchen sink during the day, then drain the aboveground pipes so they don't freeze. There's a thousand-gallon storage tank for Richard and Beth's house, which Doug, his North Carolina love Martha, and her three kids have moved into, and there's a smaller tank at Bill's house for Annie and the baby. The word is Bill isn't coming back. He went down to Peter's zome to confront Peter about his carrying on with Annie, and no one was there, although a big pot of spaghetti sauce was simmering on the stove. Bill went berserk and flung the sauce all over the white walls. He left the valley soon after that. After the Great Spaghetti Massacre, Peter and Annie's affair is still going strong, but I'm betting Peter will stay with Nancy while they spend her money on the Libre water system. David says I have a bad attitude, I'm too negative and don't appreciate Peter's generosity with Nancy's money, which has changed our lives. He's right. Peter gave up on the Libre well in his meadow, and we got Philbert to dig out the spring box in Dry Creek to have water most of the year. Libre bought a more powerful pump and thousands of feet of one-and-a-quarter-inch PVC pipe, and we can pump up the ridge and fill all the tanks when the water's high. It's like having money in the bank.

This evening David, Doug, and I drive around Gardner in the pickup drinking cold Cokes. It's like old times, like our drives the first summer, when we bopped around the valley together, windows down, the smell of sage sifting in, the breeze evaporating the sweat off our faces, separating our damp hair at the roots. We're not going to finish the house this year either. A lot of things have diverted our energy—maintaining an equilibrium while I had an affair with Paul, my summer movie career, the Dog Brothers' gigs, work on the water system. Since he's been back, Doug helps with the goats and small projects once in a while, but Martha and her three small kids naturally take most of his time. But this evening it's a replay of our first summer, and we sip the chilled Cokes as the songs of meadowlarks on the fence posts zip through the open windows as we drive past. That first year we felt like Che, Fidel, and Sonia in the Sierra Maestra, and we knew even then that those were memorable times. At the outdoor pay phone in Gardner, we pull up next to Mary, Brooke, and their baby girls. Bad Eddy, Mary, and baby Molly live with Brooke and her daughter over in Malachite now. There was some kind of scene at the Red Rockers, and Bad Eddy and Donny, Benjo's felonious twin, had to leave. I can't imagine the Red Rocks without Mary, or vice versa.

She calls over the engines, "Did you hear?"

"Hear what?" Doug asks.

"Nixon's about to resign! We're heading for Steve Dump's. He's got a TV!"

"See you there!" David says. Steve Dump rents a falling-down adobe in Gardner that looks over the arroyo in which rusted washing machines, busted bedsprings, and cracked tires bob on a current of more nondescript trash. When we get there, the small front room is packed with Adrienne and Stewart from the Triple A, some Ortiviz Farm and Archuletaville people, and a Denver couple who've just rented an adobe nearby. We squeeze in along the walls, and almost immediately Nixon's onscreen, sitting at his big desk, saying, "Good evening."

"Still getting your Danish bacon?" Mary whispers, and I step on her foot. She yells, and Adrienne tells her to shut up. The TV reception isn't great, and we can barely hear Nixon over the static. We've listened to some of the hearings on our portable radio since Watergate broke, but we didn't believe Nixon would quit. His face is pastier than usual, remarkably like the complexion of the huge papier-maché Nixon head that the Bread and Puppet Theater carried at the Moratorium in Washington five years ago, when his big head and the head of his attorney general, John Mitchell, wobbled on poles as we chanted, "Impeach them! Impeach them!" until we were hoarse. Now Mitchell's gone and Nixon's going. We're in a crumbling adobe in Colorado, the American troops are out of Vietnam, North Vietnam's marching south, and Nixon's face fills the screen before he leaves in ignominy. All across America, watching Nixon's resignation, is anybody saying, "Hey, those kids were right after all"? My mother's probably sitting on the porch next to my dad, legs crossed, sipping her scotch, saying, "Tsk, tsk, I don't know," in a noncommittal way. In our last call she didn't try to defend Nixon. Just as I gave up on my dreams of victory over Nixon, he quits.

"This is so unreal," says David, "so unreal," looking at me.

"Yeah. I only wish it had been unreal tens of thousands of lives sooner," Mary says.

"Shuddup and listen," Adrienne says, but the wisecracks keep coming as Tricky Dick reads his last presidential speech. When he says, "Therefore, I shall resign the presidency effective at noon tomorrow," we whoop like it's New Year's Eve, and Adrienne passes around beers, but it's still like a strange dream.

"This sounds weird," David says, holding his forehead. "He brought this on himself, I know, but I can't help feeling like we did this too."

"I know what you mean," I say. "It's his karma and our karma." Distracted by the TV, I add, "Ford looks like one of those old-fashioned honest Republicans, doesn't he? It's going to be hard to hate him, you know?"

"This is all so anticlimactic," says Mary. "The wind's out of our sails, kind of."

"I almost feel sorry for them," I say, watching the Nixon family. Mary looks shocked, so I add, "Okay, I almost feel sorry for *Pat*, but not Tricia. My mother always compared me to her." When Batista left Cuba, Che, Fidel, and Sonia rode down from the mountains into Havana triumphantly. We're not going back to reclaim Washington. We'll regroup in the Huerfano, still hoping to change the world through art and a new way of life.

The following weekend we have a Sunday community dinner and celebrate Nixon's fall. We defrost and cook the last pork roast from Tricky Dick, a pig we raised last year. The dinner's at the Grow Hole, in the meadow across from Libre's trash arroyo. We like having community dinners outside there in warm weather because the house is small and half greenhouse. It smells of overheated earth, plants, manure, compost, and bugs, and the decor's early Cro-Magnon. Martha and I fixed manicotti with goat ricotta and tomatoes from the three bushels we bought for canning at our new co-op in Gardner. Last week a private investigator hired by Martha's husband drove up, disguised in a light blue, tight-fitting bell-bottom suit and platform boots, a new style of dress catching on in the cities. It's a young, polyester, patent leather countercultural style which doesn't seem counter or cultural to us. He punctuated his speech with a lot of "hey man's" and thought his cover was successful. Over Texaco's low growls, Jim and Dean stood in the parking lot with their arms crossed over their chests and said no, no one here fit Martha's description. He wasn't convinced, but he gave up and made his way awkwardly in his platform boots over the rocks back to his car.

"Maybe that wasn't a disguise," Dean mumbled to Linda and me after he drove away.

"That's a horrible thought," Linda said.

We stop and wait while Matt, Martha's youngest, catches up as we walk to the Grow Hole. "Come on, Matt," says his sister Maura, exasperated, hands on her hips, like a mother who's had a long day. Walking with Doug and his new family feels good. We're a comfortable tribe. David and I are relaxed. Despite our difficulties, there are rewards for sticking it out. The dinner's perfect. Linda's made a big salad, and the pork roast is great. Nancy couldn't do much, since she's busy building a little house in a grove of trees a stone's throw from the zome. While Nancy was telling me that Annie and baby Julep were moving into the zome with Peter, and that she was moving out and building her little house two hundred yards north of the zome, Peter sat at the table and smiled as if he'd swallowed something hard to keep down but didn't want to offend his hostess. Most of the time Nancy supervises Billy, Dallas's brother, whom she's paying to build the house. She talks as he works, sometimes about how Peter and Annie and she are all friends, and it's better this way, and sometimes about how Peter has taken her for a ride and she hasn't been fooled for one minute. She's still using the zome as a base while her house goes up, per her separation agreement with Peter. I stopped by earlier when she was lopping tops off carrots and peeling them with swift, jerking motions. No one else was there. Nancy wants to remain part of a family here, too.

Monty's brought homemade paté and crackers. Jim and the very pregnant Christine baked some bread, twisting the dough exuberantly into a Sanskrit letter which became unreadable once the bread rose and swelled. They forgot butter, but Peggy has half a stick, although it smells like her refrigerator. Dallas brings what he calls rice salad, which is leftover rice with raw onions in it. Billy has been working hard all day on Nancy's house, so all he brings is local grass. A couple visiting from New York brings jugs of wine. Tom and Peggy got half a bushel of Paonia peaches at the Gardner Cooperative, and Muffin drove to the Malachite Farm and bought two quarts of thick, fresh cream. We borrowed the Red Rockers' ice cream maker, and we take turns cranking it after dinner. The kids dance with excitement.

There's really not much to discuss at the meeting. Peter scolds, "People, the spring box is getting low, and we've got to be more careful about coordinating when we fill our tanks." All the improvements have helped, but the spring box still gets low, causing a low-grade panic, and every other day somebody (including Peter) gets up before dawn and secretly tops off his new personal tank in case the spring runs completely dry. No one responds to Peter. We're busy cranking ice cream, and it's too nice an evening. Besides, there are the guests from New York. We nod, each of us deciding we'll sneak down to top off our tanks before daybreak tomorrow.

The pipe goes around, and Tom Grow takes the last turn at the ice cream maker, cranking faster and faster, and the kids laugh at him. His baggy pants, held up with a tie-dyed scarf, are sitting so low you can see the crack of his butt as he jerks and cranks. He stops suddenly and stumbles backwards, almost tripping over Texaco, who's licking all the empty dinner pans. Muffin takes the top off the ice cream maker and announces, "It's ready!" The kids push against one another, and the mothers yell, "Be patient! There's enough! *Share, share!*" In the twilight, we sit down and eat our bowls of ice cream as a few bats swoosh above us. Linda gives baby Luz a little taste, and everyone laughs when his eyes widen. Our ice cream's a unique color, a mix of rose-yellow peach flesh and pale yellow farm cream. We take our first spoonfuls, then look around the circle.

"This is the best ice cream I've *ever* tasted!" the dark-haired visitor from New York says incredulously. He shakes his head and looks at the thin, curly-haired lady he's with. They're wrestling with the idea of leaving their old life and moving here.

"Naturallllly!" says Peter, his mouth full. The ice cream, supernaturally perfect in texture, taste, and aroma, sits on the back of our tongues and melts, a consummate miracle of peachiness. On a perfect late summer night, as our spoons scrape our bowls, I think, "*I'll always remember this,*" although it's possible I'll be somewhere else remembering it.

Up in Denver two weeks later, I'm regrouping at Dr. Frank's. The remaining *Bite the Bullet* money is in an envelope beside me as I sit on Frank's couch and comb through the *Denver Post* classifieds, looking for a six- or seven-year-old mare. I call a number in Longmont. The mare sounds good, so I drive out into the plains. The bay mare is in a corral and looks fine, but a little sorrel horse hitched nearby catches my eye.

"What about that horse hitched to the fence over there?" I ask Curly, an old cowboy who's been showing me the mare. He was about to saddle her so I could try her out.

"Oh, that one," Curly puts the saddle down. "That's a two-year-old stallion, not broke," he says. "Nice little horse, though." I walk closer to the young coppery red horse. His thick tail almost touches the ground, and he's got a little white diamond on his forehead and one white sock. He stands patiently, mouth open, not used to a bit. He doesn't flinch as I smooth my hand along his beautiful neck.

"He's like a Morgan, so compact, his neck's so strong," I say. This is no way to bargain.

"That little horse is a full-blooded quarter horse," Curly says, "but you know Morgans are one of them breeds they used to make the quarter horse." I comb the coarse hair of the stallion's fetlock with my fingers, then clump it all to one side. His eyes are a shiny, rich brown, and he looks at me calmly. I stroke his nose, a cross between velvet and a baby's bottom, and he sighs a little. I haven't ridden in years. My plan was sensible: get an older mare, breed her, and get a colt eventually, but have an experienced horse to ride first.

"How much is this one?" I ask Curly.

"Well, even though he's not broke, he's got better blood lines than the mare, as you can tell, although she's a good horse, too. He costs a little bit more."

"How much?"

"Four hundred and eighty-five dollars."

I have five hundred dollars, and I was also planning to buy a saddle. "I'll take him," I say quickly, and count the bills out onto Curley's leathery palm. The little red horse watches the money pass hands curiously.

"How're you gonna get him down south?" Curley asks.

"I just have to make a few calls. Can you keep him here a couple of days while I get things organized?" I hadn't planned ahead again. I thought I was going to do a lot more shopping around. Back at Frank's, I have to spend some time calming down Frank's girlfriend, Cream Cheese. She's a little upset about yesterday, when Nancy had dropped me off and asked Dr. Frank if he'd please right away check out her vagina to see if she had a yeast infection or what. Frank had sighed and taken her into the spare bedroom, and I'd had to make small talk with Cream Cheese. Later I start working the phone, calling Johnny Bucci first. He picks up quickly and says, "Hell-O!" above the TV noise in the background. Since Alta May left him, the TV's always on. Johnny says I can borrow a horse transport cage that fits on the back of a pickup, then adds, "Hey, you know that feller Brian, the caretaker at that Buddhist place near you? He's got a nice, new, big Dodge truck, and he always seems a little lonely up there, yunno?"

"Yeah, yeah, Johnny, that's a great idea! I gotta go—thanks. Bye-bye." I say.

"Good luck," says Johnny.

Brian's the caretaker at Dorje Khyung Dzong, the Buddhist retreat a few canyons over from Libre that was Roger Randolph's land. Roger practiced oil and gas law in Oklahoma and wasn't at the cabin much. The local vandals couldn't resist his new washer, dryer, and other appliances. They left behind Tibetan tonkas much more costly than the appliances, and Roger took this as a sign to give his land to Trungpa Rimpoche, a Tibetan lama in Boulder. I've only met Brian once or twice, but Johnny's right. When I ask Brian if he'll drive two hundred miles up to Denver to transport my new horse, he says sure, why not?

Two days later Brian and I drive to Longmont, and Curly helps us load the horse. Brian stays in the truck. He's a little too cosmopolitan and doesn't know horses, but that's okay, he's done enough. I put the new brown halter over my horse's head and lead him up the ramp. He doesn't hesitate to get into the trailer.

"That horse sure has a wonderful disposition," says Curly. "Look at that, never been loaded on anything before! Just followed you like a lamb."

"What are you going to call him?" Brian asks as we drive away. The horse didn't act up when the truck started moving.

"Rufus. That's Latin for 'red,'" I say. On the ride back to the Huerfano, Brian and I talk about how we ended up in the valley, about Trungpa Rimpoche, the lama who heads Naropa Institute, which owns Dorje Khyung Dzong. The window's down, so I reach my hand back to Rufus as we talk, and he lowers his nose through the bars to touch it. A little later I reach back with an apple slice on my palm, and Rufus's soft lips swipe it up. At a gas station in Colorado Springs, Rufus neighs at me when I walk away to the bathroom, and later he neighs in the wind at some horses we're passing near Huerfano Butte, and Brian and I laugh at the sheer joy of the sound. My cheeks are flushed, I'm happier than I've been in a long time. I've always loved horses, and now I have one of my own. It's a mixed blessing playing out your dreams one by one. As you get really old, dreams of the past replace dreams of the future, but I'm still a long way from that, as I put my hand back to feel Rufus's warm breath on my palm, heading west into the Huerfano.

I'm not worried about having a young stallion that's not saddle broken. He has a gentle, trusting nature, and I spend hours brushing, talking, leaning on him. I lean more heavily on his back each day, and he turns his head and looks at me curiously. I give him oats and lie on his neck as he chews. I put his bit on him and lead him around the ridge, talking to him all the time. Sometimes Martha's kids sit on the fence of the corral or stand in the sturdy horse shed David and Doug built next to the goat yard when I showed up with Rufus. One day I lean over his back and push up onto him. He looks back at me calmly.

I don't have enough money for a saddle at first, and we spend the first few weeks with nothing between us. I ride him bareback down on Pando's fields—it's a little softer landing on the ground there. He throws me once when we're galloping at sunset, when he twists and bucks suddenly out of high spirits and sheer delight. He seems surprised when I plop down off his neck, and he stops and nuzzles me on the ground, and then I get back up. I don't believe all the Freudian stuff about penis envy and power tied up with women and horses. It's more sensual and spiritual, and I suspect women are more susceptible to cross-species love.

We speak without words. With a nervous toss of his head and a funny, anxious snort, he shows me where to look for a mountain lion, high up in a ponderosa ten feet from the trail. The tawny cat lies spread across some branches, watching us climb the Turkey Creek trail. His gold-green eyes look right into mine. Maybe he's the cat who jumped Clawed years ago.

Rufus doesn't like branches a certain size lying across the trail because they remind him of snakes. He acts skittish and nervous when a bear's been on the trail right before us, before I see the scat. One day in late June of the following year, we come across a patch of wild strawberries, and I jump down and move through the patch on my knees, picking the tiny berries under the leaves, putting them in my mouth. They're wild and sweet, the *uber*-strawberry. I don't know how long we move in tandem up the slope. He rips at the grass, jiggling his bit, looking at me out of the corner of his eye, snorting. I save up ten tiny berries and pop them in my mouth together, and the juicy flavor dancing on my tongue is chased by the sweet smell of the buffalo grass Rufus snaps up with his big teeth. I'm on my hands and knees parallel to him, popping strawberries, and I laugh when he gives me a strange look. This moment won't come again. The bears get most of the berries on the mountain.

On hot summer days Rufus wades into Ferendelli's pond up to his chest, but no further. He's got a lot of Morgan in him, and Morgans ride into the surf to rescue people, but Rufus didn't inherit that much. He likes me to splash him, but he won't immerse. After the August rains, we spend all day on the mountain finding enough boletus mushrooms to fill two big gunnysacks, and he carries the mushrooms down the trail across his rump. David and I slice and dry most of them, saving a few to fry in butter for dinner. Rufus is happy to graze by a stream under the aspens, taking an occasional sip of springwater, while I lie on my back watching the clouds scud over us, the sound of the rippling water washing through my head. He walks calmly and politely through a herd of elk near the top of Greenhorn right before hunting season, and his ears perk up when I scold a big old elk with huge antlers, telling him to be more careful about humans, for God's sake.

Rufus likes it when it gets cooler and we ride up the creeks under the quivering yellow aspen leaves. He stops and listens to the crows with me when they gather in the big trees above us, calling to one another from branch to branch at sunset. When the first winter snows come, he's extra-frisky, shaking his neck when the fat flakes accumulate on his mane, picking his feet higher out of the snow, galloping through the snowfall. The flakes hit our faces and stick to our eyelashes as we run faster across the white fields in the muffled winter silence. At a creek, he breaks the thin ice with his nose and takes a long drink, and the warmth of his body heats me, though my feet stay cold.

There's a spot under his jaw he loves me to scratch, and he rests the entire weight of his head on my shoulder when I scratch there. One day, after I buy the used child's saddle that fits me just fine, I take a handful of psilocybin mushrooms, and we ride up Williams Creek. He turns when I think about it, before I tell him with reins or knees. I experiment more, thinking, not moving my hands or my body, and every time he anticipates my direction. I don't tell anybody about our telepathy, not even David. Rufus and David have a somewhat formal relationship, but this is the best triangle I've been in so far. Rufus loves Sibylla, the German actress who's building a house on the knoll down below with her German architect husband, Kim. She walks up in her black fur coat and croons in her Marlene Dietrich accent to Rufus over the corral fence, and he eats it up. One day Kim tries to pet him too, and Rufus nips at him—he wants Sibylla all to himself. At Dean and Linda's dome, Linda holds little Luz up in the saddle, and Rufus stands as still as a carousel horse while we talk.

Some horses take advantage of accidents and hurt you, but Rufus doesn't have a mean bone in his body. When the edge of an arroyo collapses on our way back from the Red Rockers, we fall sideways, and my leg's pinned under him, but he lies on his side without moving until I tell him what to do. The sandy ground was soft enough that my leg wasn't hurt. Another time, near the top of the mountain, we almost ride into a pool of quicksand, but he rears back in time and we get out.

I can't remember not seeing the valley from Rufus's back at top speed. I've joined Hoppy, Roy, Cisco, Pancho, and Gene, riding the trails, righting all the wrongs in my head. I've got more in common with Johnny Bucci now than I do with some hippies in the valley. One time Johnny says, "That horse is so gentle, he'd sit in your lap if he could!" Mick Montano pats Rufus's neck and with unusual loquaciousness tells me my little horse is *one good horse*. At Sporleder Feeds, Sig and

I talk about whether I should change Rufus's feed, and Sig tells me when the Trinidad blacksmith will be up visiting the big ranches near us so I can get him to stop by and shoe Rufus inexpensively.

If I didn't have Rufus, I might never have met Nick Faris, but that's a different kind of encounter from these random, cordial meetings with Huerfano locals.

41 : Me and Bobby McGee

At the biggest Thanksgiving ever at the Red Rockers, there are more than two hundred of us, so we need to go outside the big dome for our circle. We stand in the old snow, holding hands in a straggly Möbius strip weaving around the meadow. The mood's festive, in spite of a bitter, cold wind, and we grin across the circle at one another. When somebody yells "Thank you!" we all say "Thank you!" dropping hands, running together, hugging and laughing in a big clump. I see this place as we dreamed it, a new society based on love. David and I had a little piece of windowpane acid when we got here, but maybe that was a mistake. I feel like I've seen something wonderful inside a big room just before a door closes, or I'm looking up at the top of the mountain just as it gets socked in with clouds.

I feel so raw and jagged today—maybe because I've spent most of my time on Rufus's back, not down on this level. Paul's opposite me in the circle, and although we stopped seeing each other months ago, I feel awkward with him at the Red Rocks, trying to treat him like a Huerfano regular. Mary's down the circle from me, holding baby Molly, putting up a brave front on her visit back to the dome she built with her old friends four years ago. I don't see Bad Eddy. When I was helping her ice her chocolate cake before the circle, she cried quietly, and I started crying too, and our tears fell into the vanilla frosting as we scraped out the bowl. Bill's back from New York for Thanksgiving, in the false holiday hope he'll get back with Annie and their baby, but Annie and Julep live in Peter's zome now, and Nancy's moved into her little house nearby. Bill's cheeks are red. He's determined to

Marilynn and me in the Red Rocker dome, Thanksgiving 1974. Photo by David Perkins.

show everyone what a great time he's having. Nancy looks tired, and Peter looks tired, but pleased with himself.

As the acid comes on more, I walk around the dome restlessly, unable to eat, feelings roiling through me. I sit next to Marilynn in a big overstuffed chair in the middle of the crowd, hugging my knees fetally, taking it all in. Johnny Bucci leaves early with the Lenczes the way the locals always do. Strider, in his ancient biker blacks, puts his arms around Stella, who—surprise, surprise—hasn't gotten spiffed up at all. She looks wind- and sunburned, like she hasn't taken a bath or combed her hair too recently. Was she barefoot outside in the snow for the circle? I heard her parents are both Park Avenue psychiatrists—analyze that! The dome buzzes like a hive, and everyone turns into insects, but I can't describe it to Marilynn. She pats me on the shoulder softly. Where's David? I struggle up and look for him, then find him and Henry sitting on the steps of the kitchen smoking. We laugh a little, but I can't stay, I'm coming out of my skin.

When I walk past Bill as he's carving turkey, he puts a big chunk of white meat in my mouth. It's overdone, and my mouth and the turkey are so dry that I choke and walk around clenching my throat, until Dean notices and thumps me on the back. If I'd collapsed, no one would have noticed. A few bodies are sprawled around the dome already, passed out before dinner. It's just what I'm choosing to see—that happens on acid. I take a deep breath and make myself look at Linda smiling at Dean, who's cradling Luz to his chest. Hickory's old lady is pregnant and beaming. Doug has his arm around Martha and looks so happy. Adrienne's happy at last with her new girlfriend.

Late in the evening, when the crowd's thinned out, I'm calmer and more subdued, sitting next to David and Henry as they trade songs. David's been working on "Me and Bobby McGee" lately. His version doesn't sound like Janis Joplin's or Kris Kristofferson's—as usual, it's got his own stamp on it. Everyone used to call me Bobbi through college. At Buffalo I decided I wanted to be called Roberta. My friends had a hard time switching from Bobbi, but David called me Roberta as soon as I said I wanted a change. I sit next to him on the big couch in the darkened dome with Henry, beside Mary and Brooke, their two daughters asleep on their laps. Some Red Rockers are already in bed. Doug and Martha and the kids are bundled up, ready to go home, hanging around for one more song.

As David sings, "*Bobby thumbed a diesel down just before it rained, / Took us all the way to New Orleans . . . ,*" I think of when we hitched to Miami: I can't remember the name of the truck driver who leered at me from eastern Texas to western Florida that first trip. I look down at the last of my cup of coffee with damp eyes, when he sings,

> *Then somewhere near Salinas, Lord, I let her slip away,*
> *Lookin' for that home and I hope she finds it,*
> *Well I'd trade all my tomorrows for a single yesterday*
> *Holdin' Bobby's body close to mine . . .*

We'll hold each other tonight, and I don't sing the blues. Despite my name change and minor inaccuracies, there's a personal truth in the music. We don't look at each other as he sings, and I avoid anyone else's eyes. It's embarrassing, and a little flattering, and almost too sad, but I love to listen to him sing. That's one reason I'm still here, besides whatever else keeps me. If he can sing our story, I can listen to it. His voice has just the right amount of irony and emotion:

Freedom's just another word for nothing left to lose,
Nothing, that's all that Bobby left me, yeah,
But feeling good was easy, Lord, when she sang the blues,
Hey, feeling good was good enough for me, hmm, hmm,
Good enough for me and Bobby McGee.

For Christmas, we go east to my parents' again. Lately I've had the feeling something was ending or changing, but I couldn't tell what, or what was next. We leave early to show our slides to Yale students, and there's a change in them, too. When we showed my Huerfano slides at Yale before, most of the students stayed around to talk excitedly about what we were doing, what it meant. This time, most of them looked at their watches and left. Back at my parents' house, it's the same base camp we always rest up in before we take another run at the mountain, and there's the usual sense of time travel. The stairs Jimmy and I tumbled down Christmas morning. The Mobil Christmas candles made right after the war—wax Santas, angels, soldiers, and reindeer made in the postwar hope and pleasure in plenty and peace. My mother's never lit them. Their colors are fading, and more glitter falls off them each year.

My dad and I lied about the price of the Christmas tree again. When we're decorating it, Uncle Carl calls and says they won't be driving down to visit after Christmas. Aunt Mabel's not doing too well. I ask my mother how long Aunt Mabel has, and my mother shakes her head and says she doesn't know, not long enough. That night I dream I'm in my bedroom here with Hoss Cartwright, the hulking, not too bright but kind middle brother in *Bonanza*. In the dream I sit on the flowered bedspread talking to him. Hoss's hat is off, and he's looking down at his spurs, and then Aunt Mabel opens the door. I'm embarrassed she's walked in on me and Hoss in the bedroom, even though we're only talking. It's so easy to feel naughty back home.

My years in Colorado surface in odd ways. I can't get over the food scraped off the plates into the garbage—at home the pigs would eat it all! For a minute I consider taking a garbage bag of the choicest refuse back on the plane for them. We're too warm in central heating. I drink my tea too soon and scald my mouth, because water boils at a higher temperature here at sea level. I run our clothes through the washer, and my mother runs them through another time. Just like in college, David walks around the block to smoke a joint at night. At Christmas, there's a truce in our house like the one in the Holy Land. We don't descend into the old fundamentalist debate.

The day we leave, I walk around my parents' bedroom upstairs, touching my mother's green Bakelite dresser set, the stuffed tiger from a London friend, my grandmother's lace mats. I wonder if the paperback about improving your sex life is still wrapped in my mother's lingerie drawer, but I don't check. On the mirrored dresser tray is the Art Deco diamond ring Nana wore, the three small diamonds in simple platinum squares. My mother's knuckles have gotten bigger from arthritis, and it doesn't fit her anymore, so she wears her larger diamonds, but this ring is more simple and beautiful to me. It fits loosely on my third finger, and I squint at my hand.

My mother notices the ring when I come downstairs and says, "Do you remember that ring on Nana's hand?" and I say yes. We have to check a big cardboard box on the plane, full of presents and the Thomas's English muffins not available in Colorado. My dad ties the box tightly with twine. We have turkey sandwiches before we leave for La Guardia. My mom and I have tea, and David and Dad split one of the Coors we brought east. We don't talk about the ring. Who gave it to Nana? I should ask. The Philadelphia man when she was getting a divorce to marry Pop? My mother's real father? Pop?

Mom's staying behind to clean up while Dad drives us to the airport. She's tight-lipped and stiff—the cortisone doesn't kick in until later in the day. Not saying what she'd like to makes her tired anyway, and she'll probably take a nap when we go. David loads our bags in the car with Dad. As she puts the cranberries in the refrigerator, she says over her shoulder, "You can keep that ring, if you'd like." She'd like a big Tricia Nixon response. I say I'd like that, too casually, smile and hug her good-bye, kissing her soft, papery cheek. The diesel Mercedes chugs like a coffeepot outside, and she stands in the doorway and waves. I sit next to Dad as he cruises down the hill. David's in the back seat, relieved the visit's over. I am too, but also a little sad.

"I heard on the radio that the weather's pretty cold in Colorado," my dad says, gliding the Mercedes into the steady stream of cars on the Hutchinson River Parkway.

"Yeah," says David, "it'll take a little adjustment—you've spoiled us!" Dad switches on WNYC, which plays Bach's Christmas Cantata. He puffs on his pipe and drives in a pleasant, distant reverie, his favorite state. I'm looking forward to seeing Rufus, to riding in the bright, crystalline snow. I never thought I'd wear a diamond ring. Now it will be on my right hand, under my glove, as I ride in wide circles and Rufus kicks up his heels, when a partridge takes off from a bush as we gallop too close, when a coyote with thick winter fur pauses in the drifts to look back at us over his shoulder. The ring flickers as it did on Nana's large, freckled hand. David hasn't noticed it, and I'm glad. It feels like another small betrayal to me.

42 : Nick

The first time I see Nick, he's up to his knees in spilled seeds. Minnesota came back from town and said a tractor trailer full of feed tipped over by the old Farisita schoolhouse on Highway 69, and there were three-foot drifts of high-grade cattle feed by the road. The next day Doug and I take some shovels and the old Chevy pickup to get some for the animals before it's ruined by the coming snow. Waste not, want not. When we get there, most of it's gone.

"I can't believe people!" I say to Doug.

"You mean you can't believe somebody got the same idea we did and beat us to it?" Doug asks. He has the same dimples as David.

"We weren't going to take the whole load! Just a little for the goats before it got ruined by the weather." I say indignantly. Doug doesn't answer. He never points out contradictions in people's reasoning. I'm happy he's with Martha and the kids, in his own house, but I miss him sometimes. It takes more than two people in the rock house to live our life. A new yellow Ford pickup is parked close to the side of the schoolhouse, and I stomp over. Nick Faris, one of his brothers, and another cowboy are unloading feed from the back of their pickup into the schoolhouse. The radio in the truck is blaring Willie Nelson's "Blue Eyes Crying in the Rain," and Nick's standing in the feed. He has long thighs, and his waist is narrow compared to his shoulders. He sweeps the snow shovel with big, powerful strokes, moving rippling waves of feed into the abandoned building. No one notices us at first with the music playing so loudly, and when Nick finally sees Doug and me beside him, he's startled and frowns at our shovels.

Somebody turns the radio down, and Nick introduces himself, still eying our shovels suspiciously. When he moves, the feed around his legs hisses like a snake.

"Nice to meet you," I say, nervously twisting a strand of hair. "We heard about a spill here, and we were coming down to get some feed for our goats before it snows. We had no idea it was yours—we thought some trucking company would just make an insurance claim and leave it by the road." Nick's father is Joe Faris, a big rancher in the Huerfano. Joe was a Lebanese boy who arrived on the California coast, made his way to the Huerfano, then made his fortune. Nick's the youngest of three sons and four daughters. They're sort of a Huerfano version of the *Bonanza* Cartwrights, although Ben Cartwright wouldn't have bulldozed over his Cadillac for an insurance scam. We heard a story about a cowboy looking for strays who came across two car fins sticking out of the dirt like land sharks. The winds had blown the dirt off Joe's buried car. The Faris family owns the Marlboro Inn, a lot of cows, land on both sides of the valley and on the plains south of Pueblo. They lease pasture in the national forest on Greenhorn.

Nick looks us up and down and looks at his brother. Doug stands behind me, lapsed into his cigar store Indian silence. I stop twisting my hair and pull my overall strap back up on my shoulder. "Well," Nick says, wiping the sweat off his forehead with the back of his work glove, "come by tomorrow after we've loaded most of this. There'll be enough left in here to sweep up for your goats." He's bigger than his older brother, with lighter skin, light brown eyes, and curly hair with a reddish tint. He has high cheekbones, and his nose looks like it's been broken.

When Minnesota, Doug, and I come back the next day to sweep up the feed, we fill four large bags. Afterwards, we buy root beers at Abe and Ersie's as a few big flakes of wet spring snow fall in the still silence. It's so quiet you can hear a bird's wings flutter when it flies close by at a low slant, looking for its buddies and a bush to hide in before the snow. Then the big yellow Ford truck pulls up. Nick's driving alone.

"Got what you need?" he asks, stepping out of the pickup and standing in front of me, rubbing the small of his back a little. He wears a plaid cowboy shirt, Levis, and a sheepskin vest. I tilt my head back to look up at him and a comb falls out of my hair. He picks it up and examines it like an artifact, then gently combs it through my hair and pushes it back toward him so it holds. He slides it over my scalp so gently that the hair stands up on my arms.

"Yeah, thanks a lot," I say, smiling and adjusting the comb. I blush a little and step back from him. "The goats may not eat it because they're so fussy, but my horse will."

"You got a horse?" he asks.

"Yeah, a little quarter horse stallion."

"Huh. Hey, you never told me your name," he says. I tell him, and introduce Doug and Minnesota. "Well, nice to meet you," Nick says, looking down at me. "I gotta check ditches up by the old Ortiviz Farm, where we're renting fields, before this snow gets bad. Enjoy your oats."

"Thanks again," I say.

In the truck Doug says, "I think he's a little sweet on you," and I tell Doug he doesn't know what he's talking about, and Minnesota puffs on his cigarette and smiles. On the way back I think of brothers: Nick and his brothers; David and Doug; and me and my brother, who finally got married this fall to Warrie, a woman from Texas as intense as he is. He sent us tickets to San Antonio for the wedding. David borrowed a three-piece suit from Larry Red Rocker, and my mother bought a dress for me at Lord & Taylor. We tried to look good for everyone's sake, but I'm not sure we passed. Lynda Bird, Luci Baines, and Lady Bird Johnson were there. Our arrival was scheduled the day after the wedding guests visited the new Johnson Library. They may have been worried that David and I might throw blood on it. It went smoothly, although Luci's husband pinched me hard under the table at the rehearsal dinner, which was held on barges floating down the canals, with a mariachi band floating along too. I kept calm but whispered to Jimmy to change my seat, or the next move Pat Nugent made, I'd flip him overboard. The canals were pretty soupy, and it would have ruined his dinner jacket—and the party. Jimmy moved me. Lady Bird's intelligent eyes lingered on us during the cathedral wedding. Maybe she hadn't ever been so close to Vietnam protesters, or maybe she was watching me cry. I always cry at weddings.

The Dog Brothers have changed their name to the Bionic Dog. They've been traveling around a lot this spring. A new couple's moved to Libre, career musicians from L.A. Cari's a good singer who looks great on the bandstand. She's tall, slim-boned, and buxom. Her husband, Brent, plays bass, but he doesn't travel with the band much, because Jim's been the bass from the start. With Cari belting out Tina Turner songs and crooning torch songs that split your heart, the band's in big demand. Between practices and gigs out of town, David's not home very much. I spend more time riding Rufus each day, whatever the weather. Rufus and I bump into Nick on two different days the next week, which is strange, because I've never bumped into him before. Once I'm riding over by the fields the Farises leased near the Ortiviz, so it's not that surprising. The second time, though, I'm up on Turkey Creek near the waterfall when he drives out from between the snow-laden trees. He says he's looking at fences.

"Your horse reminds me of mine—same size, same color," Nick says. "He has a lot of good blood in him, anybody can see that." Rufus lets Nick rub his nose, although Rufus usually prefers women. Nick is twenty, the youngest Faris. He went to the University of Wyoming to play football, but dropped out after one semester because he missed the Huerfano too much. I tell him I'm almost thirty, that I'm building a house on the ridge with my husband. I say, "I love the Huerfano too." The next week Nick and a sidekick ask me if I want to ride along and feed cows in winter pasture. I say yes and tie Rufus up. His friend drives, and Nick and I stand in the bed of the truck on the bales of hay, picking up a bale by the two wires binding it, splitting it out of the wires with our knees, then throwing four-inch flakes out at the cows. The bales are almost too big to handle, but I do okay. I'm flushed and sweaty from the effort, even though it's cold today.

"You're pretty strong," Nick says, and I work harder. His buddy drives about five miles an hour, bumping over the pasture, avoiding big rocks, hitting his horn, and the cows amble over toward the back of the truck when he honks. A big old scarred Brahma bull called Whitey glares and snorts at us.

Afterwards, when we're resting in the warm cab of the truck, drinking Coors and playing the radio, his friend says, "Nick teased Whitey once, and ol' Whitey just charged. Nick made it back to the truck just in time, but the driver's side door's crumpled where Whitey swiped it with his horns." I've scored a role in a modern-day *Bonanza*, one of the hired help treated almost like family. We're working the ranch, tired, laughing at Whitey as he paws the earth and looks murderously at Nick. When Nick's and my thighs touch as we sit next to each other, though, it doesn't feel familial. I remember my odd dream back home at my parents' last Christmas: Hoss sitting on my bed talking to me when Aunt Mabel walked in. Nick's too handsome to be Hoss, and too big to be Little Joe, the handsome youngest brother son in the Cartwright family.

"You're in a good mood," David says when I return from one of these outings.

"I guess I am," I smile and hug him. I'm happy, although I can't say why.

I'm not the first one to hang out with a local. Patricia's young boyfriend Vincie was born in the Huerfano, and so was Christine, who moved in with Jim and had a baby here six months ago. The day their daughter was born, Jim told me they'd named her Electra.

I asked, "Do you know the Electra story, I mean, Sophocles' play?"

"No," he smiled. "We just like it because it sounds like 'electricity.'" They were so happy that I didn't say any more, but maybe I should have told them the story. You always think back on things you could have done, but none of it matters much in cases like Christine's.

It gets ugly sometimes in March. The skies are grayer and there's more snow than in February, and mean winds. Once in a while there's a bright, warm day just to tease you into thinking that spring's here. Everyone gets a little batty, but Christine's different. All winter long, she's been getting stranger and stranger. We talk about her and wonder what to do.

Peter says, "Many tribes treated their mentally ill tolerantly. Their medicine men had special ceremonies to rid the mad person of the evil spirit that possessed his body. They just let the madness play out. That's what we have to do." I guess we've been trying to do that with Christine. She's left Electra and Jim and bounces around houses at Libre like a pinball glancing off the bumpers, but this isn't a game. One morning she knocks on our door and steps in. Her hair's disheveled and dirty, her eyes glint, and her clothes are in disarray.

We say, "Hello, Christine!" at the same time.

Christine looks at me and narrows her eyes. "I know

why you took my cowboy boots," she says, walking down into the kitchen.

"I didn't take your cowboy boots, Christine," I answer, trying to sound calmer than I feel. "You said your feet had grown when you were pregnant, and they didn't fit you, remember? You said I could have them since I had a horse. You can have them back anytime. Why don't you sit down with us for a while and have a cup of tea and something to eat?"

"I don't want the boots now," she spits. "*You've spoken to them.* And don't fool me about this 'something to eat' stuff, I know what you're doing." She smiles triumphantly, her pointed chin held up high, as if she were saying, "Bet you didn't expect so clever an opponent!"

"What do you mean, Christine?" I ask softly.

"It's not safe," she hisses. "Don't act like I'm dumb."

"Christine," I say, "it's safe, and you're not dumb. Have a piece of bread. I just baked it."

"Hah!" she says, ignoring me. "Acting like she doesn't know," she mutters, looking around and speaking to someone else, not David and me. She clutches a composition book to her chest and taps her fingers on it. She looks at David and smiles more benignly, then her face changes and she says, "I know what you've been saying. You think I'm a stupid high school dropout townie, the crazy junk man's daughter, that I've got no business being here. You've always hated me," she says, getting up and pacing between the table and the kitchen nervously.

"That's not true, Christine," David says, sounding calmer than I did. She looks as if she believes him for a minute, then slumps down on the banco and shakes her wavy, tangled chestnut hair so that it falls over her face. "Have something to eat with us," David says, looking at me over her bowed head. I pour mint tea and put big clumps of butter on a piece of warm bread. Christine's fingers twitch constantly.

"When was the last time you had something to eat, Christine?" I ask quietly.

"This morning. Yesterday. Last week!" she laughs loudly, and her laughter makes the hair on the back of my neck stand up.

"What's in that book?" David says, smiling. She holds the notebook closer to her chest. There's dirt under the nails of her long, trembling fingers.

"Why do you want to know?" she asks, her voice shaking a little.

"No reason in particular, I'm just interested," David says.

"These are messages, but not for everyone." Christine smiles knowingly. "Everyone would like to get them, but I'll never let you look," she says.

I put the tea and a plate of bread in front of her and say, "Christine, come on, have a snack with us." She looks at the cup of tea and the bread strangely. She holds her book tightly with one hand and picks up the plate with the other and looks underneath it. "Very, very clever," she says and drops the plate as if it's burned her hand. "Whoops!" she says, and smiles wickedly.

I pick up the two halves of the broken plate and take the bread off the floor.

"Try some tea," David says.

Pretending to read tea leaves, she says, "This is the water Lia drowned in!"

"No it's not, Christine," I say. The devil inside her looks at me through her eyes and smiles. She's gotten to me, and it didn't take long.

She stands up, mutters, "I know, I know, I see," pushes the teacup away. She backs off from David and me and reaches behind her to open the Dutch door, then squeezes out, still watching us. Through the window we see her loping awkwardly toward the trees.

David and I look at each other. I ask, "What can we do?"

"Nothing," he says. "Oh, I guess we could get her locked up in Pueblo. Jim's talked to her parents. I don't think anybody knows what to do. What do you think?"

"I don't know," I say, fitting the two halves of the plate back together. "I guess I could glue this . . . Boy, aren't you tired all of a sudden?"

"Yeah, that was exhausting," he says.

Christine heads for Monty's. His first aid for troubled visitors is legendary, and she even stays with him for a few days. When I stop by, she's quiet, almost normal, sitting by the fire. Later that night they take saunas and cold dips in a wooden tub Monty and Minnesota built, and Monty says to her, "There's a part of you that knows how you're mind-fucking us, isn't there? There's a part of you still watching, right?" She laughs and puts her face underwater, pushing Monty away when he wrestles with her and tries to pull her out after the joke's lasted too long.

"She almost pulled me under with her," he says later, shaking his head. Monty's a big man. "She was so goddamn strong, like a different person. *Christine* was never that strong." She exhausts us and her possibilities, goes to town to stay with her parents awhile. Jim tries to visit her with Electra. Two weeks later, on a windy spring afternoon, Christine goes to Walsenburg Sporting Goods and tells the salesman she wants a gun to hunt rabbits. Then she goes to an arroyo and shoots herself. At her funeral, the mortician is crushed because we won't view her and his handiwork.

On one of those sunny, unseasonably warm March afternoons two weeks later, Nancy, Brooke, and I sit on my deck and look out at the valley. They're so long and lithe that I feel like a pudgy kid sister between them. We've said about all there is to say about Christine, which doesn't make it better. I ask if they remember the Libre van with the engine that blew up on its second town trip. On its sliding door Jim had painted "Libre—The Last Resort." Maybe he was inspired by the Red Rockers' "Southwest's Most Elegant Commune" logo.

"Of course we remember," says Nancy, taking the cocoa butter. "What's your point?"

"She means Libre's literally the last resort for some," says Brooke. "And maybe they come here because a mental institution is the only other option." I talk about a young woman in the fifties—I can't remember her name. She was a footnote in a book about beatniks. She wanted to be a beatnik poet, but her very proper parents had her committed, and she was given forty-three shock treatments. She never wrote a poem again. I don't know yet about Nancy's hospitalization and electroshock treatments years ago. She shakes her head in disbelief and sympathy no differently from Brooke.

When we heard about Christine, David and I hugged, but I couldn't cry. There's a dead weight in my chest. Riding helps, and on one of those rides I finally see Nick. He puts his arm around me like a brother, and says, "Look, don't feel bad, there was nothing anybody could do. She was always a little strange, and her old man is, too, walking around that junkyard. There was nothing you guys could do. Her brains were junked up—"

"*Don't say anything more,*" I warn him, and he stops cold. His family's on the top rung of the Huerfano ladder, and Christine's was in the dump. Nick and Christine passed each other in the halls of Walsenburg High on separate trajectories. She was one of us for a while, and he's not. She's made me doubt the redemptive power of Huerfano life, and I'm as surprised as Nick at my protectiveness. I expect more from him than from other locals. He may be right, but I don't want to think about it, or hear him talk about her in his matter-of-fact way.

I say, "Gotta go—see you later!" I get on Rufus and ride away, going too fast, crying at last.

April 1975

The April Bionic Dog gig at the Marlboro Inn is the first one in the valley in a long time, and I feel like a high school girl getting ready for a dance. The band's pretty good these days, and I want Nick and the rest of the Farises to hear it and see what an exciting life we lead. We've got a block of rooms at the Marlboro. The band gets two rooms as part of their pay, the Red Rockers and Triple A have each rented two, and the Ortiviz Farm is renting one. Joy Faris, Nick's eldest sister and the manager of the Marlboro, puts us in one wing, away from the few tourists and businessmen passing through this time of year. The sauna in our hallway runs nonstop day and night, and everyone else in the valley uses our rooms for showers and baths.

The band's doing a sound check, and Linda, Luz, and I are alone in the room David and I are staying in. She changes Luz's diaper on one of the double beds. So many friends have taken showers that even the bedroom windows looking out at the Huajatollas are steamed up. The floor is full of backpacks, bags, wet motel towels, sequinned party clothes, empty soda and shampoo bottles. "I called Lars awhile ago," Linda says, pulling the tweed pants she made for Luz up over his diaper. She decides the jacket, made out of the same tweed with black corduroy sleeves and hood, is too hot for Luz to wear indoors. Luz lies on the bed and examines the ceiling thoughtfully. She smiles and says, "Lars has another soap opera role—*General Hospital.*"

"This isn't an April Fool's joke, is it?" I ask. She shakes her head, and I say, "Well, it's better than a major role in our Huerfano soaps. He's getting paid better. I almost want a TV!" I'm putting on jeans and a red velvet cowboy

The Bionic Dog play an outdoor party (David in foreground; from left: Henry on lead guitar, Tony and Daddy Dave Gordon on their drums, Jim on bass).

A Bionic Dog poster by Jim Fowler, April 1974.

shirt I sewed working next to Linda in the dome last week. I bring down yogurt and milk for Luz and sew shirts on my electric machine there.

"What are you so happy about, Roberta?" Linda asks, laughing.

"I don't know what you mean," I laugh. Later, at the dance, the band's better than ever. They sing old favorites and some David and Henry originals. Cari's a great addition. She wears a long moss green dress with a very low neckline, and her creamy skin glows in the lights on the bandstand. She raises her hand above her head when she sings "Proud Mary," mining her soul like clockwork. The dancers sing along, nodding as they dance, and David and Henry play their snaking, throbbing guitars, Peggy works out on her glittering piano, and Daddy Dave's drumbeat and Jim's thomping bass keep it all going.

We came of age when prophets and messiahs wore bell-bottoms and balanced guitars on their hips. They played our arias and anthems, scored our movies, prophesied with their pens. Our songs took shape in their throats, flowed into our heads, snapped through our synapses, fired our visions. At college, their music spilled out of open windows into the air we took in and turned into blood. The latest album contained the next encrypted message, and we rushed to get it. *Highway 61, Blonde on Blonde, The White Album, Are You Experienced?, Sergeant Pepper, Beggars Banquet, Absolutely Free, Moondance, Music from Big Pink* were our Mission Impossible instructions. The messages and the messengers self-destructed, but we got the word.

At four in the morning or afternoon in hotel rooms, tour buses, recording studios, in bedrooms of unkempt rural houses in the woods or at the beach, reaching for their cigarettes, hash pipes, coffee, coming down from acid, tequila, mushrooms, making love madly and popping a few more reds, our haggard young oracles with three-day stubbles or beards bent over their guitars, composing our duets, our pas de deux, our battle cry. Oh, the power, the fortune of times when followers murmur your words in their sleep and dance to your music. Even after settling in the mountains, I'm still an original groupie, and the symbiosis is pathological. We dance and press against one another in our rite of spring in the motel bar.

During a break, Nick Faris appears and says, "Hi." It's strange seeing him here instead of on the roads and fields of the Huerfano. He's not as relaxed, a fish out of water. He's wearing a freshly ironed white cowboy shirt and clean ironed jeans.

"Oh, hi," I say, as if I'm surprised he's at the motel his family owns on a night when all his brothers and sisters are working here, tending bar, collecting gate money, and clearing tables along with the usual help. "I'm glad you came," I tell him, as if there were anything else to do in Walsenburg on an April Saturday night. "Let me introduce you to David." David's drinking a beer with Henry and writing down songs for the next set on a napkin. "David," I say, "this is Nick Faris. I told you about him, remember?"

David looks at Nick and smiles. "Nice to meet you," he says.

Nick smiles and says, "Yeah, nice to meet you." They shake hands.

"And this is Henry," I say, gesturing toward Henry, who grins sardonically.

We stand there awkwardly, smiling, until Henry grabs the napkin from David's hand and starts writing again. I'm glad they've met, though it's crazy to want to be one big happy family. But how can Nick know me without knowing David?

Henry says, "What about 'Proud Mary'? That'll get 'em going."

David says, "Again? It's getting old . . . What about your new song, 'Sixty-nine, the Highway of Love'?"

"Good music," Nick interrupts. "And it's been nice meeting you, but I gotta go get some cases of beer for Joy. Everybody's thirsty!" he smiles.

"See you later," David says.

Henry mutters, "How civilized!" David and I ignore him, and I ask quietly, "Well, what do you think of him?"

David reaches for a cigarette and says, "I'd hate to get in a fight with him." Henry laughs, and David grins. When their set begins, I'm dancing in a riptide, at peace like a drowning swimmer. Something powerful's happening, and I'm swept along. Later in the evening, when Cari sings a slow number and the lights are low, Nick appears again. It's amazing how a big person like Nick can sneak up on you like that. He grabs me by the shoulders and we press against each other. He smells of beer, and I hear his heart pound as my ear rests on his chest when we dance. His chest rises and falls heavily, his large hand presses gently against my back, and our feet hardly move. When his feet stop shuffling, I look up at him, and this is our first kiss, and everything stops.

Until a voice says, "Nick, Nick, are you coming with me?" A slender blond girl with large blue eyes looks only at Nick.

Nick says in a wavering voice, "I'll see you in a while, Cheri."

"Nick, did you hear me? I said, 'Are you coming with me?'" she says louder.

"Maybe I'd better go," I say, stepping back.

"No," Nick says loudly, still looking at the girl. "Cheri, I said I'd see you later." He lists a bit, and sounds like he's talking to a disobedient child. Cheri disappears into the crowd, and the magic's gone, until Nick puts his arms around me and I feel like I'm coming home.

"Who was that, your girlfriend?" I smile ironically.

"Yeah, I guess," he says.

"Oh," I say, in the middle of the dance floor, clutching a boy-man who's put down his high school sweetheart to the soft music David plays, as David's new lover, though I don't know this yet, sings her heart out on the bandstand beside him. I suppose on some level I must know about David and Cari, but I'm preoccupied with the feeling I have about Nick, the feeling you have when you watch a tornado, a hurricane, or an avalanche, and you're safe for a moment, and deeply alive.

The next day David tells me he's got a thing going with Cari. I don't know which one of us got interested in someone else first. Maybe it's another kind of synchronicity. Things are balanced and precarious all at once. He and Cari and the band take off for gigs in New Mexico, and Nick's truck drives up the ridge from Turkey Creek as soon as Dr. Gonzo passes by Dry Creek outside Libre's front gate. Brent and Cari were already on the skids in L.A., and so Brent seems relieved. Cari's relieved, too, now that I know about her and David. I felt that displaced anger again, though, about David keeping me in the dark. I told him right away about Nick, in case he hadn't seen us in the clinch at the Marlboro, and only then did he tell me about Cari.

Mostly, I don't think of anything except when I'll see Nick next. He comes up whenever the Bionic Dog is traveling. When David's home, I ride Rufus down to Turkey Creek or the Ortiviz in the afternoons and bump into the big yellow Faris pickup. Nick's cowboy buddy drives away tactfully, mumbling about something he's got to do, and Nick and I fall into each other. After we've been together five minutes, a trap door opens and we drop down through it. We make love anywhere—in the trees by the creek, on top of Ferendelli's huge haystack where you can look straight up at my house and Greenhorn behind it. Sitting on the haystack with him one day I say, "This is like Lady Chatterley or something."

He says, "Who's that?" and I laugh, saying, "See what I mean?" David would appreciate this, if only I could tell him. Nick's not dumb, he's just not interested in books. He has an animal power, an ability to calm Rufus or a calf with his voice or a light touch of his big hand. Even

Whitey the bull sees that Nick's different and shows him grudging respect, not the belligerent indifference Whitey shows to the rest of us. Nick's rooted more in the Huerfano than anyone else I've met. He has a sixth sense for finding arrowheads. At the Marlboro, his sister Joy has a big shadow box full of arrow and spear heads he's found.

Once I ask, "How do you find all those arrowheads around here anyway?"

He looks down by my feet and picks one up from under my right boot tip, smiles, and says, "Like this." He talks about camping with his brothers and sisters and dad on top of Greenhorn as a kid, running cattle. The outline of the mountains is tattooed inside his head, and he's at peace with his childhood locations. He doesn't want to go anywhere else.

One day when the top of Greenhorn is hidden in clouds and cloud wisps float in the valley, I say, "Look! It looks like Japan or something, doesn't it?"

"It looks like Greenhorn to me," he answers smiling. I hit his arm, but he means it.

Doug and Martha and the kids leave Libre to go back to Tennessee. We're alone on the ridge until Brent and Cari, who are a couple now in name only, move up there. Monty laughs when we have coffee, and bolsters me up for a while. To him I'm an adventurous older woman who's dallying with the rancher's son, teaching him a thing or two. When I ride down to Turkey Creek for three days and don't see Nick, I ride back to Monty's to have a cup of coffee and sit in the afternoon sun coming through his window.

"Oh, Roberta," Monty chuckles in his deep, cultured voice, "you're sowing your wild oats, as they say. I've got to give you a tip of the hat!"

"Monty," I say, "you've got it wrong! I've never felt like this before."

Monty laughs drily. He doesn't like it when people cry or exaggerate, and he ignores my tears, but his voice is kinder, and he says, "I tell you what, why don't you and David come to dinner. It'll be nice for you both to get out of the house." He reaches for his battered edition of *Mastering the Art of French Cooking* and starts thumbing through the pages, muttering, "I have a beautiful venison tenderloin Peter gave me. Do you by any chance have any shallots?" as he hands me a box of Kleenex without looking up.

A week later Cheri drives up in a new Ford sedan while Nick and I are sitting in his truck in the Libre parking lot. Her father owns the Ford dealership, and all the Faris trucks are Fords.

"Nick," she says, "what are you doing?"

"Nothing, Cheri," he says. "What are you doing?" She stands there with her hands on her hips, and he says to me, still looking at her, "I'm going home." I get out of the pickup without saying good-bye, and he drives away. Cheri and I stand ten feet apart, like gunfighters at the O.K. Corral. You're uncomfortably familiar with someone in love with your lover.

"Look," I sigh, "why don't we talk?"

"Okay," she says, a little warily, and I walk over to the Chrysler and open the passenger side door for her. I get in the other side and we roll down the windows like synchronized swimmers. The Chrysler smells dusty from disuse, and it's hot inside from the sun shining through the windshield. You could write your name on the dashboard. Cheri looks straight ahead as if she doesn't trust my driving.

I sigh again. "Look," I say, "I know this is hard, and you're young. But Nick's the kind of guy who strays. Wouldn't you rather have him stray with a married woman who doesn't want to disrupt her or your life? My relationship with him exists outside my marriage, and his relationship with me has nothing to do with you."

She looks at me with her big blue mascara'd eyes, moist and shiny with tears, and says, "It just tears me up inside."

"Well," I reassure her, "that's natural. We all have possessive feelings, but we're striving to overcome that pettiness, and our love will be stronger as a result." I keep talking while she looks out the window. The Chrysler's not the only thing going nowhere, and even I'm not listening to myself anymore. Is any of this true, or is it the height of hypocrisy? Here's one thing that is true: I will think, say, and do anything to be with Nick as much as I can. Sitting next to Cheri in the Chrysler, I think of driving into the Huerfano for the first time when David and I were just a bit older than she is now, and the hope we felt for our life, the valley, and each other seems childish, vague, and distant. I'm repeating myself, and she interrupts with another "It just tears me up inside," and gets out. I say I understand and get out too, shutting the Chrysler door carefully. She gets in her Ford and guns it down the road. I roll up the Chrysler's windows before heading up the ridge to milk the goats.

September 1975

Cheri left for Florida a week after our parking lot talk. I didn't see Nick for a long time after that. Brent and Cari officially split up. Brent moved out of the house Richard built, and Cari stayed. Brent held a council and started building a new house down the ridge road. Cari and David traveled around the rest of the summer. Nick finally came to see me at the end of the summer after Cheri got back from Florida. I hated him for being too scared to see me while she was away, and I stomped around the house saying anything I could think of to hurt him. He looked at the floor and nodded, saying calmly, "I know, I know," and then we made love more intensely than ever. When he came up two weeks later, we made love more fiercely than that. Afterwards, he told me Cheri'd stopped taking the pill, that she was pregnant, and they were going to have to get married. I told him I couldn't see him anymore. He didn't argue. We were glad to go back to our corners.

At the end of the summer David gets sick, and while we're at Dr. Frank's where he's convalescing, I say, "David, I don't want to play anymore!"

He says, "What are you talking about?" although he knows.

"You're free to choose between Cari and me," I say. "I don't care who you choose." I actually think that's true. "I want a monogamous relationship now or nothing."

David says, "Free to choose, huh? You didn't feel this way when you were seeing Nick!"

I don't argue. I don't care about my inconsistency. I'm tired, and this is the way I feel now. He chooses me, and we're both relieved. I feel bad for Cari, just as I know she'd feel bad for me if he'd chosen her. Another Indian summer rolls in. The temporary walls on the lower octagon of our house have been stuck at five-eighths completion for three years, like the hands of a stopped clock. Doug and Martha write to say they've bought a farm in Tennessee and won't be back. If all the cells in our body are replaced every seven years, almost all my cells when we first came to Libre are gone. I stand at the goat shed after milking, wondering how the crest of a rising tide became a backwater, when a truck labors up the ridge and crawls over the crest. Johnny Bucci rolls down his window and grins. He looks like a cross between Slim Pickens and a patron in a Northern Italian Renaissance painting.

"Hi there, Reberter!" he says mischievously, imitating Adrienne, one of his favorite Huerfanites. "I came up to hire you and your little horse to help me move cattle out of summer pasture day after tomorrow. I sure could use help. 'Sposed to be a front coming in."

"Sure, Johnny," I tell him, brushing the hair out of my eyes.

"Twenty dollars a day okay?" he asks.

"Great! Where do I meet you?"

"Down on that field next to Antonio Pando's big alfalfa field, at eight thirty." He smiles again and then asks, "Say, what have you heard from that Mary Red Rocker?"

"She and Molly are in L.A., living in the chauffeur's apartment over the garage at her parents' house in Beverly Hills, and she's teaching history at a fashion and design school." She's coming back to visit this summer, when Lars is here too.

"Huh? Fashion. Whaddya know about that! I may go out there some day," he says. "I miss that ol' Mary. She was pretty smart, wasn't she?"

"Yeah, she still is."

"Right," he laughs, starting up his truck. "Well, see you day after tomorrow."

Two days later Rufus and I wait for Johnny not far from the haystack where Nick and I had our afternoon trysts. The bales have been replaced since then, just like the cells in my body since I got here. The forecast was right. There's a gray wall of cloud moving in, and it's about ten degrees cooler than yesterday. The cows look at Rufus and me warily through the rusty barbed wire. Rufus prances a little and tosses his head, ready to go, sensing a change in the weather, eager to do his job and run down some cows. This is my first paying job punching cows, and I'm about to join the cast of *Rawhide* again in my head. Johnny and old Mick Montaño drive up, towing two saddled horses in a beat-up trailer.

"Hey there, Reberter! Ready to ride?" Johnny calls. Mick Montaño just nods silently to me, of course, but I'm used to his silences now. Rufus is definitely the best horse of the group. Johnny's riding a heavy-boned buckskin, and Mick's on a bay with a torso too long for her legs. Rufus struts and tosses his head, his copper coat muted in the dull light of the overcast day. We get the cows out and down the road—they don't put up much resistance. Usually my imagination can work with any kind of material, but today I see we're a sad footnote to the epic cattle drives I used to read about and see in the movies. Instead of a moving wave of fat cows stretching up beyond the horizon, heading up the fenceless expanses of the West, there are Johnny's fifty cows, scrawny even at the end of summer, plodding down a dusty graded road lined with barbed wire fences and overgrazed pastures. Instead of the strong, smooth-jawed faces like those on *Rawhide* and *Bonanza,* to my right is Johnny's stubbly double chin, and to my left Mick Montaño's Brillo pad beard.

I'm ashamed that I'd rather be moving the fatter cows of Faris Land and Cattle Company with Nick, and will myself to not think about his jaw, not unlike that of Chuck Connors in *The Rifleman.* It's dusty behind the cows, and the unusually overcast day doesn't help my mood. The sunflowers bordering the road that would have been happy crowds watching our parade earlier in the summer are dry and drooping now. Rufus's ears are pricked. He's ready to outmaneuver any maverick cow, but the few that look over their shoulder to case things out decide it's not worth the effort. Mick Montaño sticks a chaw of tobacco in his mouth, and Johnny looks over and grins at me every once in a while. His life's an American dream compared to his miner dad's. We plod along convivially, and the dismal weather worsens.

When the cows are finally lowing softly in Johnny's corral, he hands me two crumpled tens, puts his head to one side, and says, "Say, I got a nice little paint mare I mated with a registered Appaloosa stallion over in Redwing, and I'd like to give her to you."

"What's wrong with her?" I ask, immediately embarrassed about sounding so cynical.

Johnny grins charmingly and tilts his head back the other way. "Aww, sometimes she gets lame if you ride her too hard, and she's small, but she's a pretty little thing, and her foal will be something else, let me tell you. To be truthful, I'd like to keep her, but I've got a lot of mouths to feed this winter. I want you to have her and her little foal. It would be nice."

"Thanks, Johnny," I say, still a little wary.

Rufus, Susie the mare, and me, fall 1975. Photo by David Perkins.

"Tell you what—she's in the far pasture. Take a look at her, see what you think. You can bring her back if you decide it's a bad idea."

"Thanks, Johnny," I say, embarrassed that I was suspicious at first.

"Her name's Susie," he calls after me as I trot Rufus up the road to Libre.

He's right, Susie's pretty. She has a fine, dark head, and her black, brown, and white markings stretch over a belly that's already big with the Appaloosa's foal. She's the same size as Pokey, the horse Johnny gave Linda after Lia died, but Susie's younger and in better shape. Of course I'll take her. That Johnny—does he think I need a new life to look forward to?

A week later, Jim comes up the ridge and says three men from Aguilar have driven up with an old burro in the back of their truck, and they're asking for me. When I get there, they've unloaded the little burro, who stands calmly with no halter, just an old rope around his neck. The three men are shooting the breeze with Dallas. The shortest and oldest asks me, "Are you Roberta?" When I nod, he says, "I'm Ron Rosso, and this here is Pablo. He worked in the mines for thirty years, and now he's retired. We thought he'd like it up here in the mountains for his retirement. You can tell he likes the view already." Ron's right. Pablo's staring at the Huajatollas, even though we're talking six inches from his nose. His fuzzy ears swivel subtly to monitor us, but he keeps gazing dreamily at the two mountains floating over the eastern plains. His nose is grizzled, and his back's a little swayed, but he's healthy and well fed.

"You know, burros don't eat much compared to horses. They're real surefooted, and they can pack just about anything." Ron smiles, showing his tobacco-stained teeth. The old lithograph of a young donkey Nana bought for me when I was ten that hung next to the print of the Triple Crown winners by my bed was printed around the time Pablo took his first trip into the mines. The little donkey in the print had a rope around his neck like Pablo, and he looked right out at you, cute as a bunny. Pablo's more aloof.

Dallas and Jim, out of their depth in a conversation about animals, stand around with their hands in their pockets. Dallas says, "I bet if he could talk he'd sure 'nuff have some tales to tell about haulin' coal that long." Whenever Dallas talks to locals, he sounds like a hillbilly.

"Yep, you betcha," says Ron, still watching me. I scratch Pablo's jowls, and he lowers his lids a little. He has long, thick eyelashes, and a few of them have turned white.

"Look, I'll tell you what, why don't I give you my phone number, and you keep him for a while and see what you think. If you don't want him, just call me, and I'll come pick him up," Ron says. Pablo's too dignified to plead.

"Okay," I sigh, as he writes his number on the back of an envelope. David's not going to be thrilled about another mouth to feed.

Handing the envelope to me, Ron says, "Well, we've got to be getting on. You won't regret this, and this little burro deserves to spend his golden years with you!" In the pickup, Ron leans out the window and adds, "He likes cigarette butts—they'll keep him from getting worms, too. And he likes tortillas a lot."

I don't know why Ron Rosso asked for me. Maybe he asked Sig Sporleder at the feed store who was an easy touch. Maybe he called up Johnny Bucci. The salesmen at Unfug Hardware, the ones who grin and make a point of calling me "*Ms.* Roberta" since *Ms.* published my article, could have told him. Dallas and Jim may have fingered me; the way they're acting, it's a definite possibility.

"Did you tell him to ask for me?" I demand as the truck moves down the road trailing dust.

"Why would we do that?" says Dallas, while Jim sucks on his cigarette and grins. I never called Ron, so I don't know if he gave me his real number. He was right. Pablo doesn't eat much, and he loves cigarette butts. I pick them out of ashtrays and take them to him, and his soft lips tickle my palm as he scarfs them up. He can catch tortillas or pancakes tossed from several feet away. He spends more time staring out across the valley than Rufus or Susie, whose heads are lowered over the alfalfa as long as there's any left. I like to think Pablo's still a little dazed by his change of fortune. He stands in the same spot for hours, staring at Mount Blanca. He keeps a polite distance from the horses in the corral, so they don't interact much, but he's taken a swift kick at a goat that gets too close. He has his own dignified place in the pecking order.

When I take Rufus out now, Pablo tags along. I don't use a lead, he just follows of his own free will. Sometimes he kicks up his heels nimbly and twists his body sideways, trotting behind me in the crisp fall air. Once, David rides Pablo over to the waterfall with Rufus and me. With his long legs, he looks like Don Quixote riding Sancho Panza's donkey. Rufus has more heart, but Pablo's smarter. Nothing can keep Pablo in if he wants to be elsewhere. Mostly he stays in the corral by choice. He sometimes gets into Peter's vegetable garden, and worse, Peter catches Pablo in his marijuana patch right before harvest. Peter's furious, shouting at me, his face ugly and gray, the sinews of his neck showing.

"If he gets in again, I'll shoot him!"

"If you shoot him, I'll kill you," I say. "And, by the way, Peace and Love, you motherfucker!" Peter slams the door of the zome.

When Mary Red Rocker, back in the valley from L.A. for a visit, hears about our exchange, she says, "You'd better watch out, somebody might shoot Pablo in the hope you'll finish Peter off!" We try singing "The Ballad of Joe Hill" to Pablo since we can't remember the lyrics of any coal mining songs. We certainly don't sound like Joan Baez. As Pablo eats oats, his ears rotate like the sonar scope of a submarine.

With the change of seasons, I feel oddly detached, as if I'm wobbling and floating over my life, watching myself move around, looking down on the valley. I float over the golden yellow aspens on the creeks, their leaves shimmering and glittering. The more I float along unsteadily, the more animals I take on for ballast.

46 : Aunt Mabel and the Owl

After David and I decide on a closed marriage, the year goes smoothly and rapidly, a rest stop, a chance to be friends again, something we need. The summer has moved at high speed, like all good times, and it's August already. Two days ago, I got a ride to Gardner with Nancy. I hadn't been speaking to her for a week. On a town trip a week ago, she'd complained over and over, biting her lip, "I don't have any money, I'm *completely* out of money." David and I don't have much ourselves, but we bought some gas for her Land Cruiser and treated her to lunch at the Central. Then, as we left town, she said, "I've just got to stop by the bank and cash a check, it will only take a minute."

I said, "*I thought you didn't have any money!*"

She said, "I don't. That's why I have to cash a check." After a week she noticed I wasn't speaking to her, and she offered to drive me to Gardner to do errands as a peace offering. In Gardner, I called my mother. I sipped a cold root beer Nancy bought me (she was feeling pretty guilty) and stared at Gardner Butte, while Nancy sat in the Toyota with the radio on. I searched the sky for two eagles that live at the butte while I talked to my mother. The rocks below their ledges are streaked white. I didn't see any big birds at all, or even a magpie.

My mother told me, "Aunt Mabel has taken a turn for the worse."

"Does that mean she's dying?" I asked.

"Don't say that," my mother said. Since then I've had disturbing dreams. In one, Aunt Mabel and I were playing Scrabble in front of her big brick fireplace the way we used to, but in the dream neither of us could spell any words with our letters, and we were sad. Then I had a

Nancy and Nanda inside the zome, circa 1974.

rerun of the Hoss Cartwright–Aunt Mabel bedroom dream, and the same awkwardness came back.

Last night I thought I was having a dream at first, but I wasn't. Some-one was moaning, and I woke up wondering what my dream meant. I lay next to David in a woozy, half-awake state until slowly it dawned on me that, if it were a dream, I'd know who was moaning and why, and the moans wouldn't continue after I woke up. My eyes fluttered, and the hair on the back of my neck prickled. I was awake, and the mournful, inhuman sounds grew louder. I wanted to wake David, but was afraid to make a sound. I couldn't tell if the cries were of pain or sorrow. I didn't know what animal was making them. Was it a bear? Could a bear get up on the deck? They climb trees all the time. I got a grip and poked David gently. He's a deep sleeper. He makes a pot of coffee before going to bed and drinks it all, just to stay perky enough to keep breathing. When he's awake, though, he's got me beat in the stamina department.

"Do you hear that?" I whispered.

"Hummmmh?"

"*Do you hear that*?" I whispered in his ear. "The moans. Outside, on the deck."

He mumbled, "Yeah, why don't you go out and see what it is," and turned over.

"Okay!" I said, grabbing the flashlight. I think I may be too open to others' suggestions at critical junctures. I opened the bedroom door onto the deck, took a deep breath, and stepped out. I saw a huge shape on one of the upright posts where the pole for my old pirate flag was nailed. The skull and crossbones David carried in Washington in 1969 was tattered and ragged now, and looked more authentic. The hulk moaned again, and I gasped and flicked on the flashlight automatically.

It was a bird—one I'd never seen before. An owl of some kind, about two feet tall. It froze in the flashlight beam, its large, intelligent eyes staring deep into mine. Tufts of feathers that looked like eyebrows quivered. It wasn't scared, and neither was I. Our eyes locked, and we stood still on the deck for a long time. Then it blinked once, with great, sorrowful dignity, looked at me one last time, spread its huge wings, and pushed off noiselessly. The wingspread was as broad as my outstretched arms. The deck shook under my feet, and the air whipped by the bird's wings rippled on my cheeks as it swooped past me. I broke into a sweat, despite the night's chill, and my knees felt weak. I collapsed on the deck. The stars winked. In the bright starlight I could see the clouds. David called to see if I was all right.

This morning I flip through our worn copy of *Peterson's Guide to Western Birds* again while David makes breakfast. The biggest owl is the great horned owl, but it looks smaller than the one I saw last night. "This is creepy," I say, closing the book. "I wish you'd seen it."

"I felt the deck move from inside," he says. "I saw it take off, and it was really big."

"It felt like a message," I say. He shrugs characteristically. After breakfast we were planning to work on some new shelves, but I can't get the bird's stare out of my mind. I walk down the hill, carefully circling Peter's zome in the piñons. If I tell Peter about it, he'll start carrying on like Chief Dan George and explain how birds are messengers of the spirit world, which is fine, but I'm not in the mood for a lecture on Native American lore. I run into Jim at the parking lot. He's on his way over to Gilbert Perino's ranch to see if a junked tractor there has a radiator he needs, and he offers to drive me to Gardner. While Jim's clunking around the old tractor, I ask Gilbert if he's ever seen any big owls. He opens his brown eyes wide and says, "No, gosh, Roberta, not in a long time, not since the night my dad died ten years ago."

At the pay phone in Gardner, I call home. "Oh, there you are," says my mom, like I'm a pair of bifocals she's misplaced.

"Hi, Mom, how are you?" I ask, feeling stupid about calling her and glad to hear her voice.

"Well, I'm glad you called," she says, meaning how ridiculous it is that I live someplace where I can't be reached by phone.

"What makes you so glad I called?" I say, trying to mask my sarcasm, which she picks up on her radar anyway.

"Well, if you must know, and I'm sorry to have to tell you *over the phone,* your aunt Mabel died last night. We got off the phone with Uncle Carl an hour ago."

"Oh, no." My throat catches.

My mother sounds gentler, "Well, I know how much she meant to you, and she was so proud you went to Vassar, since none of her girls did, you know." She acts as if I've been brainwashed like a Moonie and need to be reminded of everything.

"Yes, yes, I know." I suck in my breath, no use snapping at her now. "I'll write Uncle Carl. Please tell him. Did she ever know she had cancer?"

"Well, toward the end she said to Carl, 'I'm not going to make it, am I?' and he said, 'No.'" My mother sighs. She should have been an actress, her timing's impeccable. "I suppose you won't be making it to the funeral."

"No, I don't see how," I say. "Aunt Mabel will understand, even if you don't," I add.

"Well, maybe she will," my mother concedes. She knows I'm upset and leaves it at that.

I say, "I'll call again soon. Give my love to Dad. I love you."

"Yes, I'll tell him. He's outside, mowing the lawn. Be careful." I don't ask of what.

Aunt Mabel never let me win at Scrabble, and when I got old enough to beat her she was as happy as I was, but always demanded another game. She was an ethical humanitarian, a true bluestocking, a Vassar girl who used to sneak out of the dorm for suffragette meetings. She'd have laughed drily if she'd known I suspected her of taking an owl's shape to say good-bye. A few nights later, I'm ready to admit I jumped to conclusions. "Do you think it was Aunt Mabel?" I ask David.

"Hmm, I don't know," he says, looking out the window at the night sky. "There's the Indian lore about owls and the spirits of the dead, and all the Don Juan stuff . . . That bird was amazing, from what you say and the little I saw . . . When I was a kid, after we moved to Georgia, there was a guy who escaped from a state mental institution. He tied his sheets together and climbed out his window, an escape like in the cartoons or a Buster Keaton movie. They found him drawing big birds with a bar of soap on shop windows and brick walls. He said, 'Birds are the holes in the sky through which men get to heaven.'"

"That doesn't sound so crazy to me," I say. I've been with David ten years, and he still tells me stories I've never heard before. That's something.

In August the population of the Huerfano swells the way it does in resorts. Mary's back from L.A., Lars is here from New York, Triple A Trixie's come down from Boulder, and Brooke's up from Taos. Some of the people I like best have left the valley, but they come back for visits whenever possible. Except for Lars, who has more limited options, most of us who leave the Huerfano get involved romantically with people connected to the valley, too. Their connections are deeper and have more breadth, and it's easier to be with someone who understands your exile and your quirky history. This is the week of the Huerfano Pops Music Festival that Cari's ex, Brent, organized, and everyone's in a holiday mood. Mary, Lars, Trixie, and Brooke, visitors from the recent past, sit at our table sipping iced mint tea with Monty, Adrienne, and me. It's strange how people I saw relatively few times over relatively few years can feel like old, old friends. I tell them about Aunt Mabel and the owl. Nobody thinks it's a coincidence.

"It could be another aspect of your overdeveloped animal sense," says Mary. "Her horse acts like a cocker spaniel," she says to Lars. "Or maybe," Mary jokes, "it was just a twenty-five-pound hummingbird!" She explains to everyone else at the table, "Roberta has to fill her hummingbird feeders every day. They know she's a soft touch, and those little buggers drain them as soon as she refills them!"

"About your dream," Lars says after they all stop laughing about my jumbo hummingbirds. "Your feelings for family have always been strong—that could be part of it. You couldn't be there, so you brought her here."

"That family thing, it's your golden Republican background," Monty remarks in his blasé way. "Sometimes, Roberta, I think the reason you're still here is because of your conservative, bourgeois childhood."

"So, let me get this straight—she can't give up her *supposedly* revolutionary choices because she's bourgeois and conservative?" Mary asks. The Red Rockers never thought Libre was very revolutionary.

"It's not so far-fetched," Lars says, smiling at me. "Why don't you write about the owl you saw?" he suggests. "Work it out that way."

"Someday, somebody should write about the valley," Trixie says, sucking on an ice cube.

"Only why we all came here and why we all left is as important as what we did when we were here," Mary opines. Not all of us have left the Huerfano yet, though Monty, Adrienne, and I don't bother to point that out.

September 1976

Like the Lakota and other Plains tribes, who used every part of the buffalo, and like the Makah and other Northwestern peoples, who never let any part of a whale go to waste, we use every part of the marijuana plants we harvest. What to do with the stems and seeds is the biggest challenge and takes the most ingenuity. We chop them into manageable lengths and put them in a big canner of water to simmer for a day or two. Then we remove the stems and stalks, dump them in the compost, and strain the green, brackish fluid. We put the strained liquid back in a clean canner with a few pounds of unsalted butter and bring it to a boil, making a murky, green, greasy stock, which we cool overnight. The next day the canner has a thin layer of green butter on top, about the consistency of congealed chicken fat on cold chicken stock. I skim off the pale green grease carefully and put it in a bowl, and we dump the rest of the broth on the compost pile. I use some of the marijuana butter to make brownies for a Triple A party and put the rest in the little freezer compartment of our propane refrigerator.

I don't like to smoke, so I enjoy eating my THC. Not long after you swallow a brownie made with funny butter, a giggle starts deep inside you and grows. We couldn't resist having one brownie on the drive over to the party on the other side of the valley. The Triple A's eleven hundred acres face north, so the only time for an outdoor party is summer. The rest of the year, if the snow doesn't prevent your getting there, the cold in the canyon makes you wish it had. This was the most glorious drive to Redwing ever. Right before we turned in to the Triple A canyon, we saw an eagle teaching its young how to swoop down on prey. The two eaglets flew about twenty-five feet above their parent. The parent circled and maneuvered, and one eaglet would dive down toward the tip of its parent's wing. At the last possible moment, when it looked as if they would collide, the older eagle deftly dipped its wing, and the youngster would plummet past, pull itself up, and climb to join its sibling circling above. Then the other sibling would try it. There's nothing better than eating a dope-laced brownie on a crisp Colorado afternoon on the way to a party and stopping to watch eagles play.

All week since the Triple A party, I've been craving a donut with my morning coffee. When you get cravings up here, you can't run out to the bakery to satisfy them. Town is forty-two miles away—if you have a working vehicle at your disposal. The only donuts in Walsenburg, anyway, are machine made and slightly stale in their cellophane packaging at Safeway. If your craving doesn't go away, like mine hasn't, you have to make your own donuts. I put the *Joy of Cooking* ingredients out on the counter. I've got enough of everything except butter, and I wonder where I'll have to walk to in order to find someone with butter to spare, and then I remember the THC butter in our fridge. If I increase the nutmeg to mask its distinctive, not altogether pleasing flavor, it might work.

It's a crisp, sunny Sunday. The sun still glares strong, but at a lower angle now, hanging in the sky a little less each day, and you can still feel coolness around the edges of the sunlight late into the morning. Working over the warm cookstove with one of the kitchen's double doors open feels just right. I make the donut dough first thing, let it rise, punch it down, cut out the donuts, and let them rise. Now I'm frying them and placing the plump, golden rings on paper towels all over the counters. David's at the table reading an old *Rolling Stone*. We split a test donut and agree that the extra nutmeg did the trick.

Neither of us hears two riders stop and tie their horses outside. It's unusual that they knock—the door's open and people generally just call out and walk in. I say, "Come on in, the door's open!" over my shoulder without looking up. A moment later, I look up and see the rims of two black cowboy hats poke through the doorway. A pair of skinny young cowboys follow their hat rims inside. They look a lot like the Jehovah's Witnesses who proselytize here every Sunday, though I'm not sure.

"Afternoon, ma'am, we're looking for two strays that we're missing. You seen any?" asks the younger of the two, who wears cheap black-rimmed glasses like Clark Kent's. He's in his twenties, probably—it's always so hard to tell the age of clean-shaven young men with short hair.

This is the first time in six years anyone's come up here looking for cows, and the first time anybody's called me "ma'am." Are there really two lost cows, or are he and his companion just curious? They're surprised to see the rock in the middle of the house and crane their necks. They recover, a little embarrassed, and try to act like they're used to stopping by octagonal houses with five-ton boulders inside. They look around at the plaster cast Tibetan calendar, at the stained glass window of the unicorn turning into a Georgia O'Keeffe flower shape by the cookstove. Most of all, they look at the dozens of donuts cooling on the counter. The air's full of freshly grated nutmeg, and crisp sweet dough smells. They take off their hats.

"Making donuts?" the first one asks.

"Yes." I can't believe he called me ma'am. I'm wearing overalls, my hair's in braids, and I'm not that much older than they are. "You know, I haven't seen any strays around here," I say. "Were they pastured nearby?" I ask, buying time, dealing with a Big Dilemma. It's the Code of the West to offer coffee, at the very least, to a rider stopping by. We're a lonely, friendly people. Every driver in the valley waves when he sees anyone driving toward him on Highway 69, for God's sake. Umpteen dozen donuts are cooling on my counter, and two cowboys holding their hats are looking at them and practically drooling. It's a big sin not to offer them one. These, however, are not your ordinary donuts. You get a good buzz in ten minutes. I don't approve of people slipping hallucinogens in the party punch. I felt that way even before Tommy the Dwarf freaked out at our wedding.

David looks up and says, "Howdy, fellas." His southern roots let him get away with that sort of thing. He looks at the donuts and then at me and almost imperceptibly raises his eyebrows. I suppress a giggle. I wish I hadn't eaten the donut half, now that I have to deal with this ethical dilemma.

"*They sure look good!*" The slightly older cowboy says, ignoring my inquiry about the strays and David's greeting. On the one hand, I worry, it's terribly inhospitable not to offer them a donut. They'd be really offended. I hesitate. On the other hand, if I told them about the funny shortening, they might make a beeline for the FBI office in Pueblo. They could be narcs, though I concede that's a little paranoid. Still, if I don't offer them a donut, I'll have to explain why, and that's not a good idea regardless of who they are. They stand and shift their weight from one foot to the other, holding their hats, trying not to stare at the donuts. I imagine the little lines R. Crumb draws to show an irresistible aroma rising from the donuts and suppress another giggle.

"I'm Roberta, and that's David," I say, buying time.

"I'm Andy, and this is my brother Phil—Plover," the younger one says.

"Well, Andy and Phil, um, how about some coffee?" I ask. "And a slice of bread?" They frown a little and look at each other. "Or, say, how about a donut?" I blurt out.

"Yes, ma'am!" they say. "That's real nice of you!" Phil adds.

I nervously sprinkle cinnamon sugar on two donuts and hand them to the cowboys. Almost anything's better than not being hospitable and gracious, I guess. They gulp their coffee, eat their donuts in three bites, lick their fingers, and look over at the counter again. Another donut is out of the question. The mild buzz from one might possibly go undetected, but upping the donut dosage would be pushing it, and horribly irresponsible.

"More coffee, boys?" I ask. "I've got to get the rest of these donuts packed up for the meeting. I'm worried there aren't enough for everyone, David," I say.

David says, "What mee——" and stops when he sees my look, then adds quickly, "Oh, yeah, *the meeting!*" and laughs. I frown at him.

"Well, we'd better be going," says Phil.

"Thanks for the donuts—they were delicious," Andy says with a broad smile, pushing his Clark Kent glasses up on the bridge of his nose. I walk with them to the door. They get on their horses and ride west down the ridge road toward Turkey Creek.

"They're in for a hell of a ride," David says when I come back in. He picks up his guitar and starts to sing "Happy Trails to You," but it's not what Roy Rogers meant. We never hear whether they found the cows. They didn't come back this way.

When I take Rufus out for a ride two days later, I bump into Johnny Bucci on the middle Gardner road. He's driving his pickup, pulling a trailer with one scrawny cow and a calf in it.

"How's that little mare I gave you?" Johnny asks.

"Fine, she looks good, and her little filly is beautiful!" I answer. I look down at my reins for a minute. "Say, Johnny, did you ever see two young cowboys looking for strays a few days ago?"

Johnny smiles and says, "Why, yeah, as a matter of fact I did. The two Plover boys. They work some for Bob Hudson these days. Did they come all the way up to your house?" he asks.

"Yeah, they did. When did you see them?" I ask.

"Oh, around sunset, down on Turkey Creek, coupla days ago," Johnny says, rubbing the stubble on his chin.

"Well, uhm, how were they? I mean, how did they . . . I mean, how were they?"

"Oh, they were fine, fine," Johnny answers. "They were looking for those strays and having a great ol' time." He grins slyly, adding, "They were a little silly, you know what I mean? I guess I forget what it's like to be young! They're not the type to giggle and all, but, it's funny, they were sitting in their saddles giggling away, looking at the sunset, having a good ol' time!"

"Oh, really? Hmm!" is all I can manage, looking down at my saddle horn. "Well, it *was* a good sunset on Sunday, wasn't it? I gotta get back now, Johnny, nice to see you!" When I turn toward home, Rufus breaks into a trot and tosses his head. He likes the cooler weather. I don't come across any strays as I ride around the mountain in the following weeks, and I never see the Plover boys again.

.

48 : More Big Birds

One month later, on a crisp October morning when the air's so sharp that the mountain peaks are more precise than ever, I stop short on the way to the outhouse. A young falcon sits on top of a dead piñon right in front of me, looks in my eyes, and takes off insouciantly. When I get back to the kitchen, I tell David that my brother and Warrie just had their baby. He doesn't seem surprised when I explain how I know.

Later, my mother confirms the news when I call her from Gardner. "It's a little boy," she says, happier than she's sounded in years. "How did you know?" I don't say. She's worried enough without my telling her I get raptorgrams.

The local and hippie Huerfano populations have some joint projects now. Dr. Leonce, a doctor from San Francisco who's come here with a male nurse and some techs from a Bay Area free clinic called the Medical Opera, joined with Dr. Mai to get public funding for the first Gardner Clinic. My friends Pam and Don in New Mexico donated some money to renovate a funky adobe for the clinic. In Gardner, locals shop at the hippie co-op we started. Sibylla's husband, Kim, the German architect now building at Libre, designed plans for a badly needed addition to Gardner Elementary School. We can't get enough funding from the school district to build the addition, so we decide to raise money for it and build it ourselves. More and more locals show up at the Bionic Dog fund-raisers held at the Gardner Community Center. The school building crews are half hippie and half old Huerfano residents.

The weather changes the second week in October. In the spring and fall, there's a period of a few weeks that all

The Medical Opera (Dr. Mai second from left, Dr. Leonce second from right).

living creatures hate. Winds twenty miles an hour or more blow through the valley without stop. The goats huddle by the alfalfa feeder, the cows clump together, rumps against the wind, and the horses shut their eyes, their noses tucked into each other's tails. Outside we clench our teeth and fists, squint our eyes while walking around, and we avoid going out-side as much as possible. It's not so bad today, so far, and since autumn winds often bring storms, we want to get the clinic's new roof finished.

To replace the roof on the new Gardner Clinic, we're building as much of the new peaked roof as possible and leaving the existing flat roof undisturbed for as long as we can. That way, Dr. Leonce and Dr. Mai are still able to see patients, and the clinic stays reasonably warm and functional. We want to finish the roof, though, before the snows we can smell coming. Dean, Monty, Minnesota, and I went down to Gard-ner three days ago, and there've been big crews from the Triple A and the Ortiviz Farm since, but today it's just Monty and me. I grit my teeth as the wind gusts. The new roof's almost framed. I'm up on the struts because I like to slam nails, and I'd rather Monty use the table saw, which is fine with him. He's a little hung over, not in the best spirits, but at least he's here. I wonder where everyone else is and can't tell what the crews did the last two days. I grab a two-by-four, mark it with a pencil, and throw it down to Monty, who's singing "I Could Have Danced All Night," which is irritating, but everything's irritating in this wind. He cuts it slowly and deliberately, nursing his Cottontail hangover. I wait, squinting my eyes against the wind and covering my face with a bandanna like a bandit.

"One cut two-by-four coming up," Monty shouts, and I bend over to snag it, almost losing my balance because his throw's too weak. I try to fit the board in, but the angle's wrong.

"Maybe you didn't see my pencil. You gotta cut this again, okay?" I shout down at him.

"Whatever," says Monty. "Are you sure you marked it right?"

"Of course I'm sure," I shout, as the next big gust hits me. I'm angry at the weather, not Monty, and he understands that. When the blowing stops, your body relaxes, and you realize how tense the wind made you during the week or two it blew continuously. I mark the angle on a new board and make the line thick and black. "Okay, here it is," I yell. "Once more with feeling, please." Monty moves faster this time, but he's still a little out of it. He's an air sign, a Libra, like half the people at Libre, and air signs get more spaced out in the wind. He cuts the board, spins around like Fred Astaire on quaaludes, throws it higher this time, and I catch it easily.

"Thanks *so much*," I say, but he doesn't hear me in what's become a gale instead of a zephyr now. Once again the board doesn't fit, the angle's off. I throw it down, pick up a new one, mark it, and jump down to the existing roof and the ladder to climb down and cut it myself.

But that doesn't happen. Instead, I crash through the roof of the clinic like Hopalong Cassidy dropping through the ceiling of a saloon to stop a gunfight. For one moment I hover above the examining room like the Angel of the Annunciation, noting with surprising detachment the alarmed look on Dr. Leonce's upturned face. Sitting on the examining table, Mrs. Ortiz looks up, but not quickly enough, and I come crashing down before she realizes what's breaking through the roof like an asteroid.

"*Díos mio!*" she cries. I land on my feet, falling into a crouch. My right foot hits first, and my heel feels like a knife blade's twisting in it. I'm woozy, the kerchief falls off my face.

"*Roberta, my God, are you all right?*" Leonce asks.

"What do you have to do to get in to see a doctor these days!" I say with tears in my eyes. Lucky I'm wearing thick Dunham construction boots, lucky I landed on my feet. I try to get up and walk, but the pain's too much, and I list over onto the examining table next to Mrs. Ortiz.

"*Díos mio!*" she says again.

"Sorry," I mutter as Monty bursts through the door, and Mrs. Ortiz says "*Díos mio!*" one more time, clutching the edges of her blouse together.

"Roberta, what happened? My God, you looked like Lash Laroo," Monty says, helping me pull off my nail apron. He picks up the two-by-four I dropped.

"It's pretty obvious, Monty," I say, biting my lip. "I fell through the goddamn roof."

"Oh, shit!" Leonce says, holding my arm. "I guess no one saw you guys, and you didn't hear—yesterday the Triple A crew took out the old roof's frame and boards and just left the Celotex."

"You barely missed the other table saw in this room!" Monty says. "That was lucky!"

"I'm the luckiest gal in the world," I say sarcastically, but Monty sees I'm in pain and ignores me again, and I ask Leonce for some pain-killers.

"Let's take off your boot and look at it," Leonce says.

Two days later I catch a ride to Denver so Dr. Frank can get my heel seen to. The snow has already started south of Pueblo, and it's a four-hour trip. David hasn't come with me since the band's got a gig, but he's been sympathetic and helpful. Dr. Frank and his newish second wife, Cream Cheese, take me to General Rose for X rays Frank's osteopath friend will review. The intake clerk asks my marital status, and I say, "Shaky," and she looks confused. Frank laughs.

"Looks like you've cracked your heel," he says later, pointing to my X ray and a hairline crack winding like a river on the ghostly white peninsula of my heel. "There's nothing we can do for it. It heals by itself, not too quickly. You'd get some of the longest time off work under workers' compensation regs for a cracked heel, if you had a paying job, that is." Frank rubs his chin and says, "You know, you should stay up here awhile with us. You can't hobble around your house or the ridge on crutches, and it's fine with Cream Cheese and me."

They live in an old house on Garfield. There are oriental and Navajo rugs from his family and secondhand stores, Victorian furniture from

Denver antique shops, and oak chests from his grandparents, who had a cabin in Montana. There are big bathtubs and central heating, and you can't hear the wind when you're inside. There's friendship, good meals, and clean sheets. When your body breaks down, you appreciate these comforts. I wouldn't be able to make it up the ladder across the rock to our bedroom at home. Frank's right, I should stay here a little while. It would probably be easier for David without me.

"Ah have always relah'd on tha kahndness of strange-ahs," I say, my hand to my brow.

"We're not exactly strangers," says Frank, pouring a snifter of brandy.

"Frank, I'm so crazy I'm flinging myself off roofs!"

"Not off—*through* roofs, which you couldn't see were gone. A simple mistake, a breakdown in communication. Assumption, the mother of all fuckups! Now, try some brandy—doctor's orders!"

While I recuperate, I go to a Boulder dinner party with them and sit next to Cream Cheese's old friend Freddy, whom I've heard a lot about. He's an experienced river rafter, a master of the rapids, a mathematical genius, and an ace pilot. He owns motorcycles, fast cars, and jets, and he knows how to fix them all. He flies a lot of interesting cargo around, Cream Cheese told me, raising her eyebrow. Freddy's compact and muscular. He has small blue eyes, Winston Churchill eyebrows, and a Teddy Roosevelt mustache. He doesn't know much about literature, and I stopped studying math in ninth grade. We manage to talk anyway. He's not really a hippie, but he's made his fortune on hippie sacraments. He's more like an oldtime western outlaw entrepreneur with a heart of gold, staying one step ahead of the law, always outsmarting it, pissing it off. The law has Freddy in its sights.

Freddy pours some wine, resting his other arm on the back of my chair. "So, want to hear some music after dinner, or take a spin on my bike?" I know he doesn't mean a ten-speed.

"Thanks, no," I smile. "I'm not up to it. Maybe some other time." Another time I might have taken him up on his offer, but I'm on ice. Besides my cracked heel, I'm numb these days. I don't say that David and I agreed to be monogamous after I fell in love with a twenty-year-old cowboy, and the cowboy broke my heart before I tired of him, and that David and I were soul mates with common dreams and a common past, and that's a lot.

"So, do you think we might see each other again?" he asks quietly, holding my crutches as I slide into the backseat of Frank's BMW.

"I don't know," I say. I picked up a flyer for the Naropa Institute in the lobby of the hotel where we had dinner. The Jack Kerouac School of Disembodied Poetics takes place in Boulder every summer. Ginsberg, Corso, Burroughs, Anne Waldman, Gary Snyder, and Lawrence Ferlinghetti give readings. All our old heroes. I fold the flyer, look up at Freddy, smile. I can't picture him at a poetry reading. "Maybe. Maybe I'll be up here again sometime."

Back in the Huerfano three weeks later, the day I stop using my crutches, an airplane buzzes the ridge. "Jeesh," says David, "they haven't done that since they were looking for Patty Hearst and the Symbionese Liberation Army! Or maybe it's the Forest Service . . ."

"I don't know," Peter says. He's stopped by to apologize for his behavior during community dinner at our house last night. He denounced us in front of everyone for letting the pump run after the spring box was dry. Jim told us later that Annie was the one who'd turned the pump on, but nobody mentioned this when Peter was yelling. "This plane sounds pretty low," Peter says, looking out the window. "Maybe it's in trouble."

Linda, who's stopped by to see how I am, says, "Somebody ought to report that guy. It's dangerous flying so low." The engine gets louder till it sounds like it's right over the roof, and then it's gone. Five minutes later, Jim pulls open the kitchen door and falls inside, out of breath, unable to talk. I've never seen him breathless. I've never seen him go faster than a loping walk.

"Did you . . . did you see that plane?" he finally gasps.

"No, but we heard it," says David. "Why? What's up?"

"It . . . dropped . . . a package in your meadow!" Jim pants. David, Peter, and Jim look at each other for an instant and run out like they're in a fifty-yard dash. Linda reaches over and closes the front door, and we shrug at the same time. Through the window, we see them pick up a package and rush back in, and David hands it to me like it's an Oscar envelope. They're like seven-year-olds on Christmas morning. It's wrapped in brown paper and twine. Scrawled on top in big letters is: *TO PENNY, FROM SKY KING!*

"Whoozat?" asks Jim.

"I dunno," I stall, unwrapping it too slowly for them. The package smells a little.

"Shit!" sniffs David, "It's a kilo of grass! Oh my God, woo-hoo!" I hand him the package, and the three men start unwrapping it, cleaning it, rolling a joint. Happy Holidaze.

Linda looks at me. "Who's Sky King?" she asks.

"I think maybe he's a pilot guy I just talked to at a Boulder dinner party . . . honestly!"

"Oh, Roberta," Linda giggles, "*You talked to him at a dinner party? What am I going to have to do to top this?*"

The three men lean over the package eagerly, like goats at the alfalfa feeder. David looks over his shoulder at me, smiles ironically, and says, "Now *this* is the type of big bird that I like to see bringing you messages! Do you think you'll be seeing this Sky King guy again?"

49 : The Deerskin and the Dobie Pad

Six months after Sky King's drop, I went to Dr. Frank's in Denver to escape awhile. My seventh year at Libre began with another hot and dry June, and our water was very low. At Frank's I took lots of showers and didn't feel guilty. I asked him if it's true that after seven years all my cells are different from the ones I came west with, and he said, "Sort of." One night when he and Cream Cheese went out, I was restless, so restless I called Freddy on a whim. Over the winter he'd buzzed Libre a few times, but there were no more care packages. He didn't seem surprised to hear my voice and asked if I wanted to take a ride. We drove in his BMW, with the Eagles wailing on his Stereo about the Hotel California in the soft, Denver night, out to a little airport on the plains east of Denver, where small craft were tethered around a field like grazing cattle. We got into a sleek Cessna.

"You said you wanted to take a ride," Freddy said, his blue eyes glinting in the cockpit light. We flew over Denver with Willie Nelson singing "Blue Eyes Crying in the Rain" through our high-tech headphones, and it sounded like Willie was inside my head. Freddy banked, and we swooped high over the city studded with rhinestone lights. The traffic on Cherry Creek Parkway looked like fireflies on a conveyor belt. He efficiently produced a bottle of cold champagne, and then handed me some cocaine on a card, and I took a little, just to be polite, even though I'd tried it twice before and didn't get its appeal, and felt horribly depressed afterwards. This was the last time I gave it the benefit of the doubt. It was a new and expensive city drug that we didn't see much of in the Huerfano. Willie sang "On the Road Again," and we flew on, my heart beating as fast as a bird's. David's father said he wasn't happy unless he was above ten thousand feet. Freddy must have felt that way too. Not me.

We flew through the cool early June night, soaring over the city, at eye level with the mountains, while Willie sang from his heart, and we sipped fine French champagne and smoked strong hash, soaring like a bird, but I didn't feel carefree. Maybe I was the one person per thousand who reacts badly to cocaine, or perhaps I was just thinking too much. I couldn't fit what I was doing into any New World order, and I crashed into my puritan roots. This freedom was weighing me down. Fred nosed the plane lower and pointed out the Red Rocks Park, the Brown Palace Hotel, the observatory, Frank and Cream Cheese's neighborhood and house, but he wasn't dumb, and we descended with my mood as Willie sang "Luckenbach, Texas" lugubriously.

"Thanks, thanks for a wonderful evening," I said when he dropped me off. "I can't remember ever being that high. Ha-ha," I added, trying to sound chipper.

"Sometime I'll fly you over the Huerfano and you can look down on where you live."

"Yeah," I said, "that'd be great," but I didn't want to see it from that distance.

One week later, back at home, I decide to go to the Naropa Institute, all because of a deerskin and a Dobie scrub pad. The drought's worse. June's the driest month, and Dry Creek routinely dries up right before the rainy season. The spring box doesn't fill overnight, even though we dug it deeper two years ago when Nancy gave the ten grand for the water system. We haven't had stomach problems from low water for a long time—over the years, we've built up a resistance to stomach bugs. This June, however, almost everyone's sick, and no one knows why. The outhouse doors slam day and night. People stop mid-sentence and run doubled over to the nearest comfort station. Everyone's green under their tans and we all drink mint and papaya tea constantly. I make extra yogurt and deliver it around the land.

After three days of this mini-plague, Peter stumbles up the creek to check the pump and spring box. He leans over the hole, spots something underwater, and pulls it out with a stick. It's a fresh deerskin, tiny pieces of soggy flesh still dangling from it. He staggers down the creek bed to the garage, where Jim's up to his elbows in grease, working on Sesame's '67 Chevy van. She drove up from Taos for a change of scene, but her van threw a rod, and she's staying with Jim while he fixes it, so he's not rushing. When Peter shows Jim the deerskin, he doesn't look surprised.

"Know anything about this, Jim?" Peter asks.

"Well, sure. I got that from Johnny Bucci. I'm curing it," Jim says, smiling, slightly embarrassed. "I think I'm going to make—"

"Curing it? *IN THE SPRING BOX?*" Peter yells. Jim nods and smiles a little less. "Have you noticed that everyone around here is *SHITTING THEIR BRAINS OUT?*" Peter yells louder.

"I don't think it's because of the deerskin," Jim mumbles, looking around for a tool.

"Well, let's keep it, all animal remains, and anything else you can think of out of our water supply, okay?" Peter says, dropping the deerskin in the dirt and stomping away.

The next day, while we're proofing the new issue of *Wordworks*, a valley literary broadsheet we started last year, Peter tells us about the deerskin and his conversation with Jim. David shakes his head and says, "Man! That Jim! I think he's distracted being a single father and all, and now he may be in love!" David and Peter laugh tolerantly. A lot of tolerance is required in order to make it here, but I don't want to live with people who make me sick. I don't share my thoughts because Peter and David will think I'm too negative, too uptight, that I have a bad attitude. Come to think of it, I don't want to live with anybody who'd shoot my cat, either. If reserving judgment is a matter of infinite hope, as Nick Carraway said at the start of *Gatsby,* I guess my hope's found its limits.

Maybe my attitude is bad because I never have enough money. On a shopping trip to Walsenburg two days later, I don't have enough change for a new scrubbie. A Muzak version of "Blowin' in the Wind" plays softly for the early morning Safeway shoppers, and I bump into Adrienne and Monty chatting in the vegetable aisle.

"I wonder how much money Dylan made selling the rights to Muzak," I mutter. "Or do you think Albert Grossman got most of it?"

"Adrienne, were you perchance looking for *sour grapes?* I think I found them," Monty says, chuckling at his bon mot.

I ignore him, and Adrienne gives me forty-seven cents so I can buy a Dobie pad. I say, "Thanks. I'm sick of voluntary poverty!"

"Howdya think you'd feel about involuntary poverty?" she asks.

At the Central, I call my brother collect. "He's on the phone with London. Please hold, Miss Price," says a secretary. I want to ask her how important you have to be to talk to a whole city, but decide not to. He clicks on now and says brusquely, "Hey, Roberta, how's Colorado?"

"It's great, how are you, Jimmy?"

"Fine, fine—busy, busy! It's hot and humid today, you know that haze . . . We don't get much sleep with the baby, but he's a great kid, almost standing now."

"That's terrific. The last picture was too much, he's so beautiful."

"Yeah. So . . . anything else? I gotta go, meeting all afternoon, London tomorrow, trying to get out of here early. Have you called Mom and Dad?"

"Not yet—and there's just one more thing. There's this Jack Kerouac School of Disembodied Poetics in Boulder this summer, run by Naropa Institute. I want to go—you know, drive up and take a class—but we're short on extra cash for tuition and traveling. If I go, I can't work, and if I can't work, I don't make money, and I can't go. I could maybe pay you back when I do more movie work this fall. There's supposed to be a David Bowie movie in New Mexico . . . or I could dedicate a poem to you, like Sir Philip Sidney."

"What does Naropa mean?" Jimmy asks.

"It's a Buddhist term, it means—"

"Never mind," he interrupts. "How much do you need?"

"Well, about seven hundred dollars."

"Hold while I take this call, okay?"

Being on hold extends the humiliation I feel asking for money. At the Central, Benny mops off the bar and folds his towel carefully. Shirley walks by stiffly—her arthritis is acting up—as she carries two enchilada specials over to Strider and another Ortiviz Farmer. The door to the Central opens, and Adrienne steps into the long trapezoid of daylight. She walks past the pickled regulars at the far end of the bar, who number fewer than when we first came here. If one of them died on his barstool, no one might notice until closing time.

Adrienne says, "Reberter, got yer Dobie pad? Need lunch money?" I shake my head, and she opens a manila envelope and shows me a proof sheet, saying, "Look at this, it's pitchers of Lars. Some famous guy named Mupple-, or Mapple-, thorpe took them." They're mostly head shots: Lars in a loose crew neck, sucking in his cheeks and making his sultry, matinee idol face, Lars smiling and flashing his perfect white teeth. In others, he wears a tux.

"Do you remember him in braids, sewing that buckskin Tonto outfit for himself?" Adrienne cackles. "He should have a picture in his leathers as a p.r. photo. He could get a lot of Indian roles, har, har. But there're not too many Native Americans on soaps, are there? Maybe I should send Mupplethorpe a picture of Lars in his Tonto outfit—"

"Roberta!" my brother clicks back on. "How much was that again?"

"Seven hundred."

"Okay, I'll send seven hundred and fifty. Do you need it wired?"

"No, mail's fine. Thanks, Jimmy, thanks a lot."

"It's good you're writing again, and getting out." He makes it sound like I'm in Sing Sing.

"Well, I'm not *getting out,* I'm just going there during the week for summer classes."

"I didn't mean that, I meant seeing people, doing things, you know," he says.

"I know," I say.

Back home, as I unload groceries, David asks about my day. "Oh, fine," I tell him. "I didn't have enough money for a Dobie pad, so Adrienne gave me forty-seven cents. And Monty and I had to circle around town looking for Bella again, because she spaced out the three o'clock rendezvous. She was at the Wash-O-Mat, watching a dryer like it was a TV. I don't think it was even her clothes spinning inside. Janie Lencz gave me some homemade horseradish sauce and . . . oh, the usual." In my head I'm composing a class note for the *Vassar Quarterly,* asking if there are other Vassar-Yale couples who can't afford scrubbies.

"Hmm. That's good," David says, lighting his cigarette.

I add casually, "Oh, yeah, I spoke to Jimmy today, and he offered to lend me the money to go to the Jack Kerouac School of Disembodied Poetics, at Naropa." I make it sound like it's Jimmy's idea, as if he'd read about Naropa in the *Wall Street Journal* and thought of me.

David looks up at me for a minute. "That's great," he says.

"You'll have to milk the few days mid-week I'm up there, but it won't interfere too much with your gigs. I can put the horses and Pablo in the field by Turkey Creek."

"It'll be fine. Peter or Dallas could fill in if they had to," David reassures me.

"It'll be really great to be able to do this," I say.

Next morning, when I come back from milking, David's measuring the kitchen counters, his tools all over the floor. He says he's going to make a spice rack and put in the rest of the tongue-and-groove counter by the stove. We stopped working on the kitchen counters two years ago and never got back to it. Still, there's no question I should go to Naropa. I don't throw the *I Ching*. I cash my brother's Merrill Lynch check and put the money under the mattress. It doesn't take much to get the Chrysler ready for the weekly drives to Boulder. Jim rebuilt the engine last winter. When I get the Naropa registration materials and start filling them out, David says, "Isn't there something contradictory about an academic institution named after Jack Kerouac? Wasn't he kicked out of Columbia his freshman year?"

"Yeah," I say, sighing and putting the papers away. When he's not here, I'll take them out again and pick a course. But I'll get more than a course—I'll be part of the Naropa scene, too.

August 1977

Two months later, it's mid-August and hot, and I sit in the Boulderado Hotel lobby, soaking up the Naropa vibes. Three stories above me is a big stained glass ceiling. The cantilevered stairs and balustrade around the mezzanine are dark, carved cherry. The men who built the Boulderado, high on the crest of the silver boom, had a City of Gold vision older than Coronado and pulled out all the stops. I lie back on the shredded upholstery and squint up at the translucent patterns, thinking of the big plans and boomtown hopes at the birth of the century. The Rockies were the location for every kind of European American's desperate dream—the cities of gold, the buried treasures, the plentiful furs, the big gold strikes, the endless silver vein at the Matchless Mine, the limitless ranches, the Aquarian settlements. Now the ceiling's in disrepair, showing a few broken squares of sky. A pigeon that flew in by mistake flutters back and forth until it finds its way out. Some broken panes have been replaced with regular glass covered over with stained glass decals.

Except for the general deterioration, the lobby's pretty much the same as it was when Baby Doe and Horace Tabor arrived for the Boulderado's opening on New Year's Day 1909. There's a picture of Baby Doe in her velvets and matching ermine muff and hat, standing with the dignitaries. Horace is beside her, the gold watch chain swagging across his fat belly showing through his open fur coat. A building rising grandly in five brick stories on a dirt street, amidst wooden shacks and little stone stores in the wild mountain West! Now, in the last part of the same century, the lobby's got a different crowd: disheveled, hairy poets and pale, skinny poet groupies from back east, and a few slim Tibetan men dressed in French clothes. There are one or two wary drug dealers in Stetsons and custom-made boots, and the blond, muscular mountain girls common in northern Colorado. Two fat tourist families look out of place. The kids run between the oversized chairs, the fathers stick their restless hands into their shorts pockets, and the mothers look at vacation brochures from the hotel desk and glance nervously at the crowd.

There's a special rate for Naropa students during the week, and I have a tiny first-floor room off the back hall. I've been drunk on anonymity during my six-week Naropa course. Each week I've parked the Chrysler and lugged my bags and books in the back entrance, signed in, paid with some of Jimmy's money, and taken my room key. Through the thin walls of my seedy, monkish cell with a single bed and bad mattress, I heard the bar speakers—the wail of the Eagles and the strut of Elton John's piano, or more often just some kind of ersatz honky-tonk to make you think you're in a bar in the True West, where Bret Maverick might walk in at any moment and start smooth-talking you. I liked being on the first floor despite the noise. In this firetrap, I'd have a chance to escape.

I picked a course with Larry Fagin from the St. Mark's Place Poetry Project. He assigned Frank O'Hara, and I'd sit in a Pine Street coffeeshop reading about O'Hara's errands on Sixth Avenue on his way to East Hampton the day Lady died: the tobacconist at the Ziegfeld Theatre, the Park Lane Liquor Store, and the sudden sweat when he sees her face in the *New York Post*. It was more real than the fading light on the Rockies outside the plate glass window of the coffeeshop. Fagin smiled like Bret Maverick as he taught. He couldn't believe he was getting paid to stand in a basement room in a one-horse town and smooth-talk about poetry!

The other students were in their early twenties. I made friends with a young guy from New York named Stephen. He had frizzy red hair and protruding front teeth, and he cracked jokes like a vaudeville comedian, and I laughed longer and louder than the other kids in class. After we'd known each other awhile, when we were having a beer at the Boulderado bar, Stephen said, "You know, I'm really not that funny. I think you just need to laugh." I laughed when he said that. "How old are you?" he asked, squinting at me.

"Thirty-one," I smiled, "I—"

"No way!" he interrupted. "You can't be! That's ten years older than me!"

"*Than I*," I correct him. "I've been living in Shangri-La, Stephen, or I'm immature, or both." He was right, I felt younger than the other Naropa students.

One weekend in July I took Fagin down to Libre. He couldn't believe the view, the houses, what we'd done, and was surprised by David's tricky melodies and ironic lyrics.

"I thought David's songs were going to be like John Denver's," he told me sheepishly as we drove back up to Boulder, and I made a face at him. Fagin told all the other Naropa poets about the Huerfano, and Anne Waldman, the founder with Ginsberg of the Jack Kerouac School, came down with me two weeks later. We stood at the pools in the waterfall nude, although Anne kept her thin metal belt shaped like a snake fastened around her waist. The snake swallowing its tail had a tiny ruby eye. I liked Anne, and she liked what she saw in the Huerfano, too. Back in Boulder, she told everyone something was going on down south.

My musings on this August dog day afternoon stop abruptly. KGNU just broke in on Fleetwood Mac with a bulletin that Elvis is dead, and the news ripples through the lobby and throughout Boulder. ("Did you hear? Elvis died! I can't believe it, man!") At the impromptu poetry reading that evening, nobody reads a poem about Elvis as good as the one Frank O'Hara wrote when Billie Holiday died, but we haven't had much time. I don't read anything. I don't know what we owe Elvis, or the continent he claimed for us. I gave up on him when he met with Nixon and volunteered to be a special drug agent. He wasn't my king. Nevertheless, I understand something has ended with him.

The older poets remember more. Gregory Corso drinks a lot and shouts, "The King is dead, and Long Live the King, whoever the fuck he is! Personally, I think there's no Crown Prince!" Poets recite, looking out over an audience mostly not old enough to remember the advent of the southern boy who started everything. "Oh Elvis Oh Elvis," one poet intones, "look at you, so fat and dead on your bathroom floor!" Cosmic considerations and subtle observations waft up with the cigarette smoke in the firetrap hotel as the bards look down at their scraps of paper or legal pads and eulogize the black white boy who sang and danced poems that millions had to hear, poems that made millions, too. Allen Ginsberg reads a short poem off a dinner napkin, then opens his harmonium and chants a few sections of "Plutonium Ode." His skin is pale, almost dewy, and his nearsighted eyes blink behind his thick glasses. His belly shakes as he pulls the harmonium open and shut, and he pushes his glasses up his nose and stares out over the crowd. He chants in a rich, deep, beautiful voice.

Elvis's last words were, "I think I'll go to the bathroom and read." One rumor is that he was reading about the scientific evidence for the existence of Christ when he died. If I wrote a poem, I'd put that in. When it's over, I'm standing near Allen. On a whim, I ask, "Do you think you could come down to the Huerfano Valley, in southern Colorado, for a poetry reading to benefit our medical clinic?" I hope he's heard about the Huerfano from the other poets at Naropa.

He blinks at me, pushing up his glasses nervously, even though they haven't slid down his nose much. "Yes, yes, I think I should do that, I'd like to do that," he says. "I could get Gregory Corso, too," he adds. "And Peter, of course." I look confused, and he adds, "Peter Orlovsky!" I smile—I've won the beatnik trifecta! "Maybe two weekends from now." Allen tugs his beard, smiles slightly. "After classes are over. I wanted to do a retreat at Dorge Khyung Dzong, but it's full. Is there somewhere I could do a retreat for a few weeks with you?"

"Well, yeah," I say. "Dean built a cabin on the back of the land by the waterfall. We could get it in shape for you. It's a little more rustic than Dorge Khyung Dzong . . ."

"Umm, fine, that's fine, wonderful!" Allen says. He scribbles a phone number. "Call me later," he says, as students press up against him and his harmonium.

I feel like I've bagged a big bear for the tribe back home. When I tell David, he nods casually, as if he expected it. The Huerfano buzzes. Dean and Dallas spend days fixing up the retreat cabin. They put in a new stovepipe, shingle the roof, and replace broken windowpanes. "The beatniks are coming, the beatniks are coming," Tom Grow calls like Paul Revere as he skips through Peter's meadow. Jim draws posters to put up in town. Excitement's in the air, like the first nip of fall. Dean and Peter reminisce about Ginsberg and Kerouac as we sit at the table, planning the reading. David looks across at me while Dean talks about a New York party where Kerouac read from *Dharma Bums*. Allen's important—Corso and Orlovsky too. On dark and wintry Buffalo nights, reading Blake, Kerouac, Ginsberg, and Gary Snyder, David and I talked excitedly, their books spread out all around us. Is David remembering that now? Our life in the Huerfano began with these poets, although Nixon and Kissinger helped us along too.

Last night, Ginsberg, Corso, and Orlovsky landed in the Huerfano. A pilot friend of theirs flew them down from Boulder, and I drove the Chrysler to an obscure airstrip near Huerfano Butte to pick them up. It was a small plane, so Allen had asked me if Bobby, a young poet, could catch a ride in the Chrysler with me from Boulder. Bobby has honey-colored skin and a crown of wavy auburn hair like an Italian cherub's. He's the kind of boy Ginsberg likes to mentor. We drove down from Boulder two days ago, and he fit right in at Libre. Bobby seems both young and new and wise beyond his years.

Bobby went along with me to the airstrip out on the plains. David was still getting things ready back at Libre. They landed, and when the plane's lights hit the cholla and sagebrush, for a minute the range looked like the ghost of the ocean floor it had been millions of years ago. Ginsberg stepped out first. He seemed tired, but he was glad to see Bobby. Orlovsky was robust and muscular—he must have been something else at Bobby's age, when Ginsberg met him. He gave me a powerful hug, and his big chest burst the buttons of his shirt. Corso wore a hat like Norton's in *The Honeymooners,* and he held his jaw and complained immediately.

"Are you a docta?" he asked. "I have a horrible, horrible toothache! Can you give me something for this pain?"

"Sorry," I said, "I'm not a doctor, but maybe Mai or Leonce could help tomorrow." Corso dropped his hand from his jaw and didn't mention his tooth for the rest of the night. Spencer, the pilot, locked up the plane. He was thin and wiry, with a shock of white hair and big teeth

*Allen Ginsburg,
August 1977.*

like a Kennedy. Bobby and I jammed their bags in the trunk, and they squeezed into the Chrysler's backseat.

I'd spent enough time in Allen's company at Naropa to get over my initial awe. Despite his beard and long hair, he first seems like a mildly lunatic, down-at-the-heels insurance agent, maybe because of the cheap suit jackets and no-iron shirts he wears. He was never good-looking, like Kerouac or Neal Cassady, and he comes across darker and wilder in photographs than he does in person. He's smaller and frailer than I expected, with the pale, flabby body of a middle-aged academic. He's nervous, and mumbles sometimes, and his watery eyes blink myopically. He tugs at his beard, has a little potbelly, is losing a button on his jacket. But his mouth is rimmed with full, fleshy lips, and his voice is rich, deep, melodic. His laugh is infectious, and his words are sometimes magic. Despite this new familiarity, I was still excited Ginsberg was coming to our home.

I had half the Big Beatniks still alive piled into my back seat, but, driving them along Highway 69, I felt more like a Harvey Girl than Neal Cassady. Like a good tour guide, I told them about Libre, the Red

Rocks, the Triple A, Ortiviz Farm, the Gardner Clinic. I told them about Greenhorn's death, Mother Jones and the Ludlow Massacre, the Penitentes. I pointed to where the people who'd read Allen's and Gregory's poems as kids in city high schools were building homes. I went over the weekend schedule—the reading at Dean's, the dinners at my house. I told them how excited we all were about the reading. We pulled into Libre after midnight, when the moon was high. David met us in the parking lot, and we loaded them and their bags into the Chevy pickup and took them to Brent's new house, just down the ridge road from us. Brent's in L.A., and so they'll all stay at his house and come up to our house for meals.

After I milk the goats the next morning, I make whole grain pancakes, fresh yogurt, and sliced fresh peaches for their breakfast. When Allen finishes his second batch of pancakes, he sips some chicory coffee, looks at the rock in our house, and says, "This is marvelous!"

"Well, it's not finished yet," I say, getting up to push Little Egypt and her daughter, Frieda Peoples, away from the Dutch door, where they've been resting their front hooves on the bottom door and peeping in, making a racket all during breakfast. They know something's going on, taking up all our attention, and they object. "It'll be great when the house goes around it, full circle," I say, not looking at David.

Allen nods. "Yes, sure, but still, it's amazing! Trungpa Rimpoche told me your house felt Tibetan, did you know that?"

"Yeah," I say, "he told us, too. Only we have goats instead of yaks." Little Egypt *baa*'s outside the door again—her timing's perfect. Rimpoche's the lama who heads Naropa in Boulder. When he was a baby, Tibetan monks identified him as the umpteenth reincarnation of the Rimpoche. After the Chinese invaded Tibet, they tried to track down all the current reincarnations of Tibetan lamas. Trungpa escaped as a young man, walking over the mountains to Nepal. Now he's slowly killing himself with booze in Boulder.

"I wish Jack could have lived to see this," Allen muses.

"Kerouac?" says Gregory. "Whaddya mean? He hated hippies!" Gregory's unhappy. He's in the country and hasn't found any city drugs so far.

"I don't mean the way he was at the end, Gregory," Allen says, "I mean the way he was when he wrote, 'Pray, by God, later on in our future life we can have a fine free-wheeling tribe in these California hills, get girls and have dozens of radiant enlightened brats, live like Indians in hogans and eat berries and buds . . .'" Allen closes his eyes, smiles, tilts his head. As he quotes Kerouac, he looks more like he's talking to him. Allen also quotes Blake, the Bhagavad Gita, and Whitman after breakfast. He's memorized more poetry than I've ever read. By now he's mainly talking to David, as if David's his host in the valley, and I'm happy I've brought them together.

After breakfast they leave for a tour of Libre. I stay behind, dressed in cut-off jeans, cooking a big chicken stew and corn bread. It's hot, and I stop the slaving over the hot stove routine in the afternoon, jump on Rufus without taking the time to saddle him, and ride bareback to the pond. On the way, we gallop up to Allen and the others leaving Dean and Linda's dome. Rufus rears like Silver in the opening credits of *The Lone Ranger*. I'm happy I don't fall off and am secretly pleased they see me on Rufus. In Boulder, I felt like half of myself.

Allen looks startled and almost scared of Rufus, and then blurts out, "WHAT THIGHS!" He's not talking about Rufus, and I blush. David grins slyly, and they walk on to Peter's. Bobby hangs behind and pats Rufus on the neck.

"That was a weird thing for him to say," I tell him.

"Why?" asks Bobby. "Because he loves men?" I look down. "You're silly." Bobby can say things like that and not offend you. "Allen appreciates all kinds of beauty," he adds, moving his hand over Rufus's glistening neck.

"Gotta go," I say, turning Rufus around. "I've been working over a hot stove, and I'm going to go for a quick dip at Ferendelli's pond to cool off before dinner. Want to come?" I ask over my shoulder. "There's always a few people at the pond on a day like this."

"No, I'd just slow you down," Bobby says. "Maybe some other time, though," he calls as I gallop away. The swim's great, but the afternoon's marred by minor tragedy when a horsefly stings Dean on the dick while he's sunbathing. There are advantages to wearing a bathing suit.

There's at least twenty-five for every meal at our house. David helps, but only Bobby and Peter Orlovsky offer to wash dishes. We run out of food, and I give Jim the last of my Naropa money to buy more in Walsenburg, but we run out again.

Still, the reading's the big success we'd hoped it would be. Saturday night the dome's packed, and we sell lots of beer and wine to raise money for the clinic. Joints circulate everywhere. I look out over the crowd, feeling like I've brought my teachers home to meet the family.

The poets are having fun, and the reading runs late. The local writers want Allen to hear their poems as much as they want to hear Allen. Peter Rabbit reads a poem about killing a deer, and Dean (completely recovered) reads a long poem about the Sun Dance. Bobby reads one of his hitchhiking poems, and Annie reads a mildly feminist rant. Allen sits cross-legged in front of his instrument and listens patiently and carefully all night long. Although she's almost too drunk to stand up, Little Dawn from the Triple A sings one of her original dark and surrealistic country-and-western songs. Nancy reads a poem that stops the show, a small, bright window on her peculiar madness, and the dome is silent before the crowd claps. I read, and Mary Red Rocker reads, and some people from Gardner I've never met read. Orlovsky reads, Gregory Corso reads, then Allen reads and plays his harmonium. He looks out at the crowd, the fruit of his brain and words if not his loins, his visions in young, awkward flesh in this cranny of the Rockies. I sit behind Allen, looking out at what has been my tribe for the past seven years. I've had a little wine, too, and the halves of my brain fall together. Now that Allen's come here, I know I can leave. When a dream comes true, it's over too.

The visitors are having fun, and they drink wine freely. Cumulatively, these old poets have probably been to nine thousand poetry readings. Corso's drinking more than enough, as usual. His Norton hat is lopsided, and he looks like a cross between Chico Marx and Pinocchio's father. Corso couldn't get a prescription from Leonce or Mai, despite his theatrical moans and constant complaints of the worst toothache in the world, so he pouted and drank a lot of wine and whatever hard liquor was offered, and now he shouts occasional insults at the audience. He stops and recites a short, exquisite poem from a few decades ago by heart. Then he returns to insulting the crowd, and the audience yells and whistles and throws cups back at him. The kids are making a racket, playing their usual mad game of tag around the perimeter of the crowd. I'm a little tired, probably from cooking and washing dishes and staying up so late. Spencer the pilot reclines on some pillows behind Gregory and laughs. David slips out to change into a black turtleneck, black jeans, his Cherokee beads, and a beret, and he returns carrying bongo drums. Peter Rabbit introduces him as Allen Grinsberg, aka Jack Carwreck.

"Black, I look into the blackness and see black," David says, lids half closed, a cigarette hanging from his mouth in classic fifties style.

Allen sits up and laughs and shouts, "Yeah, go man go!"

David's high on the moment. He's so fully Allen Grinsberg/Jack Carwreck that he doesn't seem to recognize me. He's on equal footing with his gods, mocking himself and them. He lurches over his bongos, slapping them, saying,

I'm the best mind, I'm the best mind,
I'm the best mind of my generation,
I'm beat, running down the street, the sheet
In my cleats, screaming to be fixed . . .

The thing is, he's right—he is one of the best minds of his generation, though he's not screaming. He stays perfectly in character, no matter what the audience shouts and throws, and his performance is his poem. Gregory stands up and hollers, "GET DOWN, David, tell us how it really is!" and David looks at him calmly while his long, sensitive fingers rest on the bongos, and then he looks out at the crowd, which laughs and cheers. He's always known the value of silence, the pregnant pause. Allen grins and strokes his beard, chuckling. He sees that David's a poet, an original, that David will take risks and won't turn back. As Ginsberg recognizes my longtime companion, I see I can't stay with him any longer. David's act is the perfect end to a perfect evening. We cheer and stand around when it's over, and people come up and slap David on the back and crowd around the guests of honor. There's no more booze, so the crowd thins out quickly. Dean starts to sweep the dome, swaying and steadying himself on the broom. The engines rev up outside, the trucks roll down the mountain, and Bobby helps me get David, Spencer, and the three poets up the ridge to bed.

The days after the poetry reading are heady ones. I watch Gregory and Allen, Bobby and Orlovsky, David and me carefully, trying to remember everything about this time. The crisp end-of-summer weather is in sharp Technicolor. We're more familiar with one another since the successful reading. We laze around the morning after, talking and laughing over the highlights. David's parody has earned him a special membership in their club. I take pictures of Ginsberg, Corso, Bobby, and David outside the house. David closes his eyes on purpose in every shot. The next few days, we sit up late at our table until the wine runs out each night. We tell them famous Huerfano stories. *"What's time to a pig?"* Allen chuckles, stroking his beard. They tell stories starring Jack and Neal, Burroughs and Ferlinghetti, Snyder and Nanao, stories they've told many times before. Throngs come each night, eager to eat,

Group photo on the ridge (Peter Orlovsky and me in foreground;
Allen Ginsburg and Bobby in back; from left: Dean, unidentified woman, Luz,
David, Spencer the Pilot reclining, and Gregory Corso), August 1977.

drink, and party with legends. I cook and do dishes for twenty people, and only Orlovsky, Bobby, and David offer to help again.

Gregory leaves pretty quickly—there are no city drugs here. Dallas and Jim drive Allen and his provisions back to Dean's retreat cabin. Spencer asks David if he wants to fly to Navajo country with him to meet the chiefs Spencer represented years ago. Spencer was a lawyer once, but he doesn't talk about the business he's in now. My guess is he's in Freddy's line of work.

The morning David leaves, I whisper, "Don't go."

He smiles and hugs me, saying, "What do you mean? Come on, it's only for a few days! Bobby will help you." What happens next is predictable, or inevitable, if there's a difference. Orlovsky's the last poet left, and he's carefree, running around shirtless all day in the fine late summer sun. He yodels and races around Libre, staying at a different house each night. He swims in Ferendelli's pond with Nancy on hot August afternoons. One day, he makes love with her under the pines by the pond. Kind, beefcake Orlovsky, half the Adonis he must have been. Lovely, crazy Nancy, soothed by his simple strength. He chops wood nude at our woodpile, wearing only boots. Nancy rolls her eyes, and Orlovsky waits for me to grab my camera.

Bobby helps me with the goats and horses. We ride back on the ridges in the afternoons, Bobby on Susie and me on Rufus. Susie's pretty little yearling filly, Roxy, and Pablo the burro trot behind us. We ride back to the retreat house near the waterfall with supplies Allen's requested. He leaves notes under a big empty tomato can down the hill from the retreat house. We put the supplies in a lidded wooden box by the can. "More rice!" he scrawls one time. "Bigger candles, sesame oil, and apples, please! OM!" another. I sit alone with Bobby at the table every evening after dinner, and we talk about poetry, his travels across the country, the history of Libre, our personal histories. Bobby listens with smiling eyes, thoughtful questions, a goodness. Monty stops by, or Nancy and Orlovsky. Now that Allen's on retreat, there are fewer visitors.

The last night before Spencer and David are due back, I walk out the front door with Bobby to watch the meteor showers for a while, say good night, and watch him walk away across the meadow to Doug's tower, where he's sleeping now. When he's halfway across the meadow, I say quietly, "Wait." I guess he hasn't heard me, and decide that's best, turning back to the house, but then he comes back, and he puts his hands on my shoulders and we embrace under the streaking meteors in front of David's and my home.

I can't explain my motivation. Maybe Allen's sensuality is contagious. Maybe I'm in egotistical competition with Allen, or I have a ridiculous desire to claim Bobby for heterosexuality. As I get to know Bobby better, I see Allen never had a chance. Do I need Bobby's quiet strength and support to overcome gravity and blast off? Is it a way to ensure that I'll have to go? I don't see a future with him and don't feel I have to leave David for him, the way I did with Hickory, Paul, and Nick. Is that progress?

When they return, Allen and David know about Bobby and me immediately, but they don't really seem to mind. They see eye to eye on this—no petty jealousies. Allen's just been meditating for two weeks, after all. Things are relaxed and fun after dinner around the table, and at the end of the evening, I leave with Bobby and kiss him good night, then return to the house and climb up the rock to bed with David. Bobby seems to be taking all this in stride too. Everyone's doing much better with the situation than I. This is also predictable.

One day I drive Allen and Peter to see Ben Eagle and Chipita on the upper land at Ortiviz Farm. Allen knew Ben on the Lower East Side years ago, when Ben was a street kid and a member of the Motherfuckers. Ben and other Motherfuckers shouted Allen down at a poetry reading in 1965, calling him bourgeois. Now Ben's a roadman in the Native American Church, and Chipita travels across the country selling beadwork made by Plains Indian women she's organized into a mega–beading business. Movie and rock stars crave Chipita's stuff. On the way back from Ben's, we stop at a little bar in Gardner so Bobby can use the phone and Orlovsky can buy a soda pop. Inside the dark bar I see a familiar back, and Nick turns around like he knows I'm there. He stands up straight and puts his hands on his belt like a gunfighter.

"Hi," I say.

"Hi," he says back. He looks down at the paunchy black-bearded man dressed in a crumpled seersucker jacket sitting next to me. Then he looks over the large, muscular middle-aged man with the gray ponytail on my other side. He glances at the slim youth with the halo of auburn curls, who smiles guilelessly back at him.

Allen looks up at Nick and says, "Oh! My!"

"Nick, these are some friends of mine," I say quickly.

"Oh," says Nick. When he speaks, I feel his voice resonate in his chest.

"This is Nick," I say. "He's a cowboy, or rancher, or—"

"Hello, Nick," Allen says, blinking up at him.

"Hi there," says Peter, extending his big hand. Nick shakes it.

"Hello," smiles Bobby.

Allen, Peter, and Bobby use the phone and buy drinks from the bartender. I stay with Nick, disgusted with myself for being a little ashamed of them.

"So, who are they?" Nick asks.

"Just some poets," I say, looking down.

"Oh. Poets. I should have guessed," he says. "Who's that young kid?" he asks, as if he senses I've slept with Bobby.

"Nobody. He's not too much younger than you. I have to go," I say quickly.

"Yeah. Hey—take care, okay?" he sounds like he means it.

In the truck Allen asks, "Did that man come to the poetry reading? I don't remember seeing him. He certainly is . . . big."

"Uh-uh, no chance," I say to Allen. "He's just one of the natives."

Lately, I've been having trouble breathing, as if I can't get enough air. There's a weight on my chest at night. One afternoon I put my teacup down and look at Allen and sigh. "Allen, it's been great having you here," I say. "In fact, it's been wonderful, but I'm tired of cooking and cleaning for crowds every night, and we can't afford to feed this many people anymore, so I don't know . . . If you'd like to stay on and cook down at Brent's, that'd be fine, but I'm turning in my Hostess with the Mostest badge." I sound cold, and I'm ashamed of my bluntness. I'm kicking out a literary lion, and I feel like I've kicked a cat. David stares down at the table and smokes his cigarette inscrutably.

Allen blinks at me, as if I'm speaking in an unfamiliar dialect, though he's trying his best to follow along. "Okay," he says, "okay, sure." Orlovsky grins his no-hard-feelings grin.

I press on. "What do you mean?" I blurt it out louder than I intend and am embarrassed by this whole conversation.

Allen looks startled and says, "Oh, I think we can leave tomorrow. Nancy can drive us up to Boulder, right, Peter?" Orlovsky nods and shrugs.

They leave the next day. I hug them all. Allen's flesh is soft and ample, his bones small. Orlovsky feels massive, firm, a little overripe. Bobby feels supple and familiar. After they go, I can't see into my future. It's still hard to breathe. I'm not sure I want to see Bobby again. When I look at David, I'm mad or sad, although there's no blame. I don't even know for what.

A few days later I ride Rufus over to use the phone at the old Hudson Ranch, now owned by a rich hippie from Boulder. I feel like a barbarian riding up on Rufus, and I'm glad. Winnie Red Rocker drives up as I tie Rufus to the rail. He says "Hi" and looks at my face but doesn't ask what the matter is. It's not his style. When we go in, we find some northern Colorado city hippie types sitting around Bob Hudson's old living room in their two-hundred-dollar cowboy boots, smoked or coked out of their minds. Earlier, all of the lights had gone out in the living room, and the big fat Texas-size TV with the crummy reception blinked off, and everybody panicked. The new owner had sent someone over to get Winnie to fix it.

Winnie checks out the fuse box. "No fuses blown," he mutters, and he walks around the living room for a minute, then crosses over to a light switch on the wall and flips it. Presto! The lamps and TV are back on. The crowd from Boulder laughs.

"Man," the new owner says, "somebody leaned on the switch! How stupid was that?"

"Pretty stupid," laughs Winnie. Winnie and I look at each other. We built homes and lived through seven Colorado winters without electricity, chopping wood and hauling our water at first, and we're standing in a room full of hippie lookalikes who are too stoned to figure out they need to flip a light switch.

I'm not sure whom to call. My parents? Can't admit failure. My brother? Already rescued me with the Naropa money. I try Pam, my childhood friend, who's been living in New Mexico as long as I've been in Colorado. She and Don have bought a ranch on the Gila River. The connection crackles as if I'm making a transatlantic call, not one to the bottom of the next state.

"What's the matter with you?" she asks kindly. "You sound like a zombie." I choke up and can't talk for a while.

"I don't have any idea of what to do," I whisper into the phone, covering my ear to cut out the sound of the game show audience on the TV. "I don't think I can be here right now, Pammy. I can't think of anywhere else to go. And the horses . . ."

She waits through another long drawn-out pause with the patience of an old friend. "Look," she says delicately, "our house in Santa Fe's empty for a while. At least three months. It's furnished and everything. If you'd like, you could go and stay there, sort things out."

"Yeah." Now I'm crying, but just from my eyes. Although tears run down my face, my chest is still tight as a drum, and it's still hard to breathe. The Sangres outside the plate glass window of the quaint and tasteless Hudson ranch house look fake today, like mountains built by some skilled model railroad hobbyist. "Yeah. I think I might do that. Thanks. Thanks, Pam."

Nothing's unusual. I tell David I just need time and space—that stupid cliché. Does either of us know I'm leaving for good? I lack clarity, and he doesn't want to hear any more explanations anyway. At our table in the kerosene lamplight, with half his handsome face in Rembrandt shadows, he smokes his cigarette and says he understands. I bake a batch of bread for him to eat after I go. We lie cradled in each others' arms at night, although neither of us can make love.

I'm a fox chewing off her leg to escape a trap. I dismantle the goat herd in one day. David doesn't want them, I don't have to ask. I give Pablo the burro and Susie the mare to Ben Eagle. I sell the slides I took of the recording studio we built at Pass Creek last summer to Clark Dimond, its owner, for five hundred dollars. Some new people from St.

Louis buy the tipi, and David and I split the money. I'll take Roxy, my beautiful filly, over to stay on a ranch on the other side of the valley. I'll take Rufus to Nick to keep for me—that's the least he can do.

I deliver Roxy and Rufus in a borrowed horse trailer. I drop Roxy off first. Roxy's much more attached to Rufus than to her mother now. I visit with the rancher and his wife, put Roxy in the field, and drive away with Rufus. Roxy runs after us until the fence stops her, and she calls again and again to Rufus, pushing her chest against the barbed wire. Rufus answers from the trailer. I listen to the sounds of their parting as I drive to Nick's to drop Rufus off next. My chest still feels constricted, but there's a hairline crack in my heart.

September 1977

The morning of my last day in the Huerfano, I run out of dish soap. David's getting some in town today, but I go up to Cari's to borrow a little to do the breakfast dishes. Cari's not there—she must have gone to Walsenburg with David, Peter, and Annie. Cari's still in love with David, and that makes me feel less guilty about leaving. I stand on the deck outside her house, thinking of all the people who've lived there and left, and run my fingers over the hammer marks on the four-by-four uprights. Looking out over the valley I see smudges of yellow and orange halfway up the Huajatollas, where the aspens and scrub oaks have turned color already. The corral gate down the road swings open and shut. My animals are scattered around the valley now.

Bill Keidel's house stands empty back on the next ridge. He sent a postcard last week from Florida. He's running a food concession at the Ringling Brothers Circus winter home. He'll fit in at the circus, playing poker, staying up late trading stories with the Fat Lady and the Rubber Man. It's just another group of freaks and artists living together. The day's so beautiful, I look out on the valley hungrily, memorizing the view as if I'll be tested. I'm leaving, like Keidel, Lars, Trixie, Mary, Vicki, Larry and Anson Red Rocker. Sandy, Judy Rabbit, Vesey, Tony, Richard and Beth, Doug. Many valley veterans come back, like they're visiting the folks back home. None of us ever thought we owned the ideas or the landscape, and we eventually saw that the landscape and ideas had a grip on us.

Down the road, Dean's walking with a man in a white robe, and I feel happy—I don't know why. I expect Dean to be in one of his dark Flemish funks, since Linda's left him again and taken a trip to New Mexico with a musician. Dean's clean-shaven with clipped blond hair these days—it's a grim and penitent Ingmar Bergman look. But when he gets closer and grins at me, the lines in his cheeks punctuate his smile like a string of parentheses. His companion has gray hair rimming a bald crown, a curly salt-and-pepper beard, and bright blue eyes, and he looks so familiar. Then I recognize him—it's Richard, Richard Alpert! I mean Baba Ram Dass, as he's called now. Dean and I hug, something we rarely do, and laugh; we can't stop laughing. Then I hug Ram Dass, and he sighs so much as we hug I'm embarrassed. I feel his thin shoulders and his little potbelly under his robes. There's no denying how good I feel, happiness bubbling up in my chest, tears in my eyes. Whatever.

"Ram Dass came to see Libre," Dean explains, as we sit and look out over the valley, our feet hanging off Cari's deck like three kids fishing off a pier.

"I was just in Boulder, and Allen talked about what's going on down here, so I had to come see for myself," says Ram Dass smiling. "In an interview last week, Allen said what's going on in this valley is *very, very special.*" I laugh. The Huerfano's blooming in Ginsberg's head while down here I'm feeling a hard frost.

"David and I met you in Buffalo in 1968," I tell him. "You were just back from India, and it was so weird. You seemed to be talking specifically to David and me during your speech. You said, 'Don't think of yourself as an Aries!' looking at me, and I'm an Aries, and you said, 'Don't think of yourself as a green Chevy van,' looking at David, and we owned a green Corvair van. When we talked to you afterwards, you encouraged us to go west."

"It was Neem Karoli Baba talking through me," Ram Dass says.

"That's what you said then, too," I laugh.

Dean tells Ram Dass, "Trixie and Lars, some friends from the Triple A, over on the other side of the valley there, told us that when they were at Stanford in 1966, they rented your house on Homer Lane, when you and your wife were leaving. You left ten thousand hits of acid for them on the mantel, and that's how the Triple A band got started, playing with Kesey at the Acid Tests." Ram Dass closes his eyes, rocks, and smiles.

I point toward Slide Mountain and Blanca, saying, "That's where the Triple A's eleven hundred acres are. Lars is in New York, and Trixie's in Denver now, but they come back."

Ram Dass opens his eyes, says, "Trixie, oh no, and Lars!" We laugh. This is oddly funny. I tell him about JB, our friend in Buffalo who entered a detox program in 1970, who then went to Vancouver with our Buffalo friends to start a commune in the summer of that year. As we suspected, those plans ended before the summer did. JB had met Ram Dass at our house in Buffalo, and he left Vancouver for India and stayed there two years, having found Neem Karoli Baba and peace.

I say, "This is odd, too. Three years ago, we hadn't seen JB for four years. On our last day in New York City, halfway down the stairs with our suitcases at the Bleecker Street station, I said I had to go back and get a bagel at the shop we'd passed. David wasn't happy—we had to lug our heavy suitcases back up the stairs—but he went along. Meanwhile, JB, who was in New York for just that day, passed the same bagel place. Half a block beyond it, he decided he just had to go back and buy a bagel there. David and I got in line behind him! How's that for coincidences?"

"Yes, yes," says Ram Dass, "*you both knew!* He's Karuna now. He and Mirabai are in Boston, making translucent mandalas that you stick on your car windows, a big success. Oh, all the connections," Ram Dass sighs. "They're so rich, they run so deep."

"We felt we were the chosen people when we first met you," I say, swinging my feet clockwise in little circles.

"We are, we all are," says Ram Dass. He's just returned from Bali, and he tells us it's paradise. He says, "My taxi driver parked his taxi by a roadside shrine in the middle of my ride to stop and pray!"

"Roberta's leaving for Santa Fe for a while," Dean says.

"Oh?" says Ram Dass, his blue eyes dancing. "The City of Holy Faith?"

"Maybe I'll make enough money there to take a trip to Bali before it's covered with resorts," I say. "I'm a sucker for heavens on earth."

"You'll get there if you want to," Ram Dass says. "You'll get anywhere you want to go." Dean nods in agreement.

I look out over the valley and say, "I don't know why it's been so hard to leave."

"Love," says Ram Dass, smiling.

"And why I have to leave."

"Love," he says again.

"Or what I'm going to find out there—"

"*Love!*" Dean and I say before Ram Dass can, and we laugh some more. Whatever has happened to Ram Dass, you feel happy in his presence.

"It was hate that brought me here, just as much as love—hate for masters of war, for all the hypocrisy and greed," I say.

"No," says Dean. "You'd have made bombs in a brownstone if it was hate."

"Oh, it's love, no doubt about it," muses Ram Dass, his eyes half closed, gazing at the Huajatollas. When I look at him doubtfully, Ram Dass says, "Don't blame the idea for the people who espouse it."

All this is a little too Sgt. Pepperish for 1977, but I don't say anything. Ram Dass carries it off somehow. Che Guevara recognized that he risked seeming ridiculous saying that the true revolutionary is guided by feelings of great love. At a council last week, someone said, "After the revolution—" and Linda interrupted, saying, "*There isn't going to be a revolution!*"

Ram Dass, Dean, and I sit quietly, taking in the view and the late summer sun.

I'm bringing only a suitcase and my sewing machine with me to Santa Fe. David helps me carry my stuff down to the Chrysler in the parking lot in the morning. We hug formally by the car, then push each other gently away at the same time, as if we've choreographed even this. He turns to walk up the hill before I'm off the land. I don't look back, and neither does he. The faded "Visitors on Sunday Only" sign swings lopsidedly from one nail on the gate.

I'm on the road in the Chrysler alone now, staring out the window dry-eyed as I cross the valley. I feel like a tourist, noting the landmarks of my Huerfano life. No one's around today. Johnny Bucci's truck isn't outside his house. The tin roof of Johnny's barn has a big red horse head painted on it—a woman from the Red Rocks did it in a trade with Johnny. When I pass Gardner Mercantile, owned by the people who took my goat Trinity, I don't see her in the back corral and tell myself to stop worrying. On the Pass Creek road I look back through the dust I've kicked up, off to the west, where Mary, Molly, and Bad Eddy lived after they left the Red Rocks, where the Triple A played one summer for the Huerfano Pops, where Lars sang "Jumpin' Jack Flash" for the last time.

I'm numb for most of the trip into New Mexico, but it's easier to breathe. I realize I never found out where the first one hundred and eighty German families who tried to settle in the Huerfano lived before their endeavor failed and they left after two years. And I never understood why Chief Greenhorn lingered on the mountain while the Spaniards headed his way.

I stop in Taos to call my parents on the pay phone on the plaza. I say my visit to Santa Fe is just temporary, but my mother says, "Great! We're going to bring out your stereo and record albums and all your electrical appliances on our trip this fall!" It's their second trip looking for the perfect place to retire, but they won't ever leave home. Is that why it took so long for me to leave the Huerfano? I see my dad carefully packing my KLH, my electric Water Pik, my Tensor lamp, and my record collection in the back of their Mercedes. I see me helping him unload them at Pam and Don's house on Camino del Monte Sol.

"Well, just don't do anything rash or final," she counsels. She's sure I would never have left the East if I hadn't fallen under David's influence, and now she's upset that I'm leaving him even temporarily. But she's happy I'll be living with electricity, although she knows not to mention it. I hang up annoyed at her and feel more like myself.

Santa Fe's right up against a mountain, populated by Indians for millennia, Spanish for centuries, and Anglo artists for decades. Barely a city, it attracts newcomers who can't fit in elsewhere. It's the City of Holy Faith, full of hippies, some with a lot of money, a halfway house for commune refugees, where we get reacquainted with stoplights and utility bills and take jobs in restaurants. It's easier to adjust to the outside world here. We look up at the mountain less as we get absorbed into our new lives. Outside town, south of the opera, cresting the hill overlooking the city, the lights sparkle in the adobes scattered over the foothills and downtown. I'm an orphan, always from the Huerfano, never going back. You don't give yourself away again to ideas and lovers as completely as you do the first time, when your enthusiasm seems like it won't exhaust or betray you. In Jim's painting of the woman staring up, the mountains and trees and domes grew in her head. He retouched it recently, got carried away the way he sometimes does, and ruined it.

Pam and Don's big adobe looking out on Santa Fe Baldy is my decompression chamber. On the back patio under the willow tree, I sip coffee and stare at the mountain, part of the range that cuts through the Huerfano. I read somewhere that the heart's an organ that can sometimes repair itself. I wonder what to say on application forms for jobs at restaurants, where all the people with Ph.D.s and no money work in Santa Fe. That after graduate school I acquired new skills? I can mix cement, blow dynamite, bank a fire, use a chain saw, split wood, milk goats, make yogurt and Parmesan cheese, bake donuts, ride bareback, hunt mushrooms, start fires, frame roofs, cure bacon, punch cows. That I've memorized the shapes of three thousand clouds, calibrated a hundred sunset reds, catalogued one hundred eleven rainbows, and watched five babies slide out into life? That big birds bring me messages, and I've stared straight into a cougar's yellow eyes? That I lived in the Orphan Valley for seven years with friends, crazies, and some who were both, that we were heroic fools or foolish heroes—I can't say which, and maybe it doesn't matter.

Postlogue

Some of us stayed in the Huerfano. Jim and Sesame are at Libre. Dean is too; he's happy with Sibylla, the German woman Rufus liked so much. Dallas's brother Billy built a house on the knoll south of what was Peter's meadow. Over the years a few others have taken up residence in empty houses. Tom Grow's around. Muffin went to veterinary school and is the valley vet now.

Nick and his family are still in the area, of course. He's been married three times and works for Faris Land and Cattle Company selling vacation ranches. Over in La Veta, a quaint Colorado vacation town nestled against the Huajatollas, those breasts of the world, Adrienne lives with a woman above their bakery café. Patricia built and runs a restaurant/gallery in La Veta also, and Monty's down the street. He inherited enough money to buy a fixer-upper or two in town, remodel, sell, and buy more. The rumor is that now that Monty's a land speculator he's rediscovered his Republican roots and even applauded the Patriot Act. Perhaps he was always a Republican, and we didn't notice because he was such a good cook. Minnesota's in the valley; he teaches sculpture at an art school in La Veta. Monty's brother Steve married Lynn, the head of our old Ortiviz Farm school—they're in Pueblo but own a farm in Farasita. Henry lives in the eastern part of the valley. Marilynn and her second husband are back after years in Florida; she teaches school.

More of us have left the Huerfano, although it hasn't entirely left us. Doug owns a little farm in Tennessee and does fine carpentry work; he and Martha had a son. Dallas is married and lives in Pueblo, working as a jack-of-all-trades. Tony's a respected artist living in Taos. Linda is in the Bay Area, a professor and dean at the College of

Arts and Crafts. She returns to Libre in summer, to a house she built in the eighties. Her big sculptures are in galleries and museums all over the country. Dean and Linda's son Luz graduated from Bennington and started a record label in New York. Jim and Christine's daughter Electra was discovered as a teen and modeled on runways in Milan, in America and Australia. She's in graduate school in interior design and got married at Libre in July 2004.

Mary Red Rocker got a Ph.D. in history and teaches at UCLA; Harvard University Press published a book that began as her thesis on the *New Yorker.* She's a history consultant for network and HBO television shows. AA saved her life, and she spreads the word at prisons and anywhere else she's asked to talk; she's always been a great speaker. Her daughter Molly is a talented young photographer and artist in Los Angeles. Larry Red Rocker's a well-known photographer in Denver; Winnie owns a bed and breakfast in Oregon, and their sister Vicki lives in Santa Fe, where she restores ancient Indian pots with uncanny skill. Benjo Red Rocker, who married Stephanie, segued from the Peyote Church to Christian fundamentalism, despite his Jewish heritage. He's a minister, and he, Stephanie, their five children, grandchildren, and other believers live on community land in Texas. They have a successful business making furniture for the outside world. Benjo's unredeemed twin couldn't kick drugs and died in questionable circumstances. Their brother Anson is a well-known movie critic.

In Santa Fe, Brooke's a realtor, Dr. Mai has a practice, and Peggy's remarried. She's a concert pianist and piano teacher. Her daughter Lori's a doctor, and her son Lump, who changed his name to Puml, is a contractor in southern Colorado. Peter and Annie are in Taos; they started the Taos Poetry Circus. Freddy the pilot lives a reformed life. After a high-powered medical career in Denver, Dr. Frank's the top doctor at a community medical center in Montana, not too far from his grandparents' cabin. George McGovern is a friend and neighbor. Dr. Frank sometimes consults on health care and family practice issues in the Ukraine and other parts of the world. Bobby works for the Associated Press, is married, has two daughters.

There were casualties. Strider's liver gave up, and Daddy Dave's lungs. Bill Keidel's kidneys failed. He had diabetes and died in the hospital after one leg was amputated. His years in a Russian prison didn't help. Bill's flight was delayed in Moscow in the late eighties, and he killed time drinking vodka in an airport bar with a friendly man who spoke English very well. After a few drinks, Bill confided what was in his bags and learned too late that his new drinking buddy was in the KGB. Vesey died not long ago. Spencer, the poets' pilot, perished on the tarmac trying to put out a fire in his cockpit. In the early eighties, Nancy lost the fight with her demons and was found floating like Ophelia in Ferendelli's pond. Cari lost her fight with cancer. Allen Ginsberg, Gregory Corso, Johnny Bucci, and Benny from the Central Bar all are gone. Rufus was stolen from one of the Faris pastures. Dr. Leonce had the first case of AIDS in Colorado. He researched his troubling and mysterious symptoms in medical libraries, diagnosed his disease as what was then called "the gay cancer," and died.

Lars returned to the valley to start a gourmet restaurant in La Veta with Adrienne. He hired a contractor living at the Triple A, a Yale School of Architecture graduate, and built a beautiful little house on the Triple A land. In the summer of 1980, Lars directed *Huerfano,* a play based on the oral histories of old-timers in the valley compiled by Elaine Baker of the Triple A, thanks to a grant she got from the National Endowment for the Humanities. Elaine had recorded the stories of septagenarians who'd been children of striking coal miners during the Great Coalfield Wars, of an octogenarian who unwrapped and played his family's Stradivarius for her. The play was a pan-Huerfano production performed in Walsenburg on several weekends. Feed store owner Sig Sporleder's daughter was the lead.

Then Lars found out that he had AIDS too. June 1989 was the last time all of us were back in the Huerfano together. We took the steep trail he used to train on for the Pikes Peak Marathon, climbing up to a high ridge on Slide Mountain. A few people who'd been living in sea level cities too long, smoking and eating too much, collapsed along the path on the way up. Naturally, when we got to the ridge we made a circle. We reminisced about Lars, and then I stood beside Linda, Adrienne, Monty, David, Trixie, Mary, Brooke, and all the others, looking across to Greenhorn as we took handfuls of his ashes and threw them out into the valley. The wind blew some back in our faces. Mary touched her fingers to her tongue, and for a minute I wondered stupidly if you could get AIDS that way but then followed suit—I didn't want to miss anything Mary was experiencing about Lars. They were salty and gritty.

Like stars, friends and lovers come in constellations. After Lars died, Linda bumped into Michael in San Francisco, and they fell in love. Michael's a tall, handsome blue-eyed man with lots of prematurely gray

Poster for the play Huerfano *by Robert Sussman, 1980.*

hair whom Lars loved very much, only Michael was straight. Lars and Linda loved each other deeply, but he was gay, so Linda and Michael have closed that circle. At their wedding, they propped up a Robert Mapplethorpe portrait of Lars on a kilim. Besides the bride, groom, and Luz (who was giving Linda away), I was the only one who recognized the man in the photograph. I hadn't expected to see his handsome face, and tears welled up in my eyes. A tall bearded man looked at me strangely, and I wiped my cheeks and explained that I always cry at weddings.

No one lives in the big Red Rocker dome now. Our house at Libre is empty too, except for a lot of chipmunks. Houses that aren't kept up become ruins pretty quickly there. A year or so after I left, David moved in with Cari at the house Richard and Beth had built on the ridge; he kept living there after Cari died. No one lives at Bill Keidel's or the Grow Hole either. Linda built a new studio in what was once Tony and Marilynn's meadow after their dome collapsed because of structural changes Tom Grow had made while living there. After a marijuana bust at Libre in the early eighties, some members tore down Peter's zome while he was serving time in Canon City. The zome's lumber and appliances were reused in other projects. Nancy's little bungalow, the Libre library after her death, is the only building in that meadow now. A visitor couldn't tell anything else had ever been there.

As the revolution got stuck up to its hubs in the Reagan years, David got more and more interested in the paranormal—UFOs, crop circles, rods, and, his specialty, the unexplained cattle mutilations reported throughout the country for the last thirty-five years. He's always studied the extremes in our culture and believes that the paranormal is the key to understanding consciousness. He compiled his X files long before the television program. He founded and writes for a regional magazine, played a role in local politics, writes articles on the history of the West, the environment, and the paranormal, and speaks at national conferences, dividing his time between Santa Fe and Libre. Hollywood recently found him, so he has a new niche as a movie and TV script consultant. In the summer of 2003, he went to the White House with his lady, Paige, to dine with a freshman-year drinking buddy from Yale who was hosting a huge dinner for the Class of '68 before their thirty-fifth reunion in New Haven. What he saw that night was harder to believe than the possibility of little green men from outer space.

In 1980, I began law school. After graduation, I clerked for the federal district court judge in Santa Fe, worked at a fine old firm, taught law, and now have an intellectual property practice in Albuquerque. Sometimes I represent tribes on Native American cultural issues. I married a man whose heart is big enough to take in the Huerfano, and we have two sons who care about what happens in the world and occasionally make bad jokes about hippies. When I'd gone west in 1970, I'd put off doing my commune book until later. After my parents died within three months of each other, it occurred to me it was later, and I started looking through my slides. There we were, in little slices of light.

When I was a kid, my brother Jimmy used to talk to me about outer space over his science homework as Buddy Holly sang "That'll Be the Day" on the radio, which was turned down low so my mother couldn't hear Jimmy was playing rock and roll while studying. As I lay in my bed across the hall, he'd describe the galaxies and the myriad possibilities for intelligent life. I listened sleepily to his familiar voice and imagined a parallel world in which a girl like me made different choices than I at critical points. Each time, her life became another branch of the tree, growing in another direction from my branch on our mutual tree of life—like the life of the girl I dreamed of in the print on the living room wall. Maybe everyone we imagine is real and related to us, but in another galaxy. Imagination is the only reality, as William Carlos Williams pointed out.

A recent estimate of the number of galaxies in the universe is ninety billion. That's fifteen galaxies per earthling. I don't know if we have an estimate of the average number of solar systems within a galaxy or the percentage of those solar systems in which there are planets that might foster some form of intelligent life. Sometimes when I look at the western sky now, I squint my eyes and try to catch a glimpse of the solar system with a planet on which Oswald missed, Martin Luther King Jr. survived and was elected president, Bobby Kennedy grew gray and wise, Malcolm X became the mayor of New York, Allen Ginsberg was Secretary of States of Mind, Che headed the Organization of American States, the war in Vietnam ended in 1964, the War on Poverty escalated uncontrollably, conspicuous consumption was taboo, we hadn't backed corrupt sheikdoms and greedy despots for oil, and love—love for one another—grew and grew. What if the Thanksgiving moment at the Red Rockers' when we ran into each other's arms had exploded like an atom bomb into days, weeks, years, decades, generations? If, somewhere else in the universe, the things that got lip service for a while on Earth as the twentieth century wound down detonated deep inside us, and beyond the shards of our shattered egos, no one was an orphan, everyone came home, it was all love, that was all we needed, the Beatles were right, so we acted in love, we lived in love, we dreamed in love forever more.

I'm not plagued by these possibilities or preoccupied with current setbacks. So what if Bob Dylan shows up in Victoria's Secret commercials?

We still have his old words. *Yonder stands an orphan with his gun, crying like a fire in the sun . . . Name me someone who's not a parasite and I'll go out and say a prayer for him . . . I was so much older then, I'm younger than that now . . .* My life's fuller, happier, more real. Imagination's a double-edged sword. Lots of hopes and dreams failed to take root and flower in the arid West. I still hope good overcomes evil on this planet, however. And it sounds foolish these days, I know, but I wish that more of us woke up every morning thinking of the galaxies, that we never forgot the sky's the limit, and I wish that unbridled possibilities got more air time. We learned harsh lessons in the Huerfano, about selfishness, limits, and lunacy, about follies and visions that couldn't mesh. We learned so many practicalities the hard way. Yet unbridled possibilities are what we saw in the Huerfano, and what we took away.

It was so American of us, after all.

Author's Note and Acknowledgments

Each of us experienced life in the Huerfano differently. We remember different versions of the same events, and sometimes we manage to remember the same version of different events. This book is my version. It's a true account, but not always literal. I combined and folded together incidents, conversations, and minor characters. I cut and pasted our lives to serve the constraints of memory, narrative line, and page limits. I didn't remember every word of casual dialogue from three decades ago. (Then, too, there's that familiar saying that if you can remember the sixties you weren't really there!) On the other hand, to use another cliché, I remembered many images and interactions as if they happened yesterday. I changed some characters' names to help the reader keep track of a large cast. In real life, four or five Davids, Steves, and Jims were running in and out of the tipis and domes. Some dear friends and unforgettable people in the Huerfano Valley were lost from these pages when my editor said a tome-length book was out of the question. Some Huerfanites who appear haven't been fleshed out fully. From you, I ask your tolerance and understanding.

Huerfano is the result of a communal effort, largely a selfless one for all whose names aren't on the cover. It began when the now late professors Lawrence Chisolm, Leslie Fiedler, and Mac Hammond successfully championed my request for a faculty fund grant from the SUNY at Buffalo English Department in 1969. With that seed money, I bought a camera and film and headed west. It might not have been written at all without a 2001 Vassar Time Out Grant and its anonymous donor/fairy godmother/alumna. A grant from the Wurlitzer Foundation gave me a quiet adobe to write in, a view of Taos

Baldy from my desk, and the companionship of other working artists for three months. Bill Gifford, professor emeritus at Vassar and my writing teacher thirty-six years ago, read the first draft of this book. He's the best mentor and first reader you could have; his comments combined empathy, intuition, perception, attention to detail, and vast literary knowledge. The color photographs appear thanks to the characteristic generosity of Pam and Don Lichty, and Jack Weiss consulted on legal issues with similar largesse. To my great relief, I found an editor who loved *Huerfano* immediately: Clark Dougan at the University of Massachusetts Press. He's been an enthusiastic, skillful, and supportive editor, as they say editors used to be. Those pesky page limits prevent me from giving others their due (Marni Sandweiss, Kathleen Howe, Kim Griffith, Kaye Smolinsky, the Bookistas, and so many friends from the Huerfano and beyond).

My brother Jimmy, who wasn't as they say "on the bus" and didn't condone a lot of what was going on inside it, has nevertheless been loyal and supportive. My ex-husband David's thorough edits and suggestions were invaluable, and his assistance on a work with contents no doubt difficult for both of us was always gracious. My husband John offered unlimited help of all varieties—domestic, emotional, grammatical, psychological, aesthetic—you name it. Homer Price (a Briard mix) missed numerous walks and a few meals, limiting his complaints to deep sighs by my chair. Jesse Boyd helped take care of his then little brother when I was in Taos or busy writing here, and Walker Boyd helped with many computer or digital photo issues about which I didn't have a clue. They're proud I got this done and are willing to shrug off the predictable razzing they'll get from peers over a parent's tales and images of a less straitlaced age. I've been surrounded by exceptional men, women, and animals all my life, and for that I'm grateful.

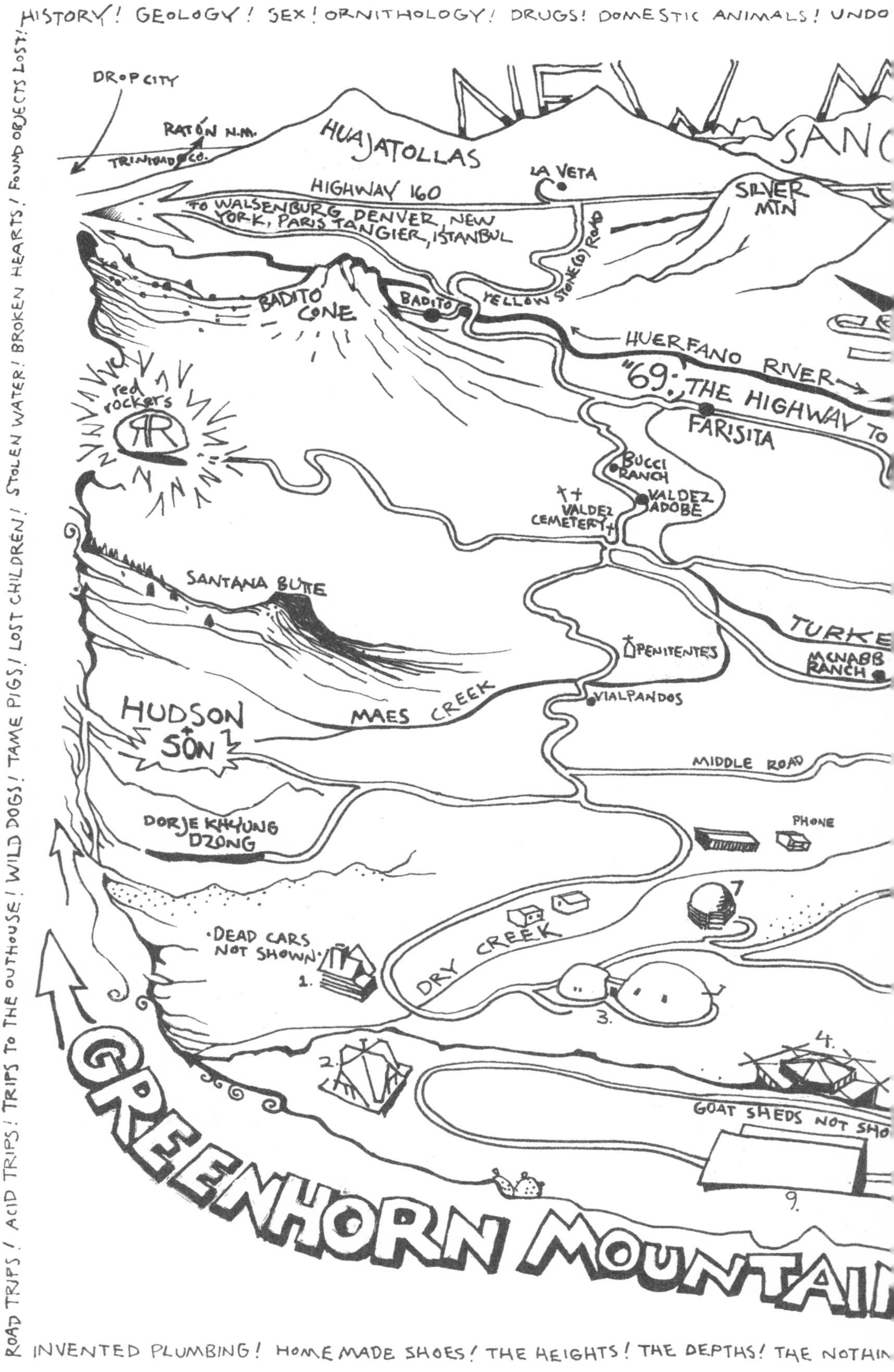

HISTORY! GEOLOGY! SEX! ORNITHOLOGY! DRUGS! DOMESTIC ANIMALS! UNDO
ROAD TRIPS! ACID TRIPS! TRIPS TO THE OUTHOUSE! WILD DOGS! TAME PIGS! LOST CHILDREN! STOLEN WATER! BROKEN HEARTS! FOUND OBJECTS LOST!
DROP CITY
RATÓN N.M.
TRINIDAD CO.
HUAJATOLLAS
SANG
LA VETA
HIGHWAY 160
TO WALSENBURG DENVER, NEW YORK, PARIS TANGIER, ISTANBUL
SILVER MTN
YELLOW STONE (D) ROAD
BADITO CONE
BADITO
HUERFANO RIVER
"69: THE HIGHWAY TO
FARISITA
red rocker's
RR
BUCCI RANCH
VALDEZ ADOBE
VALDEZ CEMETERY
SANTANA BUTTE
TURKE
MCNABB RANCH
PENITENTES
VIALPANDOS
MAES CREEK
HUDSON + SON
MIDDLE ROAD
DORJE KHYUNG DZONG
PHONE
7
·DEAD CARS NOT SHOWN
1.
DRY CREEK
3.
2.
4.
GOAT SHEDS NOT SHO
9.
GREENHORN MOUNTAI
INVENTED PLUMBING! HOME MADE SHOES! THE HEIGHTS! THE DEPTHS! THE NOTHIN